Foreword

A most interesting series of documents recently came up for auction in Israel. I was privileged to be shown them and realised their importance in the history of Jewish Sunderland. During the Second World War (1939-1945) most of the Jewish youth both men and women were called up for military service. The minister at this time was Rabbi S Toperoff. He took it upon himself to edit and send a monthly bulletin to every Jewish service man and woman from Sunderland throughout the world containing local news and also letters from all so that everybody had some contact not only with home but also with each other. Rabbi Toperoff enlisted some local correspondents to help him. This unique collection is a full series and gives a most wonderful insight not only to the serving men and women but also to the local Jewish life in Sunderland during the War Years.

Harold A Davis

Thanks are due to David Toledano, David Pearlman, Debbie Spoor and Richard Franklin for their help and advice in producing this volume.

Back Row
Leo Levin, Lionel Gillis, Mordant Cohen, Issy Levine, Cyril Behrman

Middle Row
Phivie Pearlman, Israel Winburn, Rabbi Toperoff, Joey Landau,
Maurice Minchom, Harold Magrill

Front Row
Toby Book, Norman Cohen, Nat Goodman, Solly Gillis

Contents

Note: Missing pages

Unfortunately there were three missing leaves in the original papers and these relate to the following pages:

April 1944 - Volume 2 No. 8 - page 5,

June 1944 - Volume 2 No. 10 - pages 2 & 3,

March 1945 - Volume 3 No. 6 - pages 2 & 3

Sunderland Jewish Community
Bulletin for the Forces

1942

RYHOPE ROAD SYNAGOGUE MONTHLY BULLETIN

for Members of the Forces.

Vol.1. No. 1.   Edited by the Minister, July 1942.   AV 5?

In this our debut I am endeavouring to reach our
Local men and women now serving in H.M. Forces at home and
overseas.   The team spirit has preserved the Jew through
the years of the grim struggle for existence that he has
waged against the blind forces of hate and ignorance.   The
unity of purpose and resolution of mind has encouraged him
weather the storms of racial descrimination and lying propaganda fostered by the enemies of freedom.   I firmly believe
that you can help our cause by strengthening this team spirit
so essential for the preservation of the Jewish race.   "All
Israelites are mutually accountable for each other," said our
wise sages many years ago.. You who are now serving in the
Forces can do much to spread a proper understanding of the
Jew and his problem amongst those whom you meet.   Rarely
before has such a unique opportunity presented itself, for you
are now in a different environment meeting people whom you
might never have contacted in times of peace.   Seize the
opportunity now and show our friends what contributions to
civilization the Jew has made in every sphere of life, spiritual, cultural and economic from the earliest time.   Prove by
your conduct, behaviour and bearing that the Jew is an obedient
law abiding citizen of the country of his adoption.   It is
your duty as a member of the House of Israel "not to separate
thyself from the community" but to be proud of your Jewishness
and live up to its glorious traditions and customs.   Do your
job quietly and efficiently.   Send your problems to us and
if possible we shall discuss them through the medium of this
bulletin and thus learn from each other's experiences something which may be of mutual advantage to all.
        May your efforts on behalf of Jewry be crowned with
success.
        With fervent prayers for a speedy victory and an
abiding Peace.

"The Jews - Some plain Facts."
        Have you a copy of this indispensable booklet?   It
contains in brief many facts concerning the Jew in nearly
every walk of life.   You should be thoroughly conversant

2.

with all that is in it.

"It should be carried by everyone who has the
sense of public and Jewish duty sufficiently developed to
be anxious to play his or her part in countering the
freely disseminated calumnies against Jews which are so
strenuously broadcast by Pro-Nazi and other mischievous
elements in this country and elsewhere."

If you do not possess a copy write and I shall
send one on to you.

"The Jewish Chronicle".

If you do not already receive a copy of the
Jewish Chronicle from your home write to us and I shall
endeavour to mail it on to you regularly.

We shall be pleased to print anything of
interest you may wish to send. You may like to send
a message to your friend whose address you do not know,
send it to us and use the Bulletin as your medium.

Change of Address

It is important to keep us informed of any
change of address in order to be assured of receiving
regularly a copy of the Bulletin.

Jewish War Effort.

Something of interest took place in the County
of Durham very recently when a Mobile Kitchen purchased
by the United Synagogues of Ottawa was presented to
Washington Urban District Council. This presentation
was made by the Trade Commissioner of Canada at Liverpool to Sir Arthur Lambert, Regional Commissioner and Mr.
J.J. Lawson, M.P. and then to the Chairman of the District
Council. This was one of 12 Mobile Kitchens presented
by Canadian Jewry to this country. It is a pity that no
Jewish representative was invited to the Presentation at
Washington. It sounds very odd but the Jew will nevertheless continue to give of his best for the War Effort.

The Jewish Calendar - On Thursday, July 23rd, we
commemorated the destruction of the Temple in Jerusalem
by a Fast known as Tisha Be'Av. The Jew cannot forget
the 9th of Av, it has left a deep imprint on his mind

and soul. For apart from the destruction of both the first
and second Temple and the final disintegration of the Jewish
State, a series of disasters has overtaken our people on this
day. Indeed the sequence of major tragedies associated in
Jewish history with this day is so protracted and so intense
that it hardly seems sufficient to ascribe it simply to the
long arm of coincidence. We can here refer only to a few.
Jews were expelled from England on 9th of Av in 1290, from
France 1395, from Spain 1492 and in more recent time it was
on the 9th of Av in 1929 that the Arab riots in Palestine
began their fiendish work killing and massacring innocent
people and plundering and pillaging what Jewish pioneers had
built with sweat of their brow. The reactions however were
different from what was expected. The Jews in Palestine
would not be intimidated but in the spirit of the ancient
Maccabees they fought with courage and determination and with
renewed vigour rebuilt what was destroyed, fired with
enthusiasm to make Palestine safe for the Jew. This is the
lesson of Tisha Be'Av. We must turn the tragedies of the
past into an epic of glory of the future. The Jewish State
will once again rise and we pray that it may again play its
rightful part in the comity of nations.

Palestine - During 1941, Palestine has supplied £8,000,000
worth of goods to the British Army in the Middle East.
            The number of Palestinian Jewish recruits in
H.M. Forces up to July 1st is 20,000 including nearly 2,000
women.
Economic Front - The extraction of oil from citrous peel has
been turned into a successful home industry. The oil obtained finds many uses in the manufacture of soaps, perfumes and
flavouring of fruit juices for which Italy used to be the
chief supplier. The Jews in Palestine are doing their full
share in the Allied War Effort.

Siftings from my Diary - by "The Inquisitor".

Sitting lethargically and apathetically on my office stool
during the tropical heat of the Sunderland summer (of 2 day's
duration this summer) I was aroused from my inertia by the
discordant tinkle of the telephone. Stretching a languid
hand I lifted the receiver which I left poised in mid-air
for a moment little realising what the Fates had in store,

4.

when lo! an otherwise dull, monotonous day was suddenly
brightened beyond all human comprehension by the dulcet
tones of Reverend Toperoff whispering over the ether.
I was elevated to celestial heights...... What was that
he was saying? Would I? Could I contribute a few
words to the Forces Monthly Bulletin? Dare I refuse?
Had I any desire to refuse?.... Need I say more?....
That so great a one should choose so humble a one to
write for so many! What would be of interest to so
intellectual a body? Cookery hints? Beauty problems?
Advice on affairs of the Heart? (affaires de coeur
to the linguists). Films? Books? News from the
Hometown? Interesting facts about their fellow
soldiers? That X has a commission (how did he wangle
it?) A is Grade X (a seemingly perfect specimen in
pre-war days).
FLASH:-
Is it premature to congratulate a certain soldier,
stationed in Manchester on his engagement?
Is it true that all Blackpool has become Zionist
conscious since a certain celebrity was stationed
there.
How is Mr. Daws? Still getting plenty of leave?
Is it correct that there are no yashmaks worn in Egypt
since the advent of the Sunderland Don Juan?
Rumour hath it that a very eligible S.P. is causing
as much havoc with the female population near London
as he did in Sunderland.
On dit that there is now much more that a minyan at
Gateshead. Yeshiva!
We were upset to hear from our Indian Correspondent
that all the silk stockings from there are now in the
possession of a certain fortunate married woman!!
It is said that anyone considered anyone in social
circles will be present at the 'Lit' Summer Dance,
July 26th. So the Brylcreem King has returned from
Troopship Duties, all the girls can come out of
seclusion.   Mazeltov to Cpl. Cyril Behrman who is
getting married on Aug. 18th, to Miss Judith Cohen,
formerly of Thornhill Park, now of Cheltenham.
      All correspondence should be sent to the Rev. S.P.
      Toperoff, 5 Victoria Avenue, Sunderland.

SUNDERLAND HEBREW CONGREGATION

Monthly Bulletin for the Forces.

.1. No. 2.   Edited by the Minister Aug. 1942. Ellul 5702

The month of Ellul is with us.   To no other people
do the months of the year speak each with its individual
message than to the Jewish people.   Each month is full
of spiritual content, especially the month of Ellul which
ushers in the great awe-inspiring days of Rosh Hashanna
and Yom Kaippur.   It is a month of preparation rousing
us from the slumber of the summer weeks with its restful
periods to a realisation of the approaching winter that
is coming upon us with rapid suddeness.   Nature always
prepares us, the light rolls on into the darkness, and
the darkness disappears gradually
before the light breaks through
in all its resplendent glory.
So Ellul pre- pares us for the
Penitential Season.   Are you
making preparations for the
future of your race or are you
taking the line of least resistance, oblivious of what is
happening about you.   You
must be suff- iciently interested
in the plight of your people befor
you can inter- est others.   Of the
16,000,000 Jews in the world

> The Editor sends
> New Year greetings
> to all in the Forces
> May the coming year
> herald a new era of
> lasting peace for
> which we all pray.
> May you be inscribed
> in the Book of Life.

well nigh 8,000,000, half the total Jewish population are
entombed in the vast chain of concentration camps.   The
Jew is being systematically strangled to death by a slow
process of torture.   Mass executions are taking place
everyday, whole villages including women and children are
herded together and led as lambs to the slaughter, forced
to dig their own graves.   It is estimated that in recent
months 700,000 Jews have been mercilessly killed in Poland,
scapegoats of a villainous tyranny which is determined to
wipe out the Jew who is powerless to defend himself.   You
must prepare for a saner peaceful world now.   Let the days
of Ellul and its soul stirring message awaken in you the
spirit of sacrifice.   Never tire of telling your friends
what is taking place on the Continent - the wholesale
butchery and total annihilation of communities of innocent
Jews. The Jews are everywhore in the front line.   What
preparations are the Allies taking to restore to the Jew
his independence after the war.   The shrill notes of the

Shofar sounded during the month of Ellul must strike a
responsive cord in our hearts. The least we can do is to
respond to the plaintive cries from the ghettoes of Poland
by enlightening the masses of their inhuman degradation
and pitiless torture at the hands of the Nazi herds. It
is time the conscience of the world was roused.

In Lighter Vein.

We have heard that the other night a devout and obser-
vant member of the community prepared to go firewatching,
carrying his Tallit, Tefilin, Sidur and other necessities
for the night in a somewhat unwieldy parcel. On his way
down Fawcett Street he suddenly became conscious of the
fact that his burden was gradually becoming lighter, though
he was non-plussed to know the reason for this and plied
his way unconcernedly to report for duty. It was not long
however that our friend realised that he had shed of the
religious appurtenances so dear to him, outside the Town Hall
and to his amazement and ultimate relief three different
gentlemen came hurriedly towards him anxious to return what
to them were mysterious articles, to their rightful owner.

We learn of the following incident that occurred before
Len Lerman was reported missing in the Middle East. Whilst
in Alexandria he entered a shop to make a purchase and to
his surprise he saw a pair of Tsitzis dangling from a
shelf. Len was not slow to offer to buy them but the proprietor was rather hesitant, asking him to return the next
day. Len was of course there the following day, and when
the proprietor realised that Len was not looking for a curio
but was a "Yehudi" he gladly presented him with the Tsitzis
adding that he was proud to know that a Jewish soldier, so
many miles away from home was genuinely interested in the
"law of Fringes". We pray and trust that these Fringes will
protect Len from any harm and danger and that they will
console him whilst a prisoner of war.

We are pleased to congratulate the following on their recent
promotion:-
Horace Stone, L/Cpl., Harry Black. Cpl., Norman Cohen, Cpl
Issy Levine, Sgt., Capt. Silverston, Adjutant.
We send good wishes to the following new recruits who have
entered the Forces since the issue of our last Bulletin:-
Freda Oler, W.A.A.F., Sam Isaacs, R.A.F., Joe Clarke, R.A.F.

3.

Answers to Correspondents.

Cpl. Forman. - Many thanks for your constructive suggestion, appreciated so much by "Inquisitor". You will receive more news when available.

Gwen Magrill - We are pleased you are kept guessing, it should be great fun.

I. Davis - I hope you will receive the "extra" you are asking for.

Olsberg - We trust that you will find subsequent issues as interesting as the first.

Vandervelde A. - Your long letter was very much appreciated. You certainly know what you are up against and so you have won the first round of the battle. Carry on with the good work "more strength to your elbow".

Horace Stone - Many thanks for your air-graph. I am pleased you received the book on Jewish Thoughts. I trust it will be a source of comfort to you.

P. Mincovitch - I am glad to know that you are eagerly awaiting a copy of the next issue. I trust that you will be successful in your new course.

W. Book. - Thank you for the Geruss, it was very much appreciated.

_____

En Passant - The Inquisitor.

Before giving my brief resume of uninteresting events I must first admit to what depths of despondency I have been subjected on learning that another has been basking in my reflected glory. That my style should be considered that of another is a dubious compliment - to whom? This bulletin is only in its infancy, and if I were to discard, at this early stage, my nom-de-plume I'm afraid this column would not be such a topic of concentrated, conspiratorial, conjectural conversation! It is no small matter however, that to whomsoever this effort is attributed the persons mentioned therein are wholeheartedly and frankly delighted with such publicity, and those, unfortunate enough to be omitted are eagerly awaiting this publication, because -------- who knows?

FLASH - "What great ones do, the less will prattle of".

Is it true that a smart young girl working in Sunderland tells every soldier to whom she is introduced that she is a mannequin working in London?

It comes to our notice that at a recent Social Event a married woman was seen dancing with a Captain (not her husband)

Our African Reporter tells us that a well known Sunderland Solicitor was given the honour of conducting a Court Martial. "Some have greatness thrust upon them!"

Is it true that a sergeant stationed in Poona has his heart permanently stationed in London (Comrades don't believe him!)

It has come to our ears that two members of H.M. Forces are on the 'alert' for suitable, wealthy orthodox, young, beautiful, talented and intellectual wives. Any offers?

Is the climate near Thurso the only thing portending to be cold?

Does I.B. (often L.B.) still hold the opposite sex enthralled with his usual (and unusual) witticisms?

Is it true that a teacher (obviously not the only witty person in town) has had 15 pseudo evacuations ?

Does a renowned doctor in Egypt get omelettes to his taste? We trust so.

Does the latest youthful acquisition to the R.A.F. still think Anti-Semitism is a good topic of conversation?

How is the Casanova of Glasgow? Still giving plenty of heartaches?

Did J.C. enjoy his farewell party?

Who said "TANKS for the memory?"

Rumour hath it that the "deep depression" over Sunderland has been caused by the departure of Bachelor No.1. for S.Wales (whom else could this mean?)

A certain intellectual corporal is always in the officer's mess - why. Its glaringly obvious.

Which handsome Lothario stationed near 'D' has more than a platonic interest in a girl, late of Middlesbro'?

Has a promising L.A.C.W. had any further promotion yet.

This month's two beautiful brides are Cynthia Gillis and Judith Cohen. Sorry boys.

"Impressions" - by a Visiting Soldier

During my stay here which has been one of the most enjoyable since joining H.M. Forces at the outbreak of war, I have been struck by two things which outshadow all others. In the first place, the unequalled hospitality of Sunderland's Jewish Community, which by far surpasses larger communities in this country; and secondly by the "Jew-consciousness" of everyone here. I must explain that by this, I mean, their religious outlook is very firmly interwoven with their every-day affairs. The reason for these two qualities is, I think, due to the fact, that all Sunderland Jewry are in touch with

5.

each other, quite apart from their more traditional religious
activities at their synagogues.   Another point which I
notice, is the already large and ever growing number of the
community here, who are in H.M. Forces in some capacity or
another - in fact the total effort of Sunderland Jewry is
particularly commendable especially in view of the fact that
it is relatively small.   To end in lighter vein, a word to
the boys abroad, an assurance that the young ladies are
still, I think, as charming as ever and eagerly await the
safe return of you all.

JEWISH FESTIVALS - I should like to remind you that leave
for the Festivals will be in lieu of and not in addition
to the normal periods of leave available for all personnel.
Applications for leave must be made by all ranks to their
respective Commanding Officers at the earliest possible
moment.

Jewish Handbook for Forces.
        Nearly 10,000 copies of the Jewish Pocket Handbook
have been distributed without charge, to members of H.M.
Forces.   In view of the demand, a fourth edition is to be
printed.
        The new edition will contain an Anglo-Jewish
Directory, English and Hebrew Calendars, book pages, and
notes relating to the Jewish National Home.   Those
requiring copies should write to Mr. A. Gordon, Editor,
"The Jewish Pocket Handbook", Association of Jewish Ex-
Servicemen, Woburn House, Upper Woburn Place, W.C.1.

        If you have anything interesting to write about
please send it on to us as your friends would like to hear
of it.

NOTE -Change of address must be reported to ensure regular
receipt of Bulletin.

        All correspondence should be sent to the Rev.
S.P. Toperoff, 5 Victoria Avenue, Sunderland.

THE SUNDERLAND JEWISH COMMUNITY.

Monthly Bulletin for the Forces.

Vol.1. No.3 Edited by the Minister, Sept.1942. Tishri 5703.

Tishri, the first month of the Jewish year is replete with Jewish Festivals and days of great significance. It commences with Rosh Hashannah and after more than a week of days of Penitence, the climax comes in the great Yom Kippur day. On the eve of the 15th of the month Sukkot is ushered in concluding with Simchat Torah. What connection is there between the New Year, the Great Fast and the Festival of Sukkot. They are all different in character and yet they lead to the great lesson of the Sukkah which symbolises the frailty of life and our dependence on God, the Giver of all.

In times of peace few voluntarily left their permanent homes to sit in the Sukkah under the protection of the Sechah, today many are unfortunately forced to live in temporary abodes exposed to the elements. Some of you may be billeted in huts or as we call them Sukkahs.

Some of you were fortunate to get home for either the New Year or the Great Fast, but few will have the opportunity of being at home on Sukkot. When in your hut therefore, or your camp be cheered by the beautiful thoughts of the lesson of the Sukkah. It is only a temporary abode it should make us humble and dependent on the Almighty.

What outlook on life does the Sukkah convey? Is it one of bitterness inclined towards Pessimism. No. "You shall rejoice" is the biblical comment. Sukkot is the season of rejoicing. The Festival teaches us that life with all its trials, dangers and sufferings must sound a note of cheerfulness. The theory that life is a valley of tears and our earthly existance a soul's prison is foreign to the spirit and genious of Judaism. Our religion is essentially a law of life and we are bidden to rejoice and cultivate a happy frame of mind. We have much to mourn for but we are a People of hope. Let us hope then that the Jew will not for all time live in temporary dwellings, exiled from country to country, but as a result of the war possess a Permanent Home. Let us hope that next Sukkot you will be observing the Festival of Gladness with your family at home and in lasting peace.

Here and There.

We thank all those who have sent good wishes for the New Year which we heartily reciprocate.

At an At Home held at 5 Victoria Av. at the termination of Rosh Hashannah, the following were amongst others entertained:- Dave Abrahams, Norman Cohen, Sorrel Freedman, Ralph Freedman, Zelda Gillis, Lionel Gillis, Sol. Gillis, Charles Gillis, Myer Gillis, Joe Goodman, Zelda Levin, Phyllis Mincovitch, Gwen Magrill, Freda Oler, Miriam Pearlman, Norman Pollock and Harold Schochet.

Congratulations to Dr. & Mrs. Geewater (Sonia Rawlinson) on the birth of a son.

Congratulations to Mimi Berman on her engagement to Nathan Raymen of Birmingham.

To Arnold Landau on his engagement to Miss Lowne of London.

To Eddie Levy on his engagement to Miss Rosenberg of Glasgow.

We send good wishes to the following new recruits who have recently entered the Forces:- Pearl Caplin, Austin Davis, Morris Dresner and Eric Bernstein.

The following pupils of the Sunderland Hebrew Congregation Religion Classes were successful in the Jews College preparatory examination :- Paula Neuwirth, Derrick Abrahams and Charles Cohen, the latter having gained a distinction.

Professor Norman Bentwich, the Ex-Attorney General for Palestine and now on the Legal Staff of the Air Ministry, recently visited Sunderland and spoke on the Hebrew University "Its achievements and Aims".

We are very pleased to hear Len Lerman who was reported missing in the Middle East is now in an Internment Camp in Italy. He writes that he is well.

We hear that Gerald Behrman has submitted to the War Office a plan whereby shipping will be saved.

We congratulate Sylvia Brewer and Julius Gordon on their promotion to L.A.C.

DO YOU KNOW?

1. How many Jews are fighting on the Russian Front and how many have received awards?

2. What figures are available to show production efforts in Palestine?

3. To whom did the first award of the British Empire Medal go?

4. Who was the first dominion pilot to be killed in the War?

5. How many Jews are serving in the R.A.F.?

6. What Allies has Britain in the Middle East? and how many are fighting on her side?   (Page.

Answers to the above questions will be found on the back

REPLIES TO CORRESPONDENTS.

Isaac Brewer - I am sorry but No. 1 is out of edition. Yes we send copies over-seas.

Issy Levine - I trust that your prophecy will come true. How did you spend Rosh Hashannah in Bombay?

Charles Marks - It is good to know that you meet Harry Black regularly.

Harry Black. - Was it Jerusalem Tel Aviv or Haifa?

Horace Stone - I was happy to hear of the fulsome praise by non-Jews of the work done in Palestine.

C. Kolson. - I can well understand how lonely you must feel. I shall try and send you some reading matter.

M. Doberman. - Your note is a welcome contribution to the early history of Anglo-Jewry.

Sylvia Brewer - I hope you are able to get time off and enjoy the company of your friends and relations.

J. Rosenthal - Thank you for the constructive criticisms.

B. Freedman - I trust that you are recuperating quickly.

Arnold Landau - What did the Squadron Leader mean?

I. Davis - I hope you have settled down in your new surroundings.

Freda Oler - Many thanks for your good wishes.

S. Isaacs. - I was pleased to read that you were "agreeably surprised" I trust that that the distinct improvement will be maintained.

Harold Schochet - How is the N.C.O. is he behaving himself? The Shool in Nottingham is in Chaucer Street, and our Shabbos class still meets regularly.

EXCERPTS FROM LETTERS.
"L'SHONNOR - TOWVOR".

Dear Folks,

Please accept this airgraph as my "Greetings" to all my old friends at the "LIT". Let us hope that this year, we shall be blessed with absolute and final VICTORY, and may we all be re-united to celebrate that glorious day. As you can imagine, the jolly old "Lit" has still quite a warm spot in my heart, and when things are quiet (not now!!) I often sit and wonder what's doing in the old home town. May I wish you all a VERY safe and happy New Year, and a "bumper season" at the old Shool Hall. Out here in Poona, "The Tigah" has given way to Ghandi and Congress "Wallahs" as "man's dreaded enemy!" but seriously life could be a lot worse. Perhaps when the "gang" get together once more (P.G.) the "Lit" might devote an evening to "Yarns in the Sergeant's Mess"!! If any of the boys are on there way out, please give them my address - and the girls .... I'll see them when I come back.
 Cheerio till then.
 Thumbs UP!
 ISSY   (Sgt. I. Levine).

How's Lalie?

.... Being originally Danish possessions, we get our money in Kroners, which goes a very long way here, as there is really not a great deal to spend it on. The inhabitants here are very friendly people and mostly live a very simple life, and are not burdened with the worries of people living in a modern town, and live mainly from the fish they catch, which is very plentiful here.

To give you some idea you could go down to the village, and get about 4 big cods for about 1 Kroner, which is about app. 10d in English money, also there is an abundance of other fish, and quite a number of the boys go out fishing.

At present the weather has not been too bad, and we get a great deal of rain. Just now it is practically all daylight, and in the winter is just the opposite, a few hours of daylight.............

'EN PASSANT -"The Inquisitor"

Full of rage and righteous indignation I passed my gnarled and knotted hands feverishly through my prematurely grey locks, paced the floor unmercifully, beads of perspiration stood on my lofty (though furrowed) brow, I raised my ardent, star-like orbs to the heavens my mobile lips were moving incessantly.... Had I been informed aright? Could it be true that certain members of H.M. Forces just couldn't take it... that something written, in what is hoped to be a jocular vein, has been maliciously interpreted by the Masses... So be it! We great journalists have to undergo, and be subjected to great indignities before we eventually achieve posthumous fame, perhaps I will go down to posterity as one of the martyrs who suff- ered all for his ART. I wish to express my gratitude to you all for the correspondence with which I have been inundated, I read them both last week, thank you my generous public. I also beg to draw the attention of my every-decreasing followers to the fact that all characters mentioned below are purely fictitious and any similarity to any living person is purely coincid- ental, anyone daring to identify themselves with my celebrities will be brought up for libel - so take warning.

FLASH - Is it true that the Shiek of the Barnes Hotel is still very much missed? Rumour hath it that a vital unit of the R.A.F. finds life more gay in Glasgow than in his native city. Being bored after a day at home is certainly a record. So R.A.F.V.R. is engaged - Mazeltov! On dit that Gibralter has never been so gay as since the advent of a very dynamic personality - is he still overpowered with invitations from all and sundry? Can there be any vestige of truth in the fact that the next ship to be launched

6.

from a N.E. Shipyard, is to be called "Schlemiel"(or is
that just idle gossip from all the Jewish workers there?)
How is the parcel post in Lincoln - too bad! Very "fishy"
business.   So a certain W.A.A.F. is to appear in the
Local News Reel shortly - fame in a day!   We are pleased
that Egypt is having no adverse effect on the wit of an
erstwhile benefactor, hope the currency is not causing
too much trouble.   Is the answer to a maiden's prayer still
fancy free (Scottish papers please copy).   So Durban has
been captivated by Sunderland's Own Glamour Boy (Local
Boy Makes Good).   What renowned V.P. says "Show me the
way to go Home?"   Is it true that the World's most famous
Crooner sings "Roll out the Barrel"?   Is a beautiful girl
from Glasgow shortly to become a Sunderland Bride?   Has
.... had his calling up pains again?   How is Mr. Daws the
Elder, still as entertaining as ever?   Did a charming A.T.
enjoy her 21st Birthday Party at Derby? I hope she has a
good time at Leicester.

MONTHLY PUZZLE - If a harpist plays in heaven where does
a dulciner player belong? (All entries to be handed in no
later than Oct.1983, competitors please enclose 5/- entry fee
Answers to questions on Page 3.

1. 200,000 Jews are fighting on the Russian front and although they rank 7th in the population amongst nationalitie
in the Soviet Union, they rank 4th amongst the heroes who
have received awards in recent months for exploits at the
front and for unusual feats in the arms production.
2. 29,000 Jews at present are employed in 1300 factories.
The present total in Jewish Industrial employment is 42000.
3. To a Jewish Telephonist in the A.F.S.   4. A South
African Jew falling in the very first raid over Wilhelmshave
5. About 17000, many of whom have already been decorated
for valour. 6. Egypt Irak and Turkey. So far not a single
soldier from any of them was fighting for the Allied cause
Egypt remains neutral even after Axis invasion. Irak took
up arms on the wrong side and had to be conquered. Turkey
locks on. The only country in the Middle East so far which
has given active help to the British war effort was Jewish
Palestine, where until the end of August 17000 Jewish men
and women were fighting for the Allied Cause.

All correspondence to be sent to the Rev. Toperoff,
           5, Victoria Avenue, Sunderland.

THE SUNDERLAND JEWISH COMMUNITY
Monthly Bulletin for the Forces
<u>Vol.1,No.4. Edited by the Minister, Oct.1942. Cheshvan 5703</u>

<u>Anti-Semitism</u>

It was Zangwill who explained Anti-Semitism by "the dislike of the unlike". It is the fate of minorities to suffer. National egotism comforts itself with the delusion that any failure, political or economic, cannot be due to faults of the nation but to the intruding minority. When the Black Plague ravaged Europe it was not the defective health measures that were to blame but the Jews. All their laws of cleanliness including the wonderful Jewish Dietary Laws were brushed aside. The Jews have been the prime sufferers from the unhappy human weakness referred to, because they have inherited a load of prejudice dating from the early days of Christianity and this prejudice, which has been sedulously fostered in the schools and which may also be said to have been in the blood of successive generations of non-Jews throughout the world, has enabled politicians to use them as a lightning conductor to escape from their own troubles. The Anti-Jewish tyranny of Germany rests upon the ceaselessly propagated fiction that all that country's woes following the Great War were the work of Jews and not of the German Government. How is the Jew to escape from the deadly grip of this poisonous propaganda? Only the other day there took place over the radio a discussion between a Christian Methodist Preacher and a Jewish Minister. "Why is it", the Jewish Minister was asked, "that so many Jews are guilty of sharp practices?" We find it hard to agree with the findings of our Jewish friends who explained that this was due historically to the continuous persecutions to which Jews have been subjected in every age thus sharpening their minds because they are always on the defensive. Surely the indisputable fact is that the misdeeds of a very small number are splashed in headlines in the daily newspapers; the so-called sharp practices are caught on because the Jew is disliked - these cases are brought before the public gaze by newspaper, wireless and the novel especially the latter which nearly always portrays the Jew in an unfavourable light. The same proportion of sharp practices amongst Jews is to be found amongst Christians. There <u>is</u> a wide gap between the Christian and Jewish communities in such an important matter as Juvenile Crime. Not a week passes without us reading of

2.

several cases of Juvenile Crime reported e.g. in the
Sunderland Echo. We have yet to read of one Jewish boy or
girl brought before the Juvenile Courts in Sunderland. But
what credit does the Local Jewish Community receive for
such an exemplary record? How many Christians know that
Jewish youth is comparatively free from Juvenile Delinquency?
One would expect, in all fairness that the Jewish Minister
should be asked over the Radio not only why Jews are guilty
of sharp practices but also why they are free of Juvenile
Crime. Again we might ask, how is it that The National
Society for Prevention of Cruelty to Children have not had
occasion to prosecute one Jewish parent in Sunderland?
When will the world realise that Jews are ordinary, ration-
al human beings. The world owes a great debt to the Jew
for his contributions to every sphere in life spiritual,
cultural and material. Until the world realises that we
are all children of one Father with a common lot and a
common mission to bring the Kingdom of God to pass on Earth
racial hatred will persist with all its brood of suffering
and pain and Jews will be the greatest sufferers of all.
We are waiting for the day when we shall all receive equal
treatment. In the meantime we must educate the world to
reinterpret history so that Youth may learn the true begin-
nings of the origins of Civilisation and remember that it
was the Jewish Prophet Malachi who cried," Have we not one
Father, hath not one God created us all?"

DO YOU KNOW
1. What has Palestine done for the Dig for Victory Campaign?
2. Who is the first woman in the Country to receive the
newly constituted British Empire Medal?
3. Who said the following. "Every Anti-Semite is a potential
quisling?
4. Who discovered Acetone an essential ingredient of Trini-
trotoluol T.N.T. which was unprocurable outside Germany
during 1914-18 war.
5. Who was the first Jew to be a Minister of the Crown?
6. What connection is there between Dick Whittington and the
Jews?   Answers to the above on page 5.

HERE AND THERE
We have much pleasure in making the following announcements:
Engagements-Miss Sylvia Penn to Mr. Arnold Sheckman of
N. Shields. Miss Yetta Levine to Mr.M. Jackson of London.
Dr. Katzburg (Royal Infirmary) to Dr. Shapiro.
Promotions- D. Abrahams to Cpl. I. Berg, to L.A.C. and
J. Gordon to L.A.C.
New Recruits. - Sylvia Mincovitch and Sonia Leslie.

3.

We are pleased to include the following message from our old
friend Sol Novinski. "Whilst I am looking ahead let me
express the hope that is nearest my heart, indeed it is the
earnest hope of us all "that you will soon be with us again".
Meanwhile remember that everyone of you is an ambassador of
goodwill towards your fellow Jews. Scattered throughout the
world as you are and also living in intimate contact with
those of other religions and in some cases, I'm afraid, no
religion at all, you will meet people who do not know or
understand the Jew. You must therefore rise to the occasion
and grasp the opportunity offered you to show your friends
that the Jew is worthy of respect. You can give them that
feeling of Pride that the Jew is a comrade at all times.
Stand up to your principles and beliefs as a Jew and live up
to them not only in the letter, but more important still in
the spirit.   I wish you Godspeed, my fondest thoughts are
with you always. When the day of the great Reunion of
Sunderland's Jewish Young People comes, as assuredly it will
if it is at all possible Sol Novinski will be there to
welcome you.

"TANKS," for the Memory.   by Unita J. Magrill.

This is the tale of Tefka the Trooper
If he hadn't joined up - he'd have been in the souper.
His business a weekly was falling to bits
And Tefka had creditors no one could blitz.
He went for a parley to General H.Q.,
And there told the company what he would do.
"I'd like says old Tefka to drive in a tank.
Then I'd be quite happy to stay in the rank.
"Tanks" says the C.O. - "Don't mention it" says Teff,
"With a Waltzing Matilda I'll soon prove myself."
So back to his unit old Tefka he goes
About engines and things there ain't much that he knows.
But his great tribulations I scarcely need say
Bring smiles to his comrades right up to this day.
This happened the first time they had an alert,
His prowess, our Tefka, he meant to exert.
He was sure that Herr Hitler had heard the great news
That Tefka had joined up to fight for the Jews.
Now surely he'd sent all his Black Guards and men,
To start an invasion for Hitler to stem,
So straight to the first tank that Tefka could find
One thing he remembered the starter to wind,
He then pressed a button and lo and behold!
The tank started moving and Tefka felt bold,

4.

Till the tank pushed its way through the officers mess
And Tefka felt dubious of any success.
Until his commander all panting and red
At being so roughly ejected from bed
Yelled "Muster all men - an invasion's begun.
For God's sake why can't someone fire the big gun.
A strange fate that instant caused Teff's tank to strike it
And down from the air fell a Junkers and Messershmidt
Like a miracle then fuelless Toff's tank came halt
And in pandemonium none saw Tefka's fault
So Teff for a V.C. shook hands with the king,
He's still in a daze how he won the darn thing.

INQUISITOR ?   With Apologies

WE SEEK H$_{\text{e}}^{\text{im}}$r HERE,   WE SEEK H$_{\text{e}}^{\text{im}}$r THERE,
WE READERS SEEK H$_{\text{e}}^{\text{im}}$r EVERYWHERE,
CAN (S)HE BE--? WONT YOU TELL?
THAT HALF WIT AND HALF WIT-I THINK (S)HE'S SWELL.

Lex Talionis.

En Passant   - The Inquisitor.
So I have become a back number! A nine days wonder!!
Relegates to the ranks of the forgotten men "unhonoured,
unwept and unsung". How are the mighty fallen (Tell it not
in wrath). Nevertheless I plod on valiantly hoping to fill
the few lines at my disposal, wondering if a few crumbs of
appreciation will be eventually scattered to alleviate my
hunger for a place in the Public Eye. The only inadvertent
claim to fame, I fear, is when some irate person, to whom
the barb has evidently applied, adopts a bullying, threatening attitude to my sponsor, thereby causing good feeling
all round. However to misquote a greater one than I, "Ill
feeling is better than no feeling at all."

FLASH
Who has written a new poem entitled "The DIScharge of the
Light Brigade"? (Who has "Great Expectations"?)
Which young A.T. has been responsible for placing Dalkeith
on the map once more?
Is it true that 2 persons very interested in fashions
(Limited) may soon be united in a lasting partnership?
How are Habonim in Bamburgh?
Does I.B. (invariably J.B.) still think his powers of
deduction as illuminating as he imagined? (Not married
yet?)
Does the important Shipping Magnate still present books to
all and sundry? (Did her fiance object?)

ɔ

Which re-union between two members of the R.A.F. took
place recently at Tel Aviv. "Dr. G...... I presume?"
Does a certain ex-band leader have much scope for his
talents (musical, of course) in the Highland
Regiment.
Who calls Wilmslow "The Haven of Refuge"?
Which Don Juan attracts everyone to take a Ramble to
Amble?   Is the WARK WORTH it?
If old felt hats are 1/- each, what price accountant?
(not chartered)
How is the Hebridean Dulciner Player?   Has he finished
his Thesis?.
Why has Marsden suddenly become popular again?   Can
it be............?
Are all Staff Sergeants good mathematicians or are all
mathematicians good Staff Sergeants?   (Made any good
contacts in Halifax yet?)
Which is more predominant on the I.O.M., the minx or
the manx?
Is a certain renowned doctor soon to return to England
thereby causing great joy in B.C.?
How is a certain ex-service man getting on with his
summonses?
Does M.D. still get as many games of solo since
joining the R.A.F.?
Which inmate of Blackpool bans card playing?
Was your journey really necessary D.A.?

ANSWERS TO QUESTIONS ON PAGE 2.

1. Eight new Agricultural Settlements have been created
thus helping to feed the many Allied Troops now on
Palestinian soil.
2. Miss Rosali Gassman a Jewess from London for
conspicuous bravery during a night air raid on London.
3. Lady Reading, wife of the late Lord Reading, once
Viceroy of India.
4. Dr. Chaim Weitzmann, the Zionist Leader and one time
lecturer in Chemistry at Manchester University.   Sir
Ronald Storrs wrote "Its absence appalled the British
Admiralty but not the brain of the Jewish Chemist."
5. Sir George Jessel who was Solicitor-General;   one of
the greatest English Judges and the real founder of the
Modern Chancery Court.
6. In the early 15th Century Dick Whittington when Lord
Mayor of London, was permitted to import a Jewish doctor
from the S. of France, to attend to his sick wife, Alice.

6.

EXCERPTS FROM LETTERS

Driver L. Gillis writes "Many thanks for No.3 of the Bulletin, which was very welcome and most interesting to me. You see it is the only way I can find out what the remainder of the "Gang" is doing. Their letters to me are so spasmodic and so short that it is impossible to learn or form an opinion as to their Social successes etc."
Driver Gillis by soaring to the heights of poetic fancy, concludes by quoting the following from "Thackeray.
"Ah me, how quick the days are flitting,
I mind me of a time that's gone,
When here I'd sit, as now I'm sitting
In this same place, but not alone.........."
Let's hope that those good old times will return when P.G. we can all get together and yarn about the AOMOLIKEH TZEITEN".
Gwendolin Magrill writes "Many thanks for Bulletin No.3, which I think was the best one so far. I like the Puzzle Corner idea and the questions are of the right sort to teach us something of the part Jews are playing in the world of today." She seems to be enjoying herself as she writes: "I'm still happy in the A.T.S. and I wouldn't take my discharge even if it were offered to me."
Louis Oslberg writes "I thoroughly enjoy reading the bulletin as every word seems to bring me nearer to home and my old friends in the numerous societies, they were happy days those spent with the "Lit" and the Judeans...
......Not only myself but the other Jewish boys of my Company look forward to your next issue."

Please inform change of address.   If you do not receive your Bulletin regularly, let us know.

All correspondence to be sent to the Rev. S.P. Toperoff, 5 Victoria Avenue, Sunderland.

<u>THE SUNDERLAND JEWISH COMMUNITY</u>
Monthly Bulletin for the Forces
<u>Vol. 1 No. 5 Edited by the Minister, Nov. 1942.   Kislev 5703</u>

On the Festival of Chanukah which we shall celebrate
from Thursday evening Dec. 3rd, for eight days, we would do
well to remember our indebtedness to those spiritful
Maccabees who fought for the superiority of the spiritual
over the material. The light of Judaism, the light of
knowledge and reason over the dark forces of Heathenism, of
those barbaric and uncultured days. How history repeats
itself! The dark forces of Hitlerism have forced this war
upon the world, bringing slaughter, homelessness and misery
on the greater part of humanity. As in the days of
Antiochus the Mad Dictator the Jews were his first target,
so today the Jews have been in the front line, the spear-
head of the Nazi attack.

It was the light of Jewish religion that rescued the
Jew than the light of the Maccabeans who heroically and
courageously fought for their freedom. Today too, the Jew
must bring light into the world. In olden times the lights
were placed at the door outside the home in order to publish
the miracle. For obvious reasons we cannot do the same
today. None the less it is our bounden duty to bring the
light of Judaism out into the open world so that it pene-
trates the thick darkness around us and opens the eyes of
the bigoted and fanatical Jew baiters. We must carry the
light of our religion into the highways and byways of civilization. We must take the lights of Judaism outside the
home and burn them in the sight of passersby to perpetuate
the miracle of the survival of the Jew in the midst of
incessant sufferings and persecution.

The masses are ignorant of the mission and purpose of
Judaism. Many fallacious theories and misconceptions are
spread about the Jews. It is your duty to dispel them. You
may be in camp tucked away amidst the winding country lanes
of this island, or you may find yourself in Egypt, Africa,
India, Gibraltar or Madagascar; always carry with you the
Chanukah lights of Judaism. It is in your power to kindle
the light in the hearts of your Christian friends which will
ultimately produce a warmth of feeling and a love of
mankind.

On Page 4 you will find a contribution from "Argus" of
the "Sunderland Echo".   Sport helps to break down the
artificial barriers between different peoples. We therefore
welcome all the more Argus' sporting gesture in writing a

monthly artical for our Bulletin. We all appreciate his generosity of mind and purpose and are deeply grateful to him.

_____

DO YOU KNOW?
1. What is the Quadrans Judaicus?
2. Who was the most notable Jewish figure in the newspaper world in England in the 19th Century?
3. What is "NILI"?
4. How many Jewish Generals are there in the British Forces?
5. Which Jewish Colonel was killed whilst commanding his private yacht?

Answers to the above on Page 4+5 .

HERE AND THERE

We have much pleasure in congratulating the following:-
Births: Dr. and Mrs. Lester (nee May Merskey) on the birth of a son.   Mr. & Mrs. Ratcliffe Gillis on the birth of a daughter.
Promotions: Nat Goodman - Sergeant Major.   S. Freedman - Cpl.   Issy Davis - L.A.C.   Myer Davis L/Cpl.

We hear that the Judge Advocate General in West Africa is recommending Lt. Mordant Cohen to be put on the list of potential Judge Advocates for employment on Court Martial.

From Horace Stone comes the news that a soldier friend of his has changed his religion to Judaism. What part did Horace play in this conversion?

You will shortly receive a small Chanukah gift from the Jewish Womens War Services Committee.   Mrs. Toperoff, the chairman, has expressed the wish that the gift be received, not for its intrinsic value, but as a gesture of goodwill and friendship and as an act of thoughtfulness from the Committee to the Serving men and women of Sunderland.

EN PASSANT - The Inquisitor

'Allo, 'allo ici Radio Sunderland. I 'ave very leetle to report zis, 'ow you say?, month. Per'aps you geeve ze beeg forgeeveness I make ze recovery from what you call la maladie. My time, malheureusement 'e is not my own, 'e cannot get ze, as you beeg, bold, brave airmen say, "GEN", I fall short but you 'ave ze compre'ension? Oui? Mes amis, si genereux, si aimable, merci une mille fois! I show ze obeyance and ze 'umility, I kees vos pieds, next month when I am in sante bonne....... Mais a ce moment que voulez-vous? Ze docteurs they go (and as ze comic 'e say) they come back.

Last month I observe I 'ave ze poem written to me, such 'umour so clevaire I feel ashamed when I read my si faible essai which follows, I 'ave ze great ignorance, le nom-de-plume so legal I cannot understand, am I 'aving ze compliment! ($\frac{1}{2}$ plus $\frac{1}{2}$ = 1) my knowledge of arithmetique like ze latin is negligible - mais, que faire?

Ze poetess laureaute she ver' amusante je suis jaloux (se), I am 'ow you say? Not ze only light entertainment now. I 'ave ze competition 'orrible, I no like I "TANKS" I go 'ome (with ze enormous apology for stealing le bon mot which was stolen from me! Les voleurs!)

Ze "Shipping Magnate" 'as justified my toujours 'igh opinion of 'im, 'e is, 'ow you say in zis wonderful country a SPORT. Ze money I think is for myself but ze Editor, 'e explain. I 'ave not yet ze good enough command of your so great language. A bientot.

FLASH

Did a young member of the R.A.F. and his fiancee enjoy their recent visit to the Home Town? The 48 hours at their disposal seems to have been well spent.

So you desire to be mentioned again H.B.? Do the girls still have to leave "The Rock" at a specified time? How's Bill?

Which R.A.F. officer phones his wife every night----or else

Is it true that Newcastle is soon to become the W.A.A.F. Headquarters?

Which dentist home on leave of recent months attended a "PIDYANIA BEN" - was he there in a professional capacity? Did he make a good "impression"?

Is it true that our recent successes in Egypt are due entirely to L.B., V.G., C.M., H.B., D.L., (do you know who this is?) and C.M.? Thank you, oh heroic ones!

Have 2 members of "THE GANG" met in India yet?

Did the 2 lovers home on leave last week have a good time? It must be a relief to return to your units to catch up on lost sleep!!!

Who says life in the R.A.F. is like "Holme from home"?

Did a certain Corporal and his wife have a good time at "Melrose Gardens" whilst in Sunderland recently?

Has the "Aldershot Tattoo" returned to Scotland yet? It's very gratifying to learn that your talents aren't for the exclusive use of one country.

Which Indian Accountant is known as Shepherd of the "Hills"?

Who said "Amo Madras, I love a lass"?

FLIGHTS INTO SPORT - By Argus of the "Sunderland Echo."

We don't know where flies go in the winter time, but we do know where footballers go in war time. Judging by the "stars" that shine in the many representative games they mainly disappear into nice cushie jobs on the P.T. Staff of the various Arms of the Forces. The lesser lights just disappear to be sailors, soldiers or airmen. It was ever thus.

The old Roker Park veteran, Bob Gurney, is a Sub.Lient. R.N.R., coaching the boys of the Sea Cadets in P.T. and sporting activities. The Sunderland manager, Bill Murray, who served in the Great War, is County Sports Welfare Officer with the rank of Captain, and may be seen two or three days a week out in the field coaching army teams.

Now don't say he uses the knowledge gained in the interests of his club. He has already signed three army players as professionals but keep it dark. There might be a future "star" among them. At any rate take it from me Sunderland have got some good youngsters for later on. The war years are not being wasted.

We are still awaiting the fixing of a date for Tom Smith to box Nel Tarleton for the British Championship. Originally it was to be an open air affair at Liverpool, but now it will have to be indoors. Tom is training hard again after that break due to the death of his younger brother.

Point to remember study football law in your spare time and become proficient. Many referees will be wanted when this war is over and it may be your chance to get the Cup Final one day. <u>Catch Question</u>: If a man shoots for goal, the ball bursts in transit, the bladder goes into the net and the case sticks on the crossbar. What is it?

<u>Answer to be given next month.</u>

Answers to questions on Page 2.

1. An important nautical instrument used for the determination of the sun and stars and hence gave the relative position of a vessel at any given moment. It was introduced by Rabbi Jacob ben Makhir ibn Tibbon who also compiled the Calendar used by Dante, quoted by founder of modern astronomy Copernicus Kepler and acted as Regent of the faculty of Medicine at Montpelier.

2. J.M. Levy, who created not only the Daily Telegraph but also popular journalism as a whole in England. No member of the Levy family is associated with the Newspaper world today.

3. An important organization founded for intelligence work on behalf of the British forces by Sarah Aaronson, a Jewish heroine who discovered by the Turks during the last war shot herself to escape arrest. "Nili" saved the lives of 30,000 British soldiers.

4. Brigadier W.R. Beddington recently awarded the C.B.E.; Brigadier F.H. Kisch who commands the Royal Engineers in the Western Desert and who was at one time head of Zionist Executive in Palestine and Major-General Lorie who also received the C.B.E.

5. Col. Claude Beddington who placed his yacht at the disposal of the Government and was killed recently off the Welsh coast at the age of 72.

EXCERPTS FOM LETTERS.

My dear Inquisitor;

As a keen follower of your column and an Admirer of your 'Cacoethes Scribendi', may I say that this month I was rather disappointed with your descriptive phrases, which are usually so well coined.

The ability to coin a phrase has been the making of all great column writers and your 'All and sundry' as applied to a rather attractive & charming person, seems to lack your usual punch.

Hoping that you will accept these few lines and the enclosed (towards your Services Comforts Fund) in the constructive manner in which they are intended.

Kind regards,
Yours sincerely,
Shipping Magnate.

Sorry S.M. but we "would-be journalists" (unlike the real ones with whom you seem to associate) cannot achieve the pinnacle of perfection each month.
"Inquisitor".

N.B. The editor wishes to thank S.M. for his generous contribution of 10/6 towards our comforts fund. It is highly appreciated and will be used to good purpose.

Cyril Mincovitch from Egypt writes - I was delighted with the Bulletin and must congratulate you on a very happy idea. It makes excellent reading. Of one thing you may rest assured and that is that its main message is one that has been "mantled" by every one of us and invariably discussion on those lines materialise when we can meet.

D. Levine of Egypt would like addresses of any of our chaps in Egypt and any where near Cairo.

The editor thanks the following in addition to those above for their letters: Louis Berg, Zelda Gillis, W. Book, Cpl. Freedman Horace Stone, Horace Weinthrop and A.H. Davis.

Issy Levine from India writes - Gee what a thrill it was
to receive your Forces Bulletin No. 1 and on Yom Kippur
morning too. To read of old friends and also anonymous
persons under the heading "Flash" was a feast which satisfied my natural hunger on the Day of Atonement. I think
"the road to Singapore" will soon be open so maybe I'll
come home that way. I feel sure that '43 will be our Victory year and when all the chaps (and girls too!!) meet in
your house - gee what times we'll have. Tell any lads who
may be in India to look me up they will always be welcome
in the Sgt. Mess. P.S. May I be your Indian Correspondent.
Harold Brewer of Gibralter writes - The thought of being
away from home and its social and spiritual life, no matter
how hard they are is I find softened with the arrival of
this much looked forward to Bulletin. Through the medium of
the Bulletin I should like to convey to my friends abroad
my best wishes for a safe and speedy return home in the
near future.

A Peep into the Past

As you sit on that fallen tree trunk outside the old
barn which is your billet, in some lonely spot somewhere
in England, the Middle East, or perhaps far off India, and
at sundown your thoughts turn to home, perhaps some times
you will think of the happy evenings spent at the Lit, the
Dramatic Soc., the Scouts and the many other activities of
the Communal Hall. These thoughts I am sure will be happy.

Will you let me sit beside you and help you spend a
few happy carefree moments dreaming of those times. Times
that will surely come again.

Do you remember the interfunctions with the Manchester
Lit, Liverpool Lit, Newcastle and Hull? Of course you do.
Do you remember the day we met the Liverpool folk at the
Station when we held up the tram in Fawcett St. and the
surprise of our visitors on seeing our new luxury cars? Do
you remember the Happy-Go-Lit Concert Party? The turn
calling themselves the Lit-Vacks? How one of them feared
the black grease paint would not come off his face at the
end of the show. The girls dancing Troop. That little
ballad, The Wedding of the Painted Doll and the very professional photograph taken after the show. Then those hilarious sketches with sound effects and no words but those
read by someone sitting at the side of the stage. They
were happy carefree days indeed, were they not?

At the kind invitation of Rev. Toperoff, I shall write
a number of letters in these pages giving your minds a
little touch that may stimulate happy memories. For
memories live longer than dreams.

Happy Days!   Sol Novinski.

THE SUNDERLAND JEWISH COMMUNITY

Monthly Bulletin for the Forces.

Vol. 1. No.6.   Edited by the Minister,   Dec. 1942. Tebeth 5703.

In the past few weeks Jews have been much in the news.   It seems that the world has at last aroused itself from its slumber to a realisation of the terrible tragedy that is slowly but surely annihilating millions of Jews in the Nazi occupied territories.

After a week of mourning and prayer preceded by a day of Fast a proclamation was issued by the eleven Allied powers demanding just retribution for those responsible for the bestial policy of cold blooded extermination of European Jewry.   Never before in the history of the English Parliament did all its members spontaneously rise in dead silence to pay homage to the martyrdom of the Jewish race.

The clarion call has been sounded, let us pray that its notes will not be deafened by the passage of time, but that prompt relief will be forthcoming.   For too long have we been left to struggle with our own problems.   When German Jewry was crippled out of existence and all its possessions confiscated English and American Jewry immediately launched big appeals to deal with the colossal refugee problem.   We appealed to our generous brethren three and four times, the response was magnificent, the impression thus gained was that Jews were not tied together by bonds of friendship and brotherhood but exceedingly wealthy.   It was felt that they could look after their own troubles.

The time however has arrived for the free governments of the world to realise that Jews alone cannot salvage the wreckage of Polish and Rumanian Jewry.   Superhuman efforts must be made to rescue at least some of the children that are awaiting a lingering death.   Jews are powerless to do anything themselves.   Government again alone can effect anything of lasting value.

At this season of Goodwill the Christian countries can put into practise the teaching of brotherhood by demanding that the doors of the Palestine Jewish National Home be opened wide for these innocent and helpless mites.   These children have not had the chance to breathe the air of Freedom.   The world cannot look on passively.   Thousands could be rescued if the will was there.

DO YOU KNOW?
1.   What is affixed to the Statue of Liberty in New York Harbour?
2.   Which Jewish Hymn has more musical settings than any other poem in any other language?
3.   Who brought tobacco first to Europe?
4.   Where did the Zionist colours, blue and white derive from?
5.   Who was the first Jew to become Boxing Champion of England?
6.   Which ancient Jewish Mathematician published a book on Arithmetic.
          Answers to the above questions to be found on P.3

2.

HERE AND THERE

Congratulations to Mr. & Mrs. Jack Warrentz on the birth of a son,
and to Mr. Ellis Dresner who has passed his finals in Medicine.
Promotions - A. Vandervelde, L.A.C.;   J. Schochet, Cpl.
We send good wishes to the following new recruit who has recently
entered the Forces. - Charles Winberg.
Congratulations to Dr. Ralph Collins on becoming a Major of the
Home Guard.

Requests have been received for our Bulletin from various
quarters but last week the editor received a letter from a Jewish
Padre in Southern Rhodesia for past copies of our Bulletin.

EN PASSANT - THE INQUISITOR

Can it be only six brief transitory months since I wrote my
first breathtaking article? Can so much apathy, antipathy and
sympathy have been registered in so short a time? Many belliger-
ent, unsportsmanlike remarks have been hurled at my innocent head,
BUT, may I draw the attention of those bellicose few that the pen
has always been mightier than the sword and, for the duration anyway, I hold the whip hand. If these incessant murmurings continue
I shall have to attack most violently these dissentors through the
medium of my column - so take warning. To quote a person of
almost as equal renown as myself "One can't please all of the
people all of the time."

My loyal fans from all corners of "Our Empire" continue to
besiege me with gratifying letters of adulation for which I am
eternally, internally and externally grateful. Even they, however
have the temerity to tender ONE criticism, which is that they are
unable to decipher all the flashes. At great inconvenience to my
myself I have endeavoured to make them simpler by giving more clues
and trust this will promote greater satisfaction - so be it!

As I am writing this precis I am sitting before a cheerful
roaring fuel saving fire in my study, my heavy lids close period-
ically. The warm luxurious, opulent atmosphere has a soporofic
effect on my tired and jaded nerves (it's me noives, boss) so I
must conclude as   "Sleep it is a blessed thing
                    Beloved from Pole to Pole."
                        (Not Thackeray L.G.!!!)

FLASH
So D.A. won't be intimated.

How are the suede shoes in India? (Not you Poppa, sit down.)

On dit that a certain Ambler has been Rambling quite a lot to
Scotland (It makes you think).

Did a certain Q.M. know he was going to N.I....... when he boasted
he would never leave the country?

Flash Cont'd.   3.

So A... (Ssh careless talk) is now the home of J.?. Sunderland's
Heart Throb No. 1.

Sorry N.C. pretends NOT to recognise himself in last month's
Bulletin.   But nevertheless hope he's had plenty of sleep since.....

Which proud Pappa spends his time studying the Ascot Fashions?
(with an eye to the Future?)

So the pseudo evacuee has eventually succumbed to the call of the
Yorkshire countryside in mid-winter!

Rumour hath it that the Town is to be brightened in the near future
by the return of H.B.   Nice work!

Does S.I. still fancy herself as a Public Speaker?   Much scope where
you are?

Which Public Benefactor recently bestowed Chanukah Gifts in the Town?
Is it true that all the recipients were CARD PLAYERS?

Is the Adjutant still a good judge of Indian Cosmetics?   (I hope
this flash is underlined for you).

Is it true that the C.O. of the local N.F.S. (Rectory) is Anti C.B.?
What will he think of the stripe?

Rumour hath it that a very eligible professional man in Town has
transferred his affections from Glasgow to London?

Is it true that a certain girl is filled with remorse because the
Sunderland Don. Juan does not ring the Highfield Hospital telephone
for her any more?

Is it true that a Royal Canadian Air Force Officer stationed in the
environs of Sunderland is causing quite a flutter of the feminine
hearts?

Answers to Questions on Page 1.
1.   A poem by the Jewish Poetess, Emma Lazarus 1849-1877.
2.   The Friday Night Hymn, "LECHA DODI" composed by Alkabetz early
      16th century. The musical settings number more than 300.
3.   The Jew Luis De TERRES, a companion of Columbus who settled
      in Cuba.
4.   From the Blue Stripes and White Fringes of the Tallith.
5.   Daniel Mendoza 1789.   He is credited with the introduction of
"   "Science" as opposed to the cruder tactics of the olden time
      "bruiser".
6.   Nicomachus of Gerassa in 100 C.E. whose work remained for 1,000
      years the standard work on the Subject.   Arithmetic as taught by
      the Romans was based on his work.

Answer to last month's Puzzle by "Argus"   "A Miracle".

A MESSAGE FROM PHYLLIS HEILPERN, M.A.

You will be interested to learn that Zionism continues to flourish (and be propagated) in Sunderland. Our young people are growing up "Jew-conscious" proud of the fact that they are part of that great but down-trodden, persecuted people.

The Communal Hall and the Schoolrooms in Ryhope Road are being well worn by the young and younger local Zionists. The under 15's are organised in Gedudum of Habonim and they meet on Sunday afternoo guided by one or two Rashim from 15 and upwards Groups. On Monday and Thursday evenings the Chavurah of Habonim meets and on Shabbos evenings, in members homes, there is a regular meeting of the Y.Z.A. which takes the form of a study circle. Naturally the topics under discussion are of Jewish interest. Occasionally we have meetings of a more social nature such be gramaphone recital held some weeks ago; that evening of Operatic Music proved extremely popular despit the fact that a charge was made in order to raise money for Zionist Funds, and we have had requests for further entertainments of a similar nature.

Our members have not provided us here at home with much news c themselves; the Hon. Secs. would be delighted to receive communica- tions from any of our serving men and women who care to write. Eilee E. Heilpern, 46, Ormonde Street is the Hon. Sec. of the S.Y.Z.A. What news we have about our members, we have had to glean from all l of odd sources and this, as you can imagine, is far from satisfactor

So far I have told you how those of us left at home are doing our best to keep our flag flying whilst you are away. It is no ea: job for us because our numbers are sadly depleted and blackout does interfere to some extent with our activities. Moreover, the burder of leadership falls heavily on the few to whom it accrues, for ther are not many with whom they can share it. Nevertheless we continu determined that nothing, not even air-raids, shall deter us from preparing ourselves for the upbuilding of our people and our land. Indeed so far has Sunderland Zionist Youth progressed that one of our members Leila Stone, has just gone on Hachsharah, she has realised the ambition of many a young Zionist. We wish her much happiness i her venture and hope that she is but the fore-runner of others who will follow.

Are you doing your bit towards Zionism? Do not make the mist: of assuming that it has nothing to do with you. It is an idea whic] should be part and parcel of your daily life, it must not be shelve on account of the exigencies of these times of storm and stress. Fr the furtherance of our aims for a National Home, you can gain inspi: tion and comfort. Make it your business to get into touch with the Zionist group nearest to you; there are Zionist groups in the most unexpected places and if there isn't one near to you, what about starting one. Many of the newer Zionist Societies have been begun members of H.M.F. stationed in an area where previously Zionism was practically unknown.

5.

We look forward to the time when we shall have back at our meetings all our Zionists who are now away from home. Some of them have already experienced the thrill of visiting Eretz Israel and describing in glowing terms all that they have seen there. We are waiting hoping that in the Not-too-distant future, there will be the opportunity for all who desire to go back to Palestine.

PEEPS INTO THE PAST.

About 31 years ago the committee of the Lit, decided to hold a dance on or about Simchas Torah, Chanukah and Purim. To date this has been done. Do you remember the Chanukah dances, the lighting of the candles, the happy times we had? And you who were scouts, do you remember the Chanukah Services? When you carried your beautiful flag into Shool, followed by the trim Girl Guides, under the leadership of Guide Captain Rita Olswang. How proud you felt Young Israel; carrying the noble Traditions of the Maccabeans. Now you carry your ideals to men and women who knew nothing of the Jew and cared less. You have gained their respect. Keep it. May it spread in ever widening circles until it encompasses the world. At this time of the year I am also reminded of the activities of the Jewish Arts League, the Songs and Plays. Do you remember the atmosphere alternating between sadness and joy, usually ending in hope? Is this not our life? I remember the camp fire scene depicting the young Chalutzin singing their songs when the days work is done. A most impressive performance The Choir led by the Rev. A. Oler, singing our Folk Songs, the plays mostly typifying life in the Ghetto of Europe. There was much hard work put in those shows, but we enjoyed it. Didn't we.

Happy days,
SOL.

SPORTS REFLECTIONS - BY "Argus"

Raich Carter has now been promoted to Sergeant. Promotion was promulgated two or three days after he had scored three goals for the R.A.F. against Scotland at Newcastle. Now lads stick in. A stripe a goal, you know carries with it a good bonus weekly.

Cliff Whitelum, Sunderland's centre forward is a Bombadier serving with the Ack-Ack - one of those "Z" Batteries; George Robinson now playing with Sunderland again but for many years a Charlton Athletic player, is with the R.A.F. in Northumberland.

Arthur Housam, who was married while on leave on December 15th, has of course left the Police and is serving with an Infantry Unit in the Edinburgh area. Another to "take the plunge" recently is Billy Hewison, Sunderland's centre-half.

Before these notes are in your hands a third will have taken unto himself a wife. This is Arthur Wright, who was to be married during Xmas week. He is with the D.L.I. in the south of England and has scored many goals in the Kent County League for his unit as inside left

Johnny Cochrane, Sunderland's former manager is now a Ministry of Supply official.

6.

Many former Bede School students are in the Air Force and I believe there are a round dozen across in Canada and the States training to be pilots.

Like Arthur Wright, Len Duns is also in the South of England - a P. T. Instructor with the R.A. He captained an Army eleven a few days ago.

When the war is over - when!!! You will find Sunderland has discovered a grand young back in John Robert Eves, a Redby School boy. He works overtime every night at the Forge and the only training he gets before a match each week is to run from Mackie's Corner to Fulwell three nights a week when coming home from work.

EXCERPTS FROM LETTERS.

K. DOBERMAN writes - "I wish to thank you for your last Bulletin, which I find at all times most interesting. The parts I like best are the quiz questions, as every Friday afternoon we have debates and also one may give these quiz questions."

L/C H. STONE writes - "The hospitality shown to our boys by the Jewish Community of Egypt and Palestine during the first days of Tishri should be commented on officially and brought to the notice of English Jewry".

GWEN MAGRILL says - "In my opinion each month sees an improvement in the Bulletin until now, when I think the only complaint is that there should be more of it".

DAVID ABRAHAMS says - "I receive your Bulletin regularly and enjoy its contents thoroughly. It is a very good idea and should be especially welcome to some of the boys who are not so lucky as I and are stationed away from civilisation."

HORACE WEINTHROP interests us by writing - "When in London recently I met Cpl. Ralph Freedman at the A.P. Club and want to warn the ladies back in Sunderland that Ralph is making a fine figure on the dance hall with the girls, in fact he was making me feel quite in the corner".

ISAAC BREWER writes - "Very many thanks for your Bulletin No. 5 which I can assure you I have quite enjoyed reading. I was particularly pleased to note the article by Sol Novinski. It certainly brought back very pleasant memories. It was certainly a grand gesture on your part inviting him to contribute."

ALAN FORMAN writes - "I'd like to compliment the ENTIRE staff of the Bulletin the contents of which I look forward to with avidity each month. I was promoted to full Sergeant on Oct. 14th thus missing Lance Sergeant Rank completely.

NOTE - Change of address must be reported to ensure regular receipt of Bulletin. If you do not receive your Bulletin regularly, let us know.

All correspondence to be sent to the Rev. S.P. Toperoff, 5, Victoria Avenue, Sunderland.

Sunderland Jewish Community
Bulletin for the Forces

1943

THE SUNDERLAND JEWISH COMMUNITY

Monthly Bulletin for the Forces.

Vol.1. No. 7.   Edited by the Minister.   January 1943.   Shevat 5703.

A day in the Jewish Calendar which passed by almost un-noticed was the 15th of Shevat, corresponding to Thursday, January 21st, known as the New Year of Trees.   You might think that in times of war one cannot be bothered with such minor celebrations.   Yet it is well to remember that so many think we are obsessed with greed for money and unjust gain.

How many outside our Community know that our Festivals have their origin in Nature?   Jewish Arbor Day, as it is called, is celebrated in Erez Israel with great enthusiasm by thousands of Jewish boys and girls.   "They go out into the woods and fields carrying tiny saplings, which they plant.   With songs and music they plant the baby trees.   Each makes his own sign so that he will recognise the tree he planted and then he comes day by day to care for the little tree till it grows straight and tall and strong."

Have you heard of the Jewish children murdered in cold blood by the Nazis in Eastern Europe?   These trees planted by children will be living memorials of the countless martyrs who have perished at the hand of the Hun.

A proper observance of this minor Festival would be our answer, to those who constantly brand us as materialists.   We must remind the World that even in the heat of the carnage and slaughter of total war we plant trees.   Our enemies delight in destruction, we in construction our enemies maul and trample innocent children, we plant young saplings to the Glory of God.   Let the world know that we owe our existence and hark back to a Garden tended by God Himself, where man was first planted surrounded by an abundance of trees.

We pray for the day when we shall transform this hideous world, as we know it today, into another Garden of Eden from which we shall once again receive everything that is pleasant to the sight and good for food when we shall once again be guided by the Tree of Life and the Tree of Knowledge

---

DO YOU KNOW?

1.   Who is responsible for the Jewish nose?
2.   Where is Hatikvah, the Zionist Anthem, played amongst non-Jewish people?
3.   Which is the first Jewish Colony where Jews settled?
4.   What part did Jews play in the introduction of sugar in Europe?
5.   From where does the "Star Chamber" at Westminster derive its name?
6.   Who is (a) General Dovator?   (b) Captain Israel Fisanovitch?

Answers to the above questions on P. 3.

2.

HERE AND THERE.

At the suggestion of Argus, our contributor, the Sunderland Jewish Womens War Services Committee organised on Boxing Day, a treat for the patients at a Camp Reception Station in Sunderland, all of whom were non-Jews. Each soldier was presented with a parcel. In the afternoon an elaborate tea was served by the Jewish women to the patients and the Staff. The tea was followed by a Social when there were games, dancing and singing.

Congratulations to L.A.C. Issy Berg on his engagement to Miss Lily Mandelson of Glasgow.
To Mr. and Mrs. Minchom on the birth of a daughter.

Promotions - Mordaunt Cohen to Full Lieutenant.
David Abrahams to Corporal.

EN PASSANT - INQUISITOR.

It is quite, ironical to think that some of you, my vast public are basking and baking in the torrid, tropical sunshine, whilst we, the aged and decrepit in your native city, are enveloped by cold, cutting winds with snow falling incessantly and stalactites hanging precariously from the eaves. Very few dare venture forth, nevertheless, I suppose being in England has its compensations!

Once more my post bag is unbearably heavy with epistles from H.M. Forces complaing they are still unable to identify the persons mentioned in dispatches (i.e. The Flashes). Naturally my main intention is to give unsurpassed pleasure to the persons mentioned therein, and as long as they, with their super-human intellect, can recognise the barb I am truly content. But if the plebs are desirous of probing into other peoples private affairs they will have to sharpen their somewhat dull and retarded wits, or, alternatively, they can write to me enclosing 6d. per question and I will endeavour to satiate their unseemly curiosity.

FLASH

Which member of the R.A.F. stationed near Cambridge, (home on leave this week) has expressed the sentiment that he prefers HANGERS to HANGARS?

Which Algerian Shiek is receiving mail from all but "Beth-Ivri"?

What do we infer from the fact that a certain girl in town has in her possession an R.A.F. Emergency Ration Card? Can it be - - - - - - -?

Whose HOYT is broken because the Ambler has stopped Rambling?

So the GALLANT of Glasgow has now become the Rake of Rochdale!

FLASH Continued

What is "Dr. Kildare's Strange New Case"?   So he has come over the sea from Skye!!!

Which Nigerian Solicitor is known as "The Defendant's Saviour"? So the much talked of Reunion has taken place! Elliott Smith will surely have composed and Etude, at least, to celebrate such an auspicious occasion!!

Is it true that M.D. is spending ALL his money in sending Cablegrams to his wife?

Who has been voted "The Belle of Derby"?   Don't overdo it, remember early to bed etc.

My Egyptian Agent writes much of the good long gossip between C.M. and H.B. (So they KNOW who I am.   Nice work, because even I haven't been told - - - yet!)

Which R.A.F. Officer stationed in Newcastle has as his signature tune "Open UP Dem Pearly Gates"?   -

Is it true that Cleadon was recently immersed in a deep gloom? Aren't we pleased all was normal when the Conquering Hero returned - after a day!

This is your LAST warning D.A.!

Is it purely COHENcidental that N.C. and Z.L. always have their leav simultaneously?

ANSWERS TO QUESTIONS ON PAGE 1.

1. The Jewish nose is not Jewish.   It is characteristic of the Armenoid peoples among whom were the ancient Hittites.
2. It was a folk air in the Balkans and was played as a march by one of the regiments in the Serbian Army.
3. Jamaica, which belonged to descendants of Columbus who opposed the Inquisition and therefore provided a haven for the Jews.
4. Sugar was first introduced by the Radanite Jewish Traders.   In 1548, Portugese Jews transplanted sugar cane from the Island of Madeira to South America, and Jews established sugar cane mills in the West Indies.
5. From the Hebrew "Shtar" meaning "Document", this being the repository of the documents of pre-expulsion Jewry.
6. (a) Dovator was one of Russia's Jewish Generals who was killed when leading the Cossack attack on Nazis outside Moscow thus saving the Russian Capital.
    (b) Fisanovitch is of the Russian Submarine Service who was awarded the highest decoration, the Lenin Order, the title of Hero of the Soviet Union and the Gold Star Medal.

4.

PEEPS INTO THE PAST

I received a Circular the other day informing me that a Live Newspaper Night is being held at the "LIT". Rosalie Gillow as Chairman, will be Editor and will contribute the leading article. I wish I could be there to hear it. For withering wit and hilarious humour Rosalie Gillow glitters.

As we know, the "LIT" holds a Live Newspaper Night every year and many a brilliant article has been read. Humour has never been absent. I recollect the report of a football match between the Amalakites and the Hebrews. When the Referee held up his hands the Hebrews scored and when he dropped them the Amalakites scored. The whole report was written in the venacular. The Hebrews won of course. There were serious articles also. About this time of the year a Cup Night was giving the Committee much thought. There were usually five or six Members entries. The standard of two or three was fairly good, but I always thought the summing up of the Adjudicators findings by Nathan Muscat B.A. the most masterly piece of work of the night. His calm reasoning, his tactful advice, given in that measured but kindly tone, was to my mind a delight.

I had the honour of presenting the Cup. Once handing it over to the winner he looked into it and in disgusted tones remarked "Why, there's nothing in it".

One winner's parents were so delighted with their Son's success, that they held a Party to which the Executive and Committee were invited.

Do you remember the Locum Tenens Night? The members told what they would do were they someone else. Do you remember the Mock Trials and Mock Parliaments? I had a warm time those nights, not only were the discussions heated, I was as a rule clad in gown and large wig. The wig was very hot, I assure you, and your questions and points of order hotter.

These items of our programme not only were good entertainment they were eductaional, and most important also gave us an intimate understanding of each other.

No wonder then, the Sunderland Lit was freely acknowledged as the friendliest Young Jewish Society in the North of England.

Ah well Happy Days.

SOL.

P.S. Do you know how the Communal Hall got its name?

FLIGHTS INTO SPORT - By "ARGUS" of

"The Sunderland Echo"

Well here we are again. I hope you boys are getting plenty
of exercise on the field of sport but keeping out of the road of
injuries. My experience and advice is: Never go into a tackle half
heartedly. That is the way you get a "knock". A full blooded
tackle, made when the body is well balanced is always the safe thing
to do.

I have been watching a good deal of football in the Army as the
Army Welfare Officer for the Sunderland and Seaham area, and most of
it is quite good but I find one big fault. The players do not play
the way they are facing. If that does not convey much to you, let
me explain. If you are facing your own goal and you are a forward,
never try to turn and beat your man. You can never tell what is
behind you, so put the ball back to your half-back and run into
position. Similarly if you are a half-back make a back pass to
your back, and if you are a back make it to your goalkeeper. Safety
first all the time.

The next point I wish to impress upon you is that Football
Strategy is no different to Military Strategy in this respect; Watch
and take stock of the opposition and play upon your opponent's weakness and to your own side's strength.

The censor forbids me telling you anything about weather
conditions or I might have been able to convey some idea to you how
Sunderland were beaten 4 - 2 at Middlesbrough and won 7 - 0 at Roker
in the return. But you can think it out. In the first instance
the team that took the risks attached to a fall won the points; in
the second there were no risks - just dirty knees and soiled jersey.
That should be good enough for even the proverbial blind referee who
needs his "eyes chalked".

You all probably know by now that we have started upon the cup
ties. The endeavour is to get into the 32 teams with the best
record from ten games. They are the qualifiers and they go into the
open drawer for the competition proper.

Some of you may be wondering who is this Laidman who is playing
so well for Sunderland at right-half. Well he is a Corporal at
Brancepeth Castle and a signed Sunderland player. He had a season
with Everton before war broke out when he was only seventeen and
Manager Murray discovered that he had not been placed on Everton's
retained list. So he snapped him up and signed him as a professional

Any of my readers who have been on leave and visited Roker Park
ground will have seen a big improvement in Johnny Spuhler. The
Fulwell and Redby Schoolboy is playing better than ever in his life.
That pleases me most because I was the one who signed him for
Sunderland as he was finishing school.

Cheerio until next month - and good shooting.

EXCERPTS FROM LETTERS

<u>Lt. Mordaunt Cohen</u> writes - Many thanks for Bulletin No. 2 which contained interesting local news. Keep it up, as I can assure you that I shall look forward to it every month. Is Inquisitor opening a Matrimonial Agency? It would appear so from one of the "Flashes". If so I offer to open a West African Branch. However in this part of the World it is the bridegroome who pays the NADAN to the bride's father. Anything from £6 upwards with a few goats and hens thrown in. The more one sees of its natives, the more one becomes convinced in the theory of The Lost Tribes having migrated to these parts of the World.

<u>Cpl. Ralph Freedman</u> writes - I go to Young Israel Meetings regularly at Woburn House and to the Forces Club. Recently I addressed the Richmond Jewish Literary Society, a return visit, and also the Maccabi Club.

<u>Charles Winberg</u> writes - I find the Magazine really interesting and amusing. It is grand from the point of view when one reads about people one has known most of one's life - it seems to bring home so much nearer to me.

<u>Louis Olsberg</u> writes - Your next Bulletin is looked forward by not only myself, but the other Yiddisher boys of my unit.

<u>Sammy Lerman from Colombo</u> writes - This place is very expensive for the Forces to enjoy themselves, and the climate is damp and hot. I am looking forward to your very welcome Magazine.

FAROE ISLANDS BY Charles Kolson.

One of the main events of the year in the Faroe Islands is when shoals of whales are driven into the bays and fiords from the Atlantic. The harpooning and killing of the whales is really a sight well worth seeing and contains a tremendous amount of skill and daring by the Whalers. As soon as the whales are sighted the word goes around the island quicker than telephone, and no matter with what they are occupied at the moment they all cease whatever they are doing. They generally shout as long and loud as they can "Grindergrab" the Faroese word for whales, and all rush down to the sea, not forgetting the Troops, to watch the spectacle. As soon as the whales are driven into the Bay the whalers go out in their small boats similar to canoes, and with their special knives they get ready for the fray. The handling of the boats by them is really superb and with great care and accuracy they plunge the knife into the focal point of the whale's forehead. But they must at all cost avoid contact with the tail of the whale as this in most cases proves fatal. Soon the beach is littered with as many as 600 - 700 whales which is considered a good catch by the inhabitants and the Bay is tinted bright red from the blood of the whales. Next day the cutting up of the whales begins, and as you will know they get a tremendous amount of oil from them, and of course they eat the meat which is generally left out to dry. Some of the boys who have sampled it say it is very tasty, but the majority of us prefer not to take the risk. In the evening there is a celebration and the inhabitants all "go gay" and generally finish up totally intoxicated. For such a small country there are heaps of interesting incidents one can recall and the scenery is really picturesque.

With best wishes to all friends at home and overseas.

All correspondence to be sent to Rev. S.P. Toperoff,
5, Victoria Avenue, Sunderland.

THE SUNDERLAND JEWISH COMMUNITY

Monthly Bulletin for the Forces

Vol. 1, No. 8. Edited by the Minister, February 1943. Adar 1, 5703.

What is Man?   The philosophers throughout the ages have asked
this question and each one has answered it differently.   Plato called
Man "a two-legged creature without feathers".   Pascal called Man "an
incomprehensible monster, he is a reed the feeblest thing in Nature."
Byron says, "Man is a two-legged reptile crafty and venemous".
Carlisle writes that "Man is a forked radish, a political beast."
Finally one is reminded of Diogenes searching in daylight with a
lantern to find a Man in the streets of Athens.

By studying the place held by Man in the scheme of the Universe
from the Jewish standpoint one must realise the supremacy of Judaism.
In the story of the Creation the central emphasis is placed on Man and
he is regarded as almost of an angelic rank.   Whereas Christianity
insists too much on Man as a sinful mortal fated to die an ignominious
death unless he is saved by the perfect atonement of one in whom Man
must place implicit trust and faith, Judaism says, that each man is
unique.

It is not the Jew but Man who is represented to be the aim and
goal of creation.   The Hebrew for Man is "Adam" which is akin to
"Earth".   Commenting on the verse in Genesis "And God formed Man of
the dust of the earth", the Rabbis ask "From which part of the earth's
surface did He gather the dust" and the answer is supplied by a Jewish
sage of the second century, "From every part of the habitable earth
was dust taken for the formation of Adam", was the reply.   In other
words, Man white, black or yellow is the result of the creative command
of God and all men therefore are brothers of one large society drawn
together by a common ideal and unity of purpose.

No two people are exactly alike, each individual is unique, non
the duplicate of another.   This is the reverse of the class doctrine
in which man is judged as a mere specimen of his class.   Judaism says
each man must have a chance for individual happiness.   It believes in
the equality of the rights of all people before the law.   How important is this today?   Can we understand why people of the world allow
the persecution of the Jew?   It is not the persecution of the Jew but,
an injustice is meted out to Man a human being.

Let us hope that this war will teach the world the worth of Man
and in the post-war reconstruction the dignity of Man will be upheld.
The status of Man must be a prerequisite to a final and lasting Peace.

DO YOU KNOW
1. How often in the Bible are Jews and merchants mentioned together?
2. Who are the "Saturday oil men"?
3. What was the proportion of high military officers amongst Italian
   Jewry at the end of the 19th century.
4. When and why were Jews barred from taking up arms?
5. What model did a famous tobacco manufacturing firm use to portray a
   typical English "tar".
6. Who made possible the development of modern radio?

Answers to the above on Page 3.

HERE AND THERE

Congratulations to Miss Maud Lerman on her engagement to F/O M. Cohen
of Leeds; Judith Bloomberg and Charles Kersh on their marriage;
Yetta Levine on her marriage to Michael Jackson of London; Mimi
Behrman who will be married at Darlington on February 28th to Nathan
Rayman of Birmingham. Godfrey Heilpern on his BARMITZVAH.
New Recruit - Solomon Silverman of St. Aidans (Brother-in-law of
Harry Black).

Last Sunday was a red letter day for the "Lit". Dr. Corfield
was the lecturer and the chair was taken by Sol Novinski whose
contribution giving a description of the meeting is on another page.

On Thursday, 25th March, a Mass Meeting will be held at the
New Rink to rouse public opinion to the plight of the Jew in Nazi
occupied Europe. The Mayor will preside and the Bishop of Durham will
address the meeting and Professor Brodetsky has promised to put the
Jewish case. The local M.P.'s and 12 mayors of the surrounding
boroughs (including the Lord Mayor of Newcastle) have promised to be
present.

The Sunderland Jewish Women's War Services have adopted a
Camp Reception Station in the N.E. The patients will be provided
with cigarettes, stationery, literature, cakes etc. each month.

EN PASSANT   -   THE INQUISITOR

As Spring draws nigh with the grass springing rich and verdant
beneath our feet, the trees blossoming forth and young lambs frisking
and gambolling on the fields our thoughts stray once more to our
"loved ones" fighting to make England a country fit for heroes. Soon
who knows, even I might be called upon to take arms for the defence of
our dear country, and then (horror of horrors) this delightful column
will have to come to an untimely close, so gather ye rosebuds while ye
may.
The inconsistency of my readers (both of them) is becoming
quite puzzling, one week I am rated because my contribution is too
obtuse and the identities are too well concealed etc. etc., but now my
masterpiece has suddenly become too obvious! As one who has become
a public servant and an adept at following the human barometer I am
confronted with an enigma for the solution of which I await with bated
breath, until next month when your appreciative letters come pouring
in with such rapidity and reliable advice!

FLASH
How is the Indian Accountant? Still having a "SPOT" of bother?

So the Corporal and his wife found time to visit Melrose Gardens!
Oh! to be considered worthy of such an honour!

Is it true that Canada has become "Anti-Semitism" Conscious since the
arrival of Sunderland's youthful member of the R.A.F.

FLASH Continued.

Who is the Gipsy Queen of the R.A.F. in Norwich?   Still "plotting"?

St. Helens was once famous for Beecham's Pills - - - but now A.H. A.H.

So the Rake of Rochdale is now the Beau Brummel of Bradford;   (Who has been ROBBed of his company?)

When is a Royal Box a Royal Box?   When the Battery King sits in it!

Who will have to overcome a strong aversion to his future sister-in-law?

Who is known as "The Brains Trust of Uxbridge"?   Only one shilling for the use of such magnificent brains!

Rumour hath it that the Shipping Magnate has become very cosmopolitan at dances.   Long Live The Polish Corridor!

Is the Regimental Paymaster as popular at Meerut as he was supposed to be in Manchester?

Whose recent engagement is causing much controversy?   Six months amongst the Irish Colleens is a grave risk! ! !

Is it an old African Custom to be kissed on both cheeks?   Hi-de-hi, Myer!

So the Staffordshire Student(?) is bored!   Never mind, on your next leave you can come to the "Lit" and hold forth.

So there has been a "Reversal of Situation" at Rotherham!   The old order changeth - yielding place to new?

Answers to questions on first page.

1. Only once - Hosea, Chapter 12, verse 7.
2. The white and black Jews of Cochin whose principal occupation seems to have been the manufacture and sale of oil.
3. Twice as great as amongst their non-Jewish compatriots.   One outstanding name was General Guiseppe Octolengli, Minister of War in 1902 - 3.
4. In the late Roman Empire.   As the career of arms conferred certain privileges the Church Fathers exerted themselves to have it barred to unbelievers which then included Jews.
5. The head of a Jewish sailor born in the East End of London and recognised now as one of the best known pieces of advertising in this country.
6. A German Jew, Robert von Lieben who invented the radio amplifier which was responsible not only for development of radio but also the sound film.

4.

SPORTING REFLECTIONS - By "Argus".

Last Football season, you will recall, Sunderland's team reached the Final of the Football League War Cup. At the time of writing we had reached the last week of the qualifying competition, and if Sunderland are found in the draw for the first round - well the days of miracles are not over.

They are not playing well, they cannot get a settled side owing to various calls and they have had to discard their young goal-keeper because he was giving too many goals away. You know the old story - success turns some people's head, and the way to bring it back to a normal size $6\frac{7}{8}$ is to just let them see they can be done without.

Alex Hastings announced to me a few days ago that he is giving up football at the end of the season. The way he put it to me was like this: "I have got to the stage when it takes me till half time to get my muscles loose; then it takes me until the following Thursday to recover from my exertions."

A great half-back and a gentleman. He is now a 2nd Lieut. in a Home Guard Ack-Ack Battery - one of those mystery batteries that throw up everything but the gun or rather the projector. He is doing the battery administrative work and I have heard an official whisper that Alex is to be promoted to Captain's rank.

Saw Sergt. Tom Smith a few days ago. He is still waiting for a smack at Nel Tarleton's title, but will have to wait. It's a bit rough on him that in war time another man can hang on to the title without being made to fight for it by the powers that be.

Did any of you boys ever see Shackleton, the Northern Amateur Middle-weight Champion box at Sunderland? He is in Sunderland now as a Sergt. Instructor of the A.P.T.C. Hope you heard the broadcast of his Northern Command Championship fight at York. He's a grand boxer.

Remember the man that always seemed to be smoking the stump of a cigar - the late Dr. Shaw? His son, also a Doctor is in the Middle East as a Pilot Officer. He was a member of Sunderland Harriers before the war.

The bigger game keeps rolling on. May the day not be far distant when the Hun will be rolling back and may the Red Army get into Germany before we do. They wont be so soft-hearted. Cheerio lads until next time.

PEEPS INTO THE PAST

I have been honoured with an invitation to take the chair at a meeting of the "Lit" and this is my story. Dr. Corfield was the Lecturer. At 7.10 p.m. last Sunday, February 14th, a large car pulled up at the entrance of this building. Girlie Cowan and the

Doctor jumped out, I was bundled in and away we sped.

We soon arrived at the Communal Hall, I cannot express my feelings on entering the building save to say I had a wonderful reception. I was so happy to see the old faces once again and to know that they were glad to see me. After many greetings and enquiries about my general health the proceedings commenced, some 60 or 70 people were present. As I rose to introduce the Speaker whom everybody knew I was struck by something I had never experienced before, I missed the light hearted, irresponsibility and gay laughter of the audience. The members were gay, certainly, but there was a serious undertone, I could feel it. Any Chairman of experience can "feel" his audience (I cursed Hitler once again); preliminaries over Dr. Corfield took the floor.

Slide No. 1 was flashed on the Screen, it depicted three African Natives "dressed". The centre gentleman was wearing a lady's - well er - what do you think? I am not quite sure what it was!' Pointing dramatically to the picture Dr. Corfield said "Ladies and Gentlemen - - - Niggers" and so the subject was introduced.

The Doctor is a racy speaker and he soon held his audience interested and amused. He spoke of his experiences in Hospitals among the Natives, their characteristics, and the British policy of care of the Native's rights, education and health. I was so interested I forgot the time and that the taxi was due to take us back. I had asked for questions and during an interesting discussion the Doctor and I sipped coffee. (The most delicious I had tasted for a very long time). The Rev. S.P. Toperoff saved the situation by proposing a vote of thanks to the Doctor and myself. I sincerely trust I deserve all the nice things he said about me.

The meeting was over, the taxi arrived. There were more handshakes and goodbyes, encouraging words of good cheer and some gifts including one from the dear old "Lit". The Doctor and I were whisked off. I arrived feeling tired, oh so tired, but happy. Happy to know that the "lit" is still alive. I can see the fight is hard. You dear boys and girls are missed, your younger brothers and sisters will not fail you and the "Lit" will be ready to welcome you on your return.

Cheerio for now. SOL.

EXCERPTS FROM LETTERS

Sgt. B. Taylor, Kenya, writes, "I am particularly looking forward to further editions of the Bulletin and would like you to convey my appreciation to all who help in compiling it.
A/C Landau writes "I look forward eagerly at the end of each month to the Bulletin with all its news etc. from Sunderland. The Bulletin has cheered me up immensely when, at times, like all members of the Forces I have been "browned off".

F/Lt. V.E. Gillis M.E.F. writes: "It is with profound interest that
I have received your monthly Bulletin for the month of July. On
my arrival in this country it was winter, the days rolled on summer
came and brought with it the sweltering heat of the Desert during
the daytime together with the greatest living pest of the Desert
which persists in its aggravating tactics of irritation, but as night
falls ceases its devilish acrobatics. Attention only, however, to
be replaced by a much more menacing and deadly type of aeroplane known
as the Dive-Bomber. I refer to the fly mosquitoe the latter with
its peculiar and most sinister whining before it eventually swoops
down on the unhappy individual. Again since my arrival, this is
now many months, I have hardly seen one drop of rain. One can readily understand and appreciate the reason why we Israelites prayed for
rain in the olden days. You at home may pray for sunshine but we pray
for a little rain during the summer heat.......... I went to Palestine
and paid a fleeting visit to Jerusalem, this town appears to me to
have a much more solid foundation for its existence - not the illusive
constant seeking of enjoyment and of pure selfishness which seem to be
the sole concern of the inhabitants of Tel-Aviv, the largest town in
Palestine. Indeed to me in Tel-Aviv few of them look really happy
and I am quite certain that a goodly number would be willing to return
to their native countries if permitted to do so. It was whilst perusing a notice on one of the notice boards in the Services Club that I
met a local product. I was rudely interrupted with raucous laughter
of some A/C 1, naturally enough I paid not the slightest attention to
such an outbreak of revolt and insubordination. However the uproar
and disturbance continued, it was quite evident that I would have to
use my "authority". I turned round "imposingly" to find facing me
a face wreathed in smiles, a face, with the same broad smile, that I
had known for many years and with whom I have "cracked" many a yarn.
It was indeed the smiling face of none other than that well known
personality - Cyril Mincovitch himself, smiling, not even saluting nor
at attention."

Gnr. H. Brewer, Gibralter, says - "The Bulletin arrives with clock-
work regularity. As much as I look forward to its arrival each month,
so do my Gentile billet companions. Its a pleasure to see them reading through each page with such a marked interest and then to follow
up with a short discussion on its contents, or to ask questions which
I answer as best I can. In my case I find that the Bulletin has the
effect of helping to bridge the gulf between Jew and Gentile with very
good results."

L.A.C. J. Gordon, North Africa writes "The receipt of the Bulletin has
afforded me much pleasure, but the receipt of No. 5 (November issue)
was indeed a source of great delight and a grand message of good cheer
from my home town. I believe it must be the only one coming to this
part of North Africa."

A/C C. Marks M.E.F. writes , "It was with very great pleasure that I
received your 3rd issue of the monthly Bulletin. Unfortunately owing
to the distance between us the time taken is rather long, nevertheless
the paper is very interesting and amusing as well as welcome. I wonder
who the Inquisitor is?"

―――――――――――――――

All correspondence to be sent to the Rev. S.P. Toperoff,

5, Victoria Avenue, Sunderland.

―――――――

THE SUNDERLAND JEWISH COMMUNITY

Monthly Bulletin for the Forces.

Vol.1, No. 9.   Edited by the Minister, April 1943.   Nisan 5703.

The Festival of Passover which we shall shortly be observing is full of ceremonialism and ritual. One custom which particularly appeals to us is the opening of the door on the Sedar night. We are told that the door is opened for Elijah. Now there is a number of reasons for this practice. Historically it can be explained as being due to the mediaeval edicts of the Church which ordered the Jews to have all doors and windows closed during Easter week, which nearly always co-incided with Passover. After the years rolled on and our people became walled in within the ghettos in Germany, Italy and other countries it was on Passover night in particular that they sighed for the coming of Elijah who, according to Jewish belief, is the forerunner of the Messiah and the Redeemer from all trouble. The door then was opened to welcome the Saviour and an extra cup of wine was poured out in his honour. Elijah's appearance would thus inaugurate an era of "the open door", the symbol of universal friendship and brotherly love.

Does not history move in queer cycles? The Church today has completely changed its policy towards the Jew. The wonderful lead given by the Archbishop of Canterbury has been followed by other prominent people. Never before have we had such good friends in the highest circles; yet it is a fact that the doors of Palestine, for instance, are closed to those Jews who are fortunate enough to escape from the hell hounds of Nazism. Do you remember the incident of the Struma which was sent to the bottom of the sea with a cargo of 760 innocent souls? The doors of Palestine were closed to them.

Some of us have become inured to suffering; we have resigned ourselves to our fate and the closed door policy has led to the closed mouth policy. We must not grow tired of asking for our rights. Is it not ironical that we who teach the philosophy of the open door throughout our history should have the door slammed in our face. "One law for the native and the stranger", said Moses. Did not Solomon in his famous opening prayer of the Temple invite even "the heathen who is not of the people of Israel".

We have no secrets, no mysteries, no sacraments in our religion. We welcome enquiry. "Ma Nishtanah............" "Why is this night different from all other nights?" This we are taught to ask as soon as we learn to speak.

Freedom is the keynote of Passover. This is what we long for. After this war there will be millions of homeless Jews, those that will be fortunate enough to escape the machine gun, electrocution and the lethal chamber, where will they go? You, who are fighting for freedom must clamour for the open door now.

How we all hope for the peace when the doors of our homes will once again be flung open to greet and receive you. I am sure you will join me in the prayer that Elijah may come soon and open the hearts of our friends to solve the besetting problems that confront us.

A happy and pleasant Pesach. "Now we are servants, in the year to come we hope to be free men."

<u>DO YOU KNOW</u>

1. What is the Sanhedrin and when was it convoked by a non-Jew?
2. When was a whole race converted to Judaism?
3. Who are the smallest people in Europe?
4. Who first invented a method whereby the dumb could be taught to articulate?
5. Which English literary author used the word "Gonef" meaning "Theif"
6. What is the origin of the Mogen David? (Shield of David).

<u>Answers to the above questions on Page 4.</u>

<u>HERE AND THERE</u>

We regret that owing to circumstances beyond our control, we could not publish the March bulletin.

We have much pleasure in making the following announcements.

<u>Births</u> - Sgt. & Mrs. Goodman (Mildred Mincovitch), a daughter
        Mr. & Mrs. Grantham (Trixie Rawlinson) a son.

<u>Engagement</u> - Mirriam Winberg to Dr. Goodman of Manchester.

We are pleased to report that Harry Black has arrived in Sunderland from the Middle East.

We are also happy to report that Horace Stone, who suffered injuries in the battle for Tripoli, is now well on the road to recovery.

We send good wishes to the following new recruits who have recently entered the Forces: -
        Reva Pearlman, Anette Penn and Lennie Slater.

<u>Mass Meeting</u> On Thursday March 25th a Protest Meeting against religious and racial discrimination was held at the Rink. Over 800 were present and the meeting was sponsored by the Council of Social Service. At the last moment the Mayor was prevented from presiding owing to the sudden death on active service of his son, Fl.Lt. Myers Wayman, D.F.C. Our heartfelt sympathies are with the Mayor and Mayoress in their bereavement. The chair was taken by the Deputy Mayor, Alderman Ditchburn. Those on the imposing platform included the Bishop of Durham, Major Furness M.P., Samuel Storey M.P., Professor and Mrs. Brodetzky, the Rev. Utton representing the Methodist Church, Father Dorrian, representing the Roman Catholic Church and two Jewish Mayors, Alderman Bloom of W. Hartlepool and Councillor Jackson of Darlington.

Nearly 500 copies of 'Let my people go' by Victor Gollancz were distributed and the meeting was preceded by half an hour of community singing. All the speakers made sympathetic references to the Jewish problem and urged that the government should do all in its power to facilitate the Refugee problem. A census was given of the Jewish population of Sunderland showing that there were 868 souls and over 120 in the forces.

A Purim concert was recently arranged for the pupils of the Hebrew Religion Classes at the Communal Hall. Mr. W. Morris originated the scheme and provided a cinematograph show, a conjuror and light refreshments. The older pupils of the Classes gave a presentation of "Mordecai and Esther" and the younger children gave a sketch called "The Rebbe", also a display of Palestinian dances. On the following Sunday a concert was given by the members of the

3.

"Junior Lit". The hall was crowded and all enjoyed a really
good show.

EN PASSANT - THE INQUISITOR

Can it be the effect of my literary dabblings that has
aged me beyond all human comprehension? Or is it the years taking
their rightful toll? My back, too frail to bear the burden of such
sudden popularity, has become sorrowfully bowed, my glazed orbs,
unaccustomed to reading such an influx of fan mail, have become
stationary in their sockets and my shapely hands have become the
victims of ague, due to wielding the pen so frequently.

Nevertheless whatever be the cause, I have been compelled
by my medical advisor to refrain from all cares and columns, so the
editor willing, I'm going to enjoy a well earned rest for a month
at least - I hope that this will not prevent my numerous correspondents from providing me with exhilarating reading matter. All
you would-be "gen" providers can now come out of your shells and go
gay with the knowledge that your antics will not be used in evidence
against you - yet!

FLASH

So the Brylcreem King has the wander-thirst once more. Bon Voyage!
Pleased you're touring the Lincoln countryside first.
Who was recently home on sick leave, with an "eye to the Future?
Glory of glories I.W.B. has decided to take "the plunge", is it
because he wants to be in "the swim"?
How is Newcastle agreeing with W.A.A.F. No. One?
On dit that the Shipping Magnate is proud to be so called - any
more donations forthcoming?
Is it true that André the Flea and his master are a riotous success
in Egypt?
"So D.A.
Can't stay
Long away"   Must you travel?
Which B.B.C. celebrity is incapable of parting from Sunderland or
its environs? Can it be.........?
Who is being married de bonne heure? What is la raison d'etre?
Who is said to prefer Speed Cops to Otter Cops?
How does the Yorkshire climate agree with the R.A.F. Chilblain
Addict? So he has finally discovered the identity of the writer
of this wonderful column! Better late than never.
Rumour hath it that two civilian pugilists were "daggers drawn" at
a place of worship recently. How are the Mighty Fallen!
So the Norman Conqueror has eventually taken advantage of free
travel abroad!
When is embarkation not embarkation leave? When I.D. has it.
Rumour hath it that The Girls' Last Hope is expected to leave terra
firma shortly. So gather ye rosebuds while ye may ye Cambridgeshire
Belles.

SPORTING REFLECTIONS - By "Argus"

The mayor of Sunderland who is a director of the Sunderland
Club has lost his only son - Flight Lieut. Myers Wayman D.F.C. I
believe I am right in saying the airman was in one of the Mosquito's
which went over Berlin and "put the wind up" the Nazis that Saturday

afternoon,and interfered with an anniversary event.   Flt. Lieut.
Wayman was wounded in the battle over France in mid-March, got his
machine safely home, but died of his wounds.

I suppose you all know by now that Sunderland have no more
than a passing interest in the Football League Cup.   Two points
would have kept Sunderland among the favoured 32, and strange to say
the only two points Middlesbrough had to their credit from the ten
games were from Sunderland.

But Sunderland enthusiasts are still interested, because
the young attack leader of Aston Villa is none other than their young
reserve team centre forward Davis, the fair haired boy who came to
Roker Park when he was 17 years of age.   Davis was taken from under
the nose of the Villa and Birmingham by Sunderland, and Villa
supporters are now asking: "Why!

Raich Carter, now the proud father of a daughter, has
refused to assist any other club in the competition.   His point of
view is that he earned his livelihood with Sunderland before the war,
hopes to do so after the war and therefore considers that his duty
lies in playing for Sunderland now when his Air Force duties permit.
Carter is almost a certainty to play for England against Scotland.

In March we had Arthur Wright home on leave.   Arthur is a
Corporal in the R.E.'s and he has been playing for his regimental
team in the Kent League, and scoring goals galore at inside right.
Against Middlesbrough, at his old position of left half, Arthur gave
such a polished exhibition of footcraft that one feels he is certain
to be Alex Hastings successor if he comes out of the war safe and
sound.
Jack Casey popped in to see me the other day.   Jack is
with a Scottish Regt. and now looks fit enough to start boxing again.
Jack is about the only man Pilot Officer Len Harvey feared.   Harvey
freely admits that Casey gave him the hardest fight of his career
and many of you will recall that Casey had Harvey out on his feet at
Newcastle.
Freddy Mills has handed in his British and Empire titles.
Mills is going to devote his attention to all-in wrestling, which may
or may not be a sport.   It depends upon one's point of view.   I
look upon much of it as jolly good acting.

ANSWERS TO QUESTIONS ON PAGE 2.
1. The Sanhedrin was the highest religious and political magistracy
   amongst Jews.   Napolean in 1806 invited Jews to send delegates to
   Parliament to discuss Jewish affairs.
2. The Tartars known as the Chazars.
3. The Jews are considered to be the smallest in stature the average
   height being 5 ft. 5 inches.
4. The Jew Rodrigo Pereire.   ١٩١٥ - ١٧٨٠
5. Dickens.
6. It was adopted late as a symbol of Judaism and many have been
   intended at first to represent the star of the coming Messiah in
   opposition to the Christian Cross which symbolises a Messiah who
   has already come.

5.

A PASSOVER STORY

By Heinrich Heine

Rabbi Abraham sat in the large dining room of his house surrounded by relation, disciples, and many other guests, to celebrate the great feast of Passover Eve.   Everything in the room sparkled with unusual brilliance.   Over the table spread the gaily embroidered silk cloth, whose gold fringes touched the floor;   the small plates with the symbolic food shone in a comfortable home-like way, as did the tall wine goblets, adorned with embossed images of sacred legends. The men sat in their black cloaks and black broad-brimmed hats, with white collars.   The women, in wonderful glittering garments of Lombard stuffs, wore on their heads and necks ornaments of gold and pearls while the silver Sabbath lamp poured forth its pleasant light on the smiling faces of parents and children, happy in their piety.   On the purple velvet cushions of a chair, higher than the others, and reclining as the Law enjoins, sat Rabbi Abraham, and read and chanted the Haggada, while the mixed assembly joined with him, or answered at the appointed places.   The Rabbi too, wore the prescribed black festival garments, his nobly-formed but somewhat severe features had a milder expression than usual, his lips smiled out of the dark brown beard as though they wished to tell pleasant things, while his eyes seemed to be filled with happy remembrances and anticipation. Beautiful Sara who sat on a raised chair with a velvet cushion beside her husband, wore, as hostess, none of her ornaments;   only white linen enveloped her slender form and gentle face.   Her face was touchingly beautiful, even as all Jewish beauty is of a peculiar moving kind;   for the consciousness of the deep wretchedness, the bitter scorn, and the unhappy circumstances amid which her kindred and friends dwelt, give to their lovely features a depth of sorrow and an ever-watchful apprehension of love that invariably bewitches our hearts.   So in this evening sat the lovely Sara, looking into the eyes of her husband, yet glancing now and then at the beautiful parchment edition of the Haggada which lay before her, bound in gold and velvet.   It was an old heir-loom with aged wine stains on it, which had come down from the days of her grandfather.   In it were many boldly and brightly-coloured pictures which she had often, as a little girl looked at so eagerly on Passover evenings, and which represented all kinds of Biblical stories; - how Abraham with a hammer smashed the idols of his father; how the angels came to visit him, how Moses slew the Egyptian, how Pharoah sat in state on his throne, how the frogs gave him no peace even at the table, how he - the Lord be praised - was drowned while the children of Israel walked cautiously through the Red Sea;   how they stood open mouthed before Mount Sinai with their sheep, cows, and oxen; how pious King David played the harp; and finally, how Jerusalem, with its towers and minarets, shone in the splendour of the setting sun.

The second wine-cup had been filled the faces and voices of the guests grew merrier and the rabbi, as he took a cake of unleavened bread and raised it, and with a happy greeting read the following words from the Haggada: "Behold! This is the food which our fathers ate in Egypt! Let everyone who is hungry come and eat! Let everyone who is sorrowful come and share the joys of our Passover! In this year we celebrate it here, but next year in the land of Israel.   This year we celebrate it in servitude, but next year as free men!"

6.

Then the hall door opened, and there entered two tall, pale men, wrapped in very broad cloaks. "Peace be with you," said one of them. "We are fellow-Jews on a journey, and would like to keep Passover with you!" And the rabbi replied promptly and kindly: "Peace be with you. Sit down near me!" The two strangers sat down at the table and the rabbi continued to read. While the company repeated the responses he often whispered an endearing word to his wife. Playing on the old saying that on this evening a father of a Jewish family regards himself as a king he said to her, "Rejoice, O my Queen!" But she replied smiling sadly, "The Prince is missing," meaning by that a son, who, as a passage in the Haggada requires, shall ask his father with a fixed formula of words, the meaning of the festival. The rabbi said nothing, but only pointed with his finger to a picture on the open pages of the Haggada. It was quaintly and touchingly drawn, showing how the three angels came to Abraham to announce that he would have a son by his wife Sara, who, meanwhile urged by feminine curiosity, is listening slying to it all behind the door of the tent. The little sign brought a crimson blush to the cheeks of the beautiful woman. She looked down and then glanced lovingly at her husband, who was now chanting the wonderful story how Rabbi Joshua, Rabbi Eliezer, Rabbi Azaria, Rabbi Akiba and Rabbi Tarphon sat reclining in Bne Brak and conversed all night long of the Exodus from Egypt till their disciples came to tell them it was daylight, and that the morning prayer was being read in the synagogue.

As the beautiful Sara with devotion in her eyes listened to her husband, she saw his face suddenly assume an agonized expression, his cheeks and lips grew deadly pale, and his eyes gleam with a cold stare as though they had turned icy. Almost in the same moment however, he became as calm and cheerful as before, his cheeks and lips grew red again, his eyes sparkled with cheer, and it seemed as if a mad merry mood, strange to his nature, had seized him. Sara was frightened as she had never been in all her life and a cold shudder came over her, less because of the momentary signs of blank despair which she had seen in her husband's face than because of the subsequent joyousness which now changed to rollicking merriment. The Rabbi cocked his skull cap comically from ear to ear, and pulled and twisted his beard clownishly, sang the Haggada texts like tavern ditties. In the enumeration of the Egyptian plagues, where it is customary to dip the forefinger in the full wine goblets to cast drops of wine to the floor, he sprinkled the young girls near him with the red wine and there was great wailing over spoiled collars, and ringing laughter. Sara became more and more mystified at the convulsive but apparently forced merriment of her husband, and seized with nameless fears, she stared at the buzzing swarm of gaily glittering guests who comfortably spread and rocked themselves back and forth nibbling the crisp Passover cakes, drinking wine, gossipping, or singing aloud, full of joy and merriment.

Then came the time of supper. Everyone rose to wash their hands. Sara brought in a large silver basin, richly adorned with embossed gold figures, and held it before each of the guests, while water was poured over his hands. While she held it before the rabbi he gave her a significant look, and quietly slipped out of the door. Sara followed him. He seized her hand and in the greatest of haste hurried her through the dark lanes of Bacharach, out of the city gate to the highway which leads along the Rhine to Bingen.

It was one of those calm and starry nights in spring which inspire the soul with uncanny feelings.   There was something of the church-yard in the flowers.   The birds sang peevishly and as if vexing themselves, the moon cast spiteful yellow stripes of light over the dark giant's stream as it flowed and murmured its music; the lofty masses of the Rhine cliffs looked dimly like quivering giant's heads.   The watchman on the tower of Castle Strahleck blew a melancholy tune, and with it rang in jarring rivalry the funeral bell of Saint Werner's church.   Sara carried the silver ewer in her right hand while the rabbi grasped her left.   She could feel his ice-cold fingers and the trembling of his arm, but still she accompanied him in silence, perhaps because she was accustomed to obey blindly and unquestionably; perhaps too, because her lips were mute with fear and anxiety.

Below the Sonneck castle, opposite Lotch, about the place where the hamlet of Lower Rheinbach now stands, there rises a cliff which arches over the Rhine bank.   The rabbi ascended it with his wife, peered around on every side, and gazed at the stars.   Trembling and shivering, as with the pain of death, Sara looked at his pale face, which seemed spectre-like in the moonrays, and seemed to express by turns pain, terror, piety and rage.   But when the rabbi suddenly snatched from her hands the silver ewer and threw it far away into the Rhine, she could no longer endure the agony of uncertainty, and crying out "Shaddai! Be merciful!" threw herself at his feet, and begged him to solve the dark enigma.

Unable at first to speak from excitement, the rabbi moved his lips without uttering a sound.   At last he cried, "Do you see the Angel of Death?   There below he hovers over Bacharach.   But we have escaped his sword.   Praised be God!"   And in a voice still trembling with excitement he told her that while he was happily singing the Haggada he glanced by chance under the table, and saw at his feet the bloody corpse of a little child.   "Then I noticed," continued the rabbi, "that our two guests were not of the community of Israel, but of the congregation of the godless, who had plotted to bring that corpse craftily into the house so as to accuse us of child-murder, and stir up the people to plunder and murder us.   Had I given the merest sign that I saw through the fiendish plot, I should simply have hastened out destruction; only by craft did I preserve our lives.   Praised be God!   Do not fear my lovely Sara.   Our relations and friends will also be saved.   It was only my blood for which they thirsted.   I have escaped them, and they will be satisfied with my silver and gold. Come with me Sara to another land.   We will leave our evil fortune behind us, and that it may not follow us I have thrown to it the silver ewer, the last of my possessions as an offering.   The God of our fathers will not forsake us!"

8.

EXCERPTS FROM LETTERS

L/Cpl. M. Davis, North Africa, writes - "I was delighted to receive yesterday your monthly Bulletin for November. As you can imagine, anything appertaining to the home-town is always welcome, and although perhaps I don't "catch on" to some of the cracks (presumably followed by the younger generation) it made pleasant interesting reading nevertheless.

During my stay here I took the opportunity of paying a visit to one of the many synagogues. I received an "Aliyah", and was most embarrassed when the Chazan, Parnass and Gabbai kissed me on both cheeks after the completion of the Mitzvah. Could you imagine the Parnass and Gabbai doing it in our Shool!!!"

Lt. Mordaunt Cohen from West Africa, writes - "I have just received Succot number of the Bulletin. I live in a bush hut thatched with palm leaves which more or less conforms with the essentials of a Succah even to the extent of the openings in the roof as we know to our cost when it rains. However, though this is the land of palms, I had no Lulab.

Tonight is Erev Chanukah. I have no candles to kindle but I still carry the light of Judaism in the Dark Continent and can truthfully say that the spirit and determination of Judas Maccabeus is forever in front of me as an example of a great Jewish leader and ambassador. I can foresee us having to renew his struggle after this war."

L.A.C. Vandervelde writes from Canada - "Canada is a grand country and the people here are good. It is very strange to walk about in the evening and find the street lights burning. The Jewish Community here has just opened a servicemen's club which is very comfortable."

Julius Gordon from North Africa writes - "I have the honour to be a member of the First Army. This is an amazing place for absorbing interest from a tourist's point of view and must in many respects resemble Palestine. Vineyards seem to constitute the principal item of vegetation though oranges, dates, figs etc., grow here also in abundance. Palm trees and cactus plants seem to complete a fitting setting for the angular white buildings which surprisingly enough present externally at any rate a very modern appearance though there are features which nevertheless give them a distinctly tropical flavour. It is winter here now, which means for the most part warm sunny days and nights that have a decided nip.

The population is a mixture of French and Arabs, the latter predominate and are of various types. Usually they are attired in the most amazing ragged odds and ends, dirty and of every known colour, the whole ensemble is usually completed by a head dress of an equally dirty red fez. The language spoken is of course French and at times I am afraid I am in a "flat spin" endeavouring to understand and make myself understood.

J. Charlton from India - "I am in receipt of both July and August copies of your Bulletin and cant say how much I appreciate them although I must admit that some of the subtle references in them are

too much for me.   However I am saving them up, some day, soon I hope
I will "collar" that anonymous scandal monger (bless 'im or 'er) and
I will then get full explanations."

Horace Stone from M.E.F. -   "I was amused to read of my promotion
to Lance Corporal after (for technical not punitive reasons) I lost
it.   There was an amusing incident when I applied here for a commission.   The Sergeant Major told me quite bluntly not to be a fool.
"Troopers live longest", he said.

Alan Forman writes -"I always take the Bulletin with me to our monthly
Jewish Church Parade where it always gets a warm welcome from the boy
In fact it has developed quite a reputation down here and well
deserved too!"

Staff Sergeant J. Rosenthal from Iraq and Persia writes - "Number 4
Bulletin reached me, though I have not yet heard from home. You can
therefore believe me that my thanks are real and not perfunctory. You
may be interested to know that I have stood on the soil that the
Patriarchs knew at Babylon.   I stood where our ancestors sat and
wept.   I stood and wondered at the few ruins of all that is left of
the once mighty Nebuchadnezar.   I thought to myself here stands one
of a people which refuses to be conquered.   There lies all that is
left of the conquerors.   History will repeat itself.   Our persecutors will become archaeological curiosities which our future
generations will visit some day.
        You might tell any of the boys who expect to travel East
to polish up their Hebrew.   In the Middle East it is a living
language spoken by Jews of many different countries.   Yiddish is
useless as it is not understood.

PEEPS INTO THE PAST

        February and March.   The busiest time of the season.
Concluding rehearsals for the North East Union Festival Shield and
the end of the "Lit" season's concert were in full swing.

        The lusty lads of the village, "The Gang" who gave so much
valuable if noisy help were hammering away at scenery or swinging
the paste brush, trying in vain to improve the appearance of the
proscenium.   "The front curtains wont work Sol!"   "Where should we
put the window curtains?"   "How on earth can we fix them up there?"
Or, "Where do you want the blue light?"   "Where does the fireplace
go?" and I was trying to get someone to walk like an old man, to make
a prompt entry or an effective exit.

        And the excitement of the Dress Rehearsals!   It was a
harassing time, yet good fun.   The "Lit" concerts were jolly affair
and dont you agree we always put on a good show?   The Drama Festival
alone, kept a little army of Jewish boys and girls happily busy.

10.

Memories of the past came crowding in. The plays of Sylvia Brewer, Nan Ritchenberg and the play in verse by Nita Magrill. Nan Ritchenberg is making quite a name for herself as a playwright, I hear.

I remember the beards of Isaac Brewer. How I taught Simon Light to die gracefully! Do you remember the Tenth Man? I am proud of his make-up even yet. The fine acting of Nan Ritchenberg, the one woman in the play! The problem of the candles, they had to be new at the beginning and nearly burnt out at the end of the act! In another play a most remarkable feat was making Simon Light appear 25 years older in as many seconds. At its widest, Back stage was about two feet. Did the audience ever wonder how it was done?

Do we not all feel happier when we think of those evenings spent at the Communal Hall? I do! And I think you do. If so your time and energies have not been wasted, for a smile is worth much today.

Happy days!

SOL.

NOTE: Change of address must be reported to ensure regular receipt of the Bulletin.

All correspondence must be sent to Rev. S.P. Toperoff, 5 Victoria Avenue, Sunderland.

THE SUNDERLAND JEWISH COMMUNITY

Monthly Bulletin for the Forces.

ol.1, No.10.   Edited by the Minister, May 1943.   Iyar 5703.

The Press has given much publicity of late to the case of
Rifleman Clayton, who it is alleged died from injuries inflicted by the
Regt. Sgt. Major and the Quarter Master Sgt. at a detention camp.   A
revulsion of feeling has spread throughout the country, at the cruel
treatment which this soldier received at the hands of his superiors.
Such behaviour is un-British.
          Now whatever the findings of the responsible men in authority,
one feature in this case stands out prominently - - the sense of
British justice that will not allow the mysterious death of an ordinary
Tommy to pass by unnoticed.   We marvel at the fearlessness and courage
of the Press in discussing it.   Thank God for the freedom and justice
which even in total war are not brushed aside.   So it should be, that
is what we are fighting for.   One could hardly expect such open and free
discussion of a similar case in Nazi-Occupied Europe.   There, life is too
cheap.   There, man is degraded to the level of an animal.   Many a poor
soul has had his back broken by a Storm Trooper, or a Gauleiter, but no
one knows and no one cares.
          To us as Jews, this case of Rifleman Clayton comes home with
all its poignancy.   When we read it our hearts go out to the millions of
Jews who are still left in Occupied Europe.   They are waiting to receive
treatment far worse than did Clayton, and for even less cause.   A hue and
cry has been raised because of the un-warranted punishment of one British
soldier.   What of the merciless torture and pitiless death of millions of
Jews in the hell camps of Poland?   Who is to raise a voice for those
unfortunate souls?   Is the British Government doing everything it can to
save the remnant, to rescue those that are now outside the Nazi trap but
in constant dread of being caught in the maelstrom of Nazi brutality and
wickedness?
          Compare the unjustified assault on Clayton with the premeditated
annihilation of whole communities of Jews.   In the sight of God there is
no distinction between man and man, the blood of the Jewish martyrs cries
out for help.   It is your duty to stir up the public conscience so that
reports of the Nazi extermination policy of Jews be reported fully in the
English Press.   We demand an inquest now on the death in mysterious
circumstances of over two million Jews in Europe.   We demand not only
that just retribution be meted out to the perpetrators of this wholesale
murder, but that a haven of refuge be found now for those fortunate
enough to escape from the deadly grip of the Nazi clutches.

DO YOU KNOW?

1. Who was the first house physician at St. Bart's Hospital, London?
2. What is the earliest record of a Jewish congregation in England?
3. When did Jews possess their first Town Hall?
4. Who named his seven daughters after seven conjugations of the Hebrew
   verb?
5. When was a Synagogue confiscated because of complaints of neighbours
   in England?
6. Where is there mentioned a powder puff in the Talmud?

Answers to the above on Page 3.

2.

HERE AND THERE

Congratulations to:-
Miss Maud Lorman on her marriage to F/O M. Cohen.
Dr. & Mrs. Sacks of Seaham Harbour on the birth of a son.
Sgt. & Mrs. Lewis (nee Rita Goldberg) on the birth of a son.
Engagements:-
Cpl. Natie Berg, R.A.F., to Miss Gladys Barnes of Glasgow.
Miss Celia Davis to Private Harry Phillips of Ontario, Canada.
Promotion:-
Solly Gillis to L/Bombardier.

We are very pleased to report that David Davis of the 125th Anti-Tank Regiment, who was previously reported missing in Singapore, is now safe at a Prisoner of War Camp in Malaya. We are all eagerly awaiting similar news from the other four lads.

We hear that Miss Rosalie Gillow who whilst evacuated to Thornton Watlass, Yorks, was entertained to tea by Lady Curzon-Howe at Clifton Castle. She was the first evacuated teacher to be invited to Castle and enjoyed herself immensely.

We also hear that F/O M. Olswang and P/O Charles Hall have resigned their Commissions. ‾‾‾‾‾‾‾

EN PASSANT - THE INQUISITOR.

Lying gasping belabouredly and unsuccessfully for breath I eventually pleaded with the Editor - - - Could I have a month's respite? Might I have a month's respite? Should I have a month's respite? Glancing tentatively at the Editor's unrelenting features I became horror stricken as I realised my plea was to be in vain. To the end I was expected to give of my life's blood - - - the quality of mercy is not strained???

Needless to say since my illness friends, entering my sanctum sanctorum, speak unnaturally hoarse whispers, this tense atmosphere is not conducive with NEWS - - so once more I throw myself on your never-failing good nature.

My "public informers", however, tell me that I am losing favour in the sight of one or two lesser fry--- it is with ever-increasing regret that I am cognisant of their lack of comprehension of "Who's Who" in my column.

For the paltry sum of 6d (as I mentioned some months previous) they will be informed of EVERYTHING (if I know the answer myself). So remember every cloud has a silvered lining.
FLASH
Who always has an "Eddy" fying time when in her home town?
Who sent some African "Paradise" Fruits home? Too bad (or all) ?
Is it true that a member of the R.A.F. has been inflicting "Corporal" punishment on the Sunderland girls by taking his choice from Glasgow?
On dit that a certain member of the Forces was recently entertained to unLEVINed bread.
We are very pleased to welcome the "Black" sheep to the English Fold.
This wUS WORTH fighting for?
Is it purely coinciDENTAL that everyone's teeth are now in perfect condition once more?
Who was known as "mannA (reverse) from Heaven"? He certainly seems to be travelling around England and Scotland!
Rumour hath it that one of Sunderland's Upper Strata has been having a six weeks Luxury Cruise round the South Coast of Africa - - what's

3.

happening to the "Prisoners at the Bar?"
Did Sunderland's "David and Jonathan" effect a Reunion in Bombay?
Somebody's ears must have been burning!
Which attractive W.A.A.F. is enjoying herself on one of England's most
famous battlefields?
So Seaham Harbour is now full of Commissioned Officers! Good going C.W.!
I hope that the Canadian K.C. gives satisfactory advice to the non-Anti-
Semite - keep me posted._____

SPORTS REFLECTIONS - By "Argus".

Let me commence this months article with a word of thanks to
Mr. H. Black of the R.A.F. for his letter of appreciation of previous
articles.   Welfare work for the Army and the R.A.F. takes up a great deal
of my time but if these articles keep you in touch with home and are
interesting to you, then that is all the thanks I require.   Nevertheless
that kindly little note from Mr. Black was appreciated.
          I have just finished reading a booklet published in Cairo of the
work of the 50th Division in the Middle East.   The only thing I am surprised about is that so far none of the Durham's appear to have dribbled
a football into the enemy lines and put Jerry's team offside.   However,
they may be either in the "bag" or in the "Drink" before long.
          At the time of writing Sunderland and Newcastle United look like
possible finalists for what is known as the Combined Counties Cup - Durham
Northumberland and Yorkshire.   If they are the North Riding Associations
County Cup will leave its home for the first time in history.
          Stanley Lloyd, who is filling Sunderland's outside left berth,
is the Hetton Schoolboy International.   Mark my words he will find a place
in Sunderland's team after the war.   He has a football brain.   There are
several other youngsters in the Reserve side who look like making good.
          During the war period Manager Murray has been developing friend-
ly relations with Junior and Minor clubs in the County and clearing the
air against former prejudices.   Thus the future may bring us more of the
best Durham born players.
          Jimmy Taylor who just the season before the war signed for
Newcastle United as a centre forward from Hylton Colliery Juniors went
into the R.A.F., got his Pilots wings in Canada and came home a Sergt.
Pilot, now he has been given his commission.   Taylor's home is on the edge
of the moor at Sunderland - a clear case of rising above environments.
Well done Jimmy.   He was an apprentice shipwright before enlistment and
attended the Technical College evening classes.
          Bede School boys are in the final of the John Cochrane Cup, which
is run for the funds of Monkwearmouth Hospital.   They have to meet Ryhope
Secondary School at Roker Park.   So you see while you Old Bedans are
fighting the bigger game, the youngsters are carrying on traditions.

ANSWERS TO QUESTIONS ON PAGE 1.

1. The Jew Rodrigo Lopez who on a false charge was hanged on suspicion of
having tried to poison his Royal patient Queen Elizabeth.
2. Oxford - 1075.
3. In the Ghetto of Prague. On its tower was a clock, a rare distinction
in those days. It was the only tower clock in existence and was lettered
in Hebrew.
4. Gesenius, the founder of Modern Hebrew Lexicography.
5. The Synagogue at the corner of "Old Jewry" London, because of the
wailing of Jews at prayers.
6. In the tractate Ketubot 107B. "A Jew should provide his wife with a
powder puff".

PEEPS INTO THE PAST.

Have you memories of the business-like General Meetings of the "LIT". The keenness to be elected to the committee, and the debates on balance sheet. The PURIM DANCE, usually the last event of the season h been held as usual in Wetherell's Rooms, it was always a grand affair, usually ended by the dancers forming a large circle, and singing "Auld L Sygne", "God save the King", and "Hatikvah". What happy memories I have of those dances, and I'm sure you have also, the atmosphere was so friend

But the activities were not all dances and concerts what about the lectures and debates, looking back over many years of Chairmanship I astonished at the variety of subjects covered by the guest and resident lecturers. Religion and Citizenship, were the foundation of the Literar programme, for are they not the twin loyalties of the Jew?

Do you know the first lecture held in the Communal Hall, was by the late Sir Walter Raine, Member of Parliament for Sunderland. He told about the House of Commons. The "LIT" have always made it a practice to invite the Local M.P.'s to speak at its meetings. Many an illustrious Rabbi has also lectured to its members. Then there were talks on Munici al Administration, and of course I must not forget those delightful music recitals. Do you remember how we all joined in the singing of the folk songs? There was so much done, so many people actively engaged, but I'm afraid to mention names, in case I omit someone's.

The cinema nights simply must be remembered, I'm sure you will able to recall many an amusing incident, when the Nusenbaum Twins gave a show. The Cinema Travel Lectures were very interesting and very instruc ive. Then the debates, when the precocity of youth had full sway and you poor Chairman had his work cut out to keep order. Oh yes, the "LIT." wa "alive" then. Spring time came round and your committee would be consid ering dates of Summer Activities. I shall write of these in my next letter to you, meanwhile be of good cheer, look forward to happy days to come, and spare a thought for the past.

Happy days, SOL.

DANCE ORGANISED BY THE SUNDERLAND YOUTH ZIONIST ASSOCIATIO AT THE COMMUNAL HALL ON APRIL 22nd, 1943.

By "AN OBSERVER",

A truly outstanding function in the War Diary of the Sunderland Jewish Community. The crowd began surging in about 8.30, surging I thin is really the word, for very soon couples were jostling for room to dance What actually made it such an event was the fact that friends met friends again, some after many months of absence. Another notable feature was t large number of married couples present, including amongst others, Dr. & Mrs. S. Cohen, Dr. & Mrs. R. Collins and Mr. & Mrs. M. Gillis. Happily, nearly all the "home based" members of H.M. Forces were present and every one was pleased to see them, especially the "young ladies" of Town. A ve special welcome was extended to R.A.F. Corporal Harry Black who looked ve fit and happy after his return from the Middle East, - no less was the concentrated block of femininity, around the ever increasing waist, of smiling, witty Cpl. Ralph Freedman, whose moustached brother Sam, ably he ed out the excellent band, by playing on the piano. Dashing around with his usual speed, speaking to everyone, was that now well established Londo personality, Lionel P. Altman, who acted as the most able M.C. any dance has had the privilege of obtaining.

Phyllis Heilpern, her sister Eileen, and Pearl Berg, who are to be congratulated on their organising ability, wafted round the sides of t

5.

Hall like "Will of the Wisps".   Rosalie Gillow, Thora Shechet, and
Rita Olswang, others from time to time, founded their circle to discuss
local social matters.   Dancing with as many pretty girls as he could find
- was slim, debonair Gerald Behrman.   Discussing Anglo-Soviet affairs
with various partners, and attempting to diagnose them at the same time
was Lieut. Barnett, also blonde, quiet Capt. Jacobs, who is to be found
amongst charming company at all functions.
        During the interval, to music supplied by the younger males of
the dance, and led on by lusty singing by all, many folks performed the
traditional Jewish Hora, with obvious amusement to all.   Another item was
a raffle, tickets being sold by young, red haired Blanche Book, supported
by other young saleswomen, the raffle raised over £9.   In spite of war time
conditions, I noticed the ladies looked really lovely, and to describe all
would need far more space, and many "Tatlers".   Just a few - laughing
Miriam Winberg, escorted by her brothers Charles and Philip, enthusiastic
dancer Rita Cohen, demure, wistful Phyllis Goldberg, The Grantham girls,
and others too numerous to mention.   The dance ended at 11 with the
National Anthem, followed by Hatikvah.   Such a grand function it was, that
for long after people were still in the hall and outside talking, and all
expressed how very much they enjoyed themselves.

NEWS LETTER FROM THE HOME FRONT.

        Pesach brought with it the end of another "Lit" year. A year
which as the Vice-Chairman said was "as successful as could be expected".
Certainly the membership of thirty was somewhat lower than in pre-war
times but that we can expect. The Season included five dances, all of
them being socially, if not financially successful. The other usual events
were held throughout the session including debates, a Mock Trial, Prize
Paper Night and a talk by Dr. Corfield on "African Negroes" at which Sol
Novinski was chairman. The presence in the chair of one so dear to the
"Lit" helped a great deal to recapture some of the old spirit.
        The "Lit's" general meeting was held just before Pesach when a
committee was elected - almost all new members. The Chairman is Unita J.
Magrill, Joint Vice Chairmen Esther M. Cowan and Aubrey A. Gordon, Sec.
Mrs. Charles Kersh (Judy Bloomberg) and Treas. Leslie Epstein (of Shields)
and a commitee of six. It is hoped that an attractive syllabus will be
drawn up for next session seeing that many of the younger members have
succeeded in gaining positions on the committee and executive, and a large
membership is expected.
        I notice in last month's bulletin Inquisitor refers to the R.A.F.
Chilblain Addict in Yorkshire as having discovered Inquisitor's identity.
Now we are all trying to find the Chilblain Addict to extract this hush
hush discovery!
        I hear that this Bulletin will be the first to be available to your
families at home who will be able to buy if for 6d.   It will be on sale
at the "Lit" meetings and it is expected that this month's will be on sale
at the Lag B'Omer dance which the "Lit" hopes to hold on Sunday the 23rd
May.   A new feature of 'Hall' dances is the previous sale of tickets, and
reports of sales seem to indicate that this dance also promises great
success.

        Well forces, I will keep trailing the news and will regularly
give you the 'gen' about town.
                Keep Smiling,
                        Yours,
                        Also After Gen.

EXCERPTS FROM LETTERS TO THE EDITOR

Norman Cohen from B.N.A.F. writes: As promised, I am writing to let you know that I arrived safely in North Africa after a quiet trip. At present I am stationed in a big camp outside a small town and last Saturday after quite a search I found the local Synagogue. The service differed quite a lot from ours but it was most enjoyable and I was favoured with an "Aliyah".

L.A.C. Adolphe Vandervelde from Canada writes: Thanks a lot for the Bulletin received yesterday, it was grand reading all about the local fellows, but I suggest you ask the Inquisitor to think of a topic other than ANTI SEMITISM to describe me, also Sir, I remember quite vividly when you used to write letters to the ECHO that you thought a person who used a NON DE PLUME was not worth arguing with. I am afraid I shall ad the same attitude towards the Inquisitor and also you might mention to him that I am very "pally" with a Jewish K.C. here and I intend to ask him for legal advice about what type of sentence I would get for murdering an obnoxious NON DE PLUME.

Sgt. Basil Taylor from Kenya writes: I would like to thank you for the monthly Bulletins, which I have been receiving since my return to East Africa. I cannot speak too highly of their most interesting contents and of the excellent way in which they are compiled.

L.A.C. Louis Berg from Middle East writes: I am quite settled at my new station and I am feeling fit and well again after my slight disposition. I am receiving lots of mail from home these days and from all accounts seem to be missing lots of "Simchas" but I feel sure that considering how good the news this way continues to be, that I should soon have the great pleasure of meeting all these new in-laws and babies etc.

Sgmn. R. Rosenthal from India writes: I wish to thank you, from this remote and not too civilised part of the world for No.6 of your monthly Bulletin which reached me today. This was the first I have so far received and so was the first intimation that this interesting, amusing and well done publication even existed. You will be doing me a great service to ensure that all editions are sent to me. Being completely out of touch with European Jewry out here, you will understand how much the articles are appreciated and how much I enjoy the topical news of some of the old gang. You may like to know that I attend an Asiatic Service every Shabbos. The Service is terribly strange and difficult to follow, but somehow the atmosphere is there.

Lt. Mordaunt Cohen from North Africa writes: I am glad to say that the bulletins are arriving regularly, I can imagine the amount of hard work entailed, and I can assure you that members of the Forces, especially overseas, do appreciate your efforts. I received the January number last week with more news. INQUISITOR's Flashes were quite recognisable, even by myself, who is more or less unacquainted with local gossip and the young generation. Sol Novinski's article conjured up old memories of the night I won the LIT CUP. I can also vividly recall the last Mock Parliament we had. Ralph Freedman and myself worked days looking up Parliamentary Procedure, and drafting the bills. Sol was very warm and worn out at the end of the proceedings. Argus's article is just as interesting as his column in the ECHO. Tell him that I have got my eye on an excellent goalkeeper for S'land after the war. He is just 22 and is a Sgt. in my battery and used to play for Slough.

Letters were also received from the following: L.A.C. Joey Charlton from India, A.C. Charles Winberg from Seaham Harbour, Sgnm. Solly Cohen from Huddersfield, Gnr. Charles Kolson from Faroe Islands, L.A.C. Issy Davis from Norfolk and Pte. M. Doberman from Tunbridge Wells, Pte. Gwen Magril from Northampton, L.A.C. Julius Gordon from B.N.A.F. and Tpr. Horace Stone from M.E.F.

All correspondence to be sent to Rev. S.P. Toperoff, 5, Victoria Avenue, Sunderland.

THE SUNDERLAND JEWISH COMMUNITY

Monthly Bulletin for the Forces

Vol. 1, No.11   Edited by the Minister - June 1943.   Sivan 5703.

A thrill passed through the hearts of all Jews who heard that the first person to land on Lampedusa Island was a Jew, Sgt. Sydney Cohen.   It is as well for Mussolini to know that amongst the fighting men who are contributing to the conquest of his Empire, are Jews, and they are playing a significant part.   When Egypt was threatened, Jews were ready to fight to the last to save Palestine and now too Jews are doing their share helping to bomb Italy out of the war.

It must not be thought that Sgt. Cohen is an isolated example of the heroism and bravery of the Jewish fighting men.   Feats of daring and devotion to duty are frequently met with from the highest rank to the lowest It is hardly credible that we still meet with people who think of the Jew as a shirker and not a fighter.   Is it not possible that this distorted view of the Jew is due to the fact that we have no Jewish army?   The other day I met a Palestinian sailor who is a member of the Zebulun Seafaring Society and he told me of the good work done by hundreds of Jewish sailors in every theatre of war.   But he added significantly hardly anyone has heard of this "Jewish Merchant Navy".   Our Palestinian friend told me that the Chaplain of an important port had never heard of or seen a Palestinian Jewish sailor. If the world is to hear of the exploits of the Jew in this war only through such a name as Cohen, because it is characteristically Jewish, we shall be doing an injustice to our cause and to our people.

A Jewish fighting force as a distinct entity could very well bring honour and glory to the Jewish people.   It is one thing to score a victory but another to win a truce.   We must not forget what happened in North Africa.   There, the rout of the Axis armies did not bring with it freedom for the Jew.   We were reminded that "Where the allied armies advance, liberation comes and all Jews who had suffered at the hands of the enemy would be released immediately".   We know, however, that weeks and months passed but Jews were not released entirely and unreservedly from the Nazi yoke which weighed so heavily upon them.   Why?   There was no Jewish fighting force, no Jewish General who could negotiate with the Allied Commanders.

Our plain duty is to forge ahead, demand recognition and clamour for a Jewish Army which will have an equal status with the other armies of the free fighting powers.   Our illustrious Prime Minister cried out early in the war "Give us the tools and we shall finish the job".   We have the tools, we have Jewish men and women who are ready to wreak vengeance on the Hun who is directly responsible for the cold blooded extermination policy of whole Jewish communities in German occupied Europe.   They are ready to sacrifice their lives on the altar of patriotism but they must not be denied their right to fight and die as Jews, as members of a Jewish Army and thus win dignity, status and a National Home for their kith and kin whom they leave behind.

DO YOU KNOW

1. Where does the Old Testament mention a Ferry Boat?
2. What is a "Cold Nose"?
3. How many Jews are employed in the industrial War Effort in Palestine?
4. Where and by whom was the "handkerchief" first mentioned?
5. What is "Jacob's Staff"?
6. What connection is there between the City of York and Jewish history?

Answers to the above questions on Page 3.

HERE AND THERE

<u>Congratulations to</u> Miss Miriam Winberg on her marriage to Dr. Goodman of Manchester and L.A.C. Israel Berg on his marriage to Miss Lily Mandelson of Glasgow.

We welcome to the forces Dr. Hyman Minchom, Surgeon Lieut. R.N.V.R.

We are very please to report that Sgt. Harold Magrill of the 125th Anti-Tank Regt. is safe and a prisoner of war in Japanese hands.

<u>Empire Sunday</u> On May 16th the local Jewish Girl Guides and Habonim took part in the local Parade at West Park, marching from the Synagogue, Ryhope Road and back.

A Bring and Buy sale was held on Wednesday 16th July at the Board Room of the Ryhope Rd. Synagogue for the funds of the Sunderland Jewish Women's Services Committee.   The function was a huge success and raised £44.

Eight pupils of the Hebrew Religion Classes organised a Bazaar in aid of Children in Occupied Countries.   £9.10. 0 was realised.   This is the second effort of the local Jewish Youth to raise funds for the Youth Eliy

---

EN PASSANT - THE INQUISITOR

It is Whit. Monday!   The sun is shining brilliantly on my righteous head as I drift down the river, occasionally (when enforced) making mysel responsible for an oar - but not too often, a less war-like scene it is impossible to visualise.   It could be the summer of 1939 except for the presence of so many smart uniformed figures, to right and left, in front behind, and except for the lack of discordant shrieks from a gramophone c wireless.

Mother Nature has provided her own Percussion Band, the Ripple of th water, the faint rustle of the Leaves and Grass as the gentle breeze play amongst them, the Twittering of little Nestlings, the Hum and Drone of vari-coloured Insects and lastly the almost imperceptible Tinkle of the Flower Heads as they nod gaily while watching their reflections in the riv Ah!   If only I were sufficiently gifted to conjure up these wondeful vis before your wondering eyes ' "Poems are made by fools like me.............

Much maligned and downtrodden as I am I notice that two other contri tors, in last month's issue, have emulated me by using pseudonyms - - - imitation <u>always</u> the sincerest form of flattery?   Would "Also After Gen" please refrain from mentioning The Chilblain Addict again as it is a ver "sore point" with him (or her).

FLASH

Who had a very enjoyable Engagement Party in Glasgow this week end - - lucky people!

Which eligible, handsome young doctor has become very keen on all things nau(gh)tical?

Who is shortly to become the Florence Nightingale of the Forces?

Who is <u>entirely</u> responsible for the great success of the "Balfour" (Club Declaration)?

Who is going to try and get home more often (since his recent posting) WETHER BY night or day?   Have you seen L.S. yet?

Rumour hath it that a L/Corporal stationed near here is always on "manoeu - - - good luck on his latest venture!

Which important member of the R.A.F. is so indispensable that he even ha be recalled from his <u>long over-due</u> leave?   Why Blackpool again?

3.

� Continued
◌ that another member of the R.A.F. when last home on leave was
◌ring about in his dressing gown etc. for all to see. What fools these
◌◌s be!
◌inks his recent transfer to Grimsby is "fishy business"? (It certainly
◌ standing in queues!)

SEARCHLIGHT ON SPORT - By Argus.

We are now in the "close" season, to use the official term for that
◌◌ of the year when footballers must dubbin their boots and pack away
◌ lkit. That is, officially. I still see chaps kicking a ball about
◌◌ front and if the F.A. paid a visit, two of them might find themselves
◌◌ble, officially.

Well, we landed the Combined Counties Cup - one of the best trophies
◌◌ North of England. When we won it at Huddersfield it was suggested
◌ it should be left with the County Association for safety but Billy
◌◌◌ would have none of it. He had won his first cup as manager and he was
◌◌ to have it on his sideboard. Just a few days ago he was out of his
◌◌ in lodgings. Fortunately it was a U.X.B. otherwise we might have
◌◌cted the scrap from various parts of the district.

The "Pool" from the Football League Cup brings each club £385.
◌ng that Sunderland not having reached the Competition proper, did not
◌ribute to the "Pool" its a windfall which reduces the bank overdraft.
◌◌ioning bank overdrafts reminds me of the old South Shields Club. They
◌ a deputation to the bank Manager and on being admitted to the private
◌ the club manager said: "May we have an overdraft"? The bank manager
◌ed, grasped a pile of documents on his desk and replied: "Certainly,
◌◌e will you have?"

Another one. Years ago when Manager Jack Tinn moved to Portsmouth
◌ manager I was requested by our Portsmouth paper to send them a short
◌◌graphical sketch of his career. I used the phrase "He can buy players
◌◌ old tram tickets", meaning of course he could find them without paying
◌ them. That season Portsmouth nearly went out of the First Division, so
◌ it among the spectators sent Jack Tinn about 3,000 old tram tickets and
◌◌d him to get busy.

ANSWERS TO QUESTIONS ON PAGE 1.

◌ Second Book Samuel, Chap. 19, Verse 18.
◌ A Cheese paste cooked in cream and butter, a favourite dish on Shavuot.
◌◌n milk foods are largely used.
◌ Over 40,000.
◌ It was first mentioned in the writing of an Italian Rabbi at the beginning
◌ the 14th Century.
◌ An instrument which accompanied all Explorers on their travels in early
◌◌es. It was constructed from the notes of Rabbi Levi Ben Gershon of
◌ nols, South of France. Besides being used for Navigation, Jacob's Staff
◌ the earliest form of Range-Finder.
◌ In 1190 a massacre of Jews took place when the whole of the local Jewry
◌◌ destroyed, not one being left alive.

4.

PEEPS INTO THE PAST

One 21st day of June

A sunny summer's Sunday morning a long special train streamed out of Newcastle station, a party of young men and women were aboard. They were a jolly crowd looking forward to a long happy day in the open air. At Sunderland station a similar party was on the platform awaiting a South Shields train which arrived, and another party of bright young things tumbled out. Greetings were exchanged until a long special train arrived from Newcastle. The Sunderland and South Shields party stepped aboard and the train steamed away.

Hartlepool was the next stop, a party of Hartlepool and Stockton people joined the train and it was off to Darlington, here also a party awaited the Special. As the train steamed into the station a couple of "Stop me and Buy one" ice cream boxes were spotted. With a cheer an avalanche of bright summer frocks and white and grey flannels, jumped out of the train.

Greetings with the Darlington party over, a rush for the ice cream men was made. The vendors were almost overwhelmed, soon all the ice cream was sold out. All aboard again and the train moved to its final destination. Arriving at a little station in a small cutting, the invasion of Croft began. Yes, it was a North East Union picnic party, soon re-inforcements arrived by motor and the delightful little Yorkshire village was taken by storm. Three hundred of us; what a day; glorious weather, sports, a good but rather crowded tea party. More sports and for those so inclined, lovely walks in lovely company. We knew how to organise picnics in those days. Do you remember some of them? Durham and Corbridge come to mind. The inter-sports were keenly contested, but good old Sunderland took some beating. Can you picture the figure of Ald. Bloom, now Mayor of West Hartlepool, complete with his riding breeches and straw hat? A picnic would not be complete without the champion of Jewish Youth present.

After a brilliant day a tired but happy party entered the awaiting train. Goodbyes were waved at Darlington, Hartlepool and Sunderland. Arriving home I went to bed to sleep the sleep of the tired did you? Why, yes you did. The longest Sunday of the year, North East Jewry's largest picnic over. A glorious time in glorious sunshine, to my committee I could say well done. May those times come to you again soon. Good old happy days.

SOL.

P.S. I hope you have enjoyed your "Peeps into the Past". If I have helped you to spend a little of your leisure time with happy thoughts, and given you a little comfort, then I am content.

S.N.

Our contributor will commence in the next issue a new series of articles called "In Retrospect" which will deal with different personalities.

Editor.

5.

THE DEDICATION OF THE "BALFOUR" CLUB.

By Corporal Ralph Freedman, R.A.F.

At 5 p.m. on Sunday, 2nd May, 1943, a large and brilliant cr
gathered in 41 Portland Place, London, for the dedication of these prem:
as the "Balfour" Club.   The uniforms of all ranks of all nations coul(
be seen side by side.   Colonels jostled against privates, and raw
recruits sat next to be-ribboned veterans of three and four years servj
in the field.

Lt.Colonel Dayan Gollop, who performed the dedication, was
supported by Captain Super (Chaplain to the London District), Captain
Judah Nadich (of U.S.A.) and a number of Chaplains of other Nations.   T
service was short and impressive.   In his dedication address Dayan Gol
made it clear that this was a club, maintained by the Jewish Community
the use of Forces, men and women of all the Allied Nations, regardless
race, creed or nationality, and he expressed his hope and conviction th:
Non-Jews of all Nations would enjoy its amenities.   He felt sure that
such joint use of its excellent facilities would do much to establish a
better understanding between Jews and Non-Jews.

In the speeches that followed tribute was paid to the energy ε
determination of Mrs. Sieff and her committee, and to the eagerness and
spirit of all the voluntary workers.

There is no doubt that this Club must be one of the finest in
the world.   The large panelled rooms are beautifully furnished with pil
carpets, deep easy chairs and tables bearing an amazing assortment of
magazines of all kinds and in all languages.   The magnificent library
and writing room on the first floor has a splendid collection of books,
and copies of all the daily papers, and of Jewish periodicals from all
over the world.   There are also chess sets and draughts, as well as
supplies of writing paper and envelopes.

The next room with one of the finest parquet floors in London
is used for dances (tea dance and cabaret Sundays, dancing Wednesdays)
and for literary meetings on Tuesdays and Fridays.   This Tuesday the
literary event is a Brains Trust of Seven Jewish Chaplains of seven
different countries.

Downstairs, after the two luxurious lounges, comes the table
tennis room (a very popular feature) then the Snack Bar (milk meals)
followed by the restaurant (meat meals).   In the restaurant three course
dinners and suppers are served at meal times.   Beautifully cooked and
served, the price is 1/3.   The Snack Bar is open from 8 a.m. until 10
p.m.   The Club offers sleeping facilities for 50 men.   Bath, bed and
breakfast cost 2/6.   The beds are comfortable, the sheets and rooms spot-
lessly clean, and the washrooms commodious.   Breakfast is generally a
cereal, another dish (possibly Welsh rarebit), coffee, roll and butter
and jam.

All the service is provided by a bevy of charming voluntary
workers, who do everything possible to provide a bright, homely and Jewish
atmosphere for all.

6.

To return to the dedication. Next to me sat Sylvia Mincovitch, whom I see often here. On her right, a Canadian Flight Lieu was sitting, wearing the D.F.C. - but a full description of the honours, medals and high ranking officers present would take hours. Among the committee known personally to me who were present, were Mr. & Mrs. Elton, Mrs. Bloch, Mr. and Mrs. Schwab and Mr. Gestetner. Amongst other distinguished guests were Mr. and Mrs. S.A. Golden, who "run" the West London Services Club in the Synagogue Chambers in 33, Seymour Place. Lt Louis Hammerson (Chairman) and Miss Rae Benjamin (Secretary) represented the Y.I.S. Society.

This then, was the dedication of the "Balfour" Club, and in conclusion I can do no better than join in Dayan Gollop's prayer that in these premises:
"........May all those of the Jewish Faith find in their hour of need communion and peace with the House of Israel."

NEWS LETTER FROM THE HOME FRONT

Never have I seen so sudden a change and such a striking one as I did at the 'lit' Lag B'Omer dance on Sunday May 23rd. The idea of selling tickets, already kindled by the Young Zionist dance, soon spread to the 'lit' and tickets sold for this dance brought some out-of-towners.

A renewed feature was the Running Buffet at which sandwiches and soft drinks were sold - - and sold rapidly at that! Palms placed on the stage for the wedding that afternoon (Miriam Winberg's) remained, and lent an air of exquisiteness to the Hall.

The floor was not so crowded as it had been for the Zionist dance (on Chal-Hamoed Pesach) though the atmosphere was just as, if not more, jolly. A sudden influx of wedding guests augmented the crowd as the merriment came to a climax in a Palais Glide to "Horsey, horsey, don't you stop".

The 'Lit' Secretary has already started canvassing for members who will receive membership cards this session for the first time during the war. I notice the 'lit' have returned to the use of printed circulars bearing the once familiar designed heading. It is this type of thing that makes me feel more certain that the 'lit' is going strong despite a great deal of talk last session about disbandonment.

A Ramble to Shincliffe Woods (near Durham) was planned for Sunday, May 30th, but rain was threatening about noon. The "Junior Lit", I am informed is also going strong, holding weekly meetings at private houses. These are attended usually by a gathering of about twenty and they discuss at their debates and lectures classical, political and other important subjects. Its members, whose ages range roughly from thirteen to sixteen (the lower age limit for the 'lit') scorn socials and revel in serious discussion - - - a lesson could perhaps be learned by the 'lit' on this point. The "Junior Lit" should provide some very useful members for the 'lit' in a year or two; meanwhile they're doing well and deserve every encouragement.

So news-readers also get fed up!   A B.B.C. announcer is reported to have said the other day   "Here are some new facts about the dam(n) news!"

Well that's all for the present.

Chin up, yours,

Also After Gen.

EXCERPTS FROM LETTERS.

Cpl. N. Berg writes: I look forward to receiving the Bulletin which means so much to the boys and girls serving in H.M. Forces,(especially I am sure to those serving overseas)., It is interesting to have all the news from home, especially when compiled in such a talented way, as in your Bulletin. When I think of the hard work entailed, I appreciate it even more. I am grateful to all who participate in making the Bulletin such a success. On behalf of my fiancee and myself I would like to extend to you, our thanks for the good wishes conveyed to us through your paper.

A/C Ernie Cohen writes: I would be greatly obliged if you would send me the May issue of your Magazine of news of the Sunderland Jewish lads and girls in the Services, and future monthly copies. I derive great enjoyment from them and it helps to keep me in touch with Sunderland Jewish Service personnel. I hope I too, shall have an opportunity of writing an article.

L.A.C. Julius Gordon from B.N.A.F. writes: I am sure I speak for each and everyone of the grateful recipients of the Bulletin, when I say that if appreciation and pleasure, derived from the perusal of the bulletin, each month, are sufficient justification for the work entailed in its publication and issue, then your time and labour expended on it are well worth while and it does indeed serve a most valuable purpose.

Sgm. I Rosenthal from India writes: I want to thank the J.W.W.S.C. for the parcel I got last week. Though in a somewhat dilapidated condition I certainly do appreciate the gesture - - and had an excellent shave for a change. It was a grand thought.

A.C.W.2. L. Slater writes: To Inquisitor I say:-
"I thank you kind Sir or Madam,
For your reference to me in En Passant,
But really Inquisitor you should think before
Mentioning that Battlefield of yore.

Although people know where I am stationed,
Although people know very well.
They all haven't got YOUR intelligence
To know that it referred to Cromwell".
I am afraid my attempt at poetry isn't too good but it will do for Inquisitor.

Cpl. Norman Cohen from B.N.A.F. writes: Today has indeed been a memorable occasion for myself and every other Jewish soldier who attended the first Service to be held at the Great Synagogue, Avenue de Paris, Tunis, since the Allies liberated it a few days ago. It was a service specially for the men in uniform and was conducted by Rabbi (Major) Rabbinowitz of Golders Green. There were men from the First and Eighth armies, French Troops, Americans and also members of the Palestinian Regiment. The population lined the street and gave us a welcome befitting a King.

8.

Tpr. Horace Stone from M.E.F. writes: I believe I told you that while at the South African Hospital I acquired a book of Jewish Thoughts, and A "Singer", but I do not think I told you of the comfort and consolation I derived therefrom, while I was really ill. Now I am up, and have a job to keep me busy, I am typing out a translation of a German book of Instructions about a machine captured.

Lieut. M. Cohen from West Africa writes: I was pleased to read about Sol Novinski's appearance at the Lit. He must have felt very proud indeed, and I am only sorry that there were not many of the old crowd there to welcome him. Someday in the near future P.G. we will have a grand re-union. Give Sol my regards. I was very pleased indeed to see an article by Argus in the Bulletin. I can remember when we first started the Judeans one of our first games was against Hull. Argus came along to the match (which we won 2-1) and afterwards to the dinner in the Talmud Torah.

Tel.(S.O.) Sam Lerman from Colombo writes: Going through India by train which took us five days we saw quite a lot of interesting things. India itself is very interesting, as soon as you land, they are asking for alms. Someone wants to tell you your fortune. At night the people sleep on pavements, and in the early morning they prepare their stalls for the day. Shoes and foodstuff are quite reasonable, but in Ceylon they are just the opposite.

L.A.C. I Davis writes: I am now on combined operations which no doubt you have heard and read about. Whilst I was in Scotland I was doing Commando Training for this in order to make myself tough and accustomed to such conditions. Admittedly this training nearly killed me but as you see, I survived.

Letters for which the Editor acknowledges with thanks have also been received from Pte. Doberman, Pte. Sylvia Mincovitch, A/C A. Landau, Sgt. Basil Taylor, L/Cpl. H. Winthrop, A/C M. Dresner, A/C Austin Davis, L.A.C. A. Vandervelde, Cpl. Ralph Freedman Pte. Leopold Levin and A.C.W.2 Reva Pearlman.

———

NOTE:
Change of address must be notified to ensure regular receipt of the Bulletin.

All correspondence to be sent to the Rev. S.P. Toperoff, 5, Victoria Avenue, Sunderland.

THE SUNDERLAND JEWISH COMMUNITY

Monthly Bulletin for the Forces.

Vol.1 No.12.   Edited by the Minister - July 1943.   Tamuz 5703.

I have always encouraged questions and in an interesting letter from Charles Marks from the Middle East, he asks me to deal with a query put to him by one of his non-Jewish friends.   It is not a new question and crops up ever so often.   'Why are Jews connected so much with finance?' That the Jew controls finance is a favourite weapon with the Anti-Semites.   This wicked belief has been repeated so often that some of us are beginning to believe it.   The Jew baiter is not interested in history or present day facts.   It matters little to him that the Bank of England and the big 5 Banks are controlled by Gentiles and not Jews: that the greatest international house of today is J.P. Morgan & Co. which has no Jewish partners in any of its subsidiary branches, and that out of the 30 members of the Stock Exchange only one is a Jew.

Money lending which created economic Anti-Semitism was forced upon Jews in the Middle Ages by the Church and the Crown who treated the Jew, not as a human being but as personal property.   The Jew was used as a pawn in the game of big finance, he was used as a tool with which to fill the coffers of the lordly gentry.   Those interested in the problem will find testimony from a Christian scholar and clergyman the Rev. Dr. James Parkes who wrote - "..the richest and most powerful usurers of the Middle Ages in every country and century were Christians and not Jews."   From earliest times Jews were by nature attached to the soil.   The Jewish homeland Palestine was referred to as a "Land flowing with Milk and Honey".   It is interesting to note that in the whole Bible Jews and merchants are mentioned only once and this in a figurative sense.

Judaism as a religion and a civilisation has always stressed not finance but amongst other things learning and education.   The greatest Christian Theologians and Philosophers have testified "to the charity, family feeling, industriousness, thirst for culture and knowledge which constitutes the finest traits of Jews".

He who knows history will not connect Jews with finance.   He will know that a people that have suffered martyrdom for thousands of years living through burnings at the stake, auto-da-fe, inquisitions, pogroms, persecutions and mass murder must draw its inspiration from idealism and not finance. If Jews still patiently bear the brunt of human hate and persistent suffering does this not reveal an idealism which should command the respect of the free world?

Not only in suffering and death is this Jewish idealism present but also in the creation and rebuilding of a new home in Palestine.   It is perhaps impossible to convey to our Christian friends the enthusiasm zeal and selfless devotion with which Jews of all walks of life and at all times have left secure homes and settled ways of life in order to kiss the soil of the Holy Land of Israel.   In spite of great difficulties settlements and colonies were created from the waste rocky barren land and the malaria infested swamps: the recreation of the Jewish soul goes on even now in time of war.   Whilst some of the limbs of the Jewish body are paralysed into inactivity and threatened with amputation, the heart is functioning and though seared and bruised with continuous disappointments it is awake ready to show the world that the Jew is a creative builder.

The Jew is industrious and thrifty and suffers for possessing qualities which in other people are admired.   Viscount Samuel in his recent book "An Unknown Land" wrote - "rarely in this world does advancement fail to provoke unpopularity.   Abstinence, hard work and intelligence win success

2.

in the competition, they do not win friends among the competitors. The qualities which led a people to anti-semitism were always the same, and inability to distinguish between truth and falsehood together with envy of success, an insistence of uniformity and ready resort to violence. Such qualities must inevitably lead sooner or later to national failure and downfall. The opposite qualities which preclude anti-semitism - tolerance, a care for truth and justice, a belief in persuasion rather than force - these in the long run ensure success and greatness. Throughout history and in all countries the Jews have been the touchstone of the nations". We should ponder well over these weighty words.

DO YOU KNOW?

1. Where in the Bible do we find the earliest allusion to the art of embroidery?
2. When were Jews expelled from England and how long were they not allowed to return?
3. Who wrote "Nathan the Wise" and what influenced the author to write the book?
4. What new strides have been made recently in Jewish industry in Palestine?
5. What was the first instance known in English history of death by burning for heresy?.
6. What is the "Magen David Adom"?   Answers to the above on P

HERE AND THERE.

Congratulations to Miss Phyllis Goldberg on her engagement to L/Cpl.Lionel Altman of London, to Dr. Benny Gordon and Dr. George Jacoby on their scholastic successes and to Jack Stern on attainment of degree of M.P.S.
We welcome to the Forces Mr. A. Davis of 10, Cuba Street, Miss Gwen Grantham of 13, Manila Street who has joined the W.R.N.S. and Mr. Philip Soldinger of 2, Beauclerc Terrace.
Congratulations to Kitty Ward (nee Bloom) on the birth of a son.

On a card written home, Sgt. Harold Magrill wishes to be remembered to all his friends. He is well and has not been wounded.

We are pleased to report that Bdr. Ed. Pearlman of 125th Anti-Tank Rgt. is reported safe and a prisoner of war in Japanese hands.

The Literary Society has started its Summer Session with renewed vim and vigour. On Sunday afternoon, July 4th, an "At Home" for the Forces was held, followed by a dance in the evening. In the afternoon abundant and delectable refreshments (most of which was provided gratis) were served at tables becomingly decorated and dotted attractively about the Hall. Unfortunately a number of the guests were debarred from attending at the last moment, but of those present, I can truthfully say "a good time was had by all."

Prior to the tea a short Religious Service was conducted by the Rev. S.P. Toperoff in Shool, who also gave an informal talk. The Chairman, Miss Unita J. Magrill charmingly extended a welcome to all visitors and in proposing the health of the visitors the Minister explained that these functions were to be a regular monthly event (arrangements are already in hand for another "At Home" on Sunday August 15th).

In the interval between tea and dance, various games were played and seemingly enjoyed. During the dance there was a running buffet which was exceedingly well patronised. This idea is, we trust, the nucleus of bigger and better things to come. Good luck to all responsible!

3.

EN PASSANT - "INQUISITOR"

Contrary to all expectations (my own included) I have been "reserved" once more to serve humanity in order to compose my twelfth masterpiece. During the last eventful year I have been able to retain some little popularity with a negligible number of my readers - - - those whom I have omitted to mention in my musings: what have I achieved in my year of office? (Peace for our time?) Have I given even one person (excluding myself) a little pleasure? Or, like Abraham, am I going to find difficulty in obtaining even that? I suppose it is rather gratifying to my dormant ego to realise that my name has become famous (or infamous) in at least four continents (thanks due to Anti-Semite, Andre and Amo Madras). It seems grossly unfair that neither Australia nor New Zealand have benefited , as yet, from my journalism.

FLASH

Does the Algerian Sheik still send Paradise Fruits home? The answer is six lemons. (Do you know who composed "Invitation to the Waltz"?)
It has come to our notice that the Shipping Magnate is going in for more intellectual pleasures. Enjoying yourself? Maybe:
Which influential civilian manages to obtain "Oil for the lamps of China"? (or Turkish Baths?)
Which VICTORious member of the R.A.F. (Tunisia) is expected to be on terra firma shortly? Don't DESERT us again, doctor.
On dit that D.A. takes exception to being mentioned in my column, the only way to avoid this is to refrain from coming home so often::
I'm pleased that Groucho, Chico, Harpo and Karl derive so much pleasure from my literary dabblings. And their disciples too, fame in a day (or night:)
Who doesn't feel like playing his "Tuba down in Cuba" Street now?
Who is always CONSTANT IN Everything he performs?
Is it true that there is now "Minyan" to be had at the Rectory (N.F.S.) any day?
Does I.R. find the Indian Dancers as talented as those at the Barnes? Still getting a good share?
Did the Orkney Native enjoy his special visit to the pictures? Also maybe:
Rumour hath it that the "Lit" is organising a Heavy Weight Championship - it certainly lends COLOUR to the Syllabus.
Who is exceptionally interested in HOSTELities?

ANSWERS TO THE QUESTIONS ON PAGE 1.

1. Exodus. Chapter 26, Verse 36.
2. Jews were expelled from England in 1290 and were not allowed to return for 365 years.
3. Lessing the author created in Nathan the noblest of stage-Jews.   He was influenced by two great Jewish Philosophers - Spinoza and Moses Mendlesohn, who was the personal friend of Lessing.
4. The Phoenician Glass Works of Haifa Bay have marketed its first window glass.   In addition a special process has been evolved by which building material can be made from the papyrus reeds of the Huleh swamps.
5. Robert, the Deacon of Reading deserted the Church for the love of a Jewess.   He was tried by Archbishop Langton before an ecclestastical Court and burned at the stake as a punishment for his crime.
6. The Jewish First Aid Society in Palestine founded in 1930 has a membership now of 3,500 volunteers including a Blood Transfusion Service.   It has 23 registered branches, an equal number of First Aid Stations and 16 ambulances.   It holds First Aid Courses for thousands of men and women and intends setting up Mobile Surgical Units, and Mobile Field Hospitals.

SEARCHLIGHT ON SPORT - By "Argus"

It is now possible, under censorship regulations, to say that shortly after the football season closed one of the German raiders which crossed the coast in May dropped a nice little piece of blast and metal c the Roker Park ground - just where the players came out on to the field from the dressing rooms. He planted another on the car park outside the grand stand.

Jerry or no Jerry we are still going to have our football next season. The ground drainage system was immediately repaired, the crater filled up and the ground relaid where the damage was done. True, the gra stand is the worse for wear and I am afraid the roof has more holes than cover from rain, but that's a mere detail.

When I pressed in the columns of the "Echo" for League football be resumed at Roker Park even some of the Directors thought they would lo money by it. My point was they would make players for the post war perio and they would gain money by that. As a matter of fact Sunderland made a substantial profit a year ago, and they have made a net profit of nearly £1,200 in the past season. It would have cost them £2,000 a year to kee the ground closed. So what!

Next season players are to receive £2 per match instead of 30/ which was a ridiculous sum for a man who lost a day's pay to play in away game.- with tax at 10/- in the £. Another point which will interest my o sea's readers is that in the first post war season, the League will be run an extended Regional basis without promotion or relegation. That will gi clubs a chance to get players together and bring some youngsters on. Bes all the players serving with the Forces wont be released as soon as the wa ends. When? When you are all Ex-Servicemen great day that.

Raich Carter went down to Scotland with the idea of playing for Mirren in the semi-final of the Scottish Summer Cup. But he had to sit in the stand. The Scottish F.A. would not sanction his appearance. Andy Rei Sunderland's pre-war trainer is training St. Mirren.

As I was writing these notes a letter came to me from North Afri from Cpl. Norman Cohen. Along with it was a copy of Union Jack the Forces newspaper which contained interesting experiences to the value of Carter a partner to Stanley Matthews. Thanks for your good wishes Corporal. I am glad that someone finds my articles in the Bulletin interesting and apprec iates them. Stanley Matthews is a great player - but in my opinion, one the easiest wingers in the game to stop. Just take no notice of him stop ing to kid you he is coming inside. The back who says "There is a ball an a man and one of them is mine" puts Matthews out of the game

IN RETROSPECT - by SOL NOVINSKI

I am starting my effort with a prayer for forgiveness. I sincerely b of you to forgive any error or mis-statement any omission or overstatement may make in this, my memoirs of the "Lit" and kindred young peoples societ After all, thirty two busy years are a long time. Couple this with the fa that I am writing in hospital and have only my memory to rely on and you h the reason for my plea.

That personal anecdotes may occasionally creep in, seems inevitable. hope you will bear with them, sometimes, even be interested. To my comrad of the "Lit" early days, I send my greetings and to those fellow workers o later years, my earnest thoughts and affections, especially to you boys an girls serving with the Forces in Gt.Britain and all parts of the world.

In 1911, three young men had a feeling that all was not well with Sund land's Young Jewry. A circular was drawn up, inviting the young people to meeting at the Synagogue Chambers, Moor Street - - Result--- the "Lit" was born, and Abe Rothfield, Ep.Mark Rowlands, and Sol Novinski had set in mot

5.

uch hard work, heartbreak, annoyance, joy and above all enthusiasm. Enlight
nment was on its way. My earliest memory was an interview with our Ministei
r. S. Daiches. He promised to become our Hon. President. In that first
ear, kind, helpful and jolly Rev.L. Muscat gave us a musical recital. He
as accompanied by my late sister Kate at the piano. Mr. J.J. Golding lect-
red on "Criticism". Dramatic reading, debates, a concert and a dance formed
ur syllabus. The Committee meetings were many and to put it mildly, red hot.
"It shows the thing is alive" said Chairman J.J.G. Strange as it may
eem to most of you the Literary & Debating Society, as it was then called,
ot no encouragement from the parent members of the Community, but much heart
ending discouragement. To quote only one matter: There was much opposition
o the Society using the Committee Room for debates, and the school room for
ectures and the concert. We stood our ground and eventually pulled through.

We had much snobbish sneering to put up with also, but faith in our
ause, earnestness and enthusiasm, carried us ever forward. We appealed to
he Union of Jewish Literary Societies (London), for assistance and they gave
is much valuable help. During the years before the last war, many brilliant,
ndeed famous people spoke to us. Of these, I feel I must give the name of
lkan Adler (the late Chief Rabbi's brother), first place. Never had I been
o impressed by a man. Even today to me the name of E. Adler stands for true
obility. Calling for him at the Grand Hotel, on the Sunday morning of his
risit, we went for a walk. It was an unforgetable experience for me. I
hall tell you about it next month.

NEWS LETTER FROM THE HOME FRONT

Whilst the invasion of Sicily has kept the newspapers full I find that
he "Lit" is not supplying sufficient news to fill this letter. However my
itle is wide and I am fully justified in talking about things other than the
Lit, matters I am sure that will interest you all.

The ramble that the "Lit" arranged for the 30th May had to be postponed
to the 27th June because of bad weather on the former date.

A glance at the "Excerpts from letters" section of the bulletin indicates
that several readers are abroad and they must wonder what those things in
the home town are like which, before the war, they took for granted. Most
main shops in town are more or less where they were before except perhaps
that Binns, as you must know, is now scattered throughout various parts of
Fawcett Street and Holmeside. The usual dances are still held at the Barnes
Hotel though there has been a rise in price. Barnes Park abounds in blazing
"Red Hot Pokers" stately velvet like roses and waving lupins of all colours.
Tennis is played as usual and in just as great numbers but the average standard of playing much lower than it used to be. "Whites" still dazzle the eye
though the balls are usually rather dirty as new ones are unobtainable. The
park is more or less as in peace time and is still the Shabbos walk for many.
You do not see, however, any children throwing crumbs to the swans and ducks.

The bandstand converted into a large stage is the centre of Sunderland's
"Holidays at Home" programme which includes both Shakespearean plays and opera
I have been to the sea front once or twice lately and were it not for the
coils of barbed wire and some uniforms I might have forgotten there was a war
on! One Sunday evening I strolled up and down a crowded prom. The sun shone
forth with its warm reddish rays and the chilly sea breeze made me uncertain
whether it were warm or cold. I said the prom was fairly crowded, but though
I retraced my steps several times I saw no more than a handful of Jewish
people. By the way, if you can get good ice-cream where you are count yourself lucky. The stuff here........

An advert over a Hand laundry left me wondering the other day. It read
"Don't kill your wife - let us do it".

I'll be with you again next month so cheerio for now and keep smiling.

Yours,
Also After Gen.

EXCERPTS FROM LETTERS

S/Sgt. J. Rosenthal from Iraq & Persia writes: Quite by chance today I ca
across the little handful of our people who live in the village where I a
surrounded by fanatical Moslems. Poor people, they used to live in a car
seri, but decided that to worship their God, they should have a proper hou
One room kept apart from the rest has been made into a Synagogue. The A
plain wooden cupboard was opened that I might see the Sephar Torah. The
Scroll was opened at the weeks's Parsha which is the only one I read many
ago when I was Barmitzvah. The pleasure of these people on meeting a fel
traveller was quite touching. The Sabbath and Festivals are strictly adh
to and I was asked to come for Shavouth. So is the light kept burning in
Shushan. I have also met the head of the Zionist movement in Persia. Thi
organization had to work in secret during the old Sheikh's regime and onl
came out again when the British occupied the country. It is not easy to
cognise a Jew here, but with the greeting Shalom, instead of the Persian
Salam, there is a transformation; a coolie becomes a Jew and consequentl
brother. This country is quite rich in ancient Jewish history if one can
dig out the story. The difficulty lies in the language problem and the
pressure of Islam.

Pte. L.C. Levin from Meerut, India writes: Yom Kippur & Rosh Hashannah I
in Durban. By now the whole world must know of the kindness and generosi
the Durbanites. How pleased I am to be able to say, that the Jewish peop
there not only did their share but often led the way. Succoth I spent th
latter days in Capetown, where I had the pleasure of eating many meals in
nacles decorated with palm branches and other tropical foliage. Taken al
round we had a very pleasant journey. With food we found the Army Author
were pleased to do what they could, both on the ships we were on and now
India. Of course you cannot expect anything without asking and a little
venience may be experienced, but he who wants to do so can keep his relig
in the Army - at least to some extent. As for prayers - 4 Army Padres (C
of England and Catholic) gave us permission to use their cabin each morni
and we were able to wear our Phylacteries in peace and quiet. Here in Indi
things are very much the same, Prayers, Tephillen etc. create little diff
It is quite healthy to be a vegetarian. What I miss is a Minyan etc. Shab
the greatest trouble and I am afraid I often pray for a Sabbath which wil
a day of "Yom shekulou Shabbos" and not just a Sabbath I can keep for hal
day only. However in most other things we manage O.K. We enjoyed the thr
of searching the Bazaar for lights, suitable for Chanucah, and we were ab
kindle the lights every night, but that is old history. Recently five bo
from our unit went to Calcutta for Pesach and contrary to all reports abo
Jews in India, they did all they could for us. I am afraid most of the f
who come to India tend to forget that the Jews here are from a different
and are different in many respects from the Jews in Europe. They are mai
from Persia, Iraq, Turkey etc. and are all Sephardic. Theirs is a poor s
ard of Jewish learning and orthodoxy. But they have some beautiful custo
minhagim. They call themselves Jews, not Jewish. Their Synagogues are bu
the Eastern style, very ornate often with clock towers, 80 to 100 Scrolls
Law are the usual number in the Shools of both Bombay and Calcutta. I cou
120 in one Ark built like a small circular room. The Scrolls themselves a
encased in silver covers, a protection against rot in this climate of ext
heat and humidity.

The following letters also received and are gratefully acknowledged by th
Editor:- L.A.C. C. Marks, Tpr. H. Stone, L.A.C. J. Gordon, L.A.C. A. Vande
Sgt. A. Forman, Pte. G. Magrill, A.C.W.2. L. Slater, L/Bdr. S. Gillis, L.
A. Penn, and Surg.Lieut. H.B. Minchom, R.N.V.R.

All correspondence to be sent to Rev. S.P. Toperoff, 5 Victoria Aven
Sunderland.   N.B. Change of address must also be notified to ens
regular receipt of Bulletin.

THE SUNDERLAND JEWISH COMMUNITY

Monthly Bulletin for the Forces

Vol. 1 No. 13   Edited by the Minister - August 1943.   Av 5703.

Recently we observed the "Sabbath of Comfort". Those of you who are overseas and those not very far from home will find little real comfort doing your job. You know that it has to be done and likes and dislikes have to be brushed aside.

In spite of this you will not begrudge us here at home observing the Sabbath of Comfort. You see "comfort" in our sense has nothing to do with the accredited meaning which is mainly materialistic. The Sabbath of Comfort is supposed to herald a period when the world will awaken itself to the injustices done to Israel and give it real comfort. You have heard of "Comforting the mourners" a Jewish custom when friends visit one who is bereaved and comfort him with words and kind deeds. Don't you think that we more than any other nation in the world have lost proportionally more of our sons and daughters in the slaughter houses of Poland than others on the field of battle. Our losses remember, began not in 1939, but in 1933.

Is it not time that the nations of the world comforted us not with words alone, but with deeds of loving kindness. The Sabbath of Comfort has today an added significance. We ask not for material comfort, not for worldly riches, not even for fame or honour, but for comfort in the religious sense which according to the dictionary is defined as "assistance in time of weakness".

We as a race are weak and without power, we spend all our force and resources on the peoples in whose midst we live. We depend on them for comfort and justice. It is time that the Sabbath of Comfort be generally made known and the Allied Powers make it a present reality.

DO YOU KNOW?

1. Where are the words "God Save the King" first found?
2. Who said the following:- "May I remind the honourable Gentlemen that whilst their ancestors were savages on the Banks of the Thames, mine were Princes in Solomon's Temple"?
3. Who was Preuss?
4. Do you know of three Jews who aspired to high position in Australia?
5. Where was the first Jewish Club in the British Empire and the United States of America founded?
6. Which Jewish Captain on the French General Staff was illegally convicted of high treason?

Answers to the above on Pages 3 & 4.

HERE AND THERE!

Congratulations to:-
Mr. & Mrs. J. Pean on the birth of a son.
Celia Leslie on her engagement to Jacques Grunblatt of Belgium.
Adolph Vandervelde on obtaining his Observer's Wing.
Sam Lerman on his promotion to Acting Leading Tel.(equal to Sgt. in the army) and to
Dr. Ellis Dresner on entering the Forces.

Issy Levine asks that his address be passed on through the Bulletin - here it is:- S/174060 Sgt. I. Levine, I.A.O.C., Quetta Arsenal, Indian Command.

2.

A Reminder!

Will those who have not made application for leave for the High Holy Day please do so. New Year 30th September and 1st October and the Day of Atonement, 9th October. In each case the leave should commence at suns on the previous day.

In the recent Jews College Preliminary Certificate for Teachers Diploma, the following pupils of the Ryhope Road Hebrew Classes were successful:- Moses Feld and Harold Merskey - Distinction, Godfrey Heilpern and Suzie Neuwerth - Pass.

A Certificate of Honour has been presented to the Sunderland Jewis Women's War Services Committee for their splendid achievement in War Savings during Wings for Victory Week.

We are pleased to report that Sgt. Maurice Mincovitch and Nathan Ernstone are both safe and well and prisoners in Japanese hands.

EN PASSANT

Time marches on. From being a figure of worshop and adulation I ha become a thing of the past! My name is no longer continually being hea from everyone's lips, war news and other trivial items have usurped my unenviable position! King for a day! Unhonoured, unwept and unsung.

I start my second year of journalism a sadder and wiser person. Las year I was full of joie de vivre and youthful exuberance feeling I was doing my "bit", perhaps being responsible for an occasional smile, which filtered across the stern mobile features of my indifferent readers who were bent on more serious tasks.

To say I am disillusioned is a mild form of speech, I am disconsola nay, heartbroken. No more maligned, misjudged or misunderstood person can there be.

Ah! One bright spot looms across my otherwise dull horizon, my Editor still smiles (if a trifle wearily) upon me, what greater reward cou I ask? I feel re-instated once more, I am oblivious to all, I have fou my haven of refuge. One word of timely advice, be more tolerant as it seems you're going to have the doubtful pleasure of reading my literary dabblings for some more months to come. (Long live extensions and calli up pains!)

On with the motley..........

FLASH

So the Shipping Magnate still has a roving eye. He has now ascended to W.A.A.F. s. Don't give up in despair, oh fair sex. Who knows ....

Who engaged the Bridal Suite at the Cumberland Hotel? Hope the Staff h a restful holiday?

Rumour hath it that an eminent person, recently invalided home, has becom most interested in the ALGERIAN question.

Which attractive member of the A.T.S. has not DROPped a STAIN on her impeccable behaviour? Do hope you have a really good week's leave.

Who is the latest Queen of Sherwood Forest?

Who is entrusting a very valuable parcel from Egypt to Sunderland? A very neighbourly act.

Rumour hath it that a very popular Q.M. will soon be leaving terra firma. Take it easy Middlesbro'.

Which member of the R.A.F. always spends his leave at another aerodrome? Morpeth for instance? Dancing feet.

Does H.B. still find "Les Femmes de la Roche" irresistible?

On dit that South Africa has adopted the Brylcreeme King ,,. please kee him safe for us, or else!

3.

propos of the Question from Quetta, the answer is in the negative.
o Norman the Conqueror has been tete a tete with royalty. We hope it
ortified him on his way.
o C.M. Very many thanks for The Tripoli Times which made very interest-
ng reading, particularly Astrid's glamorous form!
o all that glitters is not GOULD, sorry you can't find a better person
ith whom to become photographed. (When you return to Sunderland........)
ho has become "toffee nose" since taking a course at Cleadon?
tumour hath it that L.M. has now made my "song go round the world".

SEARCHLIGHT ON SPORT - By "Argus"

By the time these notes are in your hands another football season
rill have opened. Both Darlington and Hartlepools United have "joined-
ip" again after being out of action since the opening of hostilities, so
;here are more "Derby" games for the North-East - Hitler willing.
Mr. Bevan and Mr. Dalton are of course, gradually reducing the number
of spectators - and probably the important conferences in Quebec at the
noment may also have the effect of not only reducing the spectators but
also the service players available.
Spectators, of course, have always been the silly people - just wasting
their time to watch 22 players run about an enclosed field kicking a ball
bout. Football first started by some inmates of a lunatic asylum kicking
piece of paper about. The warders thought it a good idea so they start-
d to play with a rubber ball. And the lunatics have been looking on ever
ince. That's an Aberdeen story.
Well, Alex Hastings has football in his blood and he has changed his
lind. Any Scotsman is liable to do that when £2 is at stake, but Alex is
lot that type of Scot. He would play for the love of playing, and he is
joing to Captain the team again this season - much to the disgust of Mrs.
lastings. I can image the reply when Alex comes home and says: "By my
Legs are sore". It will be something like: "Serves you jolly well right".
During the close season, Manager Murray has been signing a few
youngsters and I shall be able to tell you more about them and their possibilities as the season advances. One of them, an outside left named
Thompson, is a son of a Sunderland player of a quarter of a century ago,
out his father was an outside right.
"Raich" Carter will still be available to play when the R.A.F. do not
rant him, and we may see more of Ralph Rodgerson this season. He seems
;o have fully recovered from a knee injury received in a Police game last
geason, and is keen to play.
Arthur Housam who did so much to help St. Mirren defeat Rangers in the
Scottish cup last season is to play for Hearts this term. Bob Gurney is
also in Scotland, but there is no indication as to who he will assist. He
played a few games for Aberdeen after he went into the Air Force.
I am looking forward to giving you much news of the Sunderland club's
doings, but believe me when I say I am much more interested in the time
rhen you will all be back home watching Sunderland play. Then I may have
in opportunity of visiting the "Lit" and seeing some of you in person, as
Ex-Servicemen. That's the title you are all waiting for.

Answers to Questions on Page 1.

1. In the Bible, 2nd book of Samuel, 16th Chapter, 16th Verse.
2. When Disraeli was attacked in the House of Commons for his Jewish
origin, this was his retort.
3. The first Jewish Minister of the Republic in Germany, he was the
Creator of the Weimar Constitution. (Continued on next page.)

4.

Answers Contined

4. (a) V.L. Snowman, early explorer, who in 1899 became Prime Minister of South Australia. (b) Sir Isaac Isaacs, at one time Chief Justice of the High Court of the Commonwealth, and later appointed Governor General. (c) General Sir John Monash, Commander in Chief of Australian Corps.
5. In Newport in 1761.
6. Alfred Dreyfuss in 1895.

IN RETROSPECT - BY SOL NOVINSKI

We met Dr. Salis Daiches on the stairs in the Hotel, he had decided to accompany us. By the time we arrived at the Roker Promenade, Mr. Elkan Adler and I were discussing the relative values of cycling and walking. I had just finished telling him one of my cycling adventures, when Dr. Daiches started a discussion on some Jewish matter of great moment. "I have come out to enjoy the sea breezes and the view of your beautiful N.E. Coast", was Mr. Adler's response.

Arriving at Sea Lane (there were no early Sunday morning trams in those days) our guest hinted that we might go farther on. In high glee suggested Marsden, we turned to the Reverend Doctor, he agreed. Almost all the way, Mr. Adler kept the level of the conversation down to that of an ordinary, fairly intelligent young man. His tact and graciousness, his kindliness and ability to set me at ease, earned my gratitude and later my admiration. His method was to draw on my observation and general knowledge. There was also something buoyant and boyish about him. There are many stories I could tell you, but space does not allow me. One tale I must tell you though. It illustrates, I think, his delightful modesty. On our way home he admired the beautiful village of Whitburn, and a little later the Bents Cottages, he turned and gazed at the view we all know and love. The old church tower peeping over sweeping line of trees, the serene sky of "a beautiful scene" Mr. Adler said. The remainder of the conversation went something like this: "If you wrote a book about the beautiful places you have seen, it would be very interesting" said Dr. Daiches. "My dear Doctor", came the reply "Could I write a book about the beautiful places I have not seen, it would be much more interesting.

Mr. Adler is a very widely travelled man. Our visitor was the guest of Dr. Daiches for lunch and spent the remainder of the afternoon playing with their baby on the hearthrug. The meeting (a lecture on a visit to the Balkans) was held in the Park Hall, Toward Road.

Next month I will write about the late Miriam Regina Bloch.

So Cheerio for now.

SOL.

NEWS LETTER FROM THE HOME FRONT.

On Sunday July 18th a most enjoyable day was spent at Shincliffe Woods by a dozen or so of "lit" members. As the buses were packed we went as far as Durham in separate buses from where we rambled along the river in two parties. The first was led by Girlie Cowan and the second, by Unita Magrill. The two parties met in the woods at a place chosen by the first party and which incidentally was swarmed with flies. But at least it was not as bad as when we went to Hylton last year and had to contend with spiders. Still it was a really enjoyable ramble and we are looking forward to the next.

A word of thanks must be recorded to Mrs. Judy Kersh who so ably started the Season off as Secretary. Owing to leaving the town she has

...igned her position in favour of Ena Stone to whose efforts the success ...our second Forces Day was partly due.

The Forces Day was held on Sunday 15th August. Minoha was read and ...y. Toperoff spoke on the importance of us all, but especially soldiers, ...aving a good name. This short service was followed at 4.30 by a ...lendid tea which was kindly arranged for the "lit" by three sisters who ...rm the "Catering Committee". They are Mrs. Dan Levine, Mrs. Joseph and ...s. Morriss. The tea was followed by a table tennis tournament and ...ganised by Jack Louis. This was won by Lieut. (Dr.) Barnett Barnard ...d was watched by an enthusiastic audience. The dancing started about ...O o'clock to Arthur Smith and his band. The function was most success-...l there being about a dozen members of the forces at the service and the ...mber increased to nearly double during the evening. The tea was attend-...by about forty people including the forces and the floor was full for ...e dance. The dance was one of the best the "lit" has had for a long ...ime. As usual there was a running buffet with soft drinks and sandwiches ...e latter being free to forces. We should mention the kind people who ...ontributed food for the tea and also the work of Girlie Cowan and Ena ...tone in helping serve the tea. Also Jack Louis and David Cohen who ...rranged the table tennis and M.C'd the dance whilst it was the watchful ...ttention of Leslie Epstein and Aubrey Gordon that saw to the smooth ...unning of the whole affair. Unita Magrill, Chairman, welcomed the guests ...nd Rev. Toperoff said that though there was a marked increase in the ...umber of guests since last time, he hoped to see still more at the next. ...most successful day.

So the clocks have been put back an hour. No longer will we hear it ...announced in Shool that the afternoon Service tonight will be at....."

Well, forces everywhere, look after yourselves and be cheerful, I'll ...be with you again next month so,

Cheerio for now, Yours,
Also After Gen.

EXCERPTS FROM LETTERS.

L.A.C. C. Marks from M.E. writes:- As the Inquisitor once mentioned that his/her Egyptian correspondent kept him/her in touch with discussions which took place between C.M. & H.B., I would like to point out that I am not under the jurisdiction of that correspondent anymore. As you will have observed, my address has altered, and I think I am the only member of the gang (at the moment) in this district, therefore I would like to consider myself your Tripolitanian Correspondent. I haven't been here very long to be able to tell you very much about the place, and in any case owing to censorship regulations, I couldn't say very much if I wanted to.

The first Friday I was here, I saw an advertisement of Services held in a local Military Synagogue, and after an awful amount of trouble eventually located this Synagogue. So along I went on Shabbos morning, and there met the Senior Jewish Chaplains of the M.E.F. and Eighth Army, and being one of the first of the Congregation present, they came over and spoke to me. Perhaps the fact that I was the only R.A.F. representative present was more of an incentive for them to "come over", anyway I was asked where I came from and and on learning that I came from Sunderland, Rabbi Rabinowitz turned to his Colleague and said - "In that case he should know something about Yiddishkeit", and turning back to me said - "Will you have an Aliyah - take Chamishi". I'm glad to say that my Cheder training stood me in good stead and I was able to prove to the Clergy, that coming from Sunderland did mean something as far as the Jewish Religion is concerned. In five weeks time it will be the anniversary of my Barmitzvah,

6.

and I asked the Chaplain whether or not it would be possible for me to have Maftir that week. The way in which my question was taken very much surprised me, because they seemed so pleased that they did everything but kiss me on both cheeks.

With regard to your bulletins I am in receipt of Nos. 7,8,9, the latter number giving me that number of consecutive issues to date. They are certainly getting better and better. I enjoy especially the contributions by Sol, whose articles are all very memorable, those concerts, do I remember them? Didn't I have to wrestle with a lamp and pieces of red and black tissue paper to make a camp fire. Those were the days, and how I wish they were back again, I suppose by the time we all get back, the younger generation will have taken complete command under the very able guidance of the "elders" who will of course include the Inquisitor, still memories will always remain. I read your bulletins at every opportunity and they are read with avid interest by my three non-Jewish room mates who are quite interested in the more religious side of the paper.

L.A.C.W. Gillis writes: Many thanks for the Monthly Bulletin, I am delighted to receive them as they are always full of items of interest. The boys abroad must certainly get a thrill when reading the local gossip and scandal of which your "gen men or women" seem to have an inexhaustible supply. The articles so kindly contributed by Argus and Sol bring back pleasant memories or pre-war days and of days which we all hope will return very soon.

Cpl. Norman Cohen B.N.A.F. writes: I am receiving the Bulletins fairly regularly and am expecting the June issue any day now. I am very pleased to hear that Harold Magrill is safe and alive although a prisoner of war and I hope that similar news comes through about the rest of the boys about whom no news has yet arrived. Both the King and Winston Churchill passed through this part of the country during their visit to NorthAfrica.

Pte. Lorna Maccoby writes: In one of your articles the writer mentions that the paper goes all over the world except to New Zealand and Australia I have sent my last three months copies to Melbourne, Australia, to Cpl. Bernard Meyer. He used to come regularly to the Lit and welcomes any news of the Sunderland people.

Lt. Mordaunt Cohen, India Command writes: I had a few days in South Africa I visited the local Jewish Club, it is a marvellous place as any of the boys will tell you if they have visited it. It contains a beautiful library and writing room, showers, squash court, table tennis, billiards etc. free to the forces. It has a fine canteen at which meals are served all day long, and twice a week there are concerts. The beauty is that it is non sectarian and a large number of non-Jewish soldiers visit it because of repute. Quite a number of my Sgts. (Non-Jews) visited it several times were full of praise. It is run at a loss of £6,000 per annum. One soldier who visited it said "I shall never say a bad word about the B- Jews again so it only goes to show.

Sgt. Issy Levine from Quetta writes: Quetta is really a delightful spot still bears evidence of the big earthquake in 1934 when that awful catastrophe occurred, The climate is almost like home up here in the hills and in the winter we will wear the jolly old battledress.

Other letters were received from Sam Lerman, Joe Clarke, Max Pearlman, Charles Marks, Julius Gordon, Adolphe Vandervelde, P. Soldinger, Nat Goodman, Lonnie Slater, Gwen Magrill, Barry Gould, I. Rosenthal, Sylvia Minkovitch, Issy Davis, Reva Pearlman, Miriam Gillis and Sonia Leslie.

Word has just come in that Tpr. Horace Stone has arrived in England from the Middle East.

All correspondence to be sent to Rev. S.P. Toperoff, 5 Victoria Avenue, Sunderland.

SUNDERLAND Jewish COMMUNITY

BULLETIN for the FORCES

EDITED AND ISSUED MONTHLY

BY THE MINISTER

AND SENT TO YOU

WITH THE GOOD WISHES OF

YOUR FRIENDS AT HOME.

September, 1943.   Vol. 2, No. 1.   Ellul, 5703

A Happy New Year to you.   This greeting with which Jews all over the world welcome each other-on Rosh Hashannah - will have a new meaning this year.   To all of us it will be not a hackneyed greeting that is used perhaps unconsciously but a short prayer for the future. How we all hope and look forward to the next year being happy and new. Can you imagine anything happier than being re-united with your families and friends and beginning not only a new year but a new life.   This short greeting is not an empty phrase but full of the hopes and aspiration of the Jewish People.   For we are haunted by the fear that all the Jews in the accursed lands of Nazi Occupied Europe will be wiped out before Peace comes.   Hitler and his satellites are determined that defeat for them will mean extinction for the Jew throughout the whole of Nazi-dom.   That means that nearly eight million Jews, half of the total Jewish population will be annihilated even if peace, for which we all hope and pray, comes soon.   In these circumstances, how is it possible for us to inaugurate a Happy New Year.   We cannot possibly be blind and deaf to the havoc wreaked on defenceless Jewish towns and villages in Poland and Russia, and to the pitiless cries of the thousands of its innocent inhabitants who have committed no crime, but against whom the Nazis are determined to vent their spleen.   Our only hope is a recognition by the Allied Powers of the supreme sacrifices endured by our People.   May the New Year 5704 open the eyes and hearts of the free world to appraise to the full the heroism and doggedness of the masses of the Jewish people, who though unarmed as in the Warsaw Ghetto, fought against the Hun exacting punishment and laying down their lives fighting in the spirit of the Maccabees of old.

The box in the middle reads:

> The Editor and Staff send New Year Greetings to all serving in the Forces. It is our Prayer that the coming year herald a new era of lasting Peace. May you be inscribed in the Book of Life.

The Jews in the Warsaw Ghetto, as in the concentration camps littered all over Nazi Europe, are the silent warriors.   Their feats of selfless devotion to the Allied Cause will not earn them even the smallest decoration for valour, but will, we hope, teach Hitler and his gang that the Jewish spirit is indestructible and immortal.   Phoenix-like it will rise from the ashes of the scorched earth of Poland and Russia.   We demand that the millions of Jewish lives be sacrificed not in vain.   The new era must be different from the old, racial discrimination and all forms of Anti- Semitism must be outlawed for all times.   We demand that the blood of the Jewish martyrs be the seed of the future that will bring not suspicion and hatred, not even toleration, but true and lasting happiness.

DO YOU KNOW?

1. Who first introduced meals for school children?
2. What new researches are now being worked upon in the Hebrew University of Palestine?
3. Who said - "The League of Nations was first of all the vision of a great Jew almost 3,000 years ago - the Prophet Isaiah"?
4. Who were Visigithes and for what were the responsible?
5. Who was Walter Rathenau?
6. What is the proportion of Jews and Arabs in the Forces in Palestine?

Answers to the above on Page 5

2,

HERE AND THERE!

Mazeltov!
Congratulations to Dr. Bendett Gordon on his engagement to Miss Joyce Bloom.

New Recruits!
Welcome to the Forces (R.A.F. Crew) Arnold Bloomberg and David Rosenthal.

At Home!
Will those who are fortunate enough to get leave for Yomtov please reserve Sunday evening October 3rd for an "at home" at the residence of the Rev. and Mrs. S.P. Toporoff.   All forces will be welcome from 8 p.m.

Cover for Bulletin!
It is very opportune that with our New Year number the Bulletin should be issued in a new format.   We are all grateful to Morris Dresner for the elaborate design on the cover and to Argus, our contributor who inspired its idea.

Educational!
We learn that a notice has been published by the Military Authorities concerning Correspondence Courses of Jewish subjects which will be as follows:- Biblical Hebrew and History, History of the Jews in England, and Jewish Religion.   I strongly advise you to take advantage of the above courses.   You should make application to your C.O. or to the Education Officer of the Unit for the necessary forms and particulars.   Here is an opportunity to learn more about your Religion and History.

EN PASSANT - by "INQUISITOR"

News is at its lowest ebb, my "snoopers" have sorely let me down, not that it really matters anyway as half of my readers have no idea to whom my flashes refer.   But the big moment is almost upon us, when Rosh Hashanah arrives I will be sated with real "hot" gen, seen with my own over-open orbs.   Do not try to hide from me as I will trail you down somehow and somewhere.   I always "get my man", so act and behave naturally.....once you become furtive, ill at ease, or too nonchalant you are as good as "in the bag".   Any "date" (broken or otherwise) will not evade my sleuths, the telephone wires will be tapped, the post-bag will be pilfered and conversation unashamedly listened to, any lift of an eyebrow, wink of an eye, sign or whisper will not pass unnoticed.   Hi-de-Hi.

FLASH!
On dit that Anti-Semite (the Little Dictator) does not forget his Faithful Correspondent.

Rumour hath it that J.G. said "It's all in the bag (leather)".

Does Also After Gen believe in bestowing(her/his worthwhile affections on one family only?

How many more times will a certain ex Q.M. Sergeant "do it again"?

Why has there been a sudden rush to be on duty at the Local Canteen?

Is it true that an important member of the R.A.F. (stationed way up North) does not receive as many letters as he would desire?

Who has as his signature tune "I belong to Glasgow"?   Everything comes to him who waits.

3.

FLASH (Continued)

Who are sending silk and rayon stockings over the Seas to the C's?

Is L.L. still "carrying a torch" for a girl in Manchester?

On dit that a renowned chemist in town has become very interested in a special W.A.A.F.

Why hasn't D.A. been home once a week as he used to? Isn't his journey really necessary? Do come home for Yomtov.

Will C.M. No. 1 of the Middle East not identify himself with C.M. No.2-- it is causing a lot of confusion.

Who expects to HALT ON the way home? How is Robin Hood and the Sherwood Forest?

SEARCHLIGHT ON SPORT - By "Argus".

I am writing these notes after the third game of the season had been played. All had been won by Sunderland and with a record of 15 goals to 3. Well that surely is a good enough start for the season but I cannot imagine that it can be maintained. That is too much to hope for or expect.

One of the most amazing things is that Raich Carter played in the first two games in which 12 goals were scored by Sunderland and Carter did not get a single goal. On the day of the third game he was playing for the R.A.F. against Civil Defence Services and scored four out of six. The explanation seems to be that in the two games he played for Sunderland he "made" most of the goals and in the R.A.F. game he decided to get some for himself.

Clifford Whitelum has made a grand start - nine goals in the three games. I have long been of the opinion that Whitelum is rather temperamental - if he gets an early goal he takes some stopping, if he has any bad luck with his shooting, it dogs him right through the game.

One of the most amazingly versatile players is Bradwell, the R.A. gunner who signed the season before last. He began as an inside forward, was developed into a wing half back, and as Jimmy Gorman had a "hang-over" from last season in the form of a 14 days suspension, Bradwell played splendidly as a right back in the first two games. Then in the third he went right half back and was the best half back on the field at Hartlepool. That surely denotes Football ability, plus adaptability.

Laidman, the D.L.I. Corporal P.T. instructor is the same type. He has already played half back and forward this season, but it is at half back I like him most. He is the same type of player as Sandy McNab - short stride, always on the move and can start another 90 minutes game immediately one is ended.

How we fare depends to a large extent upon how manager Murray is able to keep the team together. That is the secret of success in wartime football, just as it is in peace time.

Bobby Eves lost his father by an accident at work. Our sympathies with him. Mr. Eves sen., had been over 40 years in the choir at St. Peter's Church, Monkwearmouth and was always known as "the little man with the big voice." Earlier in the year Eves and his mother and father had been bombed out of their home.

4.

IN RETROSPECT.

The first lady to lecture to the Lit was Miriam Regina Bloch. This charming young lady was the guest of my parents and you can imagine my delight when she accepted my invitation to spend a few hours with me on the Sunday morning of her visit. We went to Sea Lane and returned by the rocks and the sands to the Lower Promenade, Roker. On entering Roker Marine Park I pointed out the cave known as Spotty's Hole. I could not resist telling the tale of the Pirates of the Olden Days and the theory of the underground passage to Hylton Castle. Miss Bloch seemed to listen carefully to my story and I discovered that folk lore was one of her many interests. As we were crossing Wearmouth Bridge in the tram I pointed the direction in which the old castle stands. Imagine my surprise when my companion related the legend of "The Ca'd Lad of Hylton". I heard the story for the first time and it was told me by a stranger to the district.

Dr. Radcliffe Salaman paid us a visit about this time and I have recollections of a visit by a young man whose name I have forgotten. He travelled up from Oxford or Cambridge by car and arrived late for his lecture owing to a breakdown. Now to travel from the south by car thirty years ago was an achievement and to do so in winter time in a small open sports car was well.......(I wont tell you what we thought about it). In those days we held a public reception, or the hosts of the lecturers gave a tea party in honour of their guests and delightful functions they were. Our elders were sitting up and taking notice. We were bringing brilliant Jews into their midst and we were gaining a few supporters. First and foremost amongst them was Mr. Israel Jacobs. He understood our aims and the necessity of support from our seniors. In the council he was our champion and was ever ready to identify himself with us in our undertakings Next month "Local Lecturers".

Cheerio for now.

SOL.

NEWS LETTER FROM THE HOME FRONT.

Well Forces, here I am once again with the gen about the younger folk and the lit. But really the Lit seems to concern no longer only the youth. For there were several married couples and older people at the Forces Social on Sunday, 12th September.

As usual a short service was conducted by the Rev. Toperoff and again this was followed by a tea. The number of soldiers and other forces was at first, disappointing but a sudden influx before the end of the tea brightened the doleful faces of many of the female members.

Tea was followed by amusements and games, kindly arranged by Rosalie Gillow who was assisted by Charles Cohen and his records. This proved exceedingly popular and I trust it will be repeated at future events. The dancing, from 7.0 till 11.0, was to the music of Arthur E. Smith and his band which on this occasion had a Spanish flavour lent by the "twang" of the guitar. Again there was as many people as the floor could comfortably accommodate which caused the atmosphere to be rather close. and smoking and this no doubt, accounted for the large sale of soft drinks at the Buffet. During the interval tea and coffee and eatables were provided free to forces.

A lemon, having already brought in £1 by raffle and having been given back by the winner, was auctioned, realizing a further 15/- for the Red Cross. A miniature razor was also auctioned for the same cause.

5.

As a whole the day was very enjoyable and the increasing number of guests at these Forces Days more than justifies their continuance.

It was announced that the next Forces Day is to be on Sunday 10th October, the day after Yom Kipur so I hope to see some of our own service men and women home on leave then.

The lit committee has, I understand, discussed the syllabus for the first half year which is to commence after Yom-Tov. I am told it is really attractive so I will try to find out more about it for next time, so until then,

Cheerio and best of luck,
Yours,
Also-After Gen.

WHEN OUR TURN COMES
By Cpl. E. Abrahams, 5th (Hackney) Bn.*
The Royal Berks. Regiment.

1.
Mother dear, the day may come,
When I shall go abroad,
And play my part with other men,
To slay the Nazi Horde.

2.
It's human that you'll shed a tear
I know how sad you'll be;
The day I say goodbye to you,
And sail across the sea.

3.
But think of all the years I've spent,
In this lovely land of ours,
While others fought and died for her
Against the Fascist Powers.

4.
I've had my leave quite often,
You've seen me each three months,
But our boys out East have ne'er been
In years not even once.   (home,

5.
Be brave and trust in God my dear,
That I'll come safely home
Once more to live a happy life
And never more to roam.

6.
The men whom I'll be fighting wit
For peace are all hard workers,
We'll pitch in there and win this
The famous Hackney Ghurkas. (we

7.
So have no fear dear Mother mine,
For once the "Berks" are there,
The Jerries and the Ities too,
The fate of death will share.

8.
So the sooner that we go across,
The sooner we'll return,
And a lesson 'not to wage more war
The callous Hun will learn.

9.
But if my fate should be the worst,
For I'm one just in a crowd,
I'll have fought and died for England dear,
And of this you must be proud.

---

*Readers will remember that Cpl. Abrahams often visited Sunderland whilst stationed at Durham two years ago.

Answers to the Questions on Page 1.
1. First introduced by a Jewish Community. The Jewish Services Dinner Fund was established over 60 years ago and the dinners were run extremely well in the East End of London. Later the L.C.C. took over this work and introduced it into the schools under its aegis.
2. The new method for treatment of wounds with tissue extracts. Thus great hopes are held out for the wounded of this war who will derive benefit from this discovery.
3. Field Marshal Smuts, the South African Prime Minister.

Answers Continued
4.   They were German tribes of 5th and 6th centuries who conquered Spain and created for the first time in history organised anti-Jewish legislation, which largely contributed to their downfall.
5.   An industrial statesman and philosopher of Germany, who was assassinated when as Foreign Secretary he tried to collaborate with the Western Powers.
6.   Roughly three times as many Jews as Arabs have joined the Forces though its Jewish population numbers only half of the Arab population.

EXCERPTS FROM LETTERS.

Harold Shochet from Transvaal, So.Africa writes: "There are several clubs here offering hospitality to the Services, amongst which is the Jewish Guild run entirely by the Jewish element of Johannesburg and this proves a very welcome haven at weekends and on days off.   The Jewish girls certainly devote quite a lot of time to the functions of the Guild which has acquired a respectable reputation amongst the Service personnel. It may seem rather odd but Joburg - as the city is referred to - does not create on the whole, a good impression with the R.A.F. here in general. No one quite likes the place, for apart from the manner in which cash dissolves most readily and nothing to be seen for the evaporation, there is also a most hostile element to be contended with, which makes one go around rather warily and most certainly not alone.   Out this way - in fact covering the greater part of the Transvaal - is an element or political organisation known as O.B.'s, anti-British is views, all and sundry, whose methods follow closely on the heels of the Hun.   On many an occasion the R.A.F. have been attacked and beaten up by the O.B.'s without the slightest pretext whatsoever, even in broad daylight and only naturally the scraps have been many.   They are more than delighted in giving vent to their thoughts if a mob of them happen to come upon a lone airman who is attacked and struck in the most brutal and vicious manner possible.   At the moment out here a General Election is in the making and should the opposition, comprised mostly of O.B.'s gain power - well there is a possibility - certainly not remote of our being interned.   Yes politics are a sore point and a thing we endeavour to steer clear of.
    The countryside out here in the Transvaal is composed mostly of veld, an arid, uninviting place, with a clump of trees studded here and there and grass of a dirty green growing all over.   Quite a good many of the roads are cut through the heart of the veld and where the grass has been removed this turns out to be red. A car's presence can be denoted many miles away due to the large columns of dry red dust cast up from the roads.   After a shower of rain such roads can indeed prove very dangerous for they attain a surface like that of ice.   At the moment we are in the winter season when rain is very seldom seen, the summer proving to be the very wet time.   Yet, even though there is no rain, flowers, lawns and trees go on blooming just the same.   The evenings and nights now are very very cold, so much, that overcoats and electric fires are the fast rule. Each morning one awakes to find the veld covered completely in heavy frost, which disappears when the sun arises.   I have already experienced heavy fog turning to ice on the windscreen of a car and have actually seen icicles hanging from a garden fountain.   Down Durban districts snow has ever been falling this week and judging by the cold spells of some days I would not be surprised to waken to a carpet of white one day.   Evening begins to draw on shortly after 5.30 and really it is a most amazing sight to see the colours attained during the sunset.   Out to the East, twilight practically does not exist and soon the stars and moon come out, whilst over to the West you still enjoy daylight with twilight only just apparent. To see the sun rise is another never-to-be-forgotten scene and words alone

EXCERPTS Continued

could hardly do justice to the setting, which perhaps is the nicest and friendliest thing to be seen out this way. Gold mines seem like two a penny and they are truly colossal organizations, employing mostly native labour. As at home the slag heaps are laid alongside the mines, but the seem to have a system, hence the heaps are laid out in huge square block with a pattern of stairs running alongside each block. After the rainy season, the surface is baked very hard so that the blocks now resemble gigantic concrete blocks in colour.

W.O. N. Goodman from British Somaliland writes: ...."Somaliland, at least where I am situated is not exactly a hub of civilization, such things as regular postal services, running water, and the normal amenities of life which we were accustomed to in pre-war days are a thing of the past, instead we, a handful of Europeans are living in surroundings so far removed from modern ideas and living, as to be incredible in 1943, in fa not very far removed from Biblical times. Only a few of the natives wh lived at the coast during the pre-war British occupation have seen or heard of Europeans, this was when the country was controlled by a very few officials scattered around the country, who were known by everyone, and did not travel into the interior unless it was urgently necessary, a only then under a strong guard. The Italian occupation (short as it w did not add to the opinion they had of Europeans, and it has taken some time to overcome their prejudice, but I am pleased to say we are managin them quite well now. You'd be amazed at the design of the implements, an the methods used in the manufacture of the native commodities, the mode living, and the style of dress even down to the sandals are just as you would imagine in umpteen B.C.E. This of course is in the interior, and where we are stationed at the moment the people at Berbera, the port of Somaliland are slightly more advanced, but not very much, and all live i villages comprised of mud and straw huts.

I have been stationed here fourteen months now, and when we first arrived found everything very interesting, and spent all our spare time exploring and trying to make friends with the natives, which wasn't too hard after they had received our medical treatment, and found it rather more successful than previous methods, practised by the tribal witch Dr. or the Mullah. Still it didn't stop them from ripping our tents to pieces, and robbing us at night of our few remaining belongings, the bull having been stolen by equally appreciative Somali whenever our backs were turned. This bad habit we were told, was acquired during the Italian brief command but I don't believe it, as they are too adept, and use a cunning which must have taken centuries to cultivate. However an odd thrashing coupled with strict military discipline, is gradually getting them to realise that "crime does not pay". There are even a few Yidden of the black variety, but nearly all of them live at Berbera. In conclusion I would like to convey my sincerest congratulations on the Bulletin which I think on the whole is a very fine piece of literature, and can appreciate how really valuable it is to a Sunderland born soldie Even I a "Sunderlander" by adoption find lots of local news to interest

Here is wishing you every success in your future issues, and hope it will not be long before I, and all your readers abroad, will be home personally thank you for producing a link with Sunderland which I hardly anticipated, in view of the calls that must be made upon your time and work.

Letters also received from S. Mincovitch, S. Levin, J. Rosenthal J. Gordon, J. Charlton, E. Dresner, G. Magrill, C. Winberg, I. Davis, W. Book, and B.A. Cohen.

All correspondence to be sent to Rev. S.P. Toperoff, 5 Victoria Avenue, Sunderland.

SUNDERLAND Jewish COMMUNITY

BULLETIN for the FORCES

EDITED   AND   ISSUED   MONTHLY

BY   THE   MINISTER

AND   SENT   TO   YOU

WITH   THE   GOOD   WISHES   OF

YOUR   FRIENDS   AT   HOME.

October 1943.   Vol. 2   No. 2.   Tishri   5704

SUKKOT

Few of you I imagine will get an opportunity of reliving the spi[rit] of the Festival of Sukkot and still fewer will see a Sukkot.   I do ho[pe] therefore, that you will find time at least to think of the beauty and poetry of this grand festival, even if your military duties preclude yo[u] from observing it in strict traditional style.   Sukkot is full of symbolism and we must not allow the Festival to pass without having a mental picture of the tall, stately lulav palm branch supported on eith[er] side by the willow of the brook and the myrtle.   Together with citron the[y] make a colourful picture.   But the most important is the lesson to be conveyed that these "four species" are symbolic of the unity of the rac[e] they teach us that to the Jew racial superiority is un-known.   The ric[h] and the poor, the highly and the lowly, the scholar and the ignorant, are all alike in the eyes of God.

Why should there be any racial discrimination in this world? Germany began this war thinking herself to be superior to any other race in the world.   She is the herrnvolk and she thought she had the right to enslave all the weak and small powers.

From the dawn of history we have been taught to treat all alike and the Festival of Sukkot lays particular stress on the universal character of the Jewish religion.

The Sukkot frail hut we are commanded to erect is a constant reminder to pursue simple habits and to live at peace with ourselves. Judaism always connected Sukkot with peace.   The life of the Sukkot which emphasises the quiet non-forced motive of life characterised by t[he] poorly constructed tent with its temporary roof must lead to quiet, pea[ce] ful living - the ideal of the Jew.

We have no quarrels with anyone.   We wish to lead our lives in our own way.   We pray that the world will learn the lesson of this Festival with its symbolism teaching true democracy, the same law for the native as for the stranger.

If the new post-war world is built not on the solid foundation o[f] peace and equality for all including the Jew, we shall have sacrificed t[he] flower of our youth in vain.   Such a patched up peace will lead again t[o] war.   We should like to feel that this time peace will ensure full and equal rights and privileges for the Jew.

Alongside the big, powerful nations of the world represented by [the] tall palm branch the weak and defenceless Jew should not pale into insignificance but have its rightful place in the commity of nations.

DO YOU KNOW?

1.   Where does the following come from "Better is a dinner of herbs wh[ere] love is than a stalled ox and hatred therewith".
2.   Who is Ilya Ehrenburg?
3.   Which Synagogue have the Nazis paid to rebuild?
4.   Where and when was the first Jewish Sunday School opened?
5.   When was the first Jewish Chaplain appointed to the Forces?
6.   How many Jews are there living in Sicily?   (Answers to above on P[.]

·. 2.

HERE AND THERE

Mazeltov
Congratulations to :-

Weddings - Miss Doris Burnley to Benjamin Blackstone.
Gnr. Israel Marks to Pte. Lily Franks.

Engagements - C. Goldman, M.P.S. on his engagement to Miss Cynthia Garbutt of Durham.

Births - To Cpl. and Mrs. Cyril Behrman a son at Cheltenham.
To Mr. & Mrs. G. Rabbinowitz a son.

Promotions - Harold Brewer to L/Bdr.
Phyllis Mincovitch to Cpl.

New Recruits - We welcome to the Forces Miss Rita Olswang who has taken up nursing at a Military Hospital. Her zealous and energetic work in so many branches of communal work such as Girl Guides, Literary Society, Judeans, Hostel etc., will long be remembered. We wish her good luck in her new venture.

Entertainment to Forces.
During the High Holy Days twentyfive Jewish men of the Pioneer Corp were entertained by members of the local Jewish community. I must thank all who offered their homes and am pleased to print the following letter I received from Cpl. Morley :

"Words cannot possibly express the thanks and gratitude we all feel for the kindness and hospitality of you and your congregation.

We all know that we owe special thanks to you, who in addition to your great burden, took all the trouble to make facilities for us for the Holy Days. It was a special tonic for us - the homeless, if I may say so - to spend Rosh Hashanah and Yom Kippur in Jewish homes and in a Jewish atmosphere. We felt specially what it means to have a home for the Yom Tovim which the members of your congregation so kindly offered us. We can only hope and wish that their sons and daughters in the Forces have been offered such nice homes as we had.

May I ask you to tender our profound thanks to your Congregation."

EN PASSANT   -   THE INQUISITOR

There is one huge impenetrable cloud over Sunderland and its jaded inhabitants, for the Forces in bulk (female and other species) have deserted us. Never has so much gaiety, merriment and hysteria permeated the otherwise austere atmosphere as when the Superior Beings were being feted, but now lethargy and innate dullness have descended on one and all. To what do we attribute such despondency - - - - - - - . alas!

If only I were one of H.M. Forces creating a furore wherever I deigned to honour society with my presence. Civilians would bow obsequiously. Assistants would miraculously produce unprocurable things from under the counter etc. etc. Oh, wonderful fate. What we maltreated civilians suffer whilst you enjoy life at the FRONT, you fortunate people.

I wish to take this belated opportunity of bestowing my heartfelt thanks to you for all the correspondence, which you so graciously send, my only regret is that I have not the time to answer them personally. This is the only intimation .... Forgive my prolixity but I am overcome by the morsels of benevolence which come my way.

FLASH
Many VICTORious returns on your second anniversary, doctor. Have you had your deserts yet?
Is it true that there is no more ivory or silk left in India?   Not a
MAJOR catastrophe we hope!

FLASH Continued

Rumour hath it that there has been much breaking and destroying of pots and pans of late. There is more in this than MEATS the eye.

Any more "Tripoli Times" forthcoming C.M.?

Who has been calling up pains again? How is London?

Who, recently home on leave, was jealously observed bidding a very fond farewell to a fair damsel boarding the Newcastle train?

Why has Sunderland's loss become Eggleston's gain?

Who has been bestowing rayon hose on someone very dear to him? (Hi-de-h, Myer).

Does the Cavalier of Chester still put the Sun into Sunderland?

Does a certain valuable member of the R.A.F. prefer Yatesbury to Cleadon? Of COURSE he doesn't.

I give my humble thanks to D.A. for so kindly honouring us with his presence, to think....... alone I did it.

On dit that Newcastle has been denuded for all its tropical Kit (Did you enjoy the family re-unions?

Which very attractive W.R.E.N. has become Sarah Bernhardt 2nd?

Who is known as the Little Corporal of Cheltenham?

Rumour hath it that it is now considered de rigeur to spend Yomtov leave in Glasgow. (What's Glasgow got that we haven't got?)

How's the Big Shot from Aldershot?

Answers to Questions on Page 1.

1. The Book of Proverbs, Chapter 15, Verse 17.
2. Russian Jewish Novelist and Champion of the Jewish Cause on the Rus, Radio and in the Press. In a recent interview with a Soviet Jewish Ne paper he wrote: "Whenever I talk with Nazi prisoners I always tell the that I am a Jew. I love to watch the expression on their faces."
3. The Dublin Synagogue which was damaged by a Nazi raid is being rebu and the Eire Government have insisted that the Nazis pay for it.
4. Opened in Philadelphia in 1838 and organised by Rebecca Gratz who through the suggestion of Washington Irving was made the model of the heroine of Sir Walter Scott's "Ivanhoe".
5. The first Jewish Chaplain to the Forces was recognised in 1892 whils Jews were recognised in the Army as a separate denomination in 1889.
6. Before the expulsion of Jews from Spain in 1492 over a hundred thous Jews lived in Sicily, but after 1492 those that found new homes in Italy, Turkey and other countries did not return and the small community that existed in Palermo before the war numbered about 50.

SEARCHLIGHT ON SPORT - By "Argus".

Seven games played and six won is Sunderland's record at the time of writing. Quite a good start and it means that Sunderland are bracketed top with Liverpool, the latter having a fraction better goal average - sorry goal ratio. F.A. and League rules refer to goal average but when you divide the goals against into the number of goals for you get a ratio not an average.

Sunderland have had a nasty blow. Horatio Carter was suddenly ordered away from his North East R.A.F station to Gloucestershire. The result is we have lost his services and it is doubtful whether he will even spend his leave periods here for his wife and child are staying with his wife's parents at Derby. That was the reason for his appearance for Derby County instead of West Bromwich who had asked his permission to pla him.

Our outside left problem has been worrying manager Billy Murray. On of the Barrage units nearby arranged a transfer of their P.T.I. so that

4,

Burbanks should be available to play for Sunderland.   One left for his new station but Burbanks did not arrive.   A phone call brought this answer: "Yes he has left here, but for the overseas boat".   So that's that.

During his leave we have had Len Duns for a couple of games.   No one ever suspected he had a left foot worthy of the name, but he proved in the outside left position that it is almost as good as his right.   Len is a sergeant in the Army.

Wensley, whom many of you will recall in the reserve team just before the war, has been the mainstay of the Reserves attack in the Northern Combination games.   He got a chance against Darlington and headed two perfect goals.   Probabilities are that in Carter's absence he will be given a chance to tune up to the face of the senior game.

At the moment there are some promising youngsters playing in the Reserve side, and both Hylton Colliery Juniors and Silksworth Juniors are being used as Colts Teams.   It is possible that we could win the Northern Combination by putting the strongest side into the field every week, but that is not Manager Murray's object.   It is to make players.

Well Cheerio until next time.

IN RETROSPECT.

Newcastle was very neighbourly.   Dr. Schochet spoke to us on "The Jew and Medicine".   A jolly and humorous man, his lecture was racy and full of surprises.   I particularly remembered one daring theory he propounded.   "The Ancient Hebrew", he said, "must have known something about anaesthetic for did not a deep sleep fall upon Adam when he lost that all important rib".   Mr. Sam Phillips also gave us much support.   I shall write most about him later.   In my opinion he is one of the outstanding men in North East Jewry.   Then there was Rev. Drukker.   His lectures were always the model of perfection.   There was something very earnest about him and his talks.   Nor must I forget our own Sunderland speakers.   Mr. I.J. Golding our chairman, the most even-tempered chairman I have ever known.   His addresses were full of fun, yet also full of sound knowledge.   His talk on criticism was an example of the man's worth to the Lit.   "Do not destroy unless you can build again", he said.   He would insist on what he called the 'fitness of things' and good humour in the most acrimonious debates.

The late Rev. L. Muscat spoke to the Lit several times, usually on music.   We could always expect an enjoyable night when he was speaking.   He gave us not only the benefit of his musical knowledge and his fine voice but we were sure of many hearty laughs.   He was a past master in the art of telling funny stories.   Our Honorary President, the Rev. S. Daiches, gave us a series of lectures entitled "Elementary Philosophy".   To him a spade is a spade, a Literary Society had to be a literary society in the purely literal sense.

During the years at present under review there existed a flourishing Literary and Debating Society in Newcastle.   The Hon. Sec. Mr. Mortimer Hylton, gave us much valuable assistance.   I am also reminded of two young men of forceful personality, Mr. Sandleson and Mr. M. Turner-Samuels.   We held several inter-debates with Newcastle Society both in their rooms (St. Mary's Hall) and at home.   Many North and South Shields young people joined our Lit.   The debates were about Zionism, the I.T.O. (International Territorial Organisation) and Politics.   It may seem strange to you but many a fiery discussion took place on questions such as "Desirability of Unemployment Insurance", "Health Insurance", "Womens Suffrage" and "Should a Jewish National Home be set up in a land other than Palestine".

Social Activities next month.

Cheerio,

SOL.

3.

NEWS LETTER FROM THE HOME FRONT

And so we leave the summer and return once more to the bronze leaf autumn and cold, bare winter. The winter has always been the season of the Lit, and this winter especially will be one full of jolly events. Included in the draft syllabus drawn up by the committee are such items Brains Trust (the last one was so popular), debates "B.B.C Night", "Live Newspaper Night" and all the other events that were once the usual mile-stones in the programme of the Lit. But dances have not been forgotten nor have lectures and talks on more serious subjects. The season will certainly be a pleasant blend of literary and social functions.

Forces Days have proved an excellent forerunner to the season prope and they have attracted a large crowd each time. They are more than app ciated by the boys in the forces stationed nearby and I understand they to be continued when the season starts. The first meeting of the season it was announced, will be the first Sunday after Sukkot. Following the tradition it is to be the Presidential address. From then onwards ther will be "something on at the Lit" every Sunday night during the winter months, and I am sure that the membership will increase this year despit the fact that so many of our girls and boys are being called up.

The Forces Day on Sunday 10th October, the day after Yom Kippur, wa probably the biggest success the Lit has had for a long time. The tea which over forty people sat down, was followed by a Talent Spotting Compe ition which had been exceedingly well organised by Rosalie Gillow. Seve members of the Forces took part to the very great amusement both of the would-be actors themselves and of the spectators.

As usual there was dancing from 7.0 till 11.0 to Arthur E. Smith a his band. There was a good crowd and this time I saw more Sunderland people home on leave than I have done in the past. You may like to kno just who. Well at the risk of leaving some out I will try to remember one or two. I noticed Ralph Freedman dancing with the vigour of pre-wa days; Myer Gillis (Ashwood St.) in Air-Force blue, Gwenie Grantham smart attired in W.R.N.S. uniform; Hymie Minchom who had donned his 'civvies' a few hours in place of his Naval Officer's uniform and Lorna Maccoby wearing the khaki of the A.T.S. As might have been expected this dance very jolly and several people who have known the Lit in better days came along and gave their support. Let us hope that it will not be so very before all those now serving their country and the cause for freedom re to take part in a Grand Victory Dance!

I'll be with you again next month. In the meantime keep your chin
Yours,
Also After Gen.

The Last Stand of the Ghetto - Ezekiel Gillis.

Warsaw on the Vistula night is drawing near, attack again, what do they
say, what do they see or hear?
Mighty men of Israel are rising up once more, to fight on grimly to the
end as in days of yore.

And as Samson's mighty call rang through the temple clear
O God let my soul not go but with the Phillistines here
And as his might returning making him once more strong, he the pillars
from their holds, onto the gathered throng.

And still that mighty call today is the echo of us all,
To our Father the Almighty, come, let us now call.
Are we not to you as the apple of thine eye?
That we must be trampled on by every passer-by.

6.

So gather round me comrades, for the end is drawing near
Stand and fight with all your might there is no cause to fear
For the place where we are going there we shall take them too and the
whole world shall know the courage of the Jew.

And in the cellars of the city
Where hunted men do sit
To the strategy of warfare,
They their brains do pit,

For the plan of the night is to battle as never as before
For God knows that in the morning there may be no more
To carry on that valiant fight which is to the very end,
Even tho' the flower of our youth is spent
Our spirit is strong and our faith not yet bent.

And now the field-grey horders advancing rank and file
To break down every obstacle to jump over every stile,
But the reception is awaiting
Come comrades do not tarry
For blow for blow and stroke for stroke we must the enemy parry.

And as the growing tension on our nerves begins to play,
Our leader steps forward in his gay and gallant way,
To prepare us with tactics for the coming fray,
For tonight we stand armed - and we resist come what may.

"Comrades" says he, "listen to me
For tonight we also go,
As our brother before us to face dreaded foe,
But this time it is different for tonight we are all armed
And any man who fears let him now be calmed.

For vengeance is sweet tho' the price may be dear
But tonight we must give the whole world to hear
That the Jew still exists tho' the candle of life burns low.
And he still resists
Tho' his blood doth flow
Like the mighty rivers of the whole wide world
The Flag of Zion must again be unfurled."

EXCERPTS FROM LETTERS.

A/C B.A.Cohen writes: "The excellence of the original idea of issuing this
monthly periodical is demonstrated more and more strongly as issue succeeds
issue, and the gratitude of its recipients must amply recompense you and
the staff for all the arduous work entailed. Apart from the splendid
contributions, the letters from the boys and girls in the Services are a
great source of comfort and interest, and one avidly reads accounts of
their progress and impressions. The Bulletin is the one medium whereby
we in the Forces are kept in touch, even indirectly with friends and
acquaintances of our home town, and if the extent of our eagerness in
awaiting each new issue was realised, perhaps it would necessitate an
editorial visit to the hatters."
Tpr. W. Book writes: "I find the Bulletin delightful reading these days,
with the full accounts of the S'Land Jewish Youth, and of their activities
both at home and abroad, and look forward with interest to the

EXCERPTS Continued

excerpts of letters from the boys overseas, and they are certainly ca[r]
ing the good name of the town into whichever country they find themse[l]
The articles of Sol Novinski, bringing back happy memories of the old
Lit are too, very interesting and undoubtedly appreciated, and also
Argus of the S'land Echo with his sports column."

Lt. Mordaunt Cohen, India Command writes: "When I arrived in India on[e]
of the first things I did was to go to a branch of Lloyds Bank and ope[n]
an account. In the accounts Department I noticed a sign denoting the
languages spoken by Bank Officials and it included Hebrew. Can you
imagine how proud I felt to realise that "Lashon Ameynoo" was a langu[e]
recognised by a big bank and perhaps spoken in India. Of course I
wanted to get into touch with the Jewish Community and did not quite
know where to turn. I wrote to Leo Levin, whose address I guessed an[d]
by good fortune he received it and replied giving me all the news abou[t]
the local lads. He also advised me to buy a paper called "The Jewish
Advocate" published in Bombay. I wrote to the Editor of this perio[d]
ical and received some interesting information about the Indian Jewi[sh]
Community in addition to receiving a copy of the paper. It is a ver[y]
fine journal indeed and the official organ of the Zionist Organisatio[n]
the K.H. and the J.N.F. It is one of the best publications I have r[e]
The Jewish Community is the smallest in India and although figures va[ry]
it is doubted whether the total exceeds 30,000. Compare this with a
total population of 350,000,000. No statistics are available concer[n]
the number of Jews in the armed Forces, but there are few families wh[o]
have not at least one representative in the Forces. Some have seen
service overseas and there have been a few casualties. The Navy seem[s]
to lead with popularity amongst the youth. Of course there are a goo[d]
number to be found in A.R.P. Services and there is a Jewish Division [i]
the St. John Ambulance Brigade. On the Industrial front Jews are a[l]
making their contribution. On the one hand we have the famous Hou[se]
of Sassoon and Sir Alwyn Ezra and on the other refugees who have assi[st]
ed in starting new industries and in some cases where they are techni[c]
ians have proved to be a great asset to the industries of the country.

Sir Alwyn Ezra who is the head of the Bombay Jewish Community ha[s]
been very magnanimous in his financial contributions to the war effo[rt]
There is a canteen at the Town Hall named after him. He donated a Sp[o]
Pavilion to the Royal Indian Navy in addition to a very large gift
given for the same service by Sir Alwyn to Lady Linlithgow. When Si[r]
Walter Lumley recently left for England, he handed him a cheque for t[h]
amenities if Indian Troops in the U.K. In addition to this Sir Alwy[n]
has given rent free, a cafe and a rest and reading room in Bombay fo[r]
the troops and also promoted a "Blood Bank". Bombay Jewry is very
Zionist minded and they also had a K.H. Campaign quite recently."

Other letters were received from Cpl. Phyllis Mincovitch, Gnr. A.
Abraham from Iraq, Pte. Leo Levin from Meerut, India; Fus. Freedman
from B.N.A.F.; L.A.C. J. Gordon from B.N.A.F.; Cpl. N. Cohen from
B.N.A.F.; Lt. Ellis Dresner, Middle East; Pte. Isaac Brewer and Gnr.
Charles Kolson from the Faroe Islands; A. Leading Tel Sam Lerman from
Columbo; L.A.C. H. Shochet from Transvaal, So. Africa; A.C.W. Pearlma[n]
S.R.; L.A.C. Isaacs Sam, and L.A.C. C. Marks from Middle East (for
correspondence and periodicals.)

N.B. Will readers please note that change of address must be notifi[ed]
to ensure safe receipt of the Bulletin.

All correspondence to be sent to Rev. S.P. Toperoff,
5 Victoria Avenue, Sunderland.

EDITED   AND   ISSUED   MONTHLY

BY   THE   MINISTER

AND   SENT   TO   YOU

WITH   THE   GOOD   WISHES   OF

YOUR   FRIENDS   AT   HOME.

November 1943.   Vol. 2 No. 3   Cheshvan 5704

RELIGION AND WAR

For some time now we have been affected by the religious sentimen
expressed by some of our correspondents. We cannot tell if there is
general re-awakening amongst the Forces to the importance of religio
the world.   There are signs that religion is being discussed and tre
with a seriousness and sincerity that should command the respect of a
For instance many have written complaining of the lack of sufficient
Services.   There are some who do not see a Chaplain for weeks whilst
others have not been contacted at all by a Chaplain.   This interest
religion in Services for the Forces and the spiritual comfort that a
Iain can give is very helpful.   We know the difficulties under which
Chaplains work and the distances they have to travel.

A complaint of a different kind comes from L.A.C. C. Marks whose
we publish and who was rightly disappointed during his visit to Pale
where he was shocked to see the flagrant disrespect for religion. We
his righteous indignation. We dare not acquiese in the worship of na
alism at the expense of religion. This frenzied nationalism is making
deep inroads into the very life of the Yishuv. We admire our correspo
for having the courage to write about it. Still we are inclined to th
that statistically the Sabbath is observed in Eretz Israel to a greate
extent than it is observed in England.   Of course comparisons are od
and indeed it is sad that we should have to make them.

On the other hand we must not forget the selfless devotion and m
dom of the early Chalutzim the Pioneers who braved malaria and other
diseases to lay the foundations of a National Home. The dogged persis
the self sacrifice and wonderful achievements of these Pioneers will
be remembered and will remain an inspiration to all. We admire them
their creativeness, courage and energy. Yet again we should like to
that Palestine is to be not only a National Home but a spiritual Cent
from whence the law of God will once again proceed.

Idealism is the prequisite of religion and we cannot deny the id
ism of Jewish youth in Palestine. It is possible that irreligion has
brought into the country and is not a natural growth. If this be the
we must strengthen our institutions in the Galut and make plans now fo
more virile Jewish education based on Torah-true Judaism. Criticism
healthy but more healthy still is constructive work. We need more work
more builders ready to plan, fashion build and erect the future Temple
Judaism. It must be built on the firm foundations of faith and right
ness which our Bible re-echoes persistently.

It is heartening to hear the Chairman of the National Committee
the National Bible week express the opinion that the unprecedented dem
for the Bible is due to the renewed religious feeling instilled by the
For the first time in a hundred years the demand for Bibles are exceed
the supply. We as Jews who are responsible for the Bible should find
fort in this and demand that the principles of the Bible be the backgr
of post war reconstruction. Naturally we must ourselves be imbued wit
love for our religion, its life giving laws and time honoured customs
before we can inspire others.

Lasting peace will be achieved only if our Service men and women
clamour that the Biblical ideals of justice and righteousness for all
enthroned on earth. This is what we are fighting for. We shall not
deterred even by disappointments in Palestine. We are fighting that
of different race and creed may live in harmony and peace with one ano
We are fighting that we may all enjoy the four freedoms, Freedom of Wo
Freedom of Speech, Freedom from Want and Freedom from Fear. In the wo
of the Jewish Prophet: "He hath shown thee O man what is good and what
the Lord require of thee but to do justly to love mercy to walk humbly
with thy God."

DO YOU KNOW?

What area of Palestine is still waste land and how much do Jews occupy
To whom is due the use of cocaine as an anaesthetic?
Did Jews ever practise missionary work?
What part are Jews playing in the Jugo-Slav patriot army?
What was the population of world Jewry in 1800 and again in 1880?
Who said: "The Jew who is devoted to science remains completely
indifferent to its opportunities of enrichment. The Jew who is
devoted to philosophy lives in poverty and is perfectly content so to
live."?

Answers to the above questions on Page 4.

HERE AND THERE!

MAZELTOV
Wedding - B.A. Cohen to Miss Freedman of London.
Births - Son to Mr. and Mrs. Raphael - née Molly Topaz.
          Son to Pte. and Mrs. Silverman - nee Doris Black.
Promotions - Sylvia Brewer to Assistant Section Officer.
          Myer Davis to Corporal.

The Young Zionist Society in co-operation with the Habonim hold a
Youth Rally at the Communal Hall when they were addressed by Jack Brass
Editor of the Habonim Newspaper. There was a good attendance. Playlets,
recitation, singing and dancing gave colour to the proceedings and the
Rev. S.P. Toperoff who presided announced that Sunderland Jewish Youth had
raised sufficient funds to plant more than 160 trees in Palestine,

We have just heard that the Sunderland Guardian Committee under
the presidency of the Mayor has recently disbanded and has decided to hand
over the funds at its disposal (over £100) to the Sunderland Jewish Refugee
Hostel. This wonderful gesture is much appreciated and we are glad to
know that the good work of our Hostel is receiving just recognition,

EN PASSANT - "INQUISITOR"

The wind is howling ominously as it plays fiendishly round the already
bared branches of the trees which are tap tapping mysteriously at the ice-
covered window panes! My stiff, numb and gnarled fingers are curved
awkwardly round my pen, but what of discomfort when my insatiable public
is ever clamouring for more? I have trudged wearily through snow carpeted
paths in search of illicit "dope", but this seems to be the off season
(Q.E.D.) no celebrities home on leave, no romances (or none that I would
dare nip in the bud at such an early stage) in fact no wrath-inspiring news
at all! Everything seems to be at a low ebb a circumstance over which I
have definitely no control! I feel like the Mayor of Pied Piper Fame
fearing that if I don't give my brains "a racking" I will be sent "packing"
so do your worst, even a well has been known to run dry and who am I to
deviate from custom! Hi-de-hi to you all!
ASH
(the royal) do hope that Joseph (with his socks of many colours) doesn't
tie himself in his new environ.
January 16th! January 16th! January 16th! January 16th! January 16th!
sorry that C.M. takes objection to my flights into poetic fantasy (if so
they under estimate my literary prowess.)

3.

SH Continued

s the Algerian Shiek still inspire so many "offers"? (A prophet in
own country - - - ?)   Or is the answer still a lemon?
dit that Habonim Hierarch has been conducting Sicilian Vespers! Mus
stro please!)
nk you J.R. - - I am pleased I was able to conjure happy memories
n your mysterious past.
Shipping Magnate not content with his Sunderland Spoils, must he go
-game hunting to Manchester?
our has it that the Battery King wants to "fiddle" while Rome burns!
ch member of the A.T.S. is known as "the toast of London"?   Still
ing an Eddy-fying time?
s the R.A.F. Chief think Whitley Bay is near enough to his home
erests" or is he still "browned off"?
n important W.A.A.F Officer still dreading Xmas Day?
is known as the Indian Nomad?   Would you like Cupid to do his "st
you?
it that a member of the Army and a member of the A.T.S. will soon
oined in holy wedlock!
ur hath it that Cleadon is soon to be deprived of a very interestin
tillating personality. How are the Might Fallen?

SEARCHLIGHT ON SPORT - By ARGUS

Three letters I have received from readers clearly indicates to mo
much these few notes each month are appreciated and I can only say
if they help my Jewish Friends to keep in touch with the sport i
home town and they enjoy reading them then that is sufficient "di
for me.   May I add that I thank the writers for their words of
ciation and express the hope that the day is not far distant when w
ll meet together in a real welcome home.
You will have heard that Sunderland at the time of writing these n
mistice Day, were head of the Football League - on top of the world
speak, which reminds me that on the Armistice Day of 1918, I happe
ve come down from the line to Havre to examine some machine guns a
the rest "went mad" taking possession of an electric tram car and
ng it myself with dozens of troops sitting howling on the top of i
have been told I have been mad ever since, without being certified
eally we are top of the League - at the moment.   Of course the hig
et the further you have to fall, but in this case they actually thi
ker Park they have a chance of becoming champions.   That thought
l upset by the movement of players.   For example Sid Bradwell is
transferred from Coastal Defence to a Field Regiment which means w
probably lose him, as we have lost Raich Carter.   Then Arthur Hous
is been near at hand on a course, has finished that and is to retur
otland, and Whitelum is expected to be away on a course during thre
ant weeks.   All these things have an effect, as you will apprecia
he championship games conclude at Christmas and we then start upon
n matches which qualify for the cup competition proper.   Arrangeme
e same as in the previous season the 32 clubs with the best record
he ten games go into the first round, all games being on the home
rinciple. The return of Darlington and Hartlepools United to regu
ll means that the ten qualifying games are all against the North E
We open on December 27th with the first of the series against
tle United.
ost of you will now know that the repatriated prisoners from Germa
have arrived home.   Twenty-two of them were Sunderland natives an
Murray, Sunderland's Manager did "the honours" by inviting them al

4.

as guests of the club to the home League Game against Newcastle United.
What better host could they have in the Board room than Col. Joe Prior?
It was not milk and honey which flowed. But the boys had a right royal
time and thoroughly enjoyed themselves.

By the time these notes are in your hands it will be our Christmas
and New Year. May I convey to you the compliments of the season from
Sunderland and a speedy and safe return to your loved ones.

Answers to Questions on Page 2.

1. The whole area of Palestine is 27,000,000 dunams. More than 18,000,00(
dunams are still waste land. Jews occupy 1,500 ,000 dunams that is less
than one seventh of the area of Western Palestine.
2. The Jew Carl Koller.
3. The Jews practised missionary work in the early Christian era and
before, but it was taken over largely by the Church because of the
introduction of legislation which made conversion to Judaism a criminal
offence.
4. Two Jewish physicians are members of the staff of General Mihailovitch
whilst the General's Aide-de-camp is a young Jew and a Jewish Officer
directs the operations of some 50,000 men.
5. The population of World Jewry in 1800 was 2½ million but by 1880 it
rose to 7 million.
6. Mr. Hilaire Belloc

IN RETROSPECT

The first Lit concert ever, was held in the School rooms Lawrence
Street. A sub-committee was formed to organise events. My late sister
Kate and I were members and we soon discovered our real troubles had
commenced. Our ambition was a programme comprised entirely of members.
We soon found there was very little talent in the Society. The Jewish
people we approached outside the Society were disappointing. In many
cases were amazingly sceptical and unhelpful. With the exception of one
little boy, we had to invite some Gentile friends to make up the show.
The little chappie was one David Hashman, a violinist and a talented
little lad. My sister and I took him in hand, he had to learn his two
items by heart. No music stands allowed. Nothing so amateurish for this
concert! He was taught deportment and thoroughly enjoyed the rehearsals.
His proud father and mother were very keen and helpful. One of our friends
was a comedian. Our hopes for success were centred on him. Owing to a
misunderstanding he arrived late, he was also somewhat inebriated, we were
terribly upset.

You will remember the long tables in the Communal Hall, these same
tables made our first platform. Front and side curtains, table, chairs,
tablecloths, carpet etc. were all borrowed from members parents. The
side curtains, screening the dressing rooms from the "Stage" were comprised
of coloured tablecloths and bed spreads. Little Dave Hashman, clad in a
beautiful velvet suit played the "Intermezzo" from Cavaleria Rusticana and
Braga's Serenade. A bonny boy and a bonny player, he caused a sensation.
There was the then fashionable recitations, songs and music. Then came the
Comedian's turn, he was a riot, I knew his turn, because I had done
concert work with him before. What I did not know was that when he was
drunk he was a capable and even funnier man. My mind was set at ease the
moment he stepped on to the platform. The concert was a great success.
Next month - more concerts.

Cheerio,

SOL.

5.
NEWS LETTER FROM THE HOME FRONT

Here I am once again, Forces, with the Lit's news of the month. Th
Session has started - and in the old style with a Presidential Address.
An audience of over a score and a half turned up to hear Mr. Sol Novins
talk of the Lit of the past. He spoke of the difficulties that had to
over come in earlier days and drew comparisons with the present time.
gave several ideas for future functions and hints on how to run them.
urged the Lit to partake in more constructive activities, to study dram
tics, to hold discussion groups and perhaps even present a play or a
concert. Judging from the number of questions after the address (they
mainly on dramatics) the talk attracted much attention and revealed lat
eagerness in many, to take an active part in literary affairs. It was
intimated that discussion and dramatic groups were to be formed.

The following week, October 31st, there was a Brains Trust. Those
taking part were Mr. Hadley (a Hungarian Journalist now in the Forces),
Matthews (a business man also in the Forces), Max Raine, Aaron Gillis,
Phyllis Heilpern, Nan Richenberg, Rev. Oler and the London Jewish Youth
Leader, Jack Brass. Of course the customary pungent wit of the Questi
Master was supplied by Rosalie Gillow. All kinds of questions were as
ranging from the advisability of having Jewish Day Schools to the propo
fate of Hitler; from juvenile delinquency to a federal state of Europe
from the art of painting to jazz. All questions were answered with an
air of authority much to the satisfaction of the large audience.

On November 7th, the Lit again tried its skill at entertaining. A
fine tea was provided but, though nearly 40 persons sat down to tea, on
a dozen of them were members of the Forces. This must be due, I think
to the fact that most of the Jewish lads who were stationed nearby have
now left the district. The "surprise item" between the tea and the dan
was more than surprising. Nothing had been arranged and everyone had
chance to gossip or dance to the radiogram - but this was weak compared
with the organised fun that had been arranged on previous occasions. T
was a good crowd to the dance but the band was small and the usual joll
seemed to be lacking somewhat. Some lemons were raffled on behalf of t
Ladies Guild and brought in 18/6 being won by Mrs. Dan Levine. The da
as a whole was enjoyed by most people there, including a few "out-of-
towners".

Well Forces, that brings me about up to date but here is a summary
the draft syllabus for the first half of the Season. Nov. 14th Debate,
21st B.B.C. Night, 28th Mock Trial, December 5th Dance, 12th Debate and
19th Discussion. That's all for now,
Cheerio,
Yours,
Also After Gen.

EXCERPTS FROM LETTERS

L.A.C. C.M. Marks, R.A.F. Middle East writes: 'I'm rather sorry to see t
with this issue Sol's "Peeps into the Past" have concluded, because no
matter what else he writes, I'm sure the subject couldn't be more intere
ing. No doubt the new topic "In Retrospect" will be both interesting an
entertaining, but I think there is something different in relating past
experiences, of which most of us have taken an active part. However,
perhaps I am speaking out of turn and should wait and read the first and
subsequent articles before making any comments. I'm very pleased with
"Also After Gen's" efforts too, I can almost picture the dances and the
running buffet, but in saying this I hope I'm not incurring the wrath of
the Inquisitor who seems to be sorry because he/she can't visualise for

EXCERPTS Continued

the "Tinkle of Flower-heads" or the "Nestlings Twittering" forming Natures "Percussion Band" along Durham River Banks - - Tinkles, Twitterings - Boo! Who else but a woman could write stuff like that (sorry Inquisitor but I couldn't resist it this time).

I also notice with some interest that the Lit secretary is out canvassing for members - well what about canvassing some of us overseas. Although we're unable to attend the functions (at the moment), I'm sure some of us would like to re-establish our memberships, so what about it? Apart from anything else, I expect the coffers aren't quite as swollen as they might be, so come on you overseas Lit fans and Delve into the Depths and Draw Forth those "Akkers", only 25, and you're a member.

Whilst on the subject of Clubs, I noticed and read with what I must call Grim Humour, of the Balfour Club - of 3 course dinners for 1/6 - of Bed, Breakfast and Bath for 2/6 whilst here - but I mustn't say anymore I would probably be censored.

Well Sir, Yom Kippur has once again passed us, and I'm almost ashamed to tell you that even though the reasons were unavoidable and at the moment inexplicable, I was not able to attend Shool, a thing which most grieved me, but which under the circumstances could not be helped, so let me earnestly hope and pray that P.G. next year this time may all the troubles and strife be at an end, and that my unfortunate brethren and I overseas will be if not together again at home, a long way nearer the Great Reunion.

Whilst on the subject of religion, a subject which I don't know enough about, and argue too much about, I would like to state in what a strange way a certain item seems to keep "rearing its ugly head" at me. Everywhere I look I seem to find it, and quite often find it without looking. Perhaps I should say at the outset, that my views of the Jewish Religion, are rather stabilised and perhaps to some extent old fashioned, which may be the reason for the following.

As I mentioned before I was unable to attend Shool on Yom Kippur day, for very good reasons, but I am glad to say that I obtained permission to absent myself from work, providing I didn't go out of camp etc.etc. So most of the day I spent lying on my bed, fasting and generally thinking of past Yom Kippurim, when to me again came this "ugly creature" rearing at me as it were. This time it came to me in the form of a Palestinian Jew, who occupies the next bed to me, and being on my bed all day had cause to notice him more than usual. Outwardly there was nothing different or unusual about him, he was dark skinned, rather swarthy and spoke English with a foreign accent, a typical Palestinian, so it wasn't him I noticed so much as what to me appeared to be his disrespect for his religion. That, I think sums up in three words, that "monster" whose eyes keep peering at me the Palestinian Jew's apparent disrespect for his religion. This particular case of the chap in my tent - I don't think he knew at the time that I was a Jew, not because I'm ashamed of it, far from it - but to keep him in ignorance of our co-religionship meant that I could watch him, without him realising it. Perhaps I was doing wrong, but I don't think I was doing him any harm. His reaction, like most others of his Nationality, when I told him of my faith, was just that of a disinterested spectator - sometimes they said "Shalom", but mostly they said nothing, shook their heads, and shrugged their shoulders; is this then the "Brotherhood of Jewry" which is so persistently drummed into me.

But to get back to this Palestinian friend(?) of mine in the tent, on Yom Kippur day he made no attempt to get out of camp to attend a service, and for no apparent reason as far as I could find out, but I could have forgiven him for that. I was after all in the same predicament myself, and his excuse may have been equally as good as mine. But what to my mind was most unforgivable, was that he worked all day, something which I'm sure could have been avoided, nor did he fast at all - the Greatest Day of the

EXCERPTS Continued.

Jewish Calendar, and it passed him by. But, perhaps I am wrong - perhaps he had a perfectly good reason - alright; but what about the case of the future Mothers of Israel, those girls who will, please God, bring into the world Jews and Jewesses of future generations, these Palestinian Girls who should be good representatives, should they not? Let me give you just one more example of my so-called disrespectfulness, if I may be allowed to encroach on your valuable time.

Whilst I was in Palestine, in Tel Aviv, for Posach, I had the pleasure of receiving an invitation to a Jewish A.T.S. Friday Evening. Having experienced similar things at home under the leaderships of such people as yourself, Charles Gillis, the Heilpern sisters, I went to this affair full expecting a lecture on a Jewish Subject or a Zionistic meeting, or something of a similar nature - but no, nothing of the kind, everyone sat around in arm chairs and listened with apparent eagerness to a very high-brow Symphony Concert, smoked and between overtures or whatever they're known as, talked shop. The only indication that it was "Erev Shabbos" was the fact that two candles were burning, lit by a Corporal in the A.T.S. who found time to remove the cigarette from between her lips, pronounce the Benediction, and carry on with her conversation as if nothing at all had happened. This then was the Modern Jewish Miss from our Own Land, and people want to know why I am aggravated.

Tel Aviv, supposed to be the most ultra modern Jewish City in the world - where the buses don't run on Shabbos and the cinemas are closed, because the drivers of the former and the projectionist of the latter are Jews and must have their day of rest. But, walk along the sea-front and see all the cars flashing up and down, and look into cafes and restaurants and bars, and see all the people there - are they not Jews too?

I'm afraid on re-reading this I have let my thoughts and ideas run away with me, but as any of my pals will tell I'm rather keen on the subject of Religion - but how true is the saying that a little news is harmful, still I hope that you wont think that I am a danger to our cause it's just that I have seen for myself an active quarter of Palestine and all my beliefs and ideals of the country have been shattered. If this article was printed in the Bulletin, I wonder what a storm of criticism it would get.

CFW. Magrill G. writes: I have just written a letter of appreciation to Argus. Actually I make a lot of use of his articles as the men here are very football conscious and so with the help of Argus I manage to hold my own.

Act./Leading S.Lerman writes from Colombo: We are now in the rainy season with the monsoons and yet it is far too hot for me. If you have a walk along the road or do a little shopping for an hour or so your shirt is soaking through with sweat, it is very humid here. Honestly speaking there is nothing good for the service bloke out here the only decent thing I do enjoy is your monthly Bulletin to which I look forward to reading.

Cpl. Norman Cohen of B.N.A.F. writes: Inquisitor has an unending volume of "cracks" but seeing that I have been out of touch with home affairs for a long time many of them need explaining. I suggest that he/she publishes an appendix for overseas readers. I think it would be a good idea if you could publish a special page of addresses of people in the Forces. I may be next door to somebody and not know it.

Letters were also received from the following: Gnr. A. Abrahams from P.A.I. Force, L.A.C. I Davis, A.C.W. Pearlman S.R., L.A.C. Isaacs S., Pte. L. Marks, A.C. Dresner M., Tpr. Horace Stone, Nurse Rita Olsweng, Pte. C. Kensh, Pte. M. Doberman, L.A.C. Gordon J. B.N.A.F., Pte. S. Cohen, L/Cpl. Altman, Cpl. Phyllis Mincovitch, Cpl. M. Davis B.N.A.F., CF/M P. Soldinger L.A.C. C. Gillis, C.M.F., S/Sgt. J. Rosenthal, and Cpl. Charlton.

All correspondence to be sent to Rev. S.P. Toperoff, 5 Victoria Avenue, Sunderland.

SUNDERLAND Jewish COMMUNITY

BULLETIN for the FORCES

EDITED AND ISSUED MONTHLY

BY THE MINISTER

AND SENT TO YOU

WITH THE GOOD WISHES OF

YOUR FRIENDS AT HOME.

December 1943   Vol. 2, No. 4.   Kislev 5704.

For some mysterious reason the world thinks of Judaism as a decadent and obsolete religion. It may have produced saints, pious and Rabbis but no heroes. Jewish history, say our detractors, can of no fighting men or warriors. Nothing of course is further from truth. Those that have but a smattering knowledge of Jewish history know better. This war has already furnished many an example of self devotion and heroism by the Jew on the field, in the air and on the It is a crying shame that the daring exploits of Jews on various front should be passed over in silence.

It is the irony of our fate that deeds of gallantry and self sacrifice by the Jew are hardly mentioned by the Press which seems to plenty space for the malpractices of a miserable few who are Jewish in name only. The Jewish nation is primarily a peaceful one but in its wanderings and hardened by the iron hand of persecution and racial discrimination have always produced champions who would rather die than sell their heritage for a mess of pottage.

Chanukah which we are celebrating now proves this. The Jewish Maccabees were fighters, martyrs for the cause of freedom. Already in the year 165 B.C.E., before many of the states of the modern world saw the light of day the Jews taught that it was worth fighting and dying for the supremacy of right over might. It should be remembered that Jews then fought against terrible odds. A mere handful of Jews against the invincible might of ancient Syria and Greek civilisation. It was severe trial but truth and justice had to prevail and the persecuted was victorious. .

That struggle the Jew still carries on. The world is not told how the Jew fights on every front and whilst he continually offers unknown warriors on the altar of patriotism we at home shall kindle the lights Chanukah. Hitlers one aim was to put out the lights of Europe and in urate a reign of black terror for the whole of mankind. The Jew was Hitlers enemy number 1 because he always kindled the lights of Freedom publicly. We shall continue to burn the Chanukah lights, we shall go fighting and praying for the day when the Lights of Justice, Liberty, and Freedom will burn brightly and bring lasting Peace to a darkened w

A Pleasant Chanukah to you all.

DO YOU KNOW?

1. Whose researches contributed to the invention of insulin for the treatment of Diabetes?
2. Why did Voltaire and Schopenhauer hate Judaism?
3. How often has it happened that an entire nation has emigrated from country and survived as a nation?
4. Are the Jews a race?
5. Who was Jean de Bloch?
6. What connection is there between Chanukah and Education?

Answers to the above on Page 3.

EN PASSANT - INQUISITOR

Contrary to all subterranean murmurings and expectations I do not
quit altogether public affairs" nor do I "lay down my burden" -
ure has been brought to bear so once more I carry on - - - give me
gen" and I'll finish the job!!   I've received some very exhilarating
les during the past month, they have certainly fortified me on the way.
The festive season is now in full swing so I'm going to call a
tion of hostilities pro tem - peace on earth etc.   This month I
failed to reveal any deep, dark, dangerous secrets instead of which
e kept my "flashes" consistently to news of public interest and
n knowledge, thereby giving away no vital information to the enemy.
This unwonted generosity is not the forerunner of things to come; au
aire in the next issue I expect to thrill you with tales of deeds
have never previously been divulged.   At risk of being struck off
ournalistic rolls permanently (hurrah!), I will tell you ALL.   My
which have been conditionally sealed for many months will be freed
ver more - so beware!   "Happy Inquisition" to quote one of my
ples.

s known as the R.A.F. "Cleaner Up-er", you've certainly had it!
M.M. thinks I'm a woman!   A rose by any other name - - -
r has it that a local debutante now sings "America I love you" - no
"play", be a "sport" please.
. grateful(?) coloured patient presented an important member of the
'. with a photo frame?   Or do you prefer the "brass"?
t that Norman the Conqueror and the Algerian Shiek spent a very
ant time together after the latter was released from the arms of
eus.   Thank you for including me in your conversation, I am truly
ired.
r hath it that life in British Somaliland has a deadening effect on
: usual lively wit - - n'est-ce-pas?
e Fleet's in Port Again this week!   Any more dramatic prowess
ated?
a certain Lieutenant and L.A.C. met after nearly two years separation
were the topics of conversation?   Unprintable?.
RY THE SIXTEENTH..........................!
. where is D.A.?
t that the new R.A.F. word from Iceland is "blizzard".
e new recruit going to be much in print since joining the D.L.I.?
s Louis Bromfield 11, India Command.

SPORTING REFLECTIONS - By ARGUS.

When last I penned my notes for you lads, I think I mentioned that
rland had a chance to land the championship.   You remember the story
e sapper who wrote: Dear Mother, I am sending you 5/- but not this

Well Sunderland have a chance to win the chamionship - but not this
    Our only hope now is the League Knock-out Cup and the way things
been going I do not hold out much hope.   Everything has been going
; with the team - service players either away on courses or playing in
ental games; civilian players injured or off through illness. For
on a stretch Manager Murray has been telephoning round at last
e, so to speak, trying to get a team together.
Just at the vital period Alex Hastings went down with severe influenza.
kept him out of three matches and Laidman, Whitelum and Eves were
bsent at the same time.   Now Jimmy Gorman has "got a month" for being
off in the St. James's Park game, so the first three games of the

3.

qualifying round of the cup will be over before he can play. I have bee
watching Sunderland for 45 years and this is the first time I have ever
seen a man ordered off for defending himself. No matter what his record
is, Gorman has been unjustly treated. However, there is no appeal and
that's that.

Sid. Bradwell, a grand young player whom many of you will not have
seen play, is lost to the team until the war ends - excepting leave perih
if they fit in. He has been transferred from Coastal Defence to a
Scottish infantry unit.

But it is scoring forwards that we want, and in my opinion in this we
type of football, what is wanted is two good wing men. Johnny Spuhler
would be a great player if he had a bigger heart and if Jimmy Connor was
fit and playing in present day football most backs would be running round
in circles with their tongues out.

Some of you may know that Sunderland's method of training in peace
time is the seven a side game. In pre-war days Jimmy Connor used to make
his colleagues "dizzy" running about after him. One of the greatest
players of the game was put out of it just in his prime, but I am firmly
convinced that today Connor, with one good leg, could play better than mo
outside lefts.

It is peculiar how you get periods. Sometimes you can see half a
dozen good left footed players then you can go for years without seeing
must have seen 50 this year and I have not seen a good outside left amon
hem. Raich Carter, Hastings and Sid Bradwell are the ideal in one
respect - one foot is just about as good as another. In my Schoolboy
playing days the master used to make us use both feet- and if we did not
e used to bind up the foot you were always using to make you practice wi
he other. That method today would be useful.

Well, happy shooting. See you are on the target.

Answers to Questions on Page 1.

1. Oscar Minkowski.
2. Because they said it had a super abundance of optimism.
3. Only once and this is true of the Jewish people.
4. Yes for many reasons. We have room for one only. No other race he
   gone through the process of the survival of the fittest as Jews and
   therefore they represent not only a race but a powerful race.
5. A Jew who was responsible for the convocation of the first
   International Peace Conference at the Hague.
6. The word Chanukah in Hebrew comes from a root which means to train,
   educate.

IN RETROSPECT

I remember paying a visit to the home of a young man named Gompertz
of South Shields. He was secretary or organiser of a concert party we
had invited to give us a show. After the necessary arrangements were
made, I was invited to tea. I spent a delightful cosy evening with Mrs.
Gompertz (Mr. Gomperts's mother) and family and discovered that organizin
concerts was not all work. It had its compensations. Now I must tell
you about the show itself.

I met the artists at the station. A very professional party they
looked. The men were clad in morning coats and top hats. In some case
n full evening dress, overcoat and top hats. The girls wore the then
fashionable hooded evening cloaks over their lovely frilly evening frock

The men carrying large suit cases and the girls with their small attache cases made a striking procession as we wended our way to the Park Hall, Toward Road, where the concert was held.

They gave us sketches, songs and music, really funny comedians and the inevitable recitations set to music, musical monologues. A jolly evening, the Lit had again added to its laurels. We commenced rehearsals on a Mock Trial about this time, "Trotter v Kipper, an action for libel". Mrs. Trotter, Sausage & Mash Restaurants, sued Horatio Mount Arrarat Kipper, an ex-actor turned Fish and Chip Merchant, for causing to be printed and published a poster stating that Mrs. Trotter's sausages contained flesh of captured cats. Mrs. Trotter answered to questions in "local town end Cockney". Horatio replied to cross examinations in quotations from Shakespeare using the appropriate and otherwise gesticulations. The cast including tall and short policemen were all Lit members. The Judge, Registrars and Counsel wore full evening dress under their gowns, thus giving the theatrical touch to the trial and putting the polish on a fine and finished performance. When Horatio saw the case going against him he proposed to Mrs. Trotter and "they lived happily ever after".

The Lit booked the Subscription Library Hall, Fawcett Street for the show. A bold move. The Hall was crowded, the trial was a huge success and Sol Novinski, the Hon. Treasurer and Producer netted £5 clear profit. Encouraged by this success, the Lit booked the Hall the following year and produced a three act play entitled "Checkmate". I shall write about this next month. Cheerio.

SOL.

NEWS LETTER FROM THE HOME FRONT.

There was a debate at the Lit on November 14th on the subject "That Strikers are Fifth Columnists". The Proposer was Leslie Epstein and he was seconded by Fay Merskey. The Opposition was led by Philip Winberg supported by Charles Cohen. A lively discussion took place and many points were raised for both sides of the problem, though when the house divided the opposition had a fair majority.

The following week, the 21st, saw no larger crowd for the B.B.C. Night which had been drawn up by Rosalie Gillow and Unita Magrill and was augmented during the evening by Aubrey Gordon who acted as Master of Ceremonies. The small attendance did not prevent the evening being very jolly. Charles Cohen gave a remarkably good imitation of Hutch singing "Hey diddle diddle" and Unita Magrill had to put over "Ba Ba Black Sheep" as it would have been sung by an opera singer. Others were caught out through not knowing the feminines of such words as Peacock, Horse, Executor or the composers of Faust or Madame Butterfly. Then there were some very tricky questions such as on which side of a soldier his civilian friend should walk and how many keys a piano has. I should mention that the sides were ladies against gentlemen - the ladies won 'on points'. I would like to see this repeated some time; it was great fun, even though most of us were caught out at least once during the evening.

The following week a Mock Trial was held. This was quite a success in its way, and at any rate was thoroughly enjoyed by the fair sized audience which acted as the jury. The accused was Ezekial Gillis and he was charged with using more than 5 inches of water in having a bath. Counsel were Aubrey Gordon for the prosecution and Unita J. Magrill for the defence. Ena Stone was Judge and Leslie Epstein, Clerk to the Court. The trial was carried out in style with full dress being worn by those taking part. The prisoner, with his blackened face, greatly amused the jury and the many wise-cracks that passed between counsel and witness caused endless laughter.

The Clerk using an "ultra modern" method of counting the

votes, said that the jury found the prisoner guilty and an appropriate sentence was passed! I thoroughly enjoyed this event, though it would have been even better if rehearsed before-hand and I am sure that if the next one (I'm told there is to be another one later) is more thoroughly prepared it will be an outstanding success.

On December 5th the Lit confined its tea to its own members and members of the Forces. As usual the tea "went down" well. It was followed till 11.0 by dancing to Arthur S. Smith's band, which was this time exceptionally good, no doubt helped by the electric guitar which effect a change from the usual dance band style. Perhaps it was this that livened up the proceedings but whatever it was every-body seemed to be jollier than last time and even though the floor was not as packed as some times the walls nevertheless resounded with gaiety. The 26th December is down for a Chanukah Party — so watch the date. I'll let you know all about next time.

I was pleased to read L.A.C. Marks' words in the last Bulletin encouraging forces overseas to re-establish their membership of the Lit. I am told that this matter has now been discussed by the Committee when was pointed out that all members of the Forces are considered members of the Lit without paying any subscriptions — you lucky people! Still I am looking forward to seeing you all back here in the not too distant future and I can assure you that you wont be home very long before you will be asked for your 5/- for the Lit.

Best of luck, Forces. Cheerio till next month.
Yours,
Also After Gen.

EXCERPTS FROM LETTERS.

S/Sgt. J. Rosenthal from P.A.I. Force writes: Your editorial struck a familiar note and one which cannot be overstressed. Of course it is too late now to press for a Jewish Armed Force to be of much value in this w But it is something to be worked for in the Future. We are condemned f our weaknesses and failures, (real or implied) but are not accorded our honours as Jews by the world at large, but as Englishmen etc. Thus we suffer persecution by the ignorant on the one hand as Jews and by the sa ignorance, denied the natural protection resulting from the many benefits Jews impart to the world. I think these points should be enlarged upon and stressed among our societies and clubs, so that in the future, certai selfish interests will not be able to sabotage our efforts towards regain ing our National Heritage. Many thanks to the "Inquisitor" for his/her article which brought back memories of canoeing at Belle Isle during tho bygone days I spent in the U.S.A. Gaily painted canoes they were, with bright coloured cushions to serve as a background for the fair sex in summer frocks. Thanks again for bringing back thoughts of those pleasan and carefree days.

You may be interested to know that I was invited to take part in the Yom Kippur services in the village where I am staying. Entering a small courtyard in which two sheep were tethered, I was conducted to the Shool. This consisted of a room about eighteen feet by twelve built of mud and straw with the floor covered with carpets. Only the males were allowed here and we were sixteen all told. Shoes were left outside and the men sat on the floor in Oriental style - (I had a chair). The women of cour sat on the floor outside the door and listened to the Service. Everybod took part (there being no regular officiating Rabbi) and to fill in the times that you would use for sermons, everybody chose psalms to be read. The order of service was of course somewhat different from ours, but well

6.

known and familiar.   One peculiarity I noticed was that they had no Shin or Sinn only a Toff which made the Service sound as if everybody was short tongued.   They had one Torah (which is well written) and it is kept in a shaped wooden case crudely decorated with tinsel and hung with bits of print cloth.   Conversation was carried on in Persian, Turkish and Turkish-French, which left me more or less in the sign language state.

Cf/m. P. Soldinger writes: I cannot find words to express my sincere thanks and appreciation for the Bulletin.   All the Jewish boys and girls in the Forces, our dear wives, husbands, mothers, fathers and children, we are all drawn together in one common bond within the circle of the Jewish Community of Sunderland, and a Jewish Community indeed to be proud of.   I have often longed to express my thanks to you dear Reverend, and the Jewish Community as a whole for that wonderful friendly feeling that has always been extended to me from the first day I came to Sunderland, and so I thank you all, and pray that all those whose hearts are troubled for their absent kinsfolk, may they P.G. speedily return and play their part as I hope to do to the benefit of the Sunderland Jewish Community who did not forget us at war.   We shall not forget you in Peace.

L.A.C. C. Gillis. C.M.F. writes: When I first came out I was in Camp outside Algiers and I was there for about two weeks till I found that I was posted to a unit in Tunisia, I travelled from Algiers to Sousse with an army road convoy and spent an interesting four days in a Ford truck.   We passed through Settif on a Friday where my companion on the truck (a jock from Glasgow) and myself decided to stop to have our hair cut.   I enquired from an Arab in the street where there was a barber's shop.   He told me that all the Arab shops were closed because it was Friday and that the only barber shop open was a Jewish one, but "of course" he added, "you wont go to a Jewish shop".   I asked him why and he replied simply "because they are Jews".   I then told him that I was a Jew and the conversation was suddenly interrupted by a shout from a little boy who had been playing on the pavement and who now ran up to me full of excitement.   The boy took me and my companion to a Jewish shop which seemed to act as a communal centre for the Jews of Settif who number about sixty families.   Even the local Rav was present.   They spoke only French and a little Hebrew.   They had a rough time during the German occupation but were now quite happy. Relations with the Arabs were not too good, but that did not seem to worry them at all.

Eventually I reached my unit near Monaster which is a small town not far from Sousse.   The town of Monaster itself was out of bounds because of disease and I was in camp several miles out.   However a few times a week we made a trip to the beach to bathe in the sea.   It was on the beach that I had my second encounter, again with a Jewish boy.   It was only by chance that I heard him say that one Jewish boy could easily fight three Arabs. We were soon good friends - his name was Hector.   The next time I went to the beach Hector introduced me to his friends.   They all went to a Hebrew teacher in Monaster.   I met him eventually - a first class Zionist, but sadly out of touch with events.   The children knew some Hebrew songs; I taught them some more.   It looked as though I was going to have a real Habonim group meeting on the beach, but alas the war caught up with me and without warning I was taken to Sicily.   So far as I know there are not more than about 6 Jewish families in the whole island.   Near where I am stationed at the moment there is a city which I am able to visit from time to time.   I was able to attend services there on Rosh Hashanah and Yom Kippur.   They were organised by the American Forces Chaplain, and were attended by at least a thousand American soldiers on each occasion.   The services were very impressive and were carried on more or less in orthodox manner.   A few days before Yom Kippur I was walking with some friends in the streets of the city when we were approached, quite by chance, by a young

man in civilian clothes who asked in broken English whether there we
soldiers from Palestine in the vicinity. I asked him why he wanted
know and also if he was a Jew he should speak in Yiddish or Hebrew.
those magic words the tears came into his eyes and he almost started
with me in the streets. He is a member of Hecholutz from Lwow in P
Three years ago he was on his way to Palestine when he was arrested
Italians and has spent the time since in a concentration camp in Ita
was set free when British Forces invaded Italy. We had a long talk
the various Zionist groups, he was amazed to hear that there was sti
Jewish Army as he was counting on joining it. I gave him particula
the American Jewish Chaplains office and they are now looking after
Cpl. M. Davis from B.N.A.F. writes: I remember in March and April o
year I was stationed in a well known town here, and had made severa
acquaintances and I had every hope of spending a real Jewish Seder n
in fact I had already received three concrete invitations; But it
to be. On Seder night I found myself on the move and spent a most
fortable Pesach on a cattle truck. So you can imagine how much I w
looking forward to Rosh Hashanah. Again I found myself within reas
distance of the town that can boast of the most beautiful and pictur
Synagogue in North Africa. I had arranged for myself and the other
boys in the Pen (being the senior N.C.O. - ahem) to take 3 days leave
the occasion; but again I was unlucky and I missed the boat, owing t
unforeseen illness of a clerk. However on Yom Kippur I did manag
take part in a ceremony only a couple of miles from the camp.
The service was in the American Red Cross, and there was a crow
500 or more. There was only about a dozen British soldiers, the re
comprising American soldiers, sailors, airmen and nurses. The Ser
which was surprisingly read by a British Chaplain, was most impressi
The Service was held in the evening, and I managed an hour in the mo
too, although the service did carry on right through the day. I ha
chance neither did the other British soldiers - of making the acqua
or even speaking to the Chaplain. Although I have been in this coun
nearly twelve months this is the first occasion I have seen a British
Chaplain of the Jewish faith, and I have been in places from Algiers
Tunis. It was a great disappointment to me and the other British so
that the Chaplain made no attempt whatsoever to contact us after the
was over. If there are British Jewish Chaplains, then it is a myste
me where they are. The American Jewish Chaplains are numerous (the
of course many more Jewish Americans than British) and I must say hav
much for us. I received from them - without asking - a parcel of "R
ious interest to soldiers of the Jewish Faith". This consisted of t
Bible, a Prayer Book, reading matter and a small "Mezzuzah. Nothing
that is received from the British Jewish authorities, and except for
monthly Bulletin there is nothing to help the Jewish soldier from the
religious point of view.
Don't think for one moment I am annoyed about it. I am not.
merely amazed at their (the Authorities) lack of religious interest.
Presumably the authorities in London think it unnecessary to guide th
flock as well as the other denominations do. What a mistake they ha
made, as evidenced by every Jew I have come across here.
Tonight I believe, is the 'between days' of Succoth, and perhap
the first time in my life I am sleeping in a "Succah" - at least a t
and there are plenty holes to see the stars which is according to ri
The army is indeed a great leveller and it has taught me a lot and fo
that I am thankful.
Sgt. I. Levine, Quetta Arsenal, India Command writes: I'm so happy t
that Sgt. Harold Magrill is reported safe, and all the other local n
simply a "wow". Please give a hearty Mazeltov on my behalf to Issy

and also Miriam Winborg,   Its good to know that   CUPID still refuses to
'bow the knee' for a mere war! Due to an anticipated move - (much
further EAST!!) I couldn't go to Bombay, as I had planned, for Yomtov.
However even in the seclusion of India's North West Frontier Region, it's
grand to know that all the world over, fellow Jewry is at last beginning
to see the sunshine through these years of darkness, and looking to the
future with faith and hope. I feel sure that 1944 will see the VICTORY we
all pray for so you'd better be organising the celebrations in good time!
I think you will soon have some good news from THIS part of the world.
The motto out here is 'Slap a Jap' and like so many of us, I'm expecting
to move at any time now. Please tell Sol Novinski that his articles
certainly bring back memories of those jolly old carefree days we knew at
the Lit, may they soon return. With every good wish to you all in dear
old Sunderland. MAZAL & BROCHA.

A.C.W. L.Slater writes: It is really grand to read of the doings of the
Jewish Youth of Sunderland and to think that even under these distressing
conditions and the absence of a good percentage of the girls and boys the
various Societies are still existing. It would be a good idea if the
Syllabus of the Lit was published in the Bulletin although "Also After
Gen" keeps us well informed.

Cpl. J. Charlton R.A.F. Bombay writes: I was fortunate enough to be able
to spend both Rosh Hashanah and Yom Kippur in Bombay.   It was indeed a
'tonic' to be able to attend a service again after a lapse of nearly 18
months, for the last time I was in a synagogue was during Pentecost 1942 -
in Durban.   In Bombay I located the Synagogue (which was full) and the
first evening of Rosh Hashanah I attended their overflow service - which
was Sephardic and I had the greatest difficulty in following it at all.
An enjoyable feature of the holiday was to meet Jewish lads from
various parts of the country and speak of mutual acquaintances and I found
that Sunderland and its people were by no means unknown throughout the
country.

L.A.C. J.D. Levine, R.A.F., M.E.F. writes: My thoughts are often with the
old town and I wonder what goes on at the various places - Shool, Literary
Society and the Hostel etc.   For Yomtovim (Yom Kippur and Succoth) I was
able to return to Erez Israel for the fourth time and spent most of my
vacation at Tel-Aviv, where I have made some very good friends.   We were
able to spend Succoth in a Succah and both Yom Kippur and Succoth heard a
marvellous Chazan from Warsaw, at the Great Synagogue in Allenby Road. One
day we went off to Jerusalem, and after visiting such places as Mosque of
St. Omar, Wailing Wall, Via Dolorosa and Church of Holy Sepulchre, which come
to mind we spent the latter part of the day visiting the War Cemetery on
Mt. Scopus, Jewish University, with a wonderful library (gifts from all
over the world) and the Hadassah, most up to date and the gift of the U.S.A.
My visits to Palestine have been a source of interest and pleasure to me,
although travelling facilities as well as being overtaxed are very poor
indeed. Our problem is a great one and I can see many difficulties ahead
for our people.

P.O. N.Goodman from British Somaliland writes: All our time is spent at
work, and at the moment we are quite busy building a New Civil hospital
out of mud bricks and petrol tins.   What with our Civil and Military duties
we find plenty to occupy our time, for which I thank God and hope for
nothing worse.

Pr. Horace Stone from a hospital in Herts. writes: I was in Palestine too,
in Hospital at Beer Jaacov near Tel-Aviv, and also I met many Palestinians,
perhaps more than Friend Marks, and when I said "Ani Ivri" they said far
more than just "Shalom", their pleasure was very evident, and being in
hospital I had the time to talk to them about conditions in Palestine. I
soon learnt that I could expect hospitality from Jews alone of the native

population of the Middle East. And their hospitality was truly Jewish. Lt. M. Cohen, India Command writes: Perhaps you have read or heard of a book written by Louis Bromfield entitled "A Night in Bombay", well I'm going to relate to you how I spent "A Friday Night in Bombay". It was shortly before 7 p.m. (1900 hrs) one Friday evening and I was deciding whether to go to the Fort Synagogue or the Daviv Sassoon Magen David Synagogue. There is only one Ashkenazi service held in Bombay and that is on Friday evening, mainly for the benefit of German and Polish refugees. Being accustomed to the Ashkenazi service it of course attracted me, but I had a great desire to visit the Sephardi service held in the David Sassoon Synagogue. On learning that Shabbos morning service was held 0715 hrs. (so that people could get to business) I decided to go to the Sepharde Service. On entering the Shool I was immediately conscious of a different atmosphere. There was a large marble Bimah in the centre, a great array of fans overhead. The seating arrangements were very unusual. The large wicker benches were parallel to the Bimah and widely spaced. There were several young boys in the congregation. The dress varied from European to Indian and the head dress included Yamulkes, Fez, Topees and Felt hats. Several wore for footwear Sandals which they slipped off and curled their feet up on the benches. All the congregants were descendants of what are known as the Bagdadi Jews, coming from Persia, Iraq, Iran and some even from Palestine.

After I took a seat, a Siddur was thrust into my hand. It was quite different from ours in format and contained some interesting variations from our form of service. Whilst I was perusing it, I heard a mumble from the rear of the Shool and turned to see an old man wearing a fez making towards the Bimah, when he reached it he turned towards the congregation they all burst into the Kaddish. In fact throughout the whole service they appeared to recite Kaddish every 5 minutes. By this time I realised they were reciting Mincha and managed to follow the service with a little difficulty. However when it came to Maariv I was completely lost for a and just managed to catch up with them at "veshomroo". Every now and again a man or a woman would appear and carry a baby wrapped up in a sh round the Bimah. On subsequent enquiry I was informed that it was a practise to carry round the Bimah children who were suffering from measles etc. At the conclusion of the service I enquired in Hebrew at what time the service started on Shabbos. There was a blank look on some faces t a voice spoke "Ain Medaber Kan Ivrit". At last they brought an old man who spoke "Lashon Ameynoo" and gave me the necessary information. On leaving the Shool I noticed a sign on an adjoining building which brought back old memories. It stated "Judean Club". This led to another experience which I shall relate in my next letter.

Letters were also received from the following:- A/c M. Dresner, C N. Cohen B.N.A.F., David Rosenthal & Arnold Bloomberg, Cpl. E. Abrahams, Leading Tel. S. Lerman Colombo, L.A.C. C. MARKS, C.M.F., L.A.C. J. Gord B.N.A.F., Fus. B. Freeman B.N.A.F., Sgt. B. Taylor, India Command, Pte. Pearlman India Command, Pte. A. Davis, Pte. Levin India,

We welcome to the Forces Louis Cohen.

We are pleased to report that Lenny Lerman formally prisoner of war Italy is safe in Germany.

Owing to the large number of interesting letters the Editor regrets that he has had to keep back some for next months issue..

All correspondence to be sent to Rev. S.P. Toperoff, 5 Victoria Av Sunderland.

Sunderland Jewish Community
Bulletin for the Forces

1944

note: missing pages
April - Volume 2 No. 8 - page 5,
June - Volume 2 No. 10 - pages 2 & 3

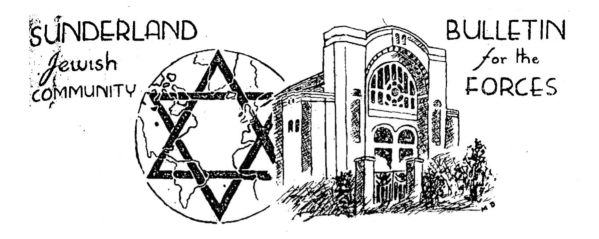

EDITED   AND   ISSUED   MONTHLY

BY   THE   MINISTER

AND   SENT   TO   YOU

WITH   THE   GOOD   WISHES   OF

YOUR   FRIENDS   AT   HOME.

January 1944.   Vol. 2, No. 5.   Tebeth 5704

With this issue we print another letter complaining of "adequacy or otherwise of Jewish Chaplains" on behalf of their personnel. It is a great pity that some of our men are deprived of the spiritual comfort th a Chaplain can offer. We do not know who is at fault but the matter certainly deserves our careful attention. The issues at stake are grav and far reaching. War in itself is not a pleasant affair. It introdu new standards, a different way of life, new friends and new contacts are made and the home influence is lacking especially to those overseas. A these changes must affect the outlook of the average service man. His spiritual equilibrium is upset and unless he is lost to all things Jewi he craves more than ever for an opportunity of meeting his own brothers and sisters in the Forces and looks forward to make new acquaintances. Even if he does not meet anyone he knows at the Service it must surel be exhilarating to be in the company of his own people, all praying in t same language all hoping and aspiring for the solution of the so-called "Jewish Problem" into which they have been born. Such services and gatherings should be an indespensable part of service life. Three or four years in the life of a young man away from home with its wonderful influence, are bound to make dangerous inroads on his outlook on religion and life unless it is checked by the guidance, advice and leader ship of the Chaplain. Where it is not possible for the Chaplain to make contacts a regular correspondence course on current Jewish topics should be initiated. In this way the Jewish position in the world could be mad known to all our men and they could be familiarised with the methods of combating Anti-Semitism.

Whilst we at home are discussing the new Education Bill and the prospects which it opens for our youth, we must not ignore the religious and cultural education of our service men and women. This is the work of the Chaplaincy Department. There is perhaps not sufficient liaison between this department and the religious authorities in London and if so it should be rectified.

There are only 360,000 Jews in England and we have well over 50,000 in the Services. Can we afford to forget about them? We owe much to the fighting man who is engaged in the twin battle of Hitlerism and Anti Semitism. We must arm them not only with weapons of destruction but also with weapons of the spirit, with an armoury of Jewish information. It is your prerogative and duty to be ambassadors of Jewry wherever you are. Do not remain silent. If the Chaplain does not ferret you out you must not sit back. You must then write to the Senior Chaplain and demand your rights. We have no doubt that your request will then receive prompt and careful attention.

DO YOU KNOW?

1. How many Jewish Special Constables are there in Palestine?
2. Who was chiefly responsible for the introduction of pasturised milk?
3. Give one proof from the Bible that the Jews are an agricultural and not a commercial people?
4. Which German General of the last war though an arch enemy of the Jew praised him for his courage on the field?
5. Which country has seen more conquerors and more foreign armies on its soil than any other in the world?
6. What is Gez?

Answers to the above questions on P. 4.

2.

HERE AND THERE!

Mazeltov!
Congratulations to Cpl. A.Berg on his marriage to Miss Gladys Berne at
Glasgow.   Congratulations to Tpr. W. Book on his engagement to A.C.W.
Miriam Gillis and to Max Gillis on his engagement to Irene Camrass of Leeds.
Congratulations to Mr. & Mrs. D. Pearlman on the birth of a son.
Congratulations to Dr. Jack Stone on gaining his Medical Degree.
Promotions - Pte. I.W. Brewer to Cpl. and Sgt. B. Taylor to Flight Sgt.
     The Chanucah celebrations this year were as successful as in previous
years.   In addition the Sunderland Jewish Womens War Services Committee
arranged a concert and tea for all the children of the town.   Nobby Clarke
and his Concert Party entertained the large gathering of young and old in
the Communal Hall.   About twenty pounds was raised for War Charities and
Mrs. M. Joseph with the help of a small sub-committee was in charge of the
arrangements.
     Recently two Memorial Tablets were unveiled at the Ryhope Road
Synagogue by Mr. A. Merskey and Mr. M. Jacoby. They are on either side of
the Bimah and contain engravings of the Prayer for the Royal Family in
English and the Prayer for the New Moon (Yehi Rotson) in Hebrew.
     A new Junior Official has been engaged by the Beth Hamedrash in the
place of Mr. Brazil who has left the town.

EN PASSANT   -   "INQUISITOR".

     Once more the town has been inundated with uniformed (and non-uniformed)
members of the Forces home for a well earned rest or a well earned sick
leave! (A rose by any other name - - - -)   It makes me feel conspicuous
and ostentatious , still a Civilian'!   (How much longer will this unhappy
state of affairs exist? How much longer will my "calling up pains"
suffice?) Nevertheless the galaxy of uniform is scintillating, the cafes
have done an unprecedented trade, the cinemas are full to over-flowing, in
fact the whole dissipated population has taken on a new lease of life
(glory be!).   I need hardly mention that a popular, palatial Dance Hall
experienced an almost pre-war boom.   Let us pray that broken hearts will
not be the order of the day as last time. (ah! but that's another story-)
By next leave who knows I also may have joined the ranks of the great
unemployed - - - I may even be one of the Fortunate Few and have an
excerpt of my letter printed!!   The thought of such **undeserved** flights
into fame fills me with confusion, so on an embarrassed note I once more
take my leave of you.   Until next time, hi-de-hi.

FLASH!
Who is the Poet Laureate of the Middle East? (Been composing any more odes
to your "trouble and strife"?)
Is three weeks the approved incubation period for an ulcer?
Who is the Home Guard Queen alias the Stalingrad Stalwart?
Does the Balfour Conqueror now adjure rings on the phone?   Did the Ring
on the Finger meet with approval?
Greetings D.A.!   Shall I say T.T.F.N.?
Who is a refugee from a Cheater Casanova? ThA.T.S. all I want to know - -
Did the Sunderland Invasion on January 16th hinder proceedings? Another
good man - - - -
Who spent a very illuminating Chanukah? Will Leeds always be as BRIGHT?
When is a certain girl to be led to the ALTMAN, sorry I meant ALTAR! (Is
it true that the Ceremony will be broadcast?)
Did "Caceothis Scribendi" enjoy his leave at B.C.?

3.

FLASH Continued

How is Tanks for the Memory?   Is he sure that this memory has only been in his mind for three weeks?

On dit that the Cumberland Hotel is out of favour, "East is East - - - remember the old quotation?

Is Berwickshire inspiring for the Muse of Poetry?

Rumour hath it that a certain Poker Fiend would rather abstain from card playing than venture through the Cedars - - - - ALONE".

SEARCHLIGHT ON SPORT   By ARGUS

Some weeks ago, at a time when Sunderland were running strongly for the League championship of the Northern Area, a well known National news paper told its readers the secret of success - team work rather than individual brilliance.   Whether that acted like good wine and went to the head I cannot say, but I can say that from that day Sunderland simply went to pieces.

Now in mid January, we are wondering whether it will be possible for the club to get into the first 32 clubs in the cup competition at the end of the ten games to qualify for the competition proper.   I am not going to attempt to don the prophetic mantle.   I might be tempted if I could pick my team and say that team will be available for every game, except for injuries, but war conditions preclude that.   Manager Murray has been having the dickens of a job to get a team at all, and he is having to keep so many reserve players back in case some selected player does not turn up that when the reserves turn out some of them do not even know each other.

For example in one reserve team game no outside left could be found but there were two goalkeepers.   Clark, who played earlier in the season for the seniors had to go from goal to outside left.

In this particular match Warrant Officer Stanley Bell of the R.A.F. just returned after a long period in Canada training young airmen, played at right back.   Stan has returned to England to go on operational duties He was a peace time N.C.O. with the week end Squadron at Usworth.

But to return to my subject.   You will have seen that Sunderland conceded ten goals to Darlington in the two games.   The home defeat was to a large extent due to Alex Hastings being ordered off for telling the referee not to be so autocratic in his manner, but on the two games the main cause was that we had two or three players who had not the courage of the men who fought and won the Battle of Britain.   Got me, Steve!

There is a very crude but expressive word - guts.   And if a football baller has not got that in his make up, he is no use to me.   I would no keep him in the team and would prefer to play a youngster who was giving all he had even if he was not so good a player.   That is my view and I hold to it.

Things might improve when we again have Gorman and Eves as the defensive pair.   Eves has had a long stretch of absenteeism through a raw wound on the top of his foot, but at the time of writing it was about better again.   Yes the luck has certainly been against us, but if you had seen the games, you would agree with me that in addition to bad luck there has been much bad play.

In conclusion let me thank those who sent season's greetings.   To them and to all I wish a safe and speedy return.   What better can I wish you for 1944 - Victory year!

IN RETROSPECT.

"Checkmates", an early Victorian 3 act play, was 60 years old when I produced it for the Lit. It had the advantage of being witty and free of copyright fees. In its early days the Society never had more than about 5/- in hand and as you can imagine every venture became a major speculation All moneys had to be laid out by the Hon. Treas., he being a very young man, caution was necessary.

In order to avoid unpleasantness at the School Rooms, the rehearsals were held in my father's workrooms. The plot - popular in its day - was the old story of the modern young man and young woman not liking the idea of their marriage being arranged by their elders. The play centred round their first meeting since early childhood. The "Hero" decided to change places with his manservant and strange to relate the "Heroine" did likewise with her maid.

They met and many awkward situations developed. One of these was when they met at dinner. A meal on the stage - a stage manager's nightmare. The fun was so fast and furious that the centre piece on the table - a lovely roast chicken - was not even touched. Between acts, music was provided by the Lit Bijou Orchestra. The Subscription Library Hall was crowded much to the Treasurer's and Producer's delight and relief.

After the show the Company spent the evening at the home of one of its members. It was a delightful supper party of happy and contented young amateur actors and actresses. The chicken - a piece of the ribbon tied round its tummy - was also there, but not for long, I assure you. "Checkmate." was also responsible for the first Lit romance, the leading lady and gentleman were married shortly after the last war.

And now please forgive me for telling a little personal story. Whilst in training with the D.L.I. at Barnard Castle, Jos. Rubins, Secretary of the Lit, the late Sydney Asher and I were entertained at the home of a canteen worker. Our hostess told us of a play she had seen at Sunderland she related the story of "Checkmate", then looking directly at me asked, "Were you the stage manager"? Such is fame.

Next month - "The Lit learns to Dance.

Cheerio.

SOL.

Answers to Questions on Page 1.

1. More than 16,000 apart from the Jewish Settlement Police.
2. The American Jew Nathan Strauss.
3. Hebrew has ten words for rain and not one for "Commerce".
4. General Ludendorff.
5. Palestine.
6. Gez is the language of Jews in Ethopia. it is a mixture of Ethiopic and Hebrew.

NEWS LETTER FROM THE HOME FRONT

On Sunday December 12th the Lit held a "Locum Tenens". Each person picked a piece of paper, bearing a profession, out of a hat and then spoke from the point of view of that profession, on "Do I want state control after the war". This proved educational and very amusing.

The next week there was a discussion group. The subject was "What I want after the war" and it was started off and led by Aubrey Gordon.

Those who took part included Unita Magrill, Esther Cowan, Jack Louis, visiting member of the R.A.F. and several others.

Half a crown was a lot, I had thought, for the Chanukah party on the 26th December. For members it was only 2/- whilst those in uniform were welcomed with open arms. But - no! I had to pay my 2/6 though I certainly did not regret it. This party was one of the jolliest affairs I have ever seen in the hall -either under the auspices of the Lit or otherwise. It started at 8.45 with a supper. There must have been round about 100 people sitting down and many came later. The hall was lavishly decorated with paper flags and streamers and there were plenty of brightly coloured paper hats, blowers, buzzers and other novelties. After the eats a presentation of three trees in the Children's Forest was made on behalf of the lit to Rev. and Mrs. Oler to mark their Silver Wedding. The games dances and fun then started and everyone joined in to make it really jolly. First was the Grand Old Duke of York followed by a novelty batton dance. Then other games such as Nursery Rhymes, "I want to be an actor", Bigamy, Elimination Dances and other novelty dances. Everyone was in a gay spirit and at midnight the party broke up and the score-and-a-half merrymakers who had lasted till then wended their weary way homeward(?) through the black of night.

Abother discussion took place on January 2nd when questions of international police forces and federal unions were discussed. Not a great many turned up to these discussions but they were worth having for the few who do. "True happiness" wrote Ben Johnson, "consists not in the multitude of friends but in their worth and choice" - but the Treasurer thinks otherwise.

On Jan. 9th there was a short play reading and the following week there was another discussion - this time on Jitterbugging - followed by dancing to the new dance records recently bought.

And now for L.A.C. Leonnie Slater and for all our other friends who want to know what's going on, here is an outline of the draft syllabus for the next few weeks.

Feb. 6th Discussion; 13th Living Newspaper Night; 20th Prize Paper Night; 27th Conversazzione; March 5th Debate; 12th Purim Dance; 19th Lecture; 26th Inter-debate and April 2nd General Meeting and elections etc.

That's all for now forces, keep smiling.

Yours,
Also After Gen.

EXCERPTS FROM LETTERS

L.A.C. Julius Gordon from B.N.A.F. writes: Some ten months had fleeted by since my arrival here and though during this period I must have visited the town some forty times and though there is, reputedly, about twenty va thousands of our co-religionists in and around it, this was my first real contact with Jews and Jewish life - and I was thrilled.

Rosh Hashannah was drawing near and I was confidently anticipating being granted leave. I just had to attend Services but to do this necessitated finding some Jewish people with whom to stay. It isn't easy to pick out people of our persuasion here - the majority are dark, and the French habit of gesticulating in speech is proverbial. I hestitated to chance the question at random "Are you Jewish?"

I recollected reading in the J.C. of the existence here of an

6.

organisation - Consistoire Israelite - which is, to all intents and purposes, the "Deputies" of North African Jewry. Here, then was my cue. I must unearth this body.

Juggling with these thoughts as I walked, the notice "English Spoken" in the window of a jeweller's shop attracted my attention, or was it not, instinctively, the familiar Hebrew characters below - very much smaller - which spelt the magic greeting "Shalom Alechem"? Without ado I entered and soon I was on my way to the office of the Consistoire.

Entering the open doorway between two stores I ascended a couple of flights of stone stairs and, reaching a large landing, saw a short corridor to the left and right, each with several doors. But what do I hear? My heart warmed as I recognised the welcome sound of Talmudic wrangling - the traditional chant I well knew. I turned left whence it emanated, tapped on the half-open door and entered as requested. There were three Baal Habatim - their prototypes could be found in Sunderland - and they returned my greeting warmly. I began to explain in halting French the immediate purpose of my call when one of them said "Can you speak "Yiddish?" The remainder of the conversation was continued in this medium without the slightest difficulty on either side.

It was an inexpressibly happy experience to be talking thus after so long. "Services? Yes of course". Rev. Berman (1st Army) was expected very shortly and combined Anglo-American Services would be arranged in the palatial Opera House for all serving Jews and Jewesses. "A shtell?" - He waved the matter aside with an appropriate gesture - "Don't worry, that will be taken care of". They evinced great interest in my home town and I told them something of its religious life which seemed to impress them. I saw they had been learning "Brochas". My curiosity apparently was observed and, turning to the Gomorah "You know something of it?" Timidly I told them it was quite a lot of years since I learned it but I tried out the first few lines or so, as best I could. I don't know which was the greater, their surprise or delight. By which you will appreciate that matters Jewish, educationally are at a rather low ebb, as we in Sunderland would judge them, among the younger generation here. I know now that lamentably few have any knowledge of Yiddish, the language, or of Yiddish-kite in general.

I took my leave feeling that at last I had got somewhere, mentally greatly refreshed and with all as pleased as Punch.

My Yom Tov experiences make a pleasant little story of themselves but the excellent hospitality I enjoyed was NOT the result of the efforts or organisation of the gentlemen of the Consistoire NOR of the Rev. Berman C.F.

Which brings me, in conclusion, to what has been, and is, a question burning within me - the problem of the adequacy or otherwise of the efforts or lack of them, of the Jewish Chaplains on behalf of their personnel. Maybe I've just been unfortunate in this respect but I regret to say it has been my experience all along to find what I can only presume to be a deplorable disinterestedness in their important work - or is it bad organ-isation or even a paucity in their numerical strength?

I would like to have the opinion of some of the Bulletin readers based on their own experiences in this direction. I regard the question as one of major importance to all serving Jews and Jewesses in their efforts to continue, by organised action, the pursuance of their faith as fully as conditions of war allow; to enable them to convene within their respective units, and areas so that they are able, the better, to reply effectively to, and combat, that undercurrent of anti-semitism which shoots to the surface so frequently endeavouring to drown with its deluge of hatred, falsehood and prejudice, the co-operative spirit of brotherly love, unity and freedom in the name of which this war is being waged.

Obviously it is the concern of all Jewry. If faults there are, the remedy must speedily be found.

Lieut. Dresner writes: At a Chanucah tea in Leeds I met Commander Br in charge of a training depot somewhere in England. He was a typical old Sea-Dog, He told me that when he entered the Navy in 1903 out total of 25,000 men only 30 were Jews. Today he alone has passed 2 Jewish youths through his one Training Ship.

Wren G. Grantham writes: I am a Cinema operator and enjoy my work as the days go by, it is an experience which I would not like to have missed. I find the Jewish Community of Glasgow most hospitable, ke an ever open door to any member of the Forces.

Pte. L. Levin, Meerut, India writes: "I thought you may like to hea our Yomtov services. We applied well in advance and were granted th days leave from duty and the use of a bungalow. When I arrived at t Meerut Shool, Yom Tov evening I had a most welcome surprise. Two of th boys had got organised and had the place thoroughly cleaned out, tabl were arranged T shape and covered with long white cloths (sheets). small desk formed the short part of the T and on it were two candlest (ashtrays) with candles ready. A little rug for the comfort of the Chazan and comfortable chairs from the barrack rooms completed the arrangements. We davened Mincha, lit the candles, and then Maariv — not forget the Kiddush, thoughtfully provided by another friend (lemon I had my Machzor, one or two boys had Siddurim and we had perhaps a do Soldiers Prayer Books. We numbered I think 16 or 17 and found the Pr Book a little inadequate at times as I read almost the full service f the Machzor. I spent the next two days very happily, Shachris in th morning at 7,30 with almost army punctuality, finished Mussaph at abou 11, only stopping for a small interval. To make up for the lack of Yo Prayer Books I would have one of the boys each in turn read a portion where normally a Mitzvah of opening the Ark would be the procedure. We also read a lot of those beautiful prayers in English as most of the bo were not too conversant with Hebrew. The portion of the Law we read English from a Bible and we managed a different 'Bal Maftir' each time the Haptarah being sung in Hebrew in the usual way. Krishma, Ashrey Ol etc. we said together in unison. The slight difference from the norm service kept everyone interested and there was no chatting or even wh ering during the service. Everything went off in great harmony, we h tallis and two capples but our greatest lack I think was the Shofar b the circumstances being a thousand miles or so from the nearest Jewis Community I think we were all very happy that we had the opportunity making our New Year and Day of Atonement really outstanding, days tha be remembered long after the usual humdrum existence out here has bee forgotten.

The letters from abroad are very interesting and I am sure all my gratitude to those who help in the publication of this paper.

Letters were also received from Pte. M. Pearlman, India Command A.C.W. Slater; Pte. S. Mincovitch; A/C A. Landau, C/FW G. Magrill, L. I Davis; Nurse R. Olswang; Act.Lead.Tel. S. Lerman, Colombo; L.A.C. J Gordon, B.N.A.F.; L/Cpl. Pearlman P., B.N.A.F.; Lt. Mordaunt Cohen, In Command, Pte. M. Pearlman; Fl/Sgt. B. Taylor, India Command; L.A.C. C Marks, C.M.F.

All correspondence to be sent to Rev. S.P. Toperoff, 5 Victoria Avenue, Sunderland,

SUNDERLAND Jewish COMMUNITY

BULLETIN for the FORCES

EDITED AND ISSUED MONTHLY

BY THE MINISTER

AND SENT TO YOU

WITH THE GOOD WISHES OF

YOUR FRIENDS AT HOME.

February 1944   Vol. 2 No. 6.   Shevat 5704.

"Why I am a Jew."   This is the title of a small book written by Edmond Fleg which I recommend you to read.   It is a statement of fact which we should all put to ourselves.   To call oneself a Jew because of accident of birth is an insult to Judaism and to God.   The author a Swiss Jew, who fought as a French volunteer in the first World War, tells us frankly that to him Israel was lost.   He drifted from Jewish thought, learning and observance, his mind was out of harmony with Jewish values.   He did not appreciate the beauty of Jewish ceremonialism and ritual, "those absurd customs", he calls them.   Then something happened that changed his out-look on life and made him find Israel again.

It began with the Dreyfus episode when the whole world shook with the trial and false conviction of Captain Dreyfus who was condemned by the French Military Court because he was a Jew.   Fleg is not the only Jew who was affected actually by the Dreyfus affair.   Herzl, the founder of modern Zionism was influenced greatly by the Dreyfus trial.   The unjust prosecution of a man because of his religion aroused in Fleg a burning desire to study his religion and ask himself why he was a Jew.   He began to regret all the years he spent in the study of strange philosophy at the expenses of Jewish learning.   "I ought to have learned Hebrew, to have studied my race, its origin, its beliefs, its role in history" he writes. This is a human document which every Jew should take to heart.   Fleg re-discovered Israel.

I suppose it happens in the life of many of us that we lose hold on our religion when suddenly we are unduly awakened by some catastrophic event.   The injustice done to Dreyfus is multiplied today a millionfold. In fact our position to-day is even more serious.   For the Dreyfus case produced a Zola who with his fiery pen wrote book after book protesting the innocence of Dreyfus.   Zola did not rest till he pierced the hard core of French anti-semitism and racial prejudices, and Zola succeeded.   To-day we have no Zola, there is a studied silence to the butcheries and untold suffering that many of our co-religionists are enduring because they are Jews.   We should therefore become imbued with the zeal of Fleg and in the first place re-discover our Judaism and learn to appreciate the eternal truth of our religion.

We belive in the justice of our cause, we have confidence we have faith.   With Fleg we know that "however numerous our exile in every age providence finds us a shelter.   First in Babylonia, then in Sicily, Spain France, Holland and so on.   The Jews who for so long lived in isolation have become integrated as citizens in all the nations and behave among them as citizens.   They kept themselves apart from all peoples, today they are the only people that includes men of all peoples; they were a nation among nations, today they are a League of Nations, . whose covenant is writ in their blood.   For we who have so long sought the proof of the existence of God and have found it in the Existence of Israel."

We should study this little book and discuss it at our Circles.   To the Jew it should act as a tonic and to the Christian it should prove that Jews have a mission to perform and that their task will be facilitated when Justice and truth reign supreme on earth.

2.

DO YOU KNOW?

1. Who is Houdini?
2. Who is Julius Rosenwald?
3. Who was one of the greatest figures of the Second Republic in France?
4. What effect did the Spanish Inquisition have on the Spanish people?
5. Which pure German poet often resorted to the use of Hebrew words in his poems to give them more colour and tone?
6. What is the motto of Durham University?

Answers to the above on P.5.

HERE AND THERE!

Congratulations.
To Corporal N. Berg on his marriage to Miss Gladys Barnes of Glasgow
To Arnold Landau on his marriage to Miss Cynthia Lowne of London.

Engagements -
To Corporal Ralph Freedman on his engagement to Miss Sylvia Grovic of London.
To Mr. Gerald Behrman on his engagement to Miss Joan Ellenbogen of Liverpool.

Births
To Mr. & Mrs. Bernstein on the birth of a son.
To Dr. & Mrs. H. Shenkin (nee Cynthia Gillis) on the birth of a son.

Promotion
Cpl. D. Abrahams on his promotion to Sergeant.

PESACH LEAVE
Personnel should make inquiries about their leave immediately.

We have just heard that Harold Brewer of Gibralter is on his way home on leave.

EN PASSANT   -   INQUISITOR

Can it be possible that four transitory weeks have elapsed since I penned my last article? Care and Old Age, which have been beckoning me successfully for some time, make the weeks pass with Mercurian Speed, so much so that secretive events seem to have taken place before my "agonised agents" are cognisant of the fact. All the "dope" with which I am plied is that of some weeks' standing in fact quite OFFICIAL, which means almost instant death to the popularity (?) of this column.

If my arithmetical prowess does not fail me I believe this is the 18th consecutive article I have contributed. If I cannot attain the standard of perfection which I have so gracefully acquired in my previous efforts I am sure you will bear with me - - a poor thing, but mine own. A permanent 100%. literary achievement is well nigh impossible in this Frozen North, believe it or not you Desert (either pronunciation) Heroes!! Hi-de-hi.

FLASH
Does Tanks for the Memory prefer the Ides of March for his Idyll? (or Ideal)?
Who is known as the Y.M.C.A. Dance Hostess?
On dit that the VICTORious Doctor had a wonderful time in Palestine. What we want to know is when is he going to return and - - - - - - -?

3.

FLASH Continued.

March 5th!.   March 5th!   March 5th!

Who prefers Canadian Capers to Incendiary Bombs? (Are you going to make CASE?)

Did the Indian LEVItes have an exciting Reunion? Roll on Pesach!

Who is always wagging his "trucking" finger in Shool??

Was the Weekend Session Barmitzvah un succes fou?

Has the Durham Evacuee made the Big Decision Yet? (Yea or Nay).

Rumour has it that the Shipping Magnate found his HAVEN or Refuge in Liverpool.   Has he been HARBOURing his affection for a long time?

Will a wellknown member of the R.A.F. (of Orkney Fame) relish his new posting?   Had he been finding competition near at hand too ominous? May be?

How are MAJOR operations in India?   Still finding silk stockings a problem?

How will the "Rock" manage without H.B.?   Our gain - - -

Which Naval Medico is known as the Cingalese Pearl?

Is the distance between Bournemouth and Glasgow still unsurmountable?

On dit that the Railway Company was recently responsible for the loss of 100 pairs of blankets (or was it only 15?)

How is D.A.   (Like being a Sergeant?)

Has C.M. met D.L. yet?

ERRATUM

In last month's issue "Cheater Casanova" should have read "Chester Casanova".

IN RETROSPECT.

At meetings and concerts of the Lit in the early days, the girls and boys would sit in separate groups and just look at each other or worse still just ignore one another.   At times one could feel an antagonism on the part of the boys and a justifiable aloofness of the girls towards the That the ice must be broken the sexes must get to know and understand each other was evident if the Society was to be a social aid to the Community. Small socials and dances were organised, members were persuaded to entertain with songs and recitations.   Dancing, games and a sit-down supper made up the programme, 2 M.C's were appointed.   It was their duty to introduce the members to each other and to see there were no wallflowers or walnuts.   Not always an easy task.   Most of the men could not dance.

Now dancing in those days was a very complicated art and the committ decided that a dancing class must be formed.   I visited Miss Locke, made arrangements and her dancing academy in Murton Street, was at our service one evening each week.   Some 30 members - an equal number of young men and women joined.   The young men were taught the correct way to ask for the pleasure of dancing with the partners of their choice and the young ladies learned to accept, or otherwise, with grace and dignity.   They were taught it was necessary to wear dancing shoes and white gloves.   The learned the steps of the waltz, valeta, polka, schottishe and the courtly minuet.   The intricacies of the waltz, cotillon, the lancers and many other dances.   Oh yes, there was much to know, a new world was being opened up to some of the members, they entered it with joy and enthusiasm After a while the committee decided the Lit was justified in holding full scale dances.   A resolution was carried to the effect that a dance be held on each of the three Festivals - Simchas Torah, Chanucah and Purim. With success came mounting ambition.   Within a couple of years the

4.

Society held its first Ball.   I will endeavour to describe a Lit Ball of thirty years ago in next months Belletin.

Four picnics were held between 1911 and 1915.   Alnwick, Hexham, Morpeth and Richmond were the places visited.   The parties seldom numbered less than 40, travel was by rail and there was much fun on the journey.   Motor coaches were unknown in those days.   Delightful walks at Alnwick.   At Hexham, Richmond and Morpeth boating also.   Most important yes, very important were the tea parties.   Fresh eggs, salad fresh country butter, bread, cakes and to finish off Strawberries and cream and I have the nerve to tell you this, in 1944.

Ah well, here's hoping.

Cheerio,

SOL.

The Editor regrets that Argus' Contribution has not yet come to hand but <u>will apear</u> in next month's issue.

EXCERPT OF LETTER FROM L.A.C. D. LEVINE, M.E.F.

A journey from Cairo to Tel Aviv per E.S.R. (Egyptian State Railways) under taken by a party of H.M.F. of which I will form a member and so will refer in tale to "we".   After all the necessary applications, passes and warrants had been made and approved the great day arrived and we set off for Cairo Main Station.   It is necessary to arrive a couple of hours prior to the departure of the train. We filter through the barrier and there is a great clamour, bells clang, and whistles blow - prelude to action in every country - but nothing happens. We secure our seats on the train, narrow wooden seats and far from comfortable for a long journey, but who worries we are only service men.   Then the fun begins, swarthy gentlemen with trays pop their heads in at the windows and dash up and down the train attempting to sell at the most ridiculous prices such thing as oranges, chocolates, hard boiled eggs and lemonade, and old and tatter- ed magazines etc.   One of the chaps decides to buy a book and the bidding commences at 30 P.T. (approx. 6/-) for a 6d novel.   He bids the "walad" down to 5 P.T. and then decides not to bother.   This displeases the old Abdul very much and with many curses and glowerings he retreats down the platform only to re-appear a few moments later as if nothing had happened Next comes an enterprising chap in his long "gallabeyah" and offers to change piastres for Palestinian money.   We are suspicious and decide to wait a while.   He disappears but turns up again later and does good busi- ness.   These interludes help to pass the time until the E.S.R. finally decide they have wasted enough time and the train very, very slowly pulls out of the station and we commence our long and tedious journey.   Stops are frequent and for no apparent reason.   When the stops are at a station we have a repetition of Cairo with natives and "chicos" dashing up and down, yelling for "backsheesh".   Slowly we proceed on our way and cross the Sinai Desert and on to Palestine.   Then the desert begins to recede and the country takes on signs of vegetation and then the famous orange and citrus groves are there and the air takes on that strange perfume familiar to these groves.   We forget our weariness and look eagerly forward to reaching our destination.   Soon now we reach the junction and board the "local" for Tel Aviv.   By now the signs are all in English and Hebrew and the language is Hebrew.   Soon we arrive in Tel Aviv, the Jewish city of the world, and almost at once we feel the "freeness" of it all just like our ancestors who also travelled from Egypt to Palestine but by a much different method.   So our journey is ended and we soon find it worth all the trouble we have taken to get there.   Of course we have the return journey - but that is another story.

5.

NEWS LETTER FROM THE HOME FRONT

A new idea was introduced into the Lit on Sunday, 23rd January.
There was a Tea Dance from 4.0 till 8.0. The dancing was interrupted at
5.0 for tea and some fifty people were served sitting down. After tea
the tables were quickly removed and dancing continued. Arthur S. Smith's
band was good and spirits were high. One feature that makes all the
difference to some of the Lit dances is the way the drummer puts over the
novelty dances. He is an ideal organiser though, being in the R.A.F.
he can only come along when he gets a "48". On this occasion he played
in uniform.

Sunday, February 6th saw another discussion, this time on Anti-anti-
Semitism and though there were nearly a score of people there it seems
they did not come to any agreement as to the causes of anti-semitism or
as to the best methods of combating this desease. The discussion, however, was lively and most of those present had something to say. Some
thought that Jews in strange lands were hated no more than any other race
in strange lands. Another opinion was that Palestine was the only solution whilst a third view was that the Nazi element was the sole cause
in this country. But as I have said there was not agreement and the
problem appears to have been left at that. I see that the question of
Palestine being an answer to the Jewish Problems is one of the subjects
set for Prize Paper Night on the 20th February so we may get an answer to
the whole question then.

On February 13th Unita J. Magrill gave a gramophone recital which
might have proved interesting had the radiogram behaved itself. Unfortunately it was not, metaphorically, (but was literally) "up to scratch".
I think the radiogram has served well these years of hard wear - perhaps
an overhaul would improve it sufficiently to keep it turning for the
duration. Good music is scarce, nowadays, in the hall, even the piano
is hopelessly out of tune. I look forward with eagerness to the day
when the lit will once again flourish and maybe then we will see a sparkling new piano and a brand new radiogram - maybe!

Well that brings me about up to date. The Bulletin Secret Service
Correspondent has just cabled me that Hitler has taken up golf - practising
the "Swing" no doubt!

Keep smiling, Forces, and I'll be with you again next month so until
then, best of luck. Yours,

Also After Gen.

Answers to Questions on Page 2.

1. Houdini who was a magician famed all over the world for his perform-
ances on the stage, was the son of an American, Rabbi Weiss. Houdini
adopted the name of the famous French conjurer, Rene Houdin and added an
"i" to the surname.
2. A Jewish benefactor who created schools and institutes for the Negro
in America.
3. Cremieux, one of the most prominent figures in French Jewry, was one
of the men called back in his old age to save France after the downfall
of Napoleon in 1876. He became a Minister of Justice in the new
Republican Court.
4. Originally it was intended to torture the Jewish people out of existence but its effects on the Spanish people were such that it reduced the
population from 11 to 8 millions in less than 200 years at a time when
other nations grew in the same proportion.
5. Heinrich Heine.
6. "Her foundations are based upon the noble hills". Psalms 87, Verse 1.

6.

IN APPRECIATION - By Cpl. N.M. Cohen B.N.A.F.

1.
A word of thanks I'm sure is due,
To each and every one of you,
Who spend much time to send to us
The Bulletin that's now famous.

2.
To Sunderland's Jews all o'er the world
Rosalie's humour is unfurled,
We like it, and we ask for more,
So keep it up Inquisitor.

3.
We're glad to hear the Lit goes strong
With Debates, Mock Trials, Dance & song,
It reminds us when we were young men
So thank you "Also After Gen".

4.
The "father" of the Lit does write
Of mem'ries which do bring delight
To all the folk of the old ecole, (Sol.
You're right, we mean our dear friend

5.
A special word of praise is due
To Argus, for, though not a Jew
He writes for us on sports events
So hats off to such Gentile gents.

6.
And lastly now to end the team,
Our Minister, for whom we've high esteem
He works for us with heart and soul,
And always will till we reach our goal.

7.
We hope that we'll all join you soon,
Perhaps in April, maybe June,
To live in peace for evermore,
So here's to Victory in '44.

EXCERPTS FROM LETTERS.

F/O Dick Cohen, R.A.F. India writes: Whilst on the ship we observed Rosh Hashanah. I went up to see the Adjutant and asked permission to put a notice in Routine orders to the effect that all Jewish personnel on board should report to my cabin. There was another R.A.F. Officer and five airmen. It was not possible to find anymore who had not read the order. We consisted of three men and I from England, the other Officer from Ireland, one airman from Canada and the other from France, so we were a very mixed lot. The O.C. Troops loaned me his sitting room and it was there we had the Service. Fortunately I had with me my Tallis and two Prayer Books. When Yom Kippur arrived we were all separated, we all took our turn to officiate and everything went off very well indeed. I have not met any Jewish fellows up here and as it is a spot of jungle country naturally there is no chance of my doing anything regarding the finding of any other Jewish boys. If an opportunity arises in the future and I can get to know from units whether any Jewish personnel are on the strength, I shall open some type of social place for us, I have no hesitation but to think the authorities will help us.

Lieut. M. Cohen, India Command writes: One Friday night on leaving the David Sassoon Synagogue, I noticed a sign "Judean Club". This conjured up old memories of home and the "Judeans". On making enquiries I was informed that an "Oneg Shabbat" was to be held that evening commencing at 9 p.m. I went along hoping to meet some of the youth of Bombay Jewry and I was not disappointed, although the "Oneg Shabbat" was not as I pictured. I was welcomed to the strains of a radiogram playing some jazz tune - I believe that it was "You are always in my Heart" - and there were one or two couples dancing. Another two were playing table tennis. This seemed all so strange for a Friday night. Gradually the place began to fill up with boys and girls, ages ranging from 17-30 years. They danced, sang and played table tennis. They were such a jolly crowd, one might have been at a "Lit" Social evening. They are mostly descended from Bagdadi Jews. There were one or two Palestinians and I had the opportunity of polishing up my Hebrew. Friday evening is the one big night of the week when the Jewish Youth meet. The Youth are very Zionist minded and several of them expressed to me their

7.

EXCERPTS Continued

wish to go and live in Palestine. Their economic outlook here is very unsettled, as neither the Hindu nor the Muslim will employ them. I've just heard from my O.C. that Mr. Gestetner - the Chairman of the Balfour Services Club in London - is to visit India shortly in connection with the Spiritual Welfare of Jewish Troops.

Sgt. I. Levine, Delhi, India Command writes:- At last Leo and I have met out here and I'm glad to say that the war has failed to change him, either spiritually mentally or physically. I was granted a 48 hrs. pass and so I decided to surprise my old pal who is stationed in Meerut. Can you imagine the expression on his face when quite casually I strolled into his billet, and said "Shalom, Leo". For the first time in all the years I have known him he was at a loss for words. Leo has had the title of the "ROV OF MEERUT" conferred on him by the many Jewish boys with him in his Unit. We have arranged to spend Pesach together in Bombay, so please tell any of the local boys out here we shall be delighted to have a "re-union" in Bombay. Meanwhile we all pray for the "PUKKAH" re-union in dear old Blighty.

Fus. B. Freeman, B.N.A.F. writes: We have a very well known Sunderland footballer here, Charlie Thompson. Some of the soldiers here - non Jews are quite interested in your Bulletin, as soon as it arrives they ask me to let them have a look through it.

A.C.W. R. Pearlman writes: It is good to read all the familiar names and especially to read the letters from the boys abroad. They are all so interesting and might I add excellently written. Can practically see the springing up of some Foreign Correspondents.

S/Sgt. J. Rosenthal, Paiforce writes: I have just completed a tour which took me through the very birth place of our people. Where the Patriarch Abraham disagreed with the religious practices of his father and became the Father of Israel. Where at the point of sacrificing his son Isaac, he saw "a ram caught in the thicket". Only there are no thickets there now, for the very face of the earth has changed and is now too barren to support life. It is my opinion that Hebrew should be taught more than it is. It should be made a living language like French and German and not as Latin and Greek. It would have proved of great practical use to our comrades who now come in to contact with Palestinian, Egyptian, Persian and Iraqi Jews and then one could have discussed the difference in religious practice and why some things are emphasised more in one place than another.

Harold Shochet from Benoni, S. Africa writes: The weather is getting hot and now with the advent of Spring the rainy season is upon us, bringing with it heavy storms of thunder, lightning, hail and winds. Quite an interesting spectacle to see is the whirlwind which carries away with it everything in the near vicinity. The other week I had a rather terrifying experience of running into a cloud of locust. The landscape was completely blotted out and the cloud that was locust covered an area of about 5 to 6 miles, eating up everything green they set eyes on, and I pitied the poor natives striving to drive the pests away from their crops but their efforts only proved futile. A locust is dark green in colour and resembles a small swallow whilst in flight.

Letters were also received from Cpl. N. Berg; Gnr. E. Kolson, Faroes; Sgt. I. Levine, India; Cpl. J. Charlton, India; Fus. B. Freeman, B.N.A.F.; L.A.C. J. Gordon, B.N.A.F.; L.A.C. C. Marks C.M.F.; Nurse R. Olswang; F/O V. Gillis, India; A/C J. Clark and L. Altman.

We have just learnt that Cpl. Sarabouski has been promoted and is now Sgt.

All correspondence to be sent to Rev. S.P. Toperoff, 5 Victoria Avenue, Sunderland.

SUNDERLAND Jewish COMMUNITY — BULLETIN for the FORCES

EDITED AND ISSUED MONTHLY

BY THE MINISTER

AND SENT TO YOU

WITH THE GOOD WISHES OF

YOUR FRIENDS AT HOME.

March, 1944.　　　　　Vol. 2　No. 7.　　　　　Nisan 5704.

　　　To those of you who are overseas I am sending this Passover message in the hope that it may arrive before Pesach.　Passover is essentially a home festival.　Believe me therefore when I tell you that we at home have you constantly in our thoughts.　We have read and heard of the wonderful hospitality that some Communities abroad shower on their visit. ors.　We appreciate the manner in which our co-religionists overseas open their homes to our sons.　But in the words of the old adage "there is nothing like home".　Do you remember the Seder nights, the thrill and expectant excitement of the youngster who is to ask "the four questions"? Perhaps many of you who asked these questions at home are now thousands of miles away amidst strange surroundings.　In the place of the comfort and warmth of home there is the camp, the hut and the barracks with its cold atmosphere.　On Pesach night we shall think of you, we know you shall be thinking of us.

　　　Do you remember that enchanting custom of filling an extra cup known as the cup of Elijah?　How some of us would fix our gaze on it and with breathless anticipation wait for the contents of the cup to disappear mysteriously when the door was opened for Elijah.　This year we shall once again fill Elijah's cup and place it in an honoured position in the centre of the table.　This is no mere empty formalism.　It is indicative of the Jewish Prayer to see the spirit of Elijah rule the earth and usher in an era of eternal peace when "nations will beat swords into plough shares and spears into pruning hooks".　This is what Elijah stands for, for he is the forerunner of the Messiah.　Though Elijah is a legendary figure, to many of us the extra cup will be a reminder of husband, father, son and brother serving away from home.

　　　We look upon you who are serving as the prototype of Elijah.　Do not think this is impossible.　It is said that every private carries the baton of the Field Marshal in his pack.　Every Jew true to his religion carries with him in his heart the spirit of Elijah.　We ask you to be fired with enthusiasm courage and bravery, and to fight for the Jewish ideals of Freedom and Liberty, the foundations of Pesach.　We do hope that wherever you may spend the Passover you will find it possible to spare a few moments and visualise the Home Seder in all its splendour and glory.　May its message and lesson inspire you to work wholeheartedly for the salvation of your people.　If you are fortunate to enjoy the hospit- ality of a co-religionist at a private communal Seder look at the cup of Elijah, we too shall look at ours on the same evening and perhaps the same hour.　In this manner though separated we shall be united in thought and spirit.　Onward then to the new era of Elijah who will attract our modern to an appreciation of the eternal truths of our historic religion.　May this be your last Pesach away from home.　Your parents, wives, relations and friends are looking forward to welcome you with the "Arba Kosos" "the four cups" and drink to your health.

　　　A pleasant and happy Yom Tov to you all.

DO YOU KNOW?

1.　What is Pupka?
2.　Who was Pinchas Rutenberg?
3.　Which was the largest elementary school in the country in the early 18th century?
4.　Which English work was hailed as the bible of the anti-semite till it was superseded by Hitler's "Mein Kampf"?
5.　When and in what country were Jews debarred from being naturalised?
6.　What was the notorious edict of Nicholas 1 of Russia in 1827?.

Answers to the above on Page 4 .

2.

HERE AND THERE.

MAZELTOV
Congratulations to Max Gillis on his marriage to Miss Irene Camrass at Harrogate.

To Dr. Bendet Gordon on his marriage to Miss Joyce Bloom.

To Gerald Behrman on his marriage to Miss Joan Ellenbogen at Liverpool.

Congratulations to Mr. and Mrs. Bergson of 3, Beauclerc Terrace on their Golden Wedding which was celebrated on Sunday, March 19th.

Birth - Congratulations to Mr. & Mrs. Myer Gillis on the birth of a daughter.

We welcome to the Forces Surg. Lieut. George Jacoby R.N.V.R.

We are pleased to record that Miss Alberta Asher has been appointed to the Panel of Headmistress for Infant Schools.

Our young lads are budding debaters as can be seen from the following prizes that have been won at the Bede Collegiate Boys Debating Society. Moses Feld won the Bi-Annual Cup Debate.

Charles Slater won the Officers Prize Debate.

Moses Feldman won the prize at the Freshers Debate.

Miss Phyllis Heilpern M.A., President of the S.Y.Z.A. writes:- The Young Zionist Society continues to meet every Saturday evening. Last summer two of the members passed the Graduate Membership Test of the F.Z.Y. the first achievement of its kind since the good old days when some of you absent chavirim entered for the awe-inspiring examination. During August 1943, Sunderland Jewish Youth showed what it could do in the way of Land work. A batch of 20 members of Habonim went to camp in Wiltshire. Two chavirim did the work on the land and stayed for nearly 3 weeks at the Kibbutz which contains 2 Chaverot originally from Sunderland. During that time they tried potato picking, threshing, stooking, peeling "spuds", washing up for about 50 people at a time and all the other unskilled jobs that are found for inexperienced agricultural workers.

If there are any Zionists who care to tell us of new contacts they have made in any part of the globe we shall be only too delighted to learn of their experiences for we like to know what our absent chaverim are doing just as they seem to like to receive news from the home front.

A local branch of the T.A.C. Trades Advisory Council, has been formed following a visit by Mr. Alec Nathan (Chairman of T.A.C.) from London. The following are the officers - the Rev. S.P. Toperoff, Hon. President; F. Minchom, Chairman; I. Share, Treasurer; and M. Burnley, Hon. Sec., and the following committee of eight: Messrs. H. Book, H. Berg, I. Bernstein, I.E. Cohen, I. Gordon, M. Jacoby, R. Share and D. Rawlinson.

EN PASSANT   -   INQUISITOR

Without appearing to neglect my other faithful admirer, I am compelled to utilise the few words at my disposal in thanking Norman "The Conqueror" for the extremely flattering way in which he brought my name to the fore (and Rosalie's too). The gratitude and humility of spirit which permeate my being I shall never fully repay (received my cheque yet Norman?) and the embarrassment with which I am clothed cannot be expressed in mere words, even by such an exponent of the literary art as I! Unlike a person of similar greatness to myself I do not wish to become "inebriated with the exuberance of my own verbosity".

I cannot conclude without re-iterating how eternally grateful I am for the unexpected (but hardly undeserved) publicity with which my poor effort has been endowed, and if, in the near future, you wish to be mentioned in my columns (id est more than your usual quota) let me know and I will willingly oblige, oh Wonderful Benefactor!

Hi-de-Hi to you all (including those who do not wish for "more").

FLASH

Which two matriarchs enjoyed a recent Home Guard Dance? (for whom the Belles toll!).

Does the Big Shot from Aldershot think 48 hours better than no leave at all?

Is it true that the Benoni Brylcreem King is now known as the Locust Lover?

Who is often seen demolishing fish and chips at a local cafe? (The eyes of the world are on - - - -)

Rumour hath it that a certain nurse from the Eye Infirmary thinks Newcastle students are "Super" (is that the correct spelling?)

How is the Whitley Bay "Storm in a Teacup"?

On dit that the Shipping Magnate does not know whether or no to LOUNGE in the MORNING (which SUITS him?)

Is the occupant of "La Maison Blanche" as important as his counterpart in Washington D.C.

Sorry B.T. is so much out of touch with Home Affairs - why not forward me some pukka gen from abroad?

It gratifies me to find that the Indian Nomad recognises himself, regret no romances in the offing - - - yet.

Does the Sarcastic Sahib of India not think it more advisable to practise spelling more correctly rather than waste valuable Shipping Space writing such "undiluted drivel".

Why is Edinburgh now called the Honeymooners' Haven?

Is Portsmouth cognisant of the honour recently bestowed thereupon. The Surgeon Lieutenant himself!!!!

Could D.C. let me know if he has any volunteers for his William Tell Act. We (the royal) hear that a very important member of the R.A.F. is expected to return to the Mother Country in October, the flags are flying already (Do you recognise this D.L.?)

IN RETROSPECT

The guests had arrived and were standing in groups chatting. Introductions were taking place and dance engagement cards being exchanged. These were folded cards with a small pencil attached by a silk cord. Programmes of the dances for the night were put in convenient places about the hall. Couples would decide which dances they preferred and marked the corresponding number by name or initial on their partner's card. These little contracts were strictly adhered to. The Committees always arranged programmes of dances and chose the music, twenty dances and possibly two extras was the standard number. For a ball commencing at 8 p.m. and finishing at 2 a.m. this was good going. Dancing was pretty strenuous thirty years ago. The orchestra usually seven professional musicians were almost hidden behind a screen of palms, they played strictly to programme and took orders only from the M.C. At his signal the orchestra struck up the opening waltz and the ball had commenced. Dancing went merrily on and the card system of engagements worked well until the refreshment room opened. Then the M.C. or steward were frequently seen looking for someone and helping an anxious dancer to find a lost partner. About 11 p.m. still lemonade and ices were served.

After the lancers or waltz-cotillion, the dancers did full justice to these refreshments. Some retired to the rest room or gallery for a short while. These set dances viewed from the gallery made a beautiful scene. The waltz-cotillion was a pretty dance. The inner circle of ladies in their long graceful many coloured gowns, now waltzing forward, now in reverse, the men making the outer circle of black and white made an unforgettable scene. After the dance the gentleman always led his partner to her seat. Then her fan fluttered as she thanked him and cooled herself. The waltz minuet, a delightful dance, always made one think of knee breeches and lace ruffles as the gentleman bowed from the waist or danced with white gloved hand on hip, his partner responding with a deep curtsey. Here was rythm, grace and dignity. In direct contrast to this dance was the polka. Very often after the polka the lady was escorted to her cloakroom for ladies did not powder their faces in public thirty years ago. The gentleman repaired to his cloakroom and donned a spare collar for he was always immaculate. The last dance always a waltz usually to the tune of "After the Ball is over", marked the end of a happy night. The orchestra played the National Anthem while the dancers stood to attention. Soon the clop, clop of horses hooves and the rumble of cab wheels or the jingle of a hansom cab was heard as the guests departed. The Janitor put out the lights, the M.C's bade Miss Wetherall goodnight and went home tired. And so ended what was soon to become a memory. Yes, a lingering, fragrant memory.

Next months contributation, "I receive a deputation".

Cheerio,
SOL.

Answers to Questions on Page 1.

1. A game of Jewish children especially at Passover. It consists of erecting a small pile of nuts in a corner of the room, the players take stands in opposite corners and try to demolish the pile by throwing nuts at it one at a time and in turn. The player who succeeds wins the game and pockets all the nuts.

2. One of the early Zionist pioneers in Palestine. He was responsible for the great electrical works at the Jordan which is now able to supply all Palestine with light and power.

3. The Jews Free School in the East End of London with more than 3,000 pupils on its roll.

4. "The foundation of the 19th century" by Houston Stewart Chamberlain: It is a work full of "perverted learning, brilliant distortion and audacious assumption".

5. In Rumania the different principalities were united in 1859 but citizenship was confined to Christians, the result being the Jews were still "resident aliens" at the end of the war of 1914-1918.

6. It forced Jews between 17 and 25 to enter military service. The children were taken to the other end of Russia and served for as long as 25 years counting from the age of 18. The conditions in which they lived were filthy and every effort was made to compel those young Jews to renounce their faith and embrace Christianity. There were examples of youths beaten till unconscious, or dead, if they refused baptism.

SEARCHLIGHT ON SPORT   -   By "ARGUS"

I very much regret that owing to so much of my time being occupied in attending the Newcastle Inquiry just about the "Press" time of the last issue, I missed sending in my contribution for the first time since I began contributing.

For some months now football legislators have been considering post war football problems. What their conclusions are may not be available for a while, but whatever they are pre-supposes conditions that may not exist.

I notice that a writer in a Forces weekly newspaper published at home puts forward the novel suggestion that to stop this transfer business clubs should be issued with "ration" coupons for players and when the coupons were used up they could get no more players that season. It's novel, so novel that the writer of it cannot have considered all the complications that might arise. After over 40 years watching first-class Football and 30 years travelling I can see many, and that it is so novel to the point of being absurd.

When full time football is resumed it wont be the scramble for players some people think. In the first place, most clubs financial resources will be at a low ebb because it has cost money to keep going now. The scramble will be for the young players, and here I would say that the most progressive football reform I can think of would be the passing of a law prohibiting the signing of any players under the age of 17. That would stop this business of signing boys when they leave school, putting them on the ground staff - veiled professionalism - and then throwing them overboard at 17 when they have not made the grade.

Sunderland were not alone among the North-East clubs to fail to reach the cup competition proper. Middlesbrough joined them and it was Sunderland who caused Middlesbrough to fail, because they took all four points out of them.

It has been arranged to bring all the North-East clubs into their own cup competition as they fall out of the League Cup. This is in preference to joining the Yorkshire Competition which Sunderland won last season. The objection against this competition is that Yorkshire clubs drew small home gates and shared in much bigger gates when they visited the North East. The North East Clubs consider they will be helping each others finances more by playing a competition amongst themselves instead of providing money for Yorkshire clubs. It seems a more sensible idea and reduces travelling. _____

NEWS LETTER FROM THE HOME FRONT

The Annual Prize Paper Night of the Lit was held on Feb. 20th. Sol Jovinski adjucated and there were four competitors. Esther (Girlie) Cowan being in the chair. First was Aubrey Gordon who spoke on "What shall we do with Hitler." He was followed by Theo Benjamin on "Recent Politics", then Jack Louis on "Science - blessing or curse" and lastly Philip Winberg on "What I want to see after the war". Awarding the prize to the first competitor, Sol said that the show put up was a great improvement over the last year. Pointing out that keenness was more important than numerical strength, he said that he was confident about the future of the Lit. I too, was pleased to see four entrants this time, for last year there were only two and the year before three. Does this show an increase in the literary ability of the Lit? I hope it does, and certainly believe it is significant that the Lit is still going strong despite so many difficulties.

The Lit had a great success the following week. There was a surprise party - bring your own grub. It started off with musical chairs which was great fun. As you were caught out you went along to the table to get your tea. The eats, as usual, were plentiful, the thirty or so guests having brought food generously. Then older games followed - spot

6.

and elimination dances, Ring on a String, Cohoots and others.   One very great attraction, enjoyed by all, was "I want to be an actor" exceedingly well organised by Rosalie Gillow.   The whole affair was very jolly indeed and everyone left at 10.30 after a really enjoyable evening.   These parties are always successful - not only socially but also financially - so let's have more of them.

On March 5th, there was a mediocre social.   It was a cold day and attendance was small.   But this was made up for by the Purim dance on the following Sunday which was an outstanding success.   It was a tea-dance commencing at 4.30.   Over fifty people were served with a splendid tea and, as usual, many came later.   The band was Arthur S. Smith's again and everyone had a jolly time.   It finished early, however, and this is, in many respects, a disadvantage for it leaves the better part of an evening - and a Sunday evening at that - blank.

That's all the local news for now but have you heard about the new navigator who was directing bombing over Berlin?   The flack was coming up thick and fast as he gave instructions - "Left, right, right, no good, run in again".   The Pilot obeyed and then "Right, right, left, left, too late try again."   The pilot had a nasty look on his face as he ran over the target for the third time. The navigator tried his best "Right, right left, left," pause "back a bit".

Best of luck Forces,
Yours,
Also After Gen.

EXCERPTS FROM LETTERS.

The Faeroes, Customs & Characteristics of the People.   By Charles Kolson.
A wedding in the Faeroes is an occasion to be remembered for many years to come by all those who attend it.   Great preparations in advance are made by all the relations and friends to feed and entertain in every available space of their homes, people of the locality whether invited or not.   It differs from the English custom, no rings, are passed, the service is according to the Lutheran Church, the bride and bridegroom cross hands and together with hymns and offerings the Pastor pronounces them man and wife.   The procession reforms and returns to the home of the bride, or if it is a big gathering to the local hall or Missionhaus where the wedding feast is set.   People crowd in about 11 p.m. some to watch, and others to participate in the famous wedding dance led by the Bride and Groom.   This one dance goes on as long as 45 minutes, this is followed by other dances, during which ancient Faeroese songs are chanted by all.   The amazing vitality of the Faeroese could not be better illus- trated than at these festivities where many do not go to bed for 48 hours on end, and are dancing all through the night in their national dress, it is a most picturesque sight to see.

Other interesting customs are those which involve the cutting and gathering of peat, the driving into special areas of all sheep for the cutting of wool.   Most of the sheep are killed in September, all the inhabitants share the kill which is divided out evenly in the village. The majority of the villages in the Faeroes are very pretty, generally sheltered from the stormy North Atlantic, at the edge of the mountain sides and most of the houses are constructed chiefly of wood, with turf covered roofs, and strings of dried fish and mutton hung around.   With the stormy climate never two days alike, and practically no vegetation through out the centuries, the Faeroese have battled against Nature for an exist- ence.   Of course since the British Force has been here conditions have improved, and with imports etc. life for these hardy people has eased considerably.   Through the medium of the Bulletin, I wish all old friends at home and overseas all the best of luck and a speedy and safe return to dear old Sunderland.

Sgt. I. Levine, Delhi , Cantt, India. writes: I was rather interested to read your article in the November issue of the Forces Bulletin. You we asking whether this war had brought about "a return to religion" well, inclined to think that it has, and I should like to keep you in the picture with regards to what is being done in this particular part of In There are many service men and women here, representatives of most of th United Nations - "Yanks", Aussies, Poles, French, Czechs, Canadians, Gr Palestinians, and of course a large section from the old home country. one would expect there is a large percentage of Jews and when we met in the cafes and canteens of India's Capital City, we recognise each other fellow Jews and brothers in arms and after the usual "SHALOM, ISH YEHUDI many friendships were born.   It was the common wish that we, the youth of the United Jews of the world, should get together and if possible hol Services every Friday evening in New Delhi. The local authorities were pleased to co-operate and a delightful building was placed at our dispos so that out here, so very far from our native lands, we could find that happiness that springs from attending a Jewish Service.   Maybe being se arated for so long from all that is dear to us has given us a more real istic aspect of the things that are worth while in this life;   perhaps th lesson of the tragedy of German Jewry has made us realise that complete assimilation would spell the ultimate doom and final disappearance of Jewry but undoubtedly there is a wave of revivalism and "Jew consciousne amongst the youth of Jewry out here in India.   Last Friday evening ther were seventy or eighty people present at the Service which was conducted by an American "doughboy". The service was really delightfully refreshi and was conducted entirely in English, apart from "ADON-OLAM" which is always sung with great gusto at any Jewish Army service. During the ser vice I was seated next to a Junior Commander in the W.A.C. (I), the Indi equivalent of our A.T.S. She is one of the many black Jews who have rallie to the Cause and like us, hopes that Nazism may soon be history instea of a menace.   As you know there is a community of Black Jews who settle in COCHIN way back in the 11th century, they are hardly distinguishable i appearance from the Indians, but preserve the customs and dietary laws o Judaism.   In addition there are the white Jews of the State of Cochin wh settled there some 2000 years ago, but unfortunately they have adopted th "caste" system of India.   They recognise the black Jews as practising the same religion, but socially, (like the Hindus and Moslems) they look up their black brothers as an inferior caste, and never inter-marry with th or attend their Synagogues.

Cadet A. Bloomberg, R.A.F. writes: The planes we fly in are Tiger-Moths which are bi-planes with a very frail appearance on the ground but once they are in the air they feel as safe as a battleship on a smooth sea. When I first went up I didn't know what kind of a sensation to expect, bu once I was in the plane I soon knew - before I knew where I was there we were 4000 feet up in the air, looking down at the ground which looked ver unreal, but the feeling up there is marvellous, it is as if the plane is hanging on nothing but it feels very solid for all that.   The best feeli I've had yet was on a fine day about a week ago with the sun shining and lots of cloud called Srato-Cumulus, this looks like cotton wool, we were flying above this cloud, it was a marvellous feeling.

Nurse R. Olswang writes: Where I am there are 230 V.A.D's and being in th Navy we go on "watch" instead of "duty" sleep in "cabins" or "bunks" which surprisingly enough are very comfortable.

Letters were also received from Sgt. Sarabouski, India; F/Sgt.Basil Taylor, India; CFM G. Magrill; L.A.C. Marks, C.M.F.; L. Altman, Fus. B. Freeman, B.N.A.F.; Cpl. Charlton, India; Lt. M. Cohen, India; W/O N.Good man, E.A. Command; Sub.Lt. B. Gould, W. Africa; Pte. S.Mincovitch; L.A.C Z. Gillis, L.A.C. J. Gordon, B.N.A.F.; A. Landau, R.A.F., P/O D.Cohen, India.

EDITED AND ISSUED MONTHLY

BY THE MINISTER

AND SENT TO YOU

WITH THE GOOD WISHES OF

YOUR FRIENDS AT HOME.

ril 1944.   Vol. 2 No. 8.   Iyar 5704.

The other day an interesting meeting took place in Sunderland
rganised by the local Council of Social Service.   The Council convened
meeting of Christians and Jews to hear an address from the Rev. W.W.
impson, Organising Secretary of the Council of Christians and Jews. The
ev. Dr. Allen, Lecturer in Theology and Religious Knowledge at Kings
ollege, Newcastle, was in the Chair.   There was a representative gather.
ng which included members of the Anglican Church, the Roman Catholic, the
ree Church Society of Friends and the Jewish Community.   No one can gain
ay the fact that this is a move in the right direction.   The conflict
3tween Church and Synagogue with disastrous results to both has been
llowed to go on far too long and the new Council hopes to arrest this and
ridge the gulf between the two Communities.

Now that Jews and Christians are faced with a common danger, the evil
: Nazi teachings, we should join hands and fight not only the common enem
it also the prejudices that are deeply ingrained in the hearts and minds
: many who are still suspicious of the Jew.   Edmund Burke wrote: "When
id men combine, the good must associate".

It is a paradox of life that the forces of evil are united whilst the
irces for good are divided and even loathe to make common cause.   Why
iould not the good of all races and creeds join, determined to uproot the
ils of mankind?

There is diversity in Nature, even in the same species we find a vary-
g number of types.   This same diversity we find also amongst human bein
have so far not arrived at that stage of universalism when we shall all
ink alike nor is it even desirable.   Diversity in nature as in human
ings is healthy. We are reminded of the famous Rabbinic saying so pregna
th thought and meaning - "In the same way that there are no two faces
actly alike in every detail so there are no two minds which agree on ever
tail."   Christian and Jew can each pursue his own philosophy of thought
t they can both combine and associate to bring about a friendship which
ould be based not on sympathy alone, but on understanding and mutual
spect.   Let us open our homes and our hearts, let us stress the things
have in common rather than those which divide us.   The Jewish historia
sephus rightly remarked; "secrecy amongst friends is prohibited for
iendship implies an entire confidence without any reserve".

The Council of Christians and Jews must cultivate this friendship
ich should be based on a frank understanding of our common problems. A
ginning has been made, we trust that the hands of the organisers will be
rengthened by the rank and file of both communities and that the well-
shers of all sections of the Community will rally and respond to the call
conscience and reason.

On the eve of the Second Front we ask our Christian friends to join us
l fortify the home front so that our lads may return to a world not torn
the conflicting ideologies of a distracted humanity but to a world
iented by ties of lasting friendship.   In the words of the Prophet
achi - "Have we not one God, hath not one Father created us all?"

DO YOU KNOW?

At what age did Einstein, the great Jewish physicist first propound the
ory of Relativity?
When did Jews first come to China?
Who is a pioneer of Trade Unionism?
Who was one of the greatest of Italy's Liberal Prime Ministers?
Who are the FALASHAS?
Which is the only entire Jewish city in the world?

Answers to above questions on P. 4.

2.
HERE AND THERE!

MAZELTOV!
Congratulations to Rev. and Mrs. Burland on the birth of a son.
We welcome to the Forces Aaron Goldblatt S.B.A. (Sick Berth Attendant) and
Radio Officer Victor Goldberg.

At the annual India Cup debate of the Bede Boys' School Debating
Society, Charles Slater was awarded the Cup.

The inaugural meeting to launch the United Palestine Appeal was held
at the residence of Mr. A. Merskey who was in the Chair. Ald. J. Cohen
addressed the meeting and the following officers were elected: A. Merskey
Chairman; The Rev. S.P. Toperoff and Mrs. M. Joseph Vicechairmen; Messrs.
H. Book and M. Jacoby, Joint Treasurers; and Miss Phyllis Heilpern, Hon.
Sec. Pro tem. Mr. Merskey opened the appeal with a donation of £100

The Council of Christians and Jews held a preliminary meeting in
Sunderland when discussion took place on the advisability of forming a
local branch of the Council. The meeting decided that four representatives
of the Church meet four representatives of the Jewish Community. His
Worship the Mayor, Councillor Milburn J.P., who attended the meeting
volunteered to help and offered the Mayor's Parlour for the first informal
meeting.

IN RETROSPECT.

I had been home just over a year when a deputation of young people
called on me with an invitation to rejoin the 'Lit' committee and help them
in their work. I asked them to return after I had had a much needed
holiday. They did. This deputation was headed by Gertrude Magrill, the
Hon. Secretary. My impressions of those youngsters were they were very
earnest. They wanted to raise the status of the Lit. They were very
desirous that the reputation of the Jew be good and a shining example to
all fellow citizens. They were sincere. They were not shy and last but
not least they had a charming and very efficient secretary. I rejoined
the Lit.
I shall never forget the Committee meetings held at the Secretary's
home in Belle Vue Park. When the agenda was just routine, the members sat
in a half circle in front of the fire, some on chairs, some on hassocks,
others on the hearth rug, but I always had the arm chair. When the business was important we sat round the dining table. Every one was very formal,
polite and business-like. Much spade work was done and mistakes of bye-
gone years were cleared away.
A Policy was clearly defined. Head quarters were moved to the Boiler
Makers' Hall, Norfolk Street and the Lit was ready for action. The syllabus
promised symposiums, debates, a couple of supper dances, Mock Parliaments
and Elections. Zionism was much in our minds then as now, the Jewish
question was also discussed.
I wish to tell you a little story. Murray Muscat (one of our
stalwarts) stood as the Yiddish Member for Whitechapel during the Mock
Parliament, his speech was entirely in Yiddish. His opponent replied, also
in Yiddish. A beautiful telling speech but he got stuck for words during
his very last argument. Thereupon Murray Muscat jumped up, finished his
speech for him (in Yiddish) and sat down. Such was the spirit of the
members who were soon to fight for the life of the Lit.
Cheerio,
SOL.

3.

EN PASSANT   -   INQUISITOR.

Amid all the rejoicings of Pesach when Everybody who was Anybody home, my thoughts were straying poignantly towards the Also Rans who "unavoidably detained at the office". It is to those unfortunate fe I address the meagre and inadequate words at my command to make them realise that they are not deprived of all the good things of Life! names were often reverently whispered from ruby lips to ruby lips, a tear would drop from a limpid orb and a moist square inch of cambric be applied daintily to the offending tear-duct! Sunderland denuded of its cream of male and female youth presents a pathetic picture which the outcasts of society are only too ready to appreciate. In a few we when the 'ban' is suspended Sunderland will be rejuvenated once more the streets will be thronged with youth at its happiest, sparkling eye and animated faces will once more be the order of the day. And we, th lesser fry, will take our normal back seats. Alas! Forgive the bre of my effort........ but....... even a well runs dry! He-de-hi till the next time!

FLASH

Rumour hath it that a certain "BIG WHITE DOCTOR" is chloroforming all insects - oh! to be an insect now that April's there!

On dit that the new "Lit" chairman was recently STRANDed in London- ho the feminine interest there? Aha!

They say that the Sunderland Darby and Joan have recently severed 'operations'? (The Doctor's Dilemma?)

We were interested to hear that the "Rock" of Gibralter was recently bestowed with a pair of silk stockings - what a small foot he has!

D.A. was home again - hurray!

So Romance has finally "caught up" with the Algerian Shiek - it's cert an extremely small world!

Does the coinciDENTAL photographer take a personal interest in his subject(s)?

Who spent an enjoyable Seder in Leeds? But there's no place like Home alas(s)!

On dit that a new Brid(g)e Instructress has come to the fore(four?) - A Daniel come to judgment!

Who refuses all invitations for Friday evening (but not Shabbos???)

Rumour hath it that a certain "deb" has a great regard for her American Cousin........? (Let us divulge no more).

Who reports news in brief (or should we say in brief-case???)

We wonder if C.M.M. has forgotten us - no more interesting periodicals are we out of favour?

On dit that "William Tell" has been promoted to the ranks of the Elite, and is his wife pleased?

It comes to our ears that our American friends were responsible for causing much disappointment in Sunderland recently (Who ordered "officer only"?)

How is the Gainsborough Lady-killer?

On dit that a certain vital force prefers Scotland to the Faroes .... Why?

4.
Answers to Questions on Page 1.

1. 23 years old.
2. It is not known definitely but according to Chinese tradition the first immegration dates back to 230 B.C.E. and it is therefore even probable that Chinese Jews are descendants of the lost ten tribes.
3. Ferdinand Lassalle 1825-1864. His enthusiasm for his race can be seen from the following note he wrote in his diary at the age of 14 - "I would not even shrink from the scaffold if I could restore my people to a position of respect among the nations. Whenever I indulge in childish dreams I love to picture myself sword in hand at the head of Jews leading them in a fight for the recovery of their independence."
4. Luigi Luzzatti 1841-1927 was a Jewish political refugee who became Professor of Political Economy at Milan, Minister of the Treasury and Agriculture and finally Prime Minister.
5. An African group of Jews in Abyssinia. They are negro Jews whose conversion to Judaism is supposed to date from the return of the Queen of Sheba from her visit to King Solomon. They maintained an autonomous Jewish kingdom until the 17th century when they were defeated by the Christian Abyssinians. Today they number about 50,000.
6. Tel Aviv in Palestine arose in 1907 from sand dunes and today has a population of 135,000.

SEARCHLIGHT ON SPORT - by ARGUS

We are near the end of April and in another fortnight the curtain will be drawn upon the season 1943-44. So I may devote a few minutes to a backward glance.

I have always maintained that you can never have a really strong senior team if you have not the reserve strength to back them up in an emergency. That is what is happening at Roker Park - the reserve strength is not there to replace men who are not available for first team duty. Consequently the football we have been watching from some Sunderland sides since the turn of the year has not been above pre-war North Eastern League standard. Whatever the potentialities of some of the reserve players most of them are very young and many of them show little sign of making the necessary grade.

Without Carter the attack is not a scoring force and without Carter and Hastings it has no pretentions of being a class side. The position is more serious than most people imagine. We have had four and a half years of war and there is no sign of it ending. All the pre-war players are that much older. Alex Hastings has no intention of playing after the war; Gorman has shown definite signs of the passing years and cannot be regarded as anything more than a reserve in post war football; Alex Hall won't come back into the game.

And so one could go on. I appreciate that most clubs are in a similar position, but that does not help us and Manager Murray won't view the prospects with any great confidence unless there is greater promise from reserve players.

Although Eves has not maintained early promise, I consider he will make the grade when he is trained. At present he works much overtime and when he is not doing that he is on Home Guard duty. Bircham is another player who will do well later and Harry Bell if he strengthens up.

6.

EXCERPTS FROM LETTERS.

Gnr. A. Abrahams, Persia-Iraq Forces writes: As is to be expected the life of the Jews and their customs are very much different from ours in England but their position is far from being an envious one. There is still a considerable hate smouldering from the days of the Iraqi Quisling (Raschid Ali). Not much English is spoken by many of them and strange again not so many speak Hebrew so that at first conversation and making friends wasnt too easy. Two years ago Jews suffered very heavily at the hands of the Quislings, every crime and atrocity was committed against then and a goodly number left in abject poverty and misery. No Hebrew is allowed to be taught and none whatever printed on cards, wedding invitations etc. Arabic is only to be used, several other restrictions are imposed on them which leaves them in a none too enviable situation. There are a few wealthy Jews who do all they can for the more unfortunate ones, every Friday the poor go from shop to shop and collect their money so that every Shabbos they will be provided for and none go without. One young Jew was pretty friendly with me and acted as a guide taking me through the Jewish Quarter. The Shools were typical of the Eastern buildings courtyard (open air) in the centre and balcony running round the building, nothing much downstairs, upstairs divided into rooms, an Eastern custom is to sit oh carpets and use them as walls and decorations. The Sefer Torah is identical the world over, but when rolled is kept in a metal cylinder and padlocked, everything of sacred value is kept behind barred and locked doors. The term "Rabbi" isn't used, "Chochom" is how they call a Rabbi. One of the wealthy Jews of Baghdad has built a school for Blind Jewish Children, this is quite a tribute.

Sgm. I Rosenthal, India Command writes: My copy of the December Bulletin reached me this afternoon as I sat resting - for a change - somewhere in the heart of the Burmese jungle, trying to avoid the heat of the fiercest sun I have ever known. Now at midnight, in my dugout - where I am fortunate enough to be at work all night - I can digest the contents of the mag. and suffer at my leisure a warranted attack of nostalgia. I'm in the thick of this campaign now, battling against the hazards of God and man, and life on the whole is one big struggle. We are becoming accustomed to this existence though, and Tommies being generally adaptable, we can still see the bright side of the toughest situation. When I read of events at home I must admit to feeling rather sorry for myself but at the same time I realise how imperative it is that we get this thing cleared up quickly so that we can return to enjoy the peace we so richly deserve - and we shall enjoy it!

A.C.1 Winberg C. writes: I have become secretary to my Commanding Officer my work is most interesting and I enjoy it a lot insomuch that I get all the 'gen' and I enjoy the trust that is placed in me. After duty hours, there is little to do in this place, but I manage to occupy my time organising fortnightly Whist Drives and Dances, cinema shows, weekly discussion groups and twice weekly Music Circles and I have been appointed Part Time Teacher of Musical Education, which I find most interesting. We simply play records, both light and better stuff and try to give an explanatory note on each. They have also appointed me Chairman of the Welfare Committee. Tonight we commence a series of tournaments, chess, billiards, draughts, darts, table tennis etc.

Sgt. I. Levine, India Command, writes: I must tell you how I spent the happiest Pesach I have had since my last one in England, way back in '41, and how thanks to our American fellow-Jews, and comrades in arms, all the British Troops in this area had the pleasure of participating at really excellent Kosher "Sedorim". At the last Friday evening Service, the

7.

American Jewish Chaplain - Rev. Horowitz, from New York, extended an invitation to all British service personnel present, to attend the Pesach Services and Sedorim which were being held at the Marina Hotel, one of Delhi's "de luxe" English hotels. Accordingly quite a crowd of us turned up, and were made very welcome, and in fact "guests of honour" by our American bretheren. Not being able to obtain many traditional Pesach dishes locally the Americans flew out from the States such items as Matzo, wine , "ingberlach" and also several hundred "Hagadahs", and so after a pleasant service we sat down to a Seder which was complete in every detail except that we were in a strange land, away from our loved and dear ones. The Chaplain solved the problem of who should ask the "four questions" by calling on the most junior member of the most Junior "Service", and so an American Pte. of the Medical Corps asked the traditional "fir kashes". The service was conducted mainly in English - with a very strong New York accent and was "covered" by Army photographers. With characteristic thoroughness, the cameramen asked the "Rabbi" to "Hold that pose", as he was holding the shankbone and narrating the story! It was indeed a pleasure to be amongst fellow Jews to celebrate our festival of Passover, and for me this was the very first Kosher Pesach since 1941 so you will realise what joy I felt at being present. In all, nearly 200 Servicemen attended, including 20 British soldiers, and we hope to arrange regular Shabbos morning services. The Hagadah, the time hallowed story of a Hitler of over 3,000 years ago, really has inspirational qualities, and just as Passover, the festival of Freedom, commemorates the deliverance of Israel from bondage, so, let us hope it will signal the final Victory of the forces of Freedom in this year of 1944.

Lt. M. Cohen, India Command writes: This is "Louis Bromfield 11" calling the Bulletin. Thank Inquisitor for the compliment (?) although no doubt if the original Louis Bromfield heard of it, he would sue the Bulletin and Inquisitor for libel. It is good to see that quite a number of the lads are writing to the Bulletin and no doubt you are not troubled like other editors searching for news to print. Somehow reading these interesting letters in the Bulletin seems to shorten the vast distances which separate us all. I'm managing to keep quite fit and well these days T.G. and have my game of football about twice a week. My Troop has quite a good European and African team. The Africans are very amusing, I'd sooner be with them than any Indian unit. They're very loyal and respectful and despite their occasional grumbles are very fine soldiers. It is hard to believe that over 50% were illiterate before they joined up and we have taught them to read numbers and some even a few words of English. We've taught them quite a bit of English, but I like to chat with them in their native tongue. - Hansa.

Sgt. Sarabouski India writes: Since leaving home I have met Jews of all types, South African, German, Russian, Baghdadis, Benei Israels., Karachi, and even Pathan Jews from the North West Frontier who wear huge turbans and baggy trousers whom one would never take for Jews. I am convinced that one of the strongest things in the world is the Jewish bond which unites all Jews of all types.

F/Sgt. Basil Taylor India, writes: For the last few weeks I have been stationed up near the North West Frontier but expect to move again at any time. The story books tell us that this district is exceptionally rich in history and adventure. Certainly the natives seem very war-like fellows and often can be seen with a sword or rifle.

Letters were also received from: L.A.C. I.Davis; A.C.W. S. Penn, Nurse R. Olswang; Cpl. P. Mincovitch; Fus. B. Freeman, B.N.A.F.; Pte. L. Levin Indian Command; F/O D. Cohen, India; Cpl. N.M. Cohen, B.N.A.F.,

All correspondence to be sent to Rev. S.P. Toperoff, 5, Victoria Avenue Sunderland.

*Edited and issued monthly by the Minister
and sent to you with the good wishes of
your friends at home.*

May 1944,   Vol. 2   No. 9   Sivan 5704

1st Anniversary of the Battle of Warsaw.

On the first night of Passover 1943 German soldiers entered the Ghetto of Warsaw with the intention of wiping it out.   The same plan put into practise on so many former occasions was to be used once again.   The Ghetto was barred and bolted, none went out and none came in.   The German could not visualise any of the ammunitions or armour being smuggled in under their eyes.   In addition the Jews were sapped of all their energy by the meagre supply of food, and daily beatings were no encouragement to live on.   In the minds of the Nazis the Jew would be praying for death, would have lost his urge to live.   Imagine therefore their surprise when the six tanks which entered the ghetto in the stillness of the night were met with a sustained volley of fire.   The Jews of the Warsaw Ghetto, were no longer passive resisters, for the first time in the history of Nazi enslavement Jews passed from passive resisters to active defenders of their people and religion, there was mutiny in the Jewish Ghetto.   The Jews rose against their erstwhile masters.   They knew they could not possibly win against the might of the German war machine, they knew they were hemmed in on all sides, they knew they could not rely on outside help they know they were doomed to extinction, but they were all steeled to fight to the last the tyranny and butchery of the taskmasters of Hitlerism

Every house was converted into a strong point, every boy and girl was instructed in the use of weapons, and trenches and underground shelter were hewn out with feverish haste.   The Jewish Ghetto was no longer ruled by the truncheon, pistol and rifle, it was no longer full of prisoners serving a life sentence.   The Ghetto became a fortress, a beleaguered town.   Here there was unity of purpose, here was opportunity to show the world that though not famed for their martial spirit, Jews could rise to the occasion and with Maccabean fortitude and selfless devotion to duty 46,000 Jews girded themselves to receive what they knew would be sure extinction - the final assault.

There was no surrender in the Jewish Ghetto of Warsaw.   Here in the Jewish Stalingrad, Jews fought and battled alone, cut off from the rest of the world, cut off from all supplies for six long weeks.   After six weeks fierce fighting, the Ghetto was liquidated and flattened into a wilderness The Ghetto of Warsaw in which Jews had lived since the 14th century - Warsaw which boasted of a Jewish culture famed throughout the world, with its museums, schools, colleges, libraries, Warsaw with its 83 Jewish newspapers and periodicals is now obliterated, it is a heap of ruins and rubble;   but from its ghost-like walls there arises the indestructible Jewish spirit.

On this day of mourning and prayer, we ask not for pity or even sympathy, a people that can fight with bare fists against terrific odds rather than die an ignoble death, a people that heroically faces sure death, a people that can proudly challenge the invincible might of the Wehrmacht - a people that can obstinately cling to life in the midst of persistent tortures - such a people does not need pity.   We demand recognition, respect and understanding.   The Jews of Warsaw gained no posthumous decorations, but what does it matter their lives will not have been sacrificed in vain, if as a result, the world will be ready to . understand the Jew and love their neighbours as themselves.

The Martyrs of Warsaw died so that Nazism be uprooted from the heart of men.   They fought and died so that Anti-Semitism be outlawed as a crime against humanity.   The Jews of Warsaw fought and died so that Christians freed from the shackles of an imprisoned Ghetto may be stirred

2.

swifter action, not only to destroy Hitlerism, but what is perhaps more important, to uproot the canker of hatred and suspicion against the Jew, and to bury for all times the hatchet of the anti-Jewish bogey which is a figment of the imagination certainly, and not based on fact or reason. Of this I am certain, the Jews of Warsaw did not fight and sacrifice their lives so that their Jewish brothers in arms should be insulted, kicked and bludgeoned by Officers and rank and file of the Polish Army in England, because of their Jewishness. Is such action in the Polish Army today the reward for the heroism of the Jewish Ghetto fighting on Polish soil for Polish independence? Then Polish Jewish soldiers would rather die than stay on in the Polish army. They are ready to face the most hazardous experiences of any front in the English army with its high code of honour and justice, rather than be members of an ungrateful people who openly exhibit racial descrimination.

We are fighting for our self-respect, we are fighting to destroy root and branch, the Fascist philosophy of life inborn in the hearts, not only of the Germans but of all our enemies and ill-wishers. At a time when we are preparing to make decisive blows to overthrow the enemy we should also be determined to demand a world free from malice, jealousy and misconception, a world which will not forget its heroes, Christian or Jew, who have laid down their lives for a better, cleaner civilization, a world which will think of the Jew not in terms of weakness or vacillation, but in terms of courage, valour and bravery.

Christians of the world, we ask you to join us in our struggle for freedom. May God harken to our prayers. Let us salute the Jewish Martyrs of Warsaw.

DO YOU KNOW?

1. Which branch of the Jewish Community styled Churches as a Nation in England?
2. When was Sunderland first represented on the Jewish Board of Deputies?
3. When was a Jew deprived of attaining the Aldermanic Chair in England?
4. Which noble lord presented to the Jews a piece of land on which to erect a Synagogue?
5. When were Jews first eligible to sit in Parliament?
6. What is the Histadrutt in Palestine?

Answers to the above questions on Page 5.

HERE AND THERE

Mazeltov
Congratulations to:-
Engagements - Miss Bertha Rosen, B.A., to Lieut. J. Priceman R.A.M.C. of Leeds.
Cpl. I.W. Brewer R.A.S.C., to Nurse Rita Olswang, V.A.D.
Promotions - Sgt. I. Levine to Warrant Officer or known as Sub.Commander in the Ordnance Corps.
L.A.C. I Davis to Corporal.

To celebrate the Golden Wedding of Mr. and Mrs. Max Bergson of 3 Beauclerc Terrace, the members, relations and friends of the family have planted in their name 50 trees in the Childrens Forest in Palestine.

We are pleased to put on record that Mr. S. Wicks is the first Jew in Sunderland to receive a commission in the Home Guard.

We regret to announce that Argus, our regular contributor, is now in hospital recovering from a recent operation. The Editor and readers of

3.

the Bulletin extend to Argus their best wishes for a speedy and full return to normal health.

We had in our midst for a short time a Jewish Bevan boy, Harry Berkovitz of London. His call-up came a few weeks prior to his sitting for the London Metriculation. Though not allowed to carry on his studies he expects to sit for the examination at the end of his training for the pits. During his stay in Sunderland he was the guest of Mr. & Mrs. I Cohen.

The Annual Meeting of the Sunderland and South Shields Refugee Committee took place at the Hostel, when a report on the year's work was given by Mr. J. Behrman as Chairman and Mr. M.B. Wolf as Hon. Secretary.

A successful meeting was held in the Communal Hall under the auspices of the United Palestine Official Committee with Mr. A. Merskey in the Chair. Professor Norman Bentwich formerly Attorney General in Palestine, and special advisor to the Emperor of Abyssinia, an international jurist, and a famous scholar, spoke on the situation in Palestine from which he recently returned. Mr. John Mack, Jewish member of Parliament for Newcastle-under-Lyme, who has put up such a spirited defence for the Polish Jews, in Parliament gave an illuminating and inspiring address before a good audience.

A special service to commemorate the "Battle of Warsaw" was held at the Ryhope Road Synagogue on Monday evening. A number of Christians were present. A few excerpts of the Minister's address will be found on Page 1.

A new circle conducted by the Minister and held at the Ryhope Road Synagogue meets every Saturday evening before Mincha. The following is a time table of the past four weeks. Mr. Ezekiel Gillis gave a paper on "The 17th century Jewish Life in Poland". Mr. Aubrey Gordon opened a discussion on "The right approach of the Jew in his contacts with the non-Jew". The Minister lectured on "The Origin and History of the Jewish Board of Deputies". Moses Feld opened a discussion on "The advisibility or otherwise of the Jewish Day School". Very interesting discussions took place at all the meetings, which we hope will prove to be successful.

EN PASSANT   -   THE INQUISITOR.

Lying contemplatively (and contentedly) in my narrow iron bedstead a kaleidoscope of past events flits before my fast dimming orbs and I begin to realise what exciting happenings are taking place in our very hometown. Engagements and marriages in galore! An involuntary sigh escapes my trembling lips as the latter thought eventually permeates my none too active brain. Whilst trying to control my features, I gaze round my garret, (a poor thing, but mine own) the watery wintry sun is manfully trying to enter the square inch of none too clean window, but only succeeds in baring, oh, so shamefully, the much faded wall-paper, the well-worn rugs the tarnished trophies (for past "scoops") -- ah! but I could continue in like vein indefinitely, why should I bore you with the sordities of my very existence! Whilst lolling in your luxurious surroundings spare me a kindly thought. . . . .and on that philosophical note I must say farewell. Hi-de-hi to you all.

FLASH
Rumour hath it that the Upper Ten are now all FLEAing to Cairo - Keep up the good work!
We hear that the Big Shot of Aldershot is having an extremely good time at the moment - - - can you guess why?

4.

<u>FLASH</u> (Continued)

Is it a STERN necessity, to wear corduroy suits? Suits him!
Are the commissioned ranks of the R.A.F. and W.A.A.F. still frantically
corresponding? Dancing? Enjoying life?
Who has been given rapid promotion in India? W.O! W.O! W.O. is he!
Which important character did Vicki Baum omit when composing "Grand Hotel"
- - why Jenny WREN of course!
We hear that celebrations of previously unknown extravagance were held in
honour of our Desert Hero - VICTORious to the end!
Has Norman the Conqueror been keeping the postman as busy as usual? Parcels?
Poems? Pleas?
Why has Barnard Castle become so dull lately. Go South young man, go
South!
So the Chester Casanova has taken the plunge at long last! Making <u>one</u>
girl happy - but hundreds miserable!!
On dit that the R.A.F. have co-opted the biggest brain power into the
C.I.D. - no UNIFORMity about this job.
Has "Karl Marx" any more problems to divulge? Or periodicals to forward?
We hear that a recently qualified Doctor (now in the Forces) was the
Newcastle R.I. Lady Killer! Did the nurses TWIN(e) themselves round his
heart strings?

IN RETROSPECT.

I have a photograph of a group of Members and Friends of the "Lit"
taken at a picnic held during 1921. It was the first open air function
since the end of the 1914-1918 War. Among others in the picture are the
"Lit" Stalwarts, Gertrude Magrill, Mary, Nathan and Murray Muscat, Bessie
Cohen (Mrs.Carmel), the Rabin Sisters, Sarah Cohen (Mrs. Slater), Abe
Mincovitch, Rev. and Mrs. Muscat, Joe Topaz, Jos. Rubin, Jack Cohen (now
Alderman) and his young lady now his wife.

Isaac Rosenberg and Elsie Louis (Now Mrs. Rosenberg) who copies
most of these articles on her visits to me in Hospital. The Picnic was
held in a wood near Whitley Bay. We had tea in the open air, sports and
a stroll through the wood, about four at this affair and it was claimed
a great success. On the way home I had great difficulty in persuading
the motor coach drivers not to stop at various Public Houses. During
the summer the Committee tried to arrange an attractive syllabus, with
very little money and no prestige. Lecturers were out of the question.
A concert was arranged, the Subscription Library Hall was booked and
Gertie Magrill got busy. To her must be given the honour of getting
together the first Variety Company consisting entirely of members of our
Community. The show was a success, the Librarian ordered the doors to
be closed as the Hall was filled to capacity. Still the Society did not
prosper, the Syllabus was not attractive, variety was scarce. The rooms
were cold and uncomfortable and attendance dwindled.

One day while looking in a shop window I felt a touch on my shoulder.
On turning I was confronted by one of our lady members, in the blunt and
straightforward way of the young people of those days she blurted out
with "Mr. Novinski, wont you give us something to do on a Sunday night.
We want some interest, we are at a loose end and bored stiff." This
girl's earnestness impressed me. Her appeal had to receive attention.
She seemed to speak for the members who absented themselves from the meetings and yet wanted a live Society. I called a Committee meeting.

SOL.

5.

NEWS LETTER FROM THE HOME FRONT

There have been no Lit meetings since I last penned my News Letter though I understand that the Committee have been busy planning new activities. Reporting on four weeks events in one Letter has not left me much room for my own opinions and general talk. I will therefore grasp this opportunity to give you a general outline of how the Lit stands. I have said before that the Lit is going strong. Do not misunderstand me, the Lit is nothing like what is was before the war. Almost every month sees one or two of our members leaving the home town to join in the struggle against Nazism. Not only the boys but also the girls are rapidly being called both into the Services and into other essential jobs. Several have answered the Government's call for more nurses - others have donned khaki or one of the two blues.

The average age of the Lit members has dropped to, I should think, around 16 or 17 and even the Executive and Committee are younger than ever before. And yet I say that the Lit is going strong. I say this because despite all of these difficulties the Lit has provided a meeting place for Jewish Youth every Sunday night during the winter months. The attendance varied from a dozen or so at Literary meetings to well over a hundred at dances - not bad for war-time! At these dances I was very glad to see that the young married couples gave their support. The average Literary standard of members has, quite naturally, lowered since the war but such events as Brains Trusts, Mock Trials, Debates, discussions and music recitals still attract a fair sized gathering.

The membership last Session was just over thirty though I feel sure that it could have been larger if all those who came to dances had joined. The Session started off full of spirit - the circulars were printed with the Lit heading at the top like the old days, and tickets were printed for dances. It was realised however that this was too uneconomical and circulars became once again duplicated and dances became to be advertised by circular. Despite this change I saw no material difference in the number of people who came along. The Hall used to look rather dismal at most dances as the blackouts in the windows gave that "Shut in" feeling. At the Chanuka party the Lit had the bright idea of decorating the Hall with streamers and bunting and this undoubtedly relieved the dismal effect.

The last Zionist Dance, during Pesach, saw a very large crowd and the Hall almost had that pre-war atmosphere - except that half of you abroad would hardly recognise many of the younger generation. At least that is what one member of the Forces said at that dance. "Some of them", he joked "were babes in arms last time I saw them".

At any rate for any of you who can get home the Lit is organising a dance in aid of the United Palestine Appeal for Sunday June 11th. I am told that a large number of tickets have already been sold. I'll tell you all about it next month so cheerio until then.

Yours,

Also After Gen

Answers to Questions on Page 2.

1. The Portugese Congregation called themselves "our nation".
2. Apart from Liverpool, Sunderland was the first provincial community to elect a Deputy in 1838. In the following year we were obliged to discontinue representation on account of the expense.
3. Mr. David Solomons in July 1839. He subsequently became Sir David Solomons, Bart.

6.

Answers Continued

4. Lord Palmerston presented a piece of land to the Jews of Dover for the erection of a Synagogue.

5. 1866.

6. The Histadrutt is a Labour organisation in Palestine which runs labour exchanges, sickness and insurance schemes and controls money of the co-operative settlements. Nearly all the bus services and the activities of the building industry are in the hands of the Histadrutt.

EXCERPTS FROM LETTERS.

Flying Officer D. Cohen from India writes: This particular part of India prior to the war, hardly ever saw a European, there being about four or five white State servants. The natives themselves are very jovial, and due to the large increase in the prices of various commodities, we often refer to them as the "laughing crooks". They are all greatly interested in their own respective religions, and many temples and mosques can be seen in the smallest villages. In the district is the palace of the local Maharajah which place we visited some time ago. Bells ring from the Palace Temple and a hollow shell is blown calling the people to worship.

Since the outbreak of war many of the local natives have adapted themselves to tailoring, road making, carpentry etc. It is the women who really do the hard work, carrying stones, unloading transports, digging sand, etc. They pay averages about one shilling and ten pence a day. They do not need much money with which to live and time to them does not mean a thing. Their homes, called "Basha's", are built of bamboo, straw and mud. It is very interesting watching them being built. First up-rights then horizontal lats through which is intertwined straw; the mud is prepared and plastered over the straw. Hinges are seldom used, wooden sockets being made for the doors and window frames to swing. The beds, if any are wooden frames with string crossed and recrossed and believe me, reverend, they are really comfortable. Of course mosquito netting is on the window frames where there is never glass.

Cpl. N.M. Cohen, C.M.F. writes: Your "leader" and Julius Gordon's letter concerning Jewish Chaplains brings forward a matter of major importance. Although I am serving in the same theatre of war as Julius I have come into contact with Jewish chaplains on a few occasions, the most memorable of which was the service of thanks-giving at Tunis shortly after the North African campaign. However I haven't met them as often as I would like to and I consider that they should "get about" a lot more. On the other hand it must be appreciated that the Jewish Chaplain has a much more difficult job to do than the Christian Chaplain in view of the fact that Jewish soldiers and airmen are spread out in twos and threes all over a theatre of operations, and chaplains are allotted according to the numbers of a faith and not according to the territory over which they are spread. I think it would be a good idea if the Senior Chaplain were requested to write an article to enlighten us on this important problem.

S/Cdr. I. Levine, India Command writes: Life in the "Imperial City" is quite pleasant, though the temperature has already rocketed up to well over the 100 mark; however as this is my 3rd summer in the Tropics, I'm quite acclimatised, and manage to keep fairly cool and comfortable. The usual Friday evening services are a source of great pleasure and spiritual comfort and are well attended by the many Jewish service personnel out here. A Jewish chaplain has just arrived from U.K. for service in India Command, so perhaps our spiritual welfare will be better catered for. I have just been told of a very lamentable case where a Jewish soldier from Leeds, unfortunately killed in a motor crash near here, would not have been buried according to Jewish custom had it not been for the intervention of a Jewish private of the same unit.   Cases of this nature stress the very great necessity for more Jewish Chaplains to come out from home. Do please use your influence and raise your voice to see that the religion we are fighting for, keeps us well supplied with several more Jewish chaplains.   Believe me they will be welcomed by the Troops.

Warrant Officer N. Goodman, East Africa Command writes: The Bulletin is running very well to form and without any doubt improves with each edition there is not a dull paragraph in it, and in my opinion should become a regular publication in Sunderland after the War.   I'm sure the entire community would welcome a little weekly local such as this, and at a small charge (all proceeds to be devoted to charity) they'd snap it up.   There would be no shortage of articles, as I should imagine you'd have as many contributors as subscribers, all you would need is a good voluntary staff and a Stationer with a charitable mind.   It would be good fun and a means of raising cash, apart from perhaps keeping the community up to scratch in many ways.

The ambulance train work is proving very interesting and I'm seeing plenty of Africa, fortunately we arrived in Nairobi last Friday afternoon so I was able to attend Shool once again yesterday.   As I had expected, the Shool was pretty bare, there being only four in the congregation myself making five, so we observed individually.   Afterwards I spoke to two old gentlemen who turned out to be two of the oldest members, and committee men.   The community was actually founded in 1904 the Synagogue being built in 1912.   Its a very nice little building very compact and airy, having been built with a high roof with a view to the heat and small ness.   It holds about 200 people each with his or her own numbered seat, so I don't quite know what they will do at Yontovim as there does not appear to be a seat vacant for any visitors, and there are quite a few Jewish soldiers here that will require accommodation at Yontof.   The interior is built entirely of African Mbau, a common type of timber used out here, and stained to a dark oak finish.   The layout is on the usual lines with a centre Bima, and a small balcony for the women, there are also some very nice memorial tablets, and the foundation stone was laid by the Governor of Kenya at that period.   On the whole it is a very comfortable little Synagogue, and scrupulously clean, this work being carried out obviously by African 'boys' the head of which, after I had spoken to him, gave me the impression that he was very proud of his position.   He no doubt is the only one employed by the Committee, but as is the rule amongst the natives, he in turn employs a few younger boys (totos, as they are called) to carry out the work.

Fus. B. Freeman, B.N.A.F. writes: I am very pleased to write that I managed to get some leave for Pesach.   Another Jewish friend and myself went to Shool in Town not very far from our camp.   The prayers are the same as ours but they pronounce the words differently.   We were both invited by a member of the Shool as well as several other soldiers to their home for the Sader night and it was quite a change, the food and wine etc. We all slept at their house and I can say they were very nice people they could not do too much for us.   Some non-Jewish soldiers here are very interested in your Bulletin as they belong to Sunderland.

Letters were also received from L.A.C. M. Dresner; S.B.A. A. Goldblatt; L.A.C. I Davis; Nurse R. Olswang V.A.D; Cpl. I.W. Brewer; L.A.C. C. Marks C.M.F; L.A.C. Gordon J. B.N.A.F.; Lt. Mordaunt Cohen, S.E.A.; Cfw. Gwen Magrill; Cpl. I.J. Charlton India; Gnr. A. Abraham, P. & I. Force.

*Edited and issued monthly by the Minister
and sent to you with the good wishes of
your friends at home.*

June 1944.   Vol. 2 No. 10.   Tamuz 5704

The news of the Invasion for which we have all waited has
naturally outshone the conquests of Rome in Italy. To Jews particula[]
the fall of Rome brings back memories of the hoary past. For Rome
possessed the oldest Jewish community in Europe; Jews settled there
already in the second century B.C.E. Battling through the vicissitud[]
of fortune Jews have lived and even flourished in Rome till modern tim[]
In the very early days the obstinacy with which Jews clung to their fa[]
and the purity of their religion proscribing all idolatrous worship an[]
superstitious practices attracted many Romans who embraced Judaism.

These converts were drawn not only from the poor but also the
nobility which included Fulvia a Senator's wife, and Flavius Clemens a[]
nephew of the Emperor Domitiam whilst Poppea the wife of Nero was very
favourably disposed towards Judaism and the Sabbath lights were kindled
in many a Roman home. But even the destruction of the Temple and the
cruel reigns of Trajan and Hadrian did not crush the Jewish spirit.
Judea was to live in spite of the invincible might of Rome. Rome with
it's lust of world conquest was materialistic, gold was it's god. Thi[]
is well expressed in Sallust's rhetorical outburst; "Venal City and soo[]
to perish if only it can find a purchaser." Judea stood for religion
and therefore outlived its erstwhile master.

Till the middle of the sixteenth century Jows in Rome were tolerat[]
but from then onwards their lot was far from happy. Paul IV forced al[]
Jews into the Ghetto in 1555 on July 26th corresponding to Tisha b'Ab.
High walls were built round the Ghetto and opposite the main entrance a
great wooden crucifix was set up so that the Jews in the Ghetto should
constantly see it. On Sabbath afternoons the Papal police would force
the Jews into the Church to listen to conversionist Sermons. Browning
satirised this in his poem 'Holy Cross Day'. As the conversionist
sermons had little effect young Jewish children were kidnapped and
forcibly converted. The climax to this age of racial discrimination
was the forcing of Jews to offer entertainment to the Christians during
the Roman Carnival.

With brief intervals the excesses of the Ghetto system affected Je[]
till 1870. After that Jews enjoyed equal status and were unmolested
even under Mussolini. But the same lust for power for which his early
forbears thirsted animated Mussolini to rob, plunder and destroy Jews.
Goaded on by his Axis partner Mussolini introduced the Jew-laws and once
again Jews were treated as pariahs of society.

Though the number of Jews in Italy is small we hail this victory
over Rome as symbolic of the future victory which we pray will bring
freedom and justice to all oppressed people. An Egyptian monument
erected about 350 years ago in the court of St. Peter's was engraved wit[]
the following inscription:- "Flee adversity. The Lion of the tribe of
Judah has conquered". We recall to mind this most appropriate inscription now that the Allied armies are slowly, but surely redeeming the
enslaved territories from the iron grip of the enemy. May the lion of
the Tribe of Judah go on conquering and through its noble teachings brin[]
to a distracted world lasting Peace.

4.

About this time Gertrude Magrill our Secretary resigned as she was about to take up Nursing. This was a serious blow to the 'Lit'. Sarah Cohen (now Mrs. Slater) was elected to be our next secretary. Keen, conscientious and a hard worker she was to help the Lit forward on its rocky road. We were also lucky in our choice of Treasurer. Sammy Tufle kept a tight hold on the Lit's cash and conserved its finances with commendable care. A home made Jellygraph was made for circulars, programmes etc., and only slips of duplicating paper were used. Postage was cut to a minimum and we decided to go hat in hand to the community and ask for donations to help us in our struggle. The result was a humiliating failure.

Still we persevered. The Lit would "never say die". A tennis section was formed, a small piece of waste ground was hired at High Southwick and with a ragged second hand net, a few balls and much enthusiasm we learned and practised the game. Playing almost every night and Sundays during the summer we played to the accompaniment of the jeers, sneers and sometimes cheers of the lads and lasses of the district. The field was bumpy but we were learning. Later on we booked two tennis courts from Hendon Cricket Club and we discovered that we could play Lawn Tennis quite well.

We spent many a happy hour at Hendon but Sunday play was barred. Rambles were arranged for Sundays and the members were kept busy. But we had the all important Winter programme to provide for and the Society had no money. One day whilst walking up Salem Road I met Rev. Muscat and we had a heart to heart talk about the Lit. Next month "We amalgamate with the Zionist Society".

Cheerio,
SOL.

Answers to Questions on Page 2.

1. "Pogrom" means "destruction". It began in Russia when peasants seeing the advantage of loot joined the mob in violent attacks upon the Jews at the end of the 19th and beginning of the 20th century.
2. About the end of the 19th century in Germany as a symbol that it was not the religion of the Hebrews but the social and political activities of the Semitic "Aliens" in European Society that was to be a trouble.
3. Treitschke occupied the Professorial chair at Berlin in the late 19th century and dominated German political philosophy. The Nazis took over his teachings and constantly used the phrase which he coined "The Jews are our calamity."
4. Cromwell's men, the French Huguenots and the Dutch soldiers read the Bible before going into battle.
5. Barcuh Shklov 1752 to 1810 translated Euclid into Hebrew, and received a letter of encouragement from the Wilna Gaon.
6. After Bonaparte had invaded the Holy Land he issued a proclamation offering to Jews their ancestral land and asked them to "take over what has been conquered and to maintain it against all comers."

5.

NEWS LETTER FROM THE HOME FRONT

The Childrens Forest Campaign was helped by the proceeds of a dance on Sunday, June 4th. The N.F.S. Band was extremely good on this their first visit to the Communal Hall. The crowd was not large but quite sufficient to make this one of the most enjoyable dances I have been to at the Hall for a long time, and I understand that the proceeds were considerable. As enjoyable as this dance was I think the one the following week was even better.

This one was run by the Lit in aid of the United Palestine Appeal and in organising it the new Committee certainly proved their worth. Arthur S. Smith's six piece band excelled and, towards the end especially very few were not dancing. There was a buffet with sandwiches, cakes, biscuits and soft drinks, and a raffle or two caused some fun. It was quite a novelty to see Mr. A. Merskey (Chairman of the local United Palestine Appeal) and his wife start off the "Snowball Waltz"! Moonlight Waltzes and other novelty dances lent themselves to the gaiety of the evening. The amount of clear profit to be handed over amounted, I understand, to about £5 and I do really think the Lit should be very proud to have raised this amount in these times and deserve every compliment.

When I think of the good work done by the Lit, in organising this dance in aid of a good cause, I know how to reply to those pessimists who, a couple of years ago, strongly insisted on the Lit going into abeyance for the duration. How glad I am that it has continued its work! "A living dog is better than a dead lion" said King Solomon, how true his words ring with regard to the Lit!

It is typical, by the way, of the calmness of this country that though the great news of the Invasion of Europe came between these two dances it did not seem to effect the Lit dance in the least - or would that account for the success of that dance?

I think that's all the 'gen' about town this month, Forces, so look after yourselves until next we meet.

Best of Luck,
Yours,
Also After Gen.

EXCERPTS FROM LETTERS.

L.A.C. Cohen, B.A., of Northern Ireland writes: One realises the inestimable value of this periodical, as apart from its literary merits and the excellence of its enjoyable reading matter it is the one medium whereby one can keep in touch with the whereabouts and welfare of one's home town. Also the various items of local news and the Serio-Comic comments of Inquisitor, we avidly lap up. So carry on with the good work.

Cpl. N.M. Cohen, with the C.M.F. writes: The Italians seem to be very short of food judging by what I have seen, although the position may be different in other parts of the country. A loaf of bread costs 100 lire or 5/- and the price of other foodstuffs are on a similar level. I have already had a glimpse of Vesuvius and visited the famous city, a more cosmopolitan crowd I've never seen. Troops from every Allied country crowd the streets, and I even noticed a Palestinian company of Royal Engineers there with the 'Magen David' prominently displayed. The ruins

<u>XCERPTS, Continued</u>

of Pompei are a big attraction and organised Army trips are arranged to
go there.   The shops have plenty of food for sale even such scarce
articles as watches and fountain pens, but they are of doubtful quality.
Prices are controlled by Amgot, to whom any cases of over-charging are
reported, and the shops concerned are closed to Allied troops for a
stipulated period.   Some of the architecture is magnificent and a
Theatre which I visited was one of the finest I have ever seen, an Opera
House in peace time.

<u>S.B.A. Goldblatt, from H.M.S. "Duke" writes:</u>   The Royal Navy places
religion before anything else.   In fact the resident Chaplain who gives
a lecture to each new group as it arrives takes a personal interest in
every one.   I was asked to make contact with new arrivals in order to
initiate them into our circle, and I hope to organise something like a
service for our men.

<u>Flt.Sgt. B. Taylor from India, writes:</u>   I paid a second visit to Cawnpore
where I met Morris Sarabouski.   It took me quite a while to find him
and as the plane in which I arrived was taking off again very shortly we
were able to have little more than a short chat.

<u>Cpl. Joe Charlton of India writes:</u>   I spent Passover in Calcutta.
Chiefly through the Chaplains efforts most of the lads American and
British totalling more than 500 were able to spend a Kosher Pesach.   A
hostel was available for those who required to sleep in and Kosher meals
were provided free in the Judean Club at the expense of the Jewish
Tobacco firm of Elias & Son.   The first Seder night was spent by some
in private homes but on the second night we had one huge communal Seder
attended by about 600 lads.   Each evening and morning the Chaplain
conducted services in the Synagogue after the usual Sephardic service
was concluded.   During the intervening days a full programme of
entertainments was arranged.   Again during the last few days services
were held;   these were almost exclusively attended by British boys,
Friday evening after the service there was the usual Dinner in the Club
and we sat till midnight singing Jewish songs and hearing stories
admirably told in true "Yiddisher" style by the Chaplain.   On Saturday
night the whole affair was rounded off by a good dance which was
thoroughly enjoyed by the huge crowd.   The thanks of the British who
were in Calcutta are due to the Americans who unselfishly shared with
us not only their Chaplain but also their supply of American Matzos
which was shipped over for them.

<u>Gunner A. Abrahams of Persia writes:</u>   Services at the Shools in
Bagdad are conducted on pretty much the same lines as at home, but more
hurried.   Maariv took ten minutes and late-comers stand to one side
when the service is repeated for their benefit.   Kaddish is recited
fairly often, it may be due to the persecutions and a atrocities that
have been committed against Bagdad Jews in olden times.   The Seder
service is the same as ours with this difference that the Matzos are
very large like thin pancakes.   Most families bake their own.   The
women folk here remain strictly in the house and raise large families.
It is not unusual for a woman of 33 to have twelve children.   There
is still felt the bitter hatred from Arab to Jew in this part of the
world.

EXCERPTS Continued
A.C.W. Leonie Slater writes: I was very sorry to read that Argus had
to undergo an operation, and send my best wishes for a speedy recovery.
Tell Sol that his articles of the Lit though a little beyond me make me
envious and I only hope that the Lit will go back to a similar standard
when peace is with us once again. "Also After Gen" certainly supplies
very snappy information about the Lit and I do enjoy the letters from
the Forces. The Editorial of course is of unfailing interest. You
will notice that I have left out "Inquisitor" in my brief summary.
Maybe it is because I am out of touch with affairs at home, but if I
can guess who she/he is talking about twice in the whole thing I think
I am doing well. However I must compliment Inquisitor this month as
I guessed eight so keep it up you are doing fine.

The following letters are also acknowledged with grateful thanks:
L.A.C. Julius Gordon, B.N.A.F.; Lt. Mordaunt Cohen, S.E.Asia; L.A.C. C
Marks, C.M.F.; Rita Olswang V.A.D; Pte. Sol. Cohen; Fus. Freeman D. Malt
Force; L.A.C. I. Davis, Army Post Office; L.A.C. Louis Berg, M.E.F.; Flt
Lt. D. Cohen, India.

PRAYER AND WAR.

When "D" day arrived we were all inspired by the noble example of H
Majesty the King who rightly asked that Prayers should be offered up fro
all places of worship. Some there are who will question the usefulness
of Prayer at this time. They will insist that tanks, aeroplanes and
ships will win this war and not prayer. What a mistaken notion they ha
of the purpose and function of prayer! We pray not to make bargains
with God, but to maintain our morale and inspire ourselves with confider
in the justice of our cause.

The cynic will retort that wars cannot be won by morale and confidence. To this our answer is "Dunkirk". If not for morale, if not for
our sincere belief in the righteousness of our cause, if not for our
prayers then which buoyed us up in the dark hours of seeming hopelessne
we should not have had the strength nor the inclination to fight on and
build the tanks, ships, guns and aeroplanes for the battle of France.

Our initial landings were successful and the battle though grim, i
proceeding according to plan. But there seems to be one natural flaw
over which we as mortals have no control and that is the weather. Milit
correspondents have forecast that with light wind and no rain we could
make swifter and more rapid progress. The time factor is important an
given fine weather we could quickly consolidate our position and what i
more important deny the enemy all hopes of counter-attacking effectivel
But science with all its miraculous achievements has not mastered the
elements. Nature is the hand maid of God and wars cannot be won by
weapons alone without the aid of the weather.

Let us therefore pray that our men be granted the opportunity of
using the superior power and might placed in their hands so that they c
very soon bring food, succour and relief to millions in the enslaved
countries who are daily praying for the healing rays of the SUN.

Will readers please notify change of address before the 20th of th
month.
All correspondence including any items of local interest should be
sent to the Editor, Rev. S.P. Toperoff, 5 Victoria Avenue, Sunderland.

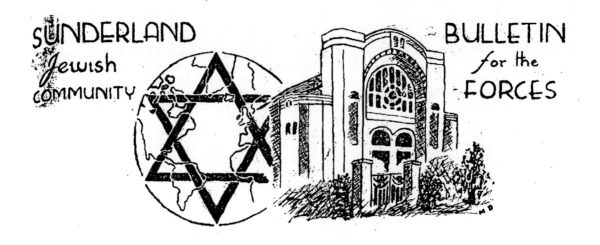

*Edited and issued monthly by the Minister
and sent to you with the good wishes of
your friends at home.*

July 1944   Vol. 2 No. 11   Ab 5704

China and Israel

The 7th anniversary of the out break of war in China took place on the 7th of July and special services were held in Church and Synagogue. From the earliest times historians have referred to the most interestin parallelism in the growth of China and Israel.   Both are peoples of antiquity and both have made a most impressive influence on the course o civilisation.

The kinship between early China and Israel is even found in the thr versions of the story of the birth of Moses one of which points to the fact of the presence of Jews in early China dating from the Chin Dynasty 265-419 C.E.

Though Jews have not lived in large numbers in China there are a number of references to Jews from the early travellers of the ninth and fourteenth centuries.   We also have a comprehensive and detailed accoun of the life of the Jewish Community in Kai-Fung-Foo one of the most ancient cities in China.   In the 17th century it boasted of having more than 600 Jews.   Another Community was traced in Harbin (Manchuria) whils in modern times Jews had settled in Shanghai, Tientsin, Hong Kong, Hsing King and Mukden.

Our interest in China is not however based on the past or on account of its 18,000 Jews before the War.   We feel with all who suffer for the cause of Freedom.   China has been at War for seven long years.   Since July 1937 fifty to sixty million Chinese have been rendered homeless. Jews have been fighting since 1933, and though numbering sixteen million in the world we have now lost eight million through death or rendered homeless.

China's problem is her isolation from the rest of the world.   The Jew is not isolated in the same sense but ethically and morally he too is isolated.   The world has no time for his problems.   Hundreds of thousands of Jews are being driven now from Hungary into the death camps of Poland.   They are isolated from the rest of the world as their brethren of the Warsaw Ghetto.   No one can help them.   The Jew has been clamoring for the opening of the gates of Palestine but their cries have fallen on deaf ears.

We can appreciate the fight of China struggling for her freedom.   In the words of Lady Cripps, President of the Aid to China Fund - "China needs friendship based on sympathetic understanding of the difficult situation in which she finds herself at the moment.   There is no doubt that we owe a great debt to China for all she has done in this world struggle for justice, and that she is destined to make great contributions to the building up of a better world".

The same words apply equally to Israel as to China.   When will the world recognise the debt it owes to Israel.   The great contributions it has made to civilisation in every sphere of culture, art and science.

Jews as Chinese need "Friendship based on sympathetic understanding". The world is torn asunder by conflicting ideologies each glorifying in its own peculiar way of life to the exclusion of its neighbour.   But Judaism teaches "Love thy neighbour as thy self".   "One law for the native as the stranger".   The Chinese may be strange to many of us for they live so many miles away, but we must love them none the less for they too are created in the image of God.

Judaism makes no distinction between man and man.   Our division is one of religious significance only.   Politically, socially and morally there is no distinction between Jew and non-Jew whatever his creed, class

2.

of colour.   In the words of the Rabbis - "Before the throne of glory
there is no difference between Jews and other people.   Goodness is the
only meteyard there, and goodness is pleasing to God in whomsoever it is
found."

China's struggle is our struggle.   Let us pray for China and work
for her salvation.

DO YOU KNOW?

1. How many Jews are in Tito's Army?
2. Who controls the English Press?
3. Who is Herbert Lehmann?
4. When was the first University degree conferred on a Jew?
5. How many Jews have been decorated for gallantry in the Russian Army?
6. Which Christian diplomats demanded that Palestine be restored to
   Jews 80 years before the Balfour Declaration?

Answers to the above questions on Page 4.

HERE AND THERE!

Mazeltov.
Engagements - Congratulation to Miss Muriel Sugden on her engagement to
                Bernard Millet of Nottingham and to Miss Gertie Kolson on
                her engagement to Pte. Harry Rosenberg of Glasgow.
Congratulations - to Doctor Aaron Gillis on his attainment of his medical
                degree and to Miss Fay Mersky on her attainment of the
                degree of B.A.

Harold Davis whose Barmitzvah took place last week won the Junior
Champion race 220, 440 and 880 yards and the long jump at the Bede Boys
School sports recently.

Mrs. Cohen wife of Ald. J. Cohen has been co-opted a member of the
Council and is to represent Monkwearmouth Shore Ward.   There is no
election owing to the Labour Party truce.

Son of a Sunderland man who went over to America when he was 16, Col.
Joseph Smith of Scranton, Pennsylvania, has been promoted Brigadier-
General in the U.S. Army.   Brigadier-General Smith's father, Mr. Jacob
Smith, was a member of an old Sunderland family and his grandfather the
late Mr. Barnett Smith, will be remembered by old Wearsiders for his
glass works in Grangetown.   He provided the collieries with glasses for
the safety lamps and held a contract with Ryhope Coal Co. for these
glasses for over 50 years.   Mr. Jacob Smith's sister - now Mrs. Rosa
Jacobs is the wife of Mr. David Jacobs of 2, Belford Road and Hon. Sec.
of Ryhope Road Congregation.   Brig.-Gen. Smith was senior Officer of Staff
at the joint conference between Pres. Roosevelt, Winston Churchill and
Marshall Stalin.

At recent meetings of the Minister's Circle on Shabbos afternoon a
Symposium on "Anti-Semitism" was held when papers were read by Harry
Berkowitz and Charles Cohen.   Miss Leonora Jacobs read a paper on
"Disraeli".

The Sunderland Young Zionist Association Meetings - the Programme in
the last month has been as follows:-
Survey of Jewish History, by Miss Eileen Heilpern.
Maimonides, by Miss Pearl Berg.

3.

Jehudah Halevy by Miss Riva Cohen.
Spinoza by Harold Merskey.
Rashi by Miss Phyllis Blakey.
Survey of Jews in England by Charles Cohen.
The Task of the Zionists, by Leon Hirschberg (of the School of
    Agriculture in Durham).
Communal Settlements by Mrs. Margaret Dent.

INQUISITOR'S Article will be resumed next
month.

IN RETROSPECT.

I knew Rev. Muscat was one of the Lit's keennest supporters. He was
a man with a big heart and ready sympathy, he saw in the young people of
his day the future members of the community and as such he thought they
should have every encouragement it was possible to give.
He took his responsibilities as Vice President seriously and often
attended Committee Meetings when his opinion and advice was listened to
with earnestness. He not only had the young folk's respect, he had
their affection! When I met him that day we talked about the Lit and
its difficulties, and this was the result of our conversation. The
Balfour Declaration had stimulated interest in Zionism in the Community.
The Zionist Society had kept that interest alive. There was a potential
audience ready and eager to listen to lectures on the subject.
Zionist H.Q. had speakers willing to lecture wherever a suitable audience
could be found.
The Local Zionist Society wanted the enthusiasm of new blood and the
experience necessary in organising propaganda meetings. What a chance
for the Lit! A General Meeting was held and the Society became known as
The Sunderland Literary and Zionist Association. Our first Committee
job was to take a census of the entire Jewish population of Sunderland in
readiness for launching the Keren Hayesod Fund. Then came the organising
of propaganda Lectures.
A Fancy Dress Ball (then very fashionable) was to be held and a Mass
Meeting (with his Worship the Mayor in the Chair) had to be arranged.
The Zionists sent a representative to the Lit Committee and I was made a
member of their Committee. The late Mr. Charles Brewer was in charge.
Kindly, courteous, tactful but very firm, he was an ideal Chairman. One
of our earliest speakers was a young Student (a new Senior Wrangler) one
Mr. Selig Brodetsky. A young scholar of note, a large crowd welcomed
him at the Boilermakers' Hall. In accordance with the policy of the
Zionists a man of standing had to occupy the Chair. On this occasion Mr
Sam Phillips, M.A., of Newcastle-on-Tyne, graced the meeting.
As I listened to Mr. Brodetsky I became aware of his facile mind,
the logical way he placed his facts before the audience and his smooth
eloquence. I was much impressed. I knew I had to move the vote of
thanks and felt very nervous. When called upon I stood up feeling
terrified and clutched the chair in front of me tightly - "I must not let
the old Lit down". I made a short speech. After the meeting Mr.
Phillips patted me on the shoulder and spoke some kindly words. These
were the first words of encouragement I had ever received.
Next month Mr. & Mrs. Israel Sieff visit us.
Cheerio,
SOL.

4.

Answers to Questions on Page 2.

1. More than 20,000 Jews have secretly fought their way to join the ranks of Tito's Army.
2. Of the 116 daily newspapers in this country 115 have no Jewish owner or Jewish Editor, and of the 17 Sunday Newspapers none is owned or edited by Jews.
3. The Director General of U.N.R.R.A. and a distinguished member of the Jewish faith.
4. The first University degree conferred on a Jew was in 1836 whilst Oxford and Cambridge abolished the tests only in 1871 which up till then had excluded all students from taking degrees unless they were members of the Church of England.
5. 32,000
6. Lord Ashley 7th Earl of Shaftesbury and Colonel Charles Churchill grandson of the 5th Duke of Malborough. Lord Ashley prepared in 1840 a Memorandum for Viscount Palmerston providing for a guarantee of settlement of Jews in Palestine and Colonel Churchill addressed a letter on the same subject to Sir Moses Montefiore in 1841.

NEWS LETTER FROM THE HOME FRONT.

And so another month has slipped by since the last Bulletin. Great changes have rolled along and the war is progressing, especially on the Russian Front, at a great speed that tempts over-optimism. But whatever we think about the war we dare not be too optimistic about the Lit.

Four difficult years for the Lit have passed and, since the war started, it has been the policy of the Lit to hold as many summer events as possible instead of closing until September as formerly. Otherwise the Lit may get forgotten in these times of worry and, should the Lit disappear, the Jewish spirit in Sunderland would have taken a big step towards its doom. Perhaps, then you will realize the importance of keeping the Lit going. To you who are fortunate enough to be at home, I am writing now (for the Bulletin has quite a large circulation at home too.)

The Lit holds meetings but how many of those who used to attend before the war come along? Have they lost interest? The reason I am sometimes given is that there are so many "youngsters" at the Lit. They forget that the age limit has not altered since 1936 and that if the older ones came along that would automatically raise the average age. But no! They have known the Lit in better days, they knew it when its membership was five times what it is today; they knew it when it had tennis tournaments, dramatic sections and art sections; they are too "proud" to "condescend" to the Lit of today! Proud - rubbish; condescend - nonsense!

To support a Lit when it is flourishing is no great feat. To serve on the Committee when matters comparatively glide along does not warrant praise. But to support the Lit today when every ounce of energetic help is needed is something for which we must admit the young members of the present Lit justly deserve praise. But praise will not keep the Lit going - they need encouragement, the co-operation of everyone left in Sunderland having the feeling of responsibility towards the Jewish Community of tomorrow. A Donation? That is not enough. It would, I feel sure be gratefully accepted but what is more urgent is that we attend Lit meetings and functions whenever we can bring along our friends.

Mr. Nathan Muscat wrote some years ago (in the Lit Silver Jubilee Souvenir Magazine) "Get the Lit Habit and, having got it, maintain it" That would be a service to our sons and daughters, brothers and sisters who are now away engaged in the fight against the enemy of Judaism and freedom. They still have a keen interest in the Lit while we at home think we have outgrown it. Perhaps they do not grow old as we who are left grow old! One word to the young Lit committee. Prepare a programme that will attract all ages and the Lit will continue in the future as in the past.

Well forces, I'm sorry I haven't any real news for you but here's smile anyway. I was waiting for a bus the other day and beside me sto a frail old woman and a young R.A.F. medical orderly. Various 'buses went by - a No. 24, No. 12, No. 15 and so on until eventually the old bewildered grandmother turned to the airman and asked "Where do I get a No. 9?" "Report sick in the morning" came the almost automatic reply!
Cheerio till next time and keep smiling.

Yours,

Also After Gen.

BULLETIN BRIGAND   By C. Vatican Doo.

Rome Correspondent.

Who's the girl that gets the gen? Rosalie?
Who is always teasing men? Rosalie?
Who's the one that makes a crack
Behind a poor soldier's back
And puts him off the beaten track? Rosalie?

Who supplies the scandal rare? Rosalie?
Who suggests an ideal pair? Rosalie?
Who knows when a parcel's sent,
And when a Shidduch's imminent,
Who knows just where to find my tent? Rosalie?

Who writes in language quite unique? Rosalie?
Who lets some information leak? Rosalie?
Who'll always stand to bear the brunt,
And open yet another Front,
Who'll think it such a splendid stunt? Rosalie?

Who writes of every girl and boy? Rosalie?
Who educates the "hoi polloi"? Rosalie?
Who knows the answer every time,
And makes the punishment fit the crime,
Who'd rather have her job than mine? Rosalie?

EXCERPTS FROM LETTERS.

Lt. Mordaunt Cohen from India writes: I arrived in Calcutta on Erev Pesach and immediately contacted Lady Ezra. I went to her house and there on my arrival I witnessed a scene that I never expected to see in the whole of India. Sir David Ezra and his household were carrying 'ou the age old custom of 'Bedikas Chametz' in such an atmosphere I immediat ly felt at home. The first Seder night I spent at the Ezra's and over sixty five people sat down at their table. It was a most impressive sight, and it demonstrated Israel's "Strength through Religion" if one

6.

EXCERPTS Continued

may coin a Goebbel's phrase. Those present who could read were given 'parshas' from the Hagaddah to recite. We sang all the traditional songs in various tunes and some of us to give extra measure sang some of the chalutz songs. Sir David and Lady Ezra kept the ball rolling the whole time, despite their prosperity and social position they are staunch Jews and orthodox. Would that some of our own in a corresponding social position immitate them. The only Sunderland friend I have met so far in India is Joe Charlton. I did not recognise him at first because he was sporting a most fierce moustache.- a la Groucho Marks. By gad, Sir, Poona, what! What!!! The service in the famous Magen David Synagogue was conducted by the U.S.A. Chaplain who in his sermon walked about the Pulpit like a D.A. (not you D.A. sit down - how about that Inquisitor?) addressing a Jury. When the service was over some of us stayed behind to daven 'Misaf'. As a result he asked us to conduct the service on the second day.

S.B.A. Goldblat writes: My training consists of first aid as we know it in the St. John's ambulance plus the use of a hypodermic syringe, the stitching of wounds, the giving of a blood transfusion and the handling of injured men. We also spend two hours each morning in the open doing practical stretcher work over rough country to the tune of a whistle which represents bursting shells or gas. Each evening when on duty we spend two hours in a ward of the hospital learning the routine. I am in a ward devoted to suspected T.B. cases and I have been shown how to test T.B. At first it was more or less terrifying to think that men's lives may depend on us but gradually we are becoming used to the idea and the practical work we do is giving us confidence.

Sgt. Norman Franks from Persia writes: As a "Sunderlander" born if not bred I feel that I should offer my congratulations to the Sunderland Jewish Community for its Bulletin to the Forces. I received several 'second-hand' copies and I wonder if I may become a further overseas man on your mailing list. Admittedly Inquisitor's witticisms are wasted on me, an exile, but there are other contributors in whose efforts I find certain pleasure not least of all the writers of "Excerpts from Letters". As a khaki clad tourist of some long standing I know many of the places to which they refer, and it is interesting to note their re-actions. I would quote in particular L.A.C. Marks who wrote in the issue of November 1943. I too discovered an apathy towards Judaism among our people, living in the cradle of our religion. They are not Jews but Palestinians. In Bagdad where I had the pleasure of staying for Rosh Hashannah among the Iraqui Jewry I discovered an "enlightened" outlook. The basic ethics of Judaism are vigorously upheld but minor variations are to be found.

Cpl. N.M. Cohen of C.M.F. writes: "How proud I feel that Inquisitor devoted 13 lines to myself in the March issue. I have not received her cheque yet. Perhaps if I disclose to her that I have got a splendid remedy for foot trouble she will rename me "Norman The Corn-curer", but on the other hand she may prefer to stick to my old name for after all Rome does not fall every day. I think that Nat Goodman's suggestion about making the Bulletin a regular publication after the war is a very good one indeed. In Italy the Magen David is to be found everywhere and makes a fallacy of the anti-semitic cry that the Jews are not in the front line. Already many graves are to be seen of Jewish soldiers who fell in the battle for Cassino. If you are ever short of news for the Bulletin you may enlist my aid as "Rome Correspondent" and I'll see "Vatican" do for you.

Letters were also received from:
L.A.C. I Davis, B.W.E.F.; W/O Nat Goodman, E.A. Command; Rita Olswang, V.A.D.; Fus. B. Freeman, Malta Force; Pte. Sylvia Mincovitch; A.C.2 Derick Cohen; Cpl. Bergson; Gnr. Abrahams M.E.F.; Gnr. Kolson; Cpl. Charlton, India; and Cpl. R. Freedman.

The Three Weeks

The period between the 17th of Tamuz and the 9th of Ab are known as
'The three weeks'. These weeks were established after the fall of the
first Temple and re-established after the destruction of the second Temp
We recall the statement of the Rabbis in the Talmud "That in times of
undisturbed peace (that is when Israel is not suffering any persecutions
disability on account of religion) the fast of Ab is optional".

Throughout the ages there have been few periods of peace and quiet
for Israel to question the retaining of the three weeks of mourning.
fact this period of semi-mourning is not observed as it was intended to be
memorial of those grim days when Israel fought to the last man for it's
independence. Jewish history is unfortunately crowded with trajedies
persecution and slaughter and this year is no exception.

We thought that with the advent of the 20th century freedom and
emancipation of the previous century would blossom and ripen into full
equality for all people on earth including Jews. We fondly imagined th
the traditional "Three Weeks" would be then of historical interest only
reminding us of our past, and keeping before us the martyrdom of our pe
who braved death rather than submit passively to a life of eternal
subjection. But this wishful thinking was short-lived.

We are witnessing today the annihilation of millions of Jews by Hit
and his henchmen. If there are degrees in suffering we are today endu
greater losses than in Judea of old. We then lost one Temple, today we
see crumbling before our eyes more than one Temple. The Warsaw Ghetto
liquidated. The Temple of Judaism in Poland which served three and a H
million Jews is crushed out of existence carrying with it as a mighty colo
death and torture to more than two million men, women and children. Th
great Yeshibot academies of learning which sustained the Jewish world wi
scholarship have been destroyed. The same picture can be seen in Germ
Rumania, and Hungary. For many Jews, their only hope in the land of
German oppression is death.

"The Three Weeks" is an institution of national mourning for Jews.
still mourn for the temple that was destroyed because we are not allowe
build a new Temple in its place. For a multitude of reasons Palestine
which was promised us by the Mandate of 52 nations is denied us as a
National Home. Plots of ground are doled out to us as though we were
charitable institution not a nation and a people with a glorious past ar
wonderful heritage to hand down to posterity.

If the authorities could with magnanimous foresight have arranged
the transfer of the 400,000 Jews of Hungary into Palestine they would h
been delivered from the hell of the German gas chambers in Poland. We
mourn these helpless souls. Another bastion of Continental Jewry is b
systematically wiped out and the world looks on. May our thoughts and
prayers during these "three weeks" strike a responsive chord in the hear
of the Allied Powers so that immediate measures be taken to help facili
the salvage of the wreck of the remnant of World Jewry.

Will readers please notify change of address before the 20th of the
month.
All correspondence including any items of local interest should be
sent to the Editor, Rev. S.P. Toperoff, 5 Victoria Avenue, Sunderland.

*Edited and issued monthly by the Minister
and sent to you with the good wishes of
your friends at home.*

August 1944.   Vol. 2 No. 12.   Ellul 5704.

The Sanctity of Charity

It is generally recognised that Jews are charitable, even some of our detractors admit this though grudgingly. Our Religion has raised the giving of charity to a Commandment. We must help not only our own but also non-Jews together with their Institutions, Hospitals and societies of every description. Jewish teaching makes no distinction between Jew and non-Jew in the realms of charity for are we not all created in the image of God. Should we not all help each other regardless of race, creed or colour?

These thoughts passed through my mind the other day when I reviewed the work done by the Ryhope Road Synagogue Charity Fund. This Fund disburses annually sums of money to a wide variety of charities mainly non-Jewish. A large number are devoted to war work such as the 125th Anti-Tank Fund, the R.A.F. Benevolent Fund, the Greek Fund, the Aid-to-China, Aid-to-Russia, the Comforts' War Fund, the Red Cross and St. John, the Soldiers, Sailors and Airmen Association. We also help the main London Hospitals, the Salvation Army, St. Dunstan's, Barnardos Homes and the principal local Charities.

This Fund is made up of voluntary contributions, and by its breadth of purpose has disproved the fallacy that Jews are interested only in their own charities. There is much truth in the old adage that "Charity should begin at home". We have enough to support amongst our own Institutions. We are also concerned very much with the plight of our unfortunate brethren where ever they may be and whom we are ready to assist. But it is right that we should think of charities outside our own 'Home'.

This virtue then should be granted to us - that we are willing to help all and sundry as far as is humanly possible. But surely a charitable person is usually kind hearted, good and generous in other respects. Can the Jew be the diabolical villain he is so often pictured and yet at the same time be charitable and ready to assist any who ask for help? This should be remembered, the Jew has no ulterior motive when he gives charity. He often gives when he cannot afford. He gives because it is part of his nature to help, because he is thus doing the will and wish of God. To strengthen the hand of the poor and the weak the helpless and the orphan the widow and the stranger is a Biblical injunction and it must apply to all human beings.

There is however another form of Charity which alas is lacking so lamentably in the world today as far as the Jew is concerned and that is charity of thought and word. Someone once wrote "Give if thou canst in alms, if thou canst not afford then give instead a sweet and gentle word". How much misery, degradation and humiliation has been heaped on the Jew because of the uncharitableness of the world at large. We have suffered much through this. We have been insulted, bludgeoned and tortured to death not for the sins we have committed but because Dictators, tyrants, rulers and their peoples have been so uncharitable towards us.

With the war reaching its climax we should like to think that the selfish way of life practised by so many will be superseded by the

2.

charitable life which with its magnanimity of purpose and breadth of vision will no longer harbour wicked and base thoughts against any section of the Community.

Such charity of thought and mind must guide all on their return from the front. 'Charity delivered from death' said Solomon. War with its holocaust of slaughter and death will be outlawed only when mankind will treat each other with CHARITY.

DO YOU KNOW?

1. Who is the director of the Savings Department of the General Post Office.
2. Who constructed the first Airship.
3. When did an Emperor present Jews with a flag in recognition of their good fighting qualities.
4. Which is one form of humanity at least which according to the Christian writer Lecky "appears more prominent in the Old Testament than in the New Testament."
5. When is a Jew permitted to transgress Jewish Law.
6. What according to Jewish teaching is the first question man is asked in the future world before the Throne of Judgment.

Answers to the above questions on Page 4.

HERE AND THERE!

Mazeltov.
Congratulations to:-
Weddings. - Cpl. Ralph Freedman to Miss Sylvia Grovic of London.
Charles Goldman to Cynthia Garbutt W.A.A.F. of Durham.
Eva Judith Maccoby to Sgt. Hiliare Gellar, U.S.A.A.F.
George Behrman (formerly of Sunderland) to Dora
Lazarus of Manchester.
Engagements - Miss Minnie Lerman to A.C.1 Leslie Stone, R.A.F. India, of Sunderland.
Births - Doctor and Mrs. Naftalin (nee Beulah Behrman) on the birth of a daughter.
Mr. & Mrs. Sid Burnley of Sheffield (formerly of Sunderland) on the birth of a daughter.

Decoration
Congratulations to L.A.C. Harold Shochet who was recently decorated with the Trooping Star 1939 to 1943.

Congratulations to Miss Alberta Asher (daughter of Mr. Harry Asher) who has been appointed Head Mistress of Chester Road Junior School. It is only several months ago that Miss Asher was placed on the Panel of Head Mistresses for Infants Schools, and we are glad to know that promotion has come so quickly.

We are pleased to hear that Corporal I.W. Brewer has had the signal honour of presenting the Chester Jewish Community with a Certificate inscribing its name in the Golden Book of Jewry.

Congratulations to Miss Dorrie Behrman (daughter of Mr. & Mrs. Max Behrman of Barnard Castle, formerly of Sunderland) who has recently

3.

gained the Bristol University Diploma of Midwife Teacher.   Miss Behrman
who is a State Registered Nurse and State Certified Midwife trained at
the London Jewish Hospital and at the Princess Mary Maternity Hospital,
Newcastle.   She also holds the Housekeeping Certificate of the Sheffield
Royal Hospital.   When in Sunderland she took a very active part in the
Literary Society and other kindred societies.

Many of our readers who have consistently asked when Argus will
resume his monthly article will be pleased to know that Argus who is
fully restored to health is once again contributing to our columns.   We
welcome him back.

EN PASSANT - INQUISITOR.

Can it be two long tedious months since you read (or ignored) my
last contribution?   Why did I refrain from writing for one month?   Was
I ill?   No.   Had I an insufficient amount of gen?   No.   Did I hope
you'd all write confessing how much you had missed the pointed witticisms
which flow in so facile a manner from my pen?   Was I disappointed?   Is
it in sheer desperation that I continue writing to my (n)ever-clamouring
followers?   Am I afraid that another month away from you all would find
my place usurped and myself relegated to the ignominious band of forgotten
men?   Whatever my reason and whatever my response (or lack of) has been,
I find myself, due to circumstances beyond my control, putting reluctant
pen to paper to sate your growing demands.   Hi-de-hi, until ....
FLASH!
Did the "also rans" run on August 9th?
On dit that the B.B.C. King is now the Indian Ingenue - n'est-ce pas?
If $x = £6$, does C.h. $= £36$?
Rumour hath it that a certain Infirmary attender has very important
documents to sign.
Does Leon the Lion(el) find his French Technique as successful as his
English?
Is a celebrated W.A.A.F. accustomed to chartering her own plane?
Well, VICTORious Doctor, to be or not to be?
Why has Maidstone recently had naval escort?
So the Indian Accountant is a pukka sahib, I feel such a cad, sir! (thanks
for the gen, Lieut.!)
Please don't be too intimated D.A. (and I don't mean District Attorney).
Give me some publicity next time, Norman the Conqueror, please or this
is the last time I mention you in despatches.   Get me pal?
Who is still King of the BARNES?

SPORTING REFLECTIONS   -   by "Argus".

The last match of last Football season is a day I shall remember -
not because of its football but because I had to leave at the interval.
Within 48 hours I had been under the surgeons knife.

On reflection of the play in the first half of that game at
Middlesbrough I feel that if it was not bad enough to give anyone an
acute appendicitis, it was certainly bad enough to give anyone a pain in
the stomach.   But I can hardly blame a football match for a much diseased
appendix, plus an abscess.   However thats that, and here I must express

4.

my gratitude to all my Jewish friends for their kindly thoughts and good wishes. I feel almost fit again, though I am not likely to break ten seconds over the 100 yards on the track.

Well here we are at the beginning of another season boys - and the war in the west well on the road to the Berlin stakes. During the close season - sounds like shooting doesn't it - Manager Billy Murray has been scouring Durham County to pick the best of the young players. The result is that the list of professionals retained and amateurs signed has passed the century mark - 105 to be precise. In addition there are Laidman, who is actually a Stockton professional; Wallbanks, the Fulham wing half and Rutherford, the D.L.I. goalkeeper who was with Newcastle and Blyth Spartans, helping the club.

You will be more interested in the younger players for it is to youth we must pin our hopes for the future. I shall have more opportunity later of giving impressions of them, but I predict good futures for Stelling, a right back with two good feet; Tulip, a centre half from Armstrong-Whitworth's; Bowes, a young outside right from the Middlesbrough area who reminds one of Stanley Matthews and Mathinson, a big boned centre forward from South Shields Boys Club.

So far as I can see there will be little change in the senior eleven in the early stages, though it is almost certain that Wallbanks will claim the right half position. The weakness will be at outside left as it has been right through the war period. Burbanks is in India so there can be no help from him.

Raich Carter is still at the R.A.F. Re-habilitation centre and can only be available on his leaves. The old War horse Bob Gurney is on an air field in Normandy and the latest to join the Forces is Freddie Bett, who has been playing with Lincoln City while on munitions.

Cheerio for now, more next month.

Answers to questions on Page 2.

1. Sir Leon Simon C.B. a noted Jewish Scholar and acting leader of the Zionist movement.
2. David Schwartz 1897 an Austrian Jewish engineer, Count Zeppelin was so impressed with the trials that he bought the patent rights.
3. Emperor Ferdinand III for the exemplary manner in which Jews defended Prague during the Thirty Years War.
4. Consideration for dumb creatures.
5. The Jew may overlook his religious scruples if necessary to come to the assistance of animals in pain or distress.
6. 'Wast thou honest in business'.

IN RETROSPECT

Eventually I was elected Chairman of the local Zionist Society and holding the same office for the Lit, the two Committees worked in harmony.

5.

There was collecting to be done, meetings to arrange, and social functions to organise. This was the Lit's work. The Zionist Committee supplied the Capital. The Association gained much publicity and prestige. The work was sometimes very exacting but very well worth while.

The Lit was now able to invite people to lecture on Jewish Religion and History. Debates were also held. The tennis section and the little Socials and Dances continued to find a place in the Syllabus. The Keren Hayesod Fund was due to be launched. A big meeting was held at the subscription Library Hall, Fawcett Street. His worship the Mayor, Ald. David Cairns J.P., opened the proceedings and then, to our surprise informed his audience "That owing to another engagement he would have to leave". He called upon the Chairman of the Association to take his place in the Chair.

Thus I was called upon to preside over my first Jewish public meeting by the Mayor of my native town. Mrs. I. Sieff was the first speaker. Her speach was heartrending, heart-searching and a piece of fine oratory. She talked of the works of the Zionist Social Services, Hospitals, Schools and much more. There was many a wet eye in the audience when she sat down. But, it was nmoney that was wanted not tears

I suggested to Mr. Sieff that a purely business like speech would now be desirable. He agreed and obliged with a verbatim speech giving particulars of the schemes in hand and the future hopes of the Zionist leaders. Then came the appeal and the fund was officially opened. Money and promises came flowing in. Collections were to be spread over a period and success was assured.

The Lit's next job was the raising of money for the J.N.F. and a fancy dress ball was organised. The Society could now afford to think big and though the Committee was still cautious it knew it could now appeal to the other communities of the North East for Zionism was strongly supported where ever Jews were to be found.

About this time a very young lady whose organising ability and energy has won the regard and admiration of everyone, joined the Lit Committee. The day Dorrie Behrman breezed into her first Committee meeting I little thought "This breath of fresh air" was in time to become the Lit's Ace secretary. Next month, The Ball that put the Lit once again on the social map. Cheerio,
                         SOL.

NEWS LETTER FROM THE HOME FRONT.

It was such a glorious day on Sunday August 6th that I had difficulty in deciding whether to join the Bank-holiday crowds at Seaburn or go to the Lit dance. I went to the dance. But I was at Seaburn during that week-end and I can say that it is literally many years since I have seen it so crowded. The beach is now open and the sands were absolutely thronged. Hundreds of kiddies built sand-castles for the first time in their lives. Buses and trains from the outlying districts and villages could hardly cope with the rush.

The dance was obviously affected by this good weather and it was not

6.

nearly as well attended as usual. However the band was good and those who were there enjoyed themselves. The buffet served delicious sandwiches and the lemonade might have been worse! It was certainly not a flop either socially or financially but I did miss the novelty dances which only "take" properly with a large crowd. I think that if a little more publicity had been provided more people might have been persuaded to come along. But as I have said those who were there did enjoy themselves and if nothing else at least there was room to dance freely.

It was in the February Bulletin that I drew attention to the hopelessness of the piano. At long last the Committee, I understand, have taken expert opinion on it and have been informed that it would be unrepairable - even in peace time - except at a cost out of all proportion to its worth. I am informed that the Committee is now looking out to buy another one. It amazes me that in a town like Sunderland, where the Communal Hall is used by many organisations and for all kinds of functions the piano should have to be bought by one Society. I should have thought that other sections of the Community would contribute towards it or maybe some generous, public minded person would think fit to present one. I feel sure there must be many a home with a piano that is rarely or never used. To present it to the Lit or to the Community would be a great service.

There's a party arranged for the 27th August and if this turns out as good as the last it's going to be fun. I believe the Lit is also having a dance on the 3rd September. I hope to be at both and will give you all the "gen" in the next Bulletin so, until then, Forces, cheerio and good luck.

Yours,
Also After Gen.

EXCERPTS FROM LETTERS.

Lt. Mordaunt Cohen S.E. Asia Command writes: If Pesach demonstrated anything it was that Jewish people no matter what country they come from are staunch in their support of our age old customs and traditions. Of course some are more orthodox than others but the Jewish 'Gefuhl' is there. Now let me relate a true Pesach story. There are several Jewish men serving on both sides of the Hump (the road or rather the air passage to China). General Chenault in command of that area wrote to Brig.Gen. Cheves stating that his Jewish personnel were desirous of celebrating Passover and could he send supplies of Matzos, wine, Haggadhas, and a good recipe for 'Gefillter Fish'. Needless to say he got the lot. It only goes to show that out here the army authorities especially that of the U.S.A. are willing to co-operate as far as possible.

St/Sgt. J. Rosenthal P.A.I. Force writes: I attended a wedding which seems to bear little relation to one of our ceremonies. The bridal pair stand in front of the guests whilst a Tallis is held behind them as a sort of background. A few Kiddushim lasting several minutes completes the Service. Each blessing is followed by cries very much like Red Indian war whoops whilst many of the oriental customs such as sprinkling salt on the bride and dipping the ring in wine are carried out. The Chuppa as we know it is not used, instead it adorns the nuptial couch to which the guests accompany the pair at the end of the wedding feast. One thing that struck me as strange was to see a Mullah stroll in on the ceremony. It transpired that he was a Rabbi of the old school who is permitted to wear the same dress as the Musilman Mullah, a long brown cloak reaching to the heels, and a white turban. Among my other discoveries is the tomb of the Prophet Haggai in a Moslem Mosque. Whether I can visit it or not remains to be seen.

EXCERPTS Continued

Cpl. Ralph Freedman, Special Investigation Branch writes: I am now something of a "G" Man or "F.B.I." as they call them in America. Indeed the branch does co-operate with American "Agents" where Americans come into picture in crimes we are investigating. We mostly work in plain clothes and are called in to deal with R.A.F. crimes more or less in the same way as Scotland Yard are called in by the local civil police all over the country.

Sgt. Sarabouski writes from India: My hobby out here is producing and acting in concert parties and plays. Some success has attended my effort as I have been on the All India Radio several times, the last time I took the part of Bob Cratchit in "Scrooge" from Radio Lucknow.

Dvr. Gillis, B.L.A. writes: I welcome the Bulletin each time as if it was a new idea. It saves a lot of correspondence, by getting all the information about home and pals in one lump. I greatly enjoy Sol Novinski's chats, and look forward to the time when he gets to the days when I and the gang began to take an interest in the Lit. Somehow although the church bells in a nearby village are pealing for the people to come to church, religion seems a long way away, especially Judaism. During the day you are far too occupied to be able to think of these things, it is only at night, when the stars shine out of a perfect moonlit sky and the red balls of tracer rise slowly and gracefully to the far heavens, that I realise that there is a God and try madly to get Mincha, Maariv and Krishmah, into one last quarter hour before diving for the dug-out. I am getting poetical, maybe it is due to the perfect weather we are at present enjoying or maybe it's the satisfaction one gets from having an egg for breakfast. We are quite fortunate to have fresh food on alternate days, and we get the papers on the day of publication, and am now looking forward to reading the 'News of the World' after tea. I had the good fortune to be able to get to a Jewish Service in one of the towns last week, where Rabbi Rabinowitz was officiating. It was very interesting to see Jews from all over England, Scotland and Canada, coming together in a Catholic Church. After we had davened, he gave a sermon of the 'parsha' and alluded to our coming tasks. There were three women, two old and one young, the remnants of the Jewish population of this WHOLE area. Before the war, there was a Jewish population in this particular town of 121 souls. This girl was hidden during the German occupation, and the 120 others were led away, some I suppose to concentration camps, and some to a pitiless death somewhere in Poland. Her name is Shalom Simcha and so it proved to her - her liberation made her very happy. The Chaplain explained to her the meaning of her name, so he told us, and she cried in happiness. Near here are a few of the new cemetries and I visited one. I found there the grave of one L/Sgt. Zimmerman of the Royal Engineers, killed in action near here. At the head of the grave a white wooden 'Magen David' had been erected by his company. I said a quiet 'El Mole Rachamim' for him and stood in tribute, to this brother.

Letters were also received from Sgt. Pearlman P., C.M.F.; A.C.W.l. L Slater, England; L.A.C. Cohen B.A., England; Fus. Freeman, Malta Force; Pte. L. Marks, England; L.A.C. M. Dresner, England; Cpl. Charlton, India; W.O. Nat Goodman, E.A. Command; A/C Landau A., B.L.A.; Cpt. E. Dresner, B.L.A.; L/Cpl. Altman P. India; A.C.W. Miriam Gillis, England and Cpl. N. Cohen, C.M.F.

The Bulletin is issued free to members of the Forces, but private subscribers at the rate of 10/- per year will be gladly accepted.

Will readers please notify change of address before the 20th of the month.

All correspondence to be sent to Rev. S.P. Toperoff, 5 Victoria Avenue, Sunderland.

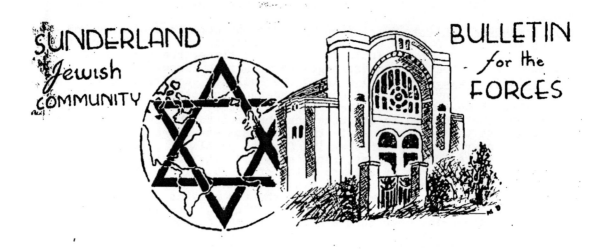

> The Editor and Staff
> send New Year Greetings to
> all serving in the Forces.
> It is our Prayer that the
> coming year herald a new
> era of lasting Peace. May
> you be inscribed in the
> Book of Life.

*Edited and issued monthly by the Minister
and sent to you with the good wishes of
your friends at home.*

September 1944   Vol. 2, No. 13.   Tishri 5705

A Rosh Hashannah Message.

According to Jewish tradition the creation of the world took place on Rosh Hashannah when the first man saw the light of day.   Let us look at the map of the world and see if there are any two countries exactly alike. Have any two countries the same geographical borders, the same shape, the same climate or the same population?   You will find this is not so.   If every country was exactly alike in every detail each would live independantly of its neighbours.   God so fashioned and formed the world that every country has need of the other.   Every people should be dependant on other people; in other words there can be no monopoly by one people over any other.

Rosh Hashannah teaches us that no one race or people should become so strong that it should ultimately enslave the rest of the world and compel it to do its bidding at the point of the bayonet.   This Jewish Festival possesses lessons of ethical and moral content which the world needs today. On Rosh Hashannah we proclaim the sovereignty of God and remind the world that it is God's wish that no one people dare reserve for itself the blessings of mankind whether it be the raw materials of the earth or the acquisition of power to bring about the destruction of any other people. On the contrary, we are all inter-dependant on each other and all must enjoy the four Freedoms to work out their own destiny and salvation in the sphere of religion, politics or economics.

This is the message of Rosh Hashannah to the world.   The Jew does not want war, nor does he seek to dominate the world, but as far as is humanly possible he is asked to imitate God to re-dedicate his life to the ideals of creation.   When God created the world he did not detach himself from this planet.   He is interested in life, better and happier life. There is an interesting anecdote that the Rabbis tell.   A Sage was one asked - "What does your God do all the time?"   And the Sage answered - "He is busy arranging marriages on earth".   A deep truth underlies these words. God wants life, not death; creation, not destruction; peace, no war. Rosh Hashannah is not a tribal festival concerning the Jewish people alone.   It has a universal message for the world.   Even now, in the midst of the welter of slaughter and death, Jews are creating, performing miracles in Palestine by creating new Colonies, building new homes, new colleges, new schools, new arable land to grow food for our soldiers in the Dominions.   Israel is still creating.   Whilst eight million Jews have been encircled by a ring of steel, caught in the maelstrom of concentration camps and mediaeval ghetto with its resultant epidemics and terrible loss of life, a small Jewish community of half a million souls is still creating a new world in Palestine and giving as of old, religion to the world.   We must create a virile and strong Palestine, we must create to defend our ancestral home, we must create to consolidate our religious position, we must create to erect a new haven of refuge for our brethren who are eager awaiting to escape from the occupied countries.   We think of our brethren more so on Rosh Hashannah because we are ushering in a New Year.   Our prayers, wishes and aspirations must be that in the New Year their lot will be eased and room will be found for them in the Jewish National Home.   The New Year has tremendous potentialities, new possibilities, great hopes and wonderful aspirations.   Let us go forward towards a better world, toward the overthrow of the destructive forces of tyranny and all forms of enslavement, towards a new world order based on the traditions of the Torah.

A Happy New Year to you all.

2.

DO YOU KNOW?

Why did Mahomet compose a special prayer to God to help him combat Jews.

Who wrote "I see now that the Greeks were only handsome striplings whilst the Jews were always men - powerful indomitable men - who have fought and suffered on every battlefield of human thought. How small Sinai appears when Moses stands upon it."

Who was Professor Martin Lamm?

Who was the author of "Tales from Hoffman"?

Who gave the first lecture in the Hebrew University of Jerusalem?

What is the WIZO?

Answers to the above questions on Page 5.

HERE AND THERE!

MAZELTOV.

Congratulations to:

Weddings - Miss Gertrude Kolson on her marriage to Pte. Harry Rosenberg
of Glasgow.
Miss Bertha Rosin, B.A. on her marriage to Lieut. Joseph
Priceman R.A.M.C. of Leeds.

Engagements - Miss Freda Oler, L.G.S.M., A.L.C.M., W.A.A.F. to Seymour
David Wiener, of U.S.A.A.F. of New York.

Educational Successes.

School Certificate Examination - Betty Schwam, Beryl Wilder.
Oxford Certificate Examination - Charles Brewer, David Levinson, Myer
Robinson.

We have just heard that Marcus Lipton an old Sunderland boy now in the Army has been promoted to the rank of Lieut. Colonel. Colonel Lipton born in 1900 was educated at the Hudson Road Council School and the Bede. He has a scholastic career, he was Exhibitioner at Merton College, Oxford and took his degree in Modern History. He became an Alderman of the Lambeth borough Council 1937 and a J.P. of the County of London 1939. He enlisted with the Territorials and rose rapidly from the ranks. His Jewish Communal activities in the past have been wide and varied. He was a Council Member of the English Zionist Federation, a member of the Board of Deputies, Hon. Secretary of the Jewish National Fund, Hon. Secretary of the Ben Uri Jewish Art Society and a Council member of the Jewish Historical Society. He was for a number of years Private Secretary to James De Rothschild M.P.

Congratulations to Major Dennis Cohen who was mentioned in Despatches in recognition of gallant and distinguished service in Italy. Major Cohen is a nephew of Mr. M. Jacoby and Mr. & Mrs. D. Cohen.

An interesting gathering took place recently at the Communal Hall when a SIYUM was held on the Kitzur Shulchan Aruch. This Jewish classic which has been studied by the Study Circle which meets under the guidance of the Minister every Shabbos afternoon between Minchah and Maariv was concluded in the presence of a representative gathering with Mr. A. Merskey in the chair. After the Minister explained the purpose and significance of the Siyum, Mr. Jacob Clarke proposed the health of the Minister and Mr. I. Gordon the success of the Circle. Mr. M. Markson responded on behalf of the Circle. Refreshments, tea and cakes and light drinks were provided by the Council of the Synagogue, Mrs. I.E. Cohen, Mr. S. Kelly and Mr. Sol Isaacs.

3.

A Public Meeting organized by the Interim Committee of Christians and Jews took place at the Town Hall with the Mayor in the Chair. The Rev. Dr. James Parkes, a scholar of note and a prolific writer on the Jewish problem spoke on "The Jews, their Future and Ourselves." The Mayor proposed that a local Council of Christians and Jews be formed and Mrs. S.P. Toperoff seconded the resolution, which was carried unanimously.

The Mayor and the speaker were thanked by the Rev. Utton (Chairman of the New Council) and seconded by Alderman J. Cohen. The Rev. R. Richardson, Vicar of St. Barnabas, who is the Hon. Secretary of the Local Council was largely responsible for the organisation of the Meeting.

We have been honoured by special mention in the "Eighth Army Jewish News Bulletin". The Editor writes:- "Contact between Congregations in Britain and members in the Forces serving abroad has been neglected by those at home, as well as other numerous aspects of welfare work for Jewish soldiers. One Community, Sunderland, is perhaps a model for all others, in that each member in the services receives a monthly magazine, edited by the Minister, Rev. S.P. Toperoff. London as the main centre of Jewish existence in Great Britain, has never been sufficiently united or organised on a real community basis to allow for this affinity between a serving man and his community. There can be no doubt, therefore, that a monthly digest of Communal and world Jewish news sent through the post to every Jewish soldier is a paramount and urgent necessity".

EN PASSANT   -   INQUISITOR.

Can it be with Victory so imminent, that I am going to take my rightful place in the background of Social activity once more? I can't explain - it is not everyone who has the opportunity of enjoying such publicity. Forgive my unwonted note of dejection and humility, but I feel very deeply, the mere thought of my transfer to the realms of the great unknown. Like greater persons even than myself I find living up to my success a great achievement and to retire into mere oblivion will be an even greater one NOW. It is bad to become accustomed to the fanfare of trumpets, plush carpets and an adulating crowd .... This may be my swan song, que faire?

Hi-de-hi until ....

FLASH
Taxi! Taxi!! Taxi!!! Taxi!!!! Tel No. 8000?
Rumour hath it that it took S. Africa to separate Sunderland's David and Jonathon (Or David and Arnold?)
America, I love you to such a DEGREE(S).
Which member of the R.A.F. celebrated his birthday on the day of National Prayer - what a celebration!
Oct. 18th! Oct.18th!! Oct. 18th!!! Oct. 18th!!!!
Nice work, Shipping Magnate.
On dit that even a worm will turn, or is it "little pup"?
Whose partiality for nurses has been finally proved?
Who is the Harrod Queen of India (evidently not one of God's frozen people!)
Comment ca va, le medecin? Aime-t-il encore les NURSE'S, peut-etre les anglais seulement, n'est-ce pas?
Will the Scottish King of Jazz have leave for Rosh Hashannah - a certain person hopes so.

4.

FLASH Continued

Has the Algerian Skoik's equilibrium been completely restored yet?   Retain a sense of humour at any cost!

We think an attractive W.R.E.N. has made a faux pas in her recent supposition - try again.

How are the THREE DAWS?

Who likes 6 eggs for 3/-.

Who is contemplating a mesalliance?   Take heed.

Argus is on Holiday.   His article will be resumed next month.

IN RETROSPECT

The Fancy Dress Ball was held in the Alexandra and Edward Halls. The Lit Committee received the guests in the vestibule.   Each invitation having been numbered the guests name was known to the Stewards welcoming them and introductions were exchanged immediately.   A great advantage when the Visitors came from a neighbouring town.

A striking change had come over the people, young and not so young. The elaborate coiffures of the ladies and the long graceful gown had departed, the shorter gown, the bobbed or sleek shingled head was now fashionable.   The men's dress shirts were semi-stiff or made of pleated and delightfully soft silk.   The open big wing collar instead of the old "choker" and larger bow was worn.   Many men wore black braided white waist-coats.   The girls looked boyish and the boys looked and felt comfortable.

Gone was the pre-war dignified and formal atmosphere..   When the young Lady met her gentleman friend a few years previously she said "Good evening Jake". He said "Goodevening Becky. How do you do".   Now it was "Hello Ray", and she replied "Hello Jack".   The Fancy Dress was negligible.   These young people had come to dance.   The long stern years of war were left behind and now they meant to have a good time.

The Dance Band engaged were all musicians from the Empire Theatre orchestra.   Mr. Streets, a fine violinist, Mr. Pillar one of the finest Flutists in the district, Mr. Jack Mackintosh, certainly the cleverest Cornetist in the North (now of B.B.C. Fame), the Theatre drummer and a powerful pianist (a lady of much ability).   This splendid combination sent a good band to play until the Theatre closed down.   So keen were they that they stayed to play with the master musicians.   This gave us a band of nine performers.   There was a feeling of expectancy among the dancers when the full combination assembled.   The M.C. announced a One Step and with a roll of the drums this crack Orchestra struck up "Alexander's Rag time band".   The effect was electrical.   In a moment the dance floor was crowded.   Everybody seemed to be dancing.   "Come on and hear, come on and hear, Alexander's Rag-time Band", everybody was singing, stepping and swinging it.   The Stewards were lined up in the gallery with stocks of coloured streamers.   "Come on and hear, its the best band in the land."

The signal was given.   A row of streamers shot out above the heads of the dancers as they swayed to the rhythm of the hit tune of the season. There were balloons, squeakers, paper hats and other novelties.   Who could resist dancing to the haunting melody of the Waltz plus lime-light effects?   The running Buffet was exceptionally good.   In fact every-

5.

thing was of the best and nothing was forgotten.   But, all goodthings
must come to an end and at 2 a.m. the dancers formed into a circle and the
M.C. was pushed into the centre.   The Auld Lang Syne was sung.
     Then followed the Hartikvah and God Save the King.   The grand ball
was ended save for the tired but happy Good-byes of departing guests, the
banging of motor car doors, the hooting of motor car horns and the sound
of early 20's accelerators as the guests were whisked homeward up the
slope of the Park Terrace.   The M.C. and Hon. Secretary said Good-morning
to Mr. Reay the caretaker, and went home very tired, but happy.   For had
not the Lit again proved it could "Deliver the Goods"!
     Next month - "Loyalty to the Chair".
                    Cheerio,
                    SOL.

Answers to Questions on Page 2.

1. He was terrified at the active opposition and the heroic qualities of
   the Jews whom he tried to overcome.
2. Heine, 1797-1856.   One of the greatest poets of modern Germany.
3. A Jewish member of the Nobel Prize Award Committee for Literature and
   Sweden's most eminent literary authority.
4. Jacques Offenbach 1819-1880, son of a Chazan.
5. Einstein who expounded his theory of Relativity.
6. Womens International Zionist Organization which looks after the
   domestic and agricultural training of women, girls and children.   The
   WIZO maintains hostels for immigrants, training farm providing
   vocational training for thousands of Jewish girls.   It also possesses
   an agricultural school at Nahalal and runs babies homes, infant
   welfare centres and day creches in Palestine.

NEWS LETTER FROM THE HOME FRONT.

     I forecast last month that the party then arranged for the 27th
August was going to be fun - and it was!   It got going about 8.0 after a
few dances to the gramophone.   Musical chairs - or rather a novel version
of it - started the programme and as each person was caught out he or she
went along to the table at the end of the Hall.   This was copiously
supplied with cakes, biscuits and sandwiches - the latter, were extremely
tasty.   More dances were interposed amongst the games and competitions of
which, perhaps the "Double or Quits" caused most excitement.   It was
arranged in the style of the well known radio novelty of that name in
"Mediterranean Merrygoround".   There was a choice of several subjects and
many competitors made their attempts worth while!   Then there was "I want
to be an Actor" again arranged by Rosalie Gillow and it went down with its
customary laughter.   And there was a Musical Quiz arranged by Jack Louis.
Time had gone faster than we thought and a few dances brought to a
conclusion a really jolly evening.   Rather as an anti-climax we left the
hall to find rain pouring down and I, for one, arrived home my spirits
high but my clothes very much damped!
     Wounded soldiers of all denominations were entertained at the Communal
Hall on 10th September from 3.0 till 8.30 p.m.   The arrangements were
made by the Lit committee ably assisted by a few social-minded ladies.
Between 20 and 30 men came along and they had, as they themselves said,
"the time of their lives".   A wonderful tea was provided and a programme

6.

of suitable games and competitions held the attention of the visitors and helpers alike. The chief events were "I want to be an actor", in which the forces themselves took part; accordian playing by Pearl Levey and her friend, and "Double or Quits" which Aubrey Gordon repeated from the party. For this eight subjects were available and, curiously enough (!) all the competitors got all of their answers correct! Rev. Toperoff welcomed the lads and a sergeant, who seemed to be their leader, expressed very warm words of thanks. I must say that the Lit committee deserved every possible ounce of credit for this affair. The team work they displayed would, I feel sure, have held even Argus spell-bound for never have I seen members of a committee co-operate in such close harmony as they did on this occasion. Before they left, the boys almost bubbled over with words of appreciation and exclaimed how much they had enjoyed themselves. This kind of thing goes a long way to aid understanding between Jews and their neighbours.

The Lit dance arranged for September 3rd was, of course, cancelled when a National Day of Prayer was proclaimed but I think one is being organised for shortly after Simchas Torah.

Cheerio for now, forces and chins up!

Yours,
Also After Gen.

EXCERPTS FROM LETTERS.

Sgt. Pearlman P., C.M.F. writes: In Algiers, a city of 30,000 Jews there are some fourteen synagogues only one of which is Ashkenazi and consisted mainly of refugees from Paris and Strasbourg. The first time in a Shool there, I was completely confused not realising that there was such a vast difference in the service, however I got used to it and developed an admiration for their ecstatic behaviour and their praying with such might and main that it called for physical effort. The Jewish quarter is in the heart of the rough district of Algiers. It was extremely interesting watching the Arabs and being pestered by beggars and vendors from silks and fruit to daggers and rusty nails. The spot I'm stationed in at the moment has the most magnificent scenery and never have I felt so close to native. I'm encamped in an orchard containing a profusion of fruit trees and grape vines, the latter unfortunately not yet ripe. A large lake nearby is like a sheet of blue glass containing fresh clear water in which I bathe once daily. The farmers are extremely friendly and seem sincerely happy. I envy them their life in some respects, living on the products of their labour. I wash under a pump from a well outside a farm house and was very impressed watching an old lady literally sorting the "wheat from the chaff" the other morning. She had cut some ears of corn and was rubbing them together, then lifting it by handfuls and letting it drop into the bowl, the wind blew the chaff away. In a crude machine the grain is ground into flour and she would have enough to feed her family for the next few days on top of what she was allowed on her ration card. Often do I think of that line in Grey's Elegy in a "Country Church yard" - 'Let not ambition mock their worldly toil.'

L.A.C. I Davis, B.L.A. writes: At a recent service I attended there were over 300 of us present, the service taking place in a special hall, "somewhere in France". Just before the beginning of prayers, the one and only Jewish A.T.S. girl who was present kindled the Friday night lights and to be able to see the Shabbos candles again gave me and no doubt the rest of us, a grand feeling.

7.

EXCERPTS Continued.

Cpl. N.M. Cohen, C.M.F. writes: I'm enclosing the latest copy of the Army Jewish News Bulletin in which you will notice Sunderland's commendation for its Bulletin. I sent a copy to Sidney Palace, the Editor, and he must have been well impressed with it. The war is going splendidly on all fronts and I don't think that you'll have many more war-time bulletins to publish. Perhaps we will have a final Chanukah war-time edition.

A/C Landau of B.L.A. writes: I don't think that anything could bind Sunderland Jewish Servicemen together more than the receipt of the Bulletin. Surely there can be no greater "mitzvah" than keeping the heart and pulse of Sunderland Jewish men and women beating even though they may be thousands of miles away. To those who are nowhere near any Jewish people such as the Burmese jungle, the Bulletin must be as mentally and spiritually comforting as food is physically comforting to a starving man.

Cpl. I.J. Charlton from India writes: Re lack of Chaplains, I suggest the co-ordination of the U.K. and American Jewish Welfare boards with a combined headquarters at some convenient centre — e.g. London. The advantage of this scheme would enable the Chaplains, whether British or American to be able to go to all the Jewish troops in their area.. In order to enable this scheme to work successfully of course, it would be necessary for the combined headquarters to be supplied with up-to-date lists of the disposition of Jewish troops. This could be done by individual efforts on the part of the men or by unit commanders by arrangements with the commander in chief of the theatre concerned. Secondly Jewish Chaplains must literally get mobile. It is in places like the Burma fronts and remoter and smaller cities that a great need is felt of the chaplains services. Thirdly, every Jewish soldier, sailor or airman must be informed of the facilities for worship and Jewish recreation available to him in his particular theatre.

Sgt. N.J. Franks of M.E.F. writes: There is a great 'drive' at the moment for a better understanding between Palestinian and non-Palestinian Jew. Rather late perhaps after four years of association in the Middle East theatre. Nevertheless there is a possible orgy of music recitals, concerts, dances and other functions designed to bring Judaism to know itself. The British Jew places Judaism above Zionism, the Palestinian Jew reverses that. In an effort to learn more of their point of view I regularly attend Onegim, each Friday evening at one or other of the Palestinian Camps. Though they will not be drawn too deeply into a discussion of religious ethics, I am learning much, and can now divide them into two classes. The farmers, fervent, proud, religious, and the city dwellers - with less likeable qualities. It is of interest to note that many of the city dwellers are post 1934 refugees from Europe.

Letters also received from Gnr. Kolson, L/C Altman, L.P., Fus. B. Freeman, Malta Force; S.Lieut. B. Gould, Sierra Leone and Warrant Officer I. Levine, India. ————

Will readers please notify change of address before the 20th of the month.

All correspondence to be sent to Rev. S.P. Toperoff, 5 Victoria Avenue, Sunderland.

```
        "Be strong and of good
     courage, be not afraid neither
     be thou dismayed, for the Lord
     thy God is with thee whitherso-
     ever thou goest".

                    Joshua, 1:9.
```

*Edited and issued monthly by the Minister
and sent to you with the good wishes of
your friends at home.*

October 1944.   Vol.3 No. 1   Cheshvan 5705.

Genesis

Once again we have begun the re-reading of our Torah from Genesis. Here we do not have a vicious circle but a happy and glorious circle of events. The end of the reading of the Torah is marked by the celebration of Simchas Torah accompanied with merriment and good fun, and the following week we again gladly commence Bereshis.

Even those of you who were fortunate to attend Services on Rosh Hashannah and Yom Kippur will not have had the opportunity to drink the toast of the Torah on Simchat Torah.

Let us then remind ourselves of the happy times these celebrations called forth. How we danced and sang clinging to our Sepher Torah and revelled in the thought that the Scroll of the Law was our mainstay and that we would hold on to it's immortal teachings at all times.

Especially in these days of war with it's resultant death and destruction should we emphasise this note of optimism so characteristic of Judaism. It is unfortunate that to many of our young people Judaism is connected with funereal customs of sadness and mourning. Religion in the minds of many is synonymous with a gloomy and sordid outlook on life.

This of course is entirely untrue especially of our Religion. "Serve the Lord with gladness", is the keynote of Judaism. Our Services may lack the decorum and quietness of the Church for we treat the Synagogue not only as a house of Prayer but a place of meeting, a friendly house where we meet God in Prayer and our neighbours and friends in convivial friendship.

This aspect of worship is unfortunately more marked in war than in peace time. From my correspondence I note with what happiness Sunderland boys have met each other at Services in France, India, Italy and more remote places. The Service then is not only an opportunity of offering grateful prayers to the Almighty, but at the same time serves as an important centre-social as well as religious for the scattered units of the Jewish personnel.

It is the fervent prayer and wish of all of us at home who have you constantly in our minds that it will not be long before you all meet again at the Reunion Service in your Home-town. In the meantime keep up your spirits and put your trust in the God of the Torah who always guards and watches over you. Strengthen your faith in Judaism which is a Religion of Life and Happiness. May this be your last "Shabbos Bereshis" away from home.

DO YOU KNOW?

1. Which Jewish Leader committed suicide in London in vain hope that his death would contribute to moving public opinion to the plight of Jews in the world?
2. Which Talmudic Rabbi became a master of Anatomy?
3. What is the percentage of Jewish recipients of awards in the lists of Nobel prize winners?
4. Which Jewish Minister delivers his sermon in the deaf and dumb language?
5. Who founded the famous International Institute for Agriculture in Rome?
6. What is the Vaad Leumi?

Answers to the above on page 3.

2.

HERE AND THERE!

MAZELTOV:
Congratulations to:-
WEDDINGS   - Rita Olswang, V.A.D. on her marriage to Cpl. Isaac Brewer.
            Muriel Sugden on her marriage to Bernard Millet of Nottingham.
ENGAGEMENTS - L.A.C. Harold Isaacs R.A.F.V.R. on his engagement to Miss
            Sheila Bloom of Leeds.
WELCOME TO THE FORCES -
            We welcome to the Forces Olga Grantham V.A.D. who has arrived
in India and Douglas Goldman of 22 Beechwood Street, Sunderland.
EDUCATIONAL SUCCESSES)-
            The following 13-14 age group have qualified for entrance to
the Bede School :- Ruth Cohen, Marion Friedlander and Gertrude Schiffman.
FROM THE JEWISH CHRONICLE.
            Reference has again been made in the pages of the Jewish
Chronicle to our boys in the Forces. Philip Pearlman was in the news
with a description of the "Yellow Badge" given him in Italy by a Dutch
Refugee.
            Reference was also made to Driver Lionel Gillis for the part
he played in organising Services in France.

IN RETROSPECT.

        The Fancy Dress Ball made more than sufficient profit to enable the
Zionist Committee to honour an ardent fellow worker by inscribing his
name in the Golden Book. About this time the "Lit" meetings were being
invaded by hordes of very naughty youngsters. Their elder brothers and
sisters objected to their presence and noisy behaviour. The Committee
did nothing in the matter so one Sunday evening the members decided to act
on their own initiative. A policeman was called and the youngsters were
evicted.
        Walking up Norfolk Street to the meeting I was surrounded by those
children. They expressed their indignation in no uncertain manner. I
replied as firmly about sympathetically as I could. Then the cry arose:
"Can't you do something for us, Mr. Novinski? We have nothing to do
and no one thinks about us".
        I promised I would do my best for them. Who could resist such a
plea? But my time was fully occupied. I was Chairman of two Societies
(including four Committees). It was two years later that the first
Sunderland group of Jewish Boy Scouts was formed, however, that is another
story.
        Some time later a number of very enthusiastic Zionists acted quite
unconstitutionally and feeling very hurt and slighted, I refused to accept
re-nomination for the Chair.
        On reporting to the "Lit" Committee and stating my case I found the
members in agreement with my action.
        At the annual General Meeting it was decided to withdraw from the
Association, and the Society was again known as the Sunderland Jewish
Literary Society. The members also decided that all lectures were to be
presided over by their own chairman. He alone would be able to invite
another to take his place should he desire it. The Committee could however suggest a guest chairman on special occasions.
        I was much affected by this mark of loyalty to the Chair.
        Next month - we move to the Unity Chambers, Athenaeum Street.
                        Cheerio,
P.S.   SOL.
On October 12th last I had the honour of presenting on behalf of the Lit a
beautiful canteen of cutlery to Rita and Isaac Brewer, the occasion was their

marriage.   Knowing the affection you absent members have, for Rita and Isaac I gave them your best wishes for a bright and happy future. The occasion was one of my unforgetable memories.

Answers to Questions on Page 1.

1. The Bundist leader Zygielbohm who committed suicide in London two years ago.
2. Samuel (175 to 254) practised dissection on dead bodies of executed slaves and thus became a master of Anatomy.
3. The percentage of Jewish recipients of awards in the lists of Nobel prize winners is nine - whereas Jews constitute less than one per cent of the total population of the world.
4. In the deaf and dumb Synagogue in New York the congregation of which is entirely composed of deaf and dumb people.
5. David Luzatto.
6. The elected assembly in Palestine which does similar work to the English County Council.   It can hold land and levy rates on it's members for educational and philanthropic purposes.

SEARCHLIGHT ON SPORT   -   By "Argus".

When I penned these notes Sunderland were still at the top of the League.   You will perhaps recall that at this time last year we were in the same position and then in November came the slump.

I am not anticipating the same thing happening, but I am just warning you, my hearties.   It is not even intelligent anticipation - just a warning.

A very well known sports writer on a national newspaper invariably used to "tip" a side to win which did not look to have an earthly chance of winning.   If the team was beaten then no one took the slightest notice If it won it gave him the opportunity to say "I was the only one to say it" - with splash headlines, of course.   I am not on that stunt.

Actually, playmates, Sunderland have been playing well, especially at half-back which has been the foundation of the teams strength.   Now however, Freddie Laidman has gone to the South and the whole front line has been upset.   A continuation of this, with the consequent throwing of more work on the defence, might just bring about that change which took place a year ago.   That is just what I am afraid of.

Raich Carter is still collecting International Caps.   He played in five Nationals before the war and ten since, so he has the distinction of having played in more Internationals than any other Sunderland born player

Bradwell, that whole hearted wing half whom Manager Murray picked up from the Coastal battery at Roker, was in Holland as a paratrooper and is back in England with a fractured leg.   I hope the surgeons make a sound job of it, because he is a great hearted player this.

Bob Gurney is over in France somewhere with the R.A.F., but Eddie Burbanks, after remaining in India a few weeks in home in England again. Ear trouble sent him home and on the journey he developed jaundice. Though he is playing he is far from fit.

4.

Johnnie Smeaton, whom we secured from Burnley, is back in Scotland. He was slightly wounded in Normandy and no doubt he will soon be ready for overseas again.

I suppose that by the time many of you receive this issue our Christmas and New Year will be upon you. May I therefore take this opportunity of conveying to you all my best wishes and season's greetings. May many of you be safely home this time next year. Good luck to you all - and good hunting of the common foe. Wish I were thirty years younger.

Inquisitor's Article will be resumed next month.

"Some Thoughts on Jews" by Lionel Altman, India.

I have met some fellows from Palestinian Units in this country, and it may be of interest to you to learn a few things about them, and how they struck me. They of course have their own Blue and White flag. I found them to be a new type of Jew - they have a tremendous pride in their achievements, and an awareness of the fight to come. They look upon themselves as the advance guard of the Jews of Europe - their language is Hebrew, and the Mogan David is on all their equipment. They helped a lot in freeing lots of people from concentration camps on the Dalmatian coast, and subsequently assisted in setting up camps in Italy for these helpless people, and out of their (roughly) £6 a month pay - they gave £1 to the rescue work that is going on.

All of us I suppose are concerned with Anti-Semitism, some believe in taking militant steps to fight it, others say, 'Hush, pay no attention to it.' There are Jews whose names are world famous, and others so humble and poor and unsuccessful and obscure, that nobody outside their own families know they are there. There are some of us who fear that regardless of which way the war ends, they will at once be the victims of persecution and discrimination, and there are others - the great majority - who have a deathless confidence in the essential integrity of the English, and American masses to see that justice is done to ALL people after the war. Really we have one thing in common, and that is we are Jews, and even that means different things to different people, it even means different things to different Jews. There is of course a minority which deplores the accident of birth that made them Jewish, such people do everything in their power to escape their Jewishness, they are I think generally scorned and despised by the great bulk of our people, like any other people do who are so justly proud of their ancient lineage and great traditions. Without (I wish to emphasise this) at all falling for the Nazi doctrine of so called "racial theory" one can say that the Jews are a people, and that is probably the only generalization one can make, whether any individual likes it or not - whether in fact he is conscious of it or not the Jewish people, despite all their incredible and colourful diversifications, have a common religious cultural, and historical heritage that goes back some five thousand years, and in those times as in these we have contributed our talents, toil and genius to mankind and civilization. Its forms are changing as they have changed elsewhere in history acclimatizing themselves to time and place which is the condition of all survival, but the content of Judaism as preserved through the ages by the people lives on.

I think we should stand for the construction of a vital patriotic, civic-minded and Jewishly informed English Jewry, and that both Judaism and Britain have democracy as their central concept and if democracy means

Continued on Page 7.

5.

NEWS LETTER FROM THE HOME FRONT.

Hello Forces, I'm here once again with a few snaps of 'gen' from the home town. As far as people on leave were concerned the Yomim-Tovim passed over comparatively quietly. Few uniforms were to be seen in either Shool.

The Lit has just launched a full scale Appeal for funds to buy a piano. Gentle propaganda paved the way and then donations were requested. Already many have generously supported this extremely worthy cause but I consider it an occasion when every Jewish person should play his or her part. A piano in the Communal Hall is used on all sorts of occasions and by many Societies and people. It is truly the concern of everyone and it is a cause where, with your own eyes, you can see the fruits of your donation. I am confident that everyone will play the game and the target will be reached.

The Lit does not however believe in relying entirely upon donations but is also helping by organising events the proceeds of which are ear-marked to aid the piano fund. The first of these was a dance on the 15th October. There was one of the largest gatherings that I have seen in the Hall for a dance since the war! Both Newcastle and South Shields were well represented and everyone had a gay time dancing to the strains of Arthur S. Smith's band which, as usual, played well. And of course there was the customary running buffet which soon ran out of sandwiches! This dance was successful socially and must have swelled the Piano Fund a good deal.

Sol Novinski, as President of the Lit, presented a Canteen of Cutlery to Rita Olswang and Isaac Brewer at their wedding on the 12th October. This, said Sol, was a token of the deep appreciation of the exceptional amount of good work the bride and bridegroom had done for the Lit. I hope that this will prove an incentive to some of our younger members!

Now here is as much of the future programme as I have been able to ascertain:- Oct. 22nd - Inter-Debate with South Shields; 29th - Social and Table Tennis Tournament; Nov. 5th - Lecture; Nov. 12th - Concert, Party and Dance.

That's all for now, Forces, but you will no doubt be wondering how long it will be before you are "demobbed". Builders think they will be out of the war first but I have it on authority that a certain paper-hanger will beat them to it!

Keep smiling, all, and good luck.

Yours,
Also After Gen.

EXCERPTS FROM LETTERS.

S/Cdr. Isadore Levine from India writes: I had the honour to get an "ALIYAH" - my first ever, on Yom Kippur. It was very pleasant to know that this may be our last year overseas. We all did justice to the huge "after the fast" meal arranged in the "MARINA HOTEL" - (one of India's finest hotels), and almost 200 people sat down to participate in this communal meal. The usual speeches, and declarations of "Anglo-American" goodwill were made, but an unusual feature was the fact that an American and British "Pte." were called upon to represent their respective Armies. Leo Levin did an excellent job in Meerut, only 50 miles away. As all the boys in his unit couldn't get leave, he stayed behind (I had expected him in Delhi) and conducted the services there. Leo is really a credit to the Sunderland Community; amongst other things he has organised Hebrew classes for the Jewish boys in his unit.

L.A.C. Charles Gillis, C.M.F. writes: I spent a few pleasant days in Naples. Amongst the Jewish soldiers present at the Jewish Services Club I spoke to Palestinians from Tel Aviv and from the Kvutzot, members of the Free French Forces, sailors in the Polish Navy, a Yugo-Slav partisan, apart from the Americans and English who were there. It was quite evident that there is a bond between us all which is in no way affected by language or the accident of birth behind some political boundary. For the second part of my leave I made a hitch hike trip to Rome. I spent only one full day in the city, but it is one which I shall never forget. As we walked amongst the ruins of Ancient Rome I pointed out to my non-Jewish companion the famous arch of Titus, telling him that it commemorated the conquest and destruction of the Jewish people. He replied that if Titus could see the "Palestinian" soldiers in Italy it would make him realise that "he'd had it!" We visited the Vatican and were duly shown the miracles of sculpture by Michael Angelo and Bernini. The wealth of art and architecture concentrated in so small a city is truly awe-inspiring. But we have lived amongst the peasants of Italy and know their plight. Even my Christian friends agree that the Vatican is a gigantic monument to the complete failure of the Catholic Church.

L.A.C. Charles Marks, C.M.F. writes: I was talking to a refugee who originates from Germany and he told me in almost perfect English that he had seen Sunderland football team when they were playing the continental matches way back; many people I have met know Sunderland as a football team, but that's all. I see my colleague in Rome has been keeping you informed as to local happenings, but his food shortage problem should be solved now. Here in Southern Italy, I'm tempted to say the uncivilised part of the country, the food situation has been relieved by the influx of American canned goods, even milk has made its appearance in tins, something which apparently has been absent for quite some time. It's remarkable that the civilian population cannot obtain sugar, yet one can see in some shops iced chocolate cakes - but at what a price. Anything from 800 to 900 lire, that is £2 to £2. 5s. I don't think anyone would believe how far behind the times they are in this part of the world, the filthy hovels which the population are pleased to call houses, the dingy smelly streets which in the majority of cases isn't wide wide enough for two vehicles to pass. I have seen Taranto, Brindisi, Bari and other places but one has to travel up as far as Bari before contacting anything like what we're used to.

L.A.C. Issy Davis, B.L.A. writes: I was literally mobbed by the people of Brussels, insisting I should return home with them and at times it was most embarrassing. However, I was eventually entertained by a young couple - their hospitality towards me was really overwhelming. They kindly presented to me a badge of the Belgium Maccabi which I appreciated very much indeed, especially as I was a staunch member of the Sunderland Maccabi pre war.

Dvr. Lionel Gillis, B.L.A. writes: I agree with one of your correspondents, in that we have all too few Chaplains in this theatre at any rate. When our Chaplain was recalled to England just before Rosh Hashannah, it left us high and dry and we just had to manage as best we could. A

Sergeant davened the first day and as he had to leave then, I officiated for the rest of the time. The men present were representative of the country we come from, and we managed quite well. Although we had been promised Kosher food, we managed just as well on bully beef and biscuits for Rosh Hashannah night. As a gift from some Germans who had overlooked them, I brought along a bunch of grapes for making 'Shehechiyonu' and also a bottle of beer for which I had waited nine weeks for making Kiddush on. We were in a Catholic Church, in a place where up till a few days previously, Germans had been ill-treating and expelling Jews, and believe me that they had done this all too well. There was not one Jew left. Usually your correspondents have remarked that on Festivals they have managed to get to a Community, or that some Community or other have done them well. But out here, where we approach the cradle of English Judaism, there is just nothing to look for. It is a sheer waste of time, I have discovered to go and look for our Brethren - they just aren't there any longer. When on the second day of Rosh Hashannah I davened, and despite its absence from the Soldiers Prayer Book, I said the 'Nsane Tokef', many strong men in that little Catholic Church had tears in their eyes. They did not need to know or try to imagine what MI VA-ESH means - they KNEW. They had gone through the Valley of the Shadow of death this last year, and were wondering what this new year held in stock for them.

The following letters are also gratefully acknowledged by the Editor: A.C.W.1. Leoni Slater, England; A.C.2 David Cohen, ENGLAND; A.C. Arnold Landau; B.L.A.; Dvr. Lionel Gillis, B.L.A.; Staff Sergeant J. Rosenthal, P.A.I.; A.C.1 Harold Shochet, SO. AFRICA; Capt. E. Dresner, B.L.A.; Pte. Leo. Levine, INDIA; Cpl. Norman Cohen, C.M.F.; Lt. Mordaunt Cohen, S.E.A.C.; S/Lieut. Barry Gould, SIERRA LEONE; L/Cpl. Lionel Altman, INDIA; Gnr. E. Kolson, ENGLAND; L/Cpl. Philip Pearlman, C.M.F.; Fus. B. Freeman, MALTA FORCE; Nurse Olga Grantham, V.A.D., INDIA; ACC D. Rosenthall, SO. AFRICA; W/O N. Goodman, SO. AFRICA COMMAND; L.A.C.W. Annette Gordon, ENGLAND; Rita Brewer, V.A.D. SCOTLAND; L.A.C. Charles Marks, C.M.F.; Cfw. Gwen Magrill, ENGLAND; and L.A.C. Julius Gordon, B.N.A.F.

Continued from page 4.

Continued from page 4.

anything, it means the right of all groups to develop the best that is within them for their own and the common good. We must remember that individuals within any society will always differ healthily, we hope, and so will groups within groups, but strengthened and richened by this diversity, the society they together compose, can march slowly forward to a better world. We Jews in Britain stand or fall with the rest of Britain, itself a symphony of peoples, if we have faults, let him cast the first stone who is without them, if we have virtues, so do all the other groups. At this terrific moment in the world's history, regardless of our almost countless differences, Jews have joined forces on the main battle we fight shoulder to shoulder on every front with our fellows - Allies of other creeds and descent, to destroy forever the monster of fascism which threatens us all. Our ability to win through is lessened by those who seek to divide our ranks through the Nazi technique of reaction - group against group. English people who really know each other, who are guided by the facts and not misled by fiction are the main hope of the world when it comes to winning the war, and more important, to us, the peace that will follow.

The Bulletin is issued free to members of the Forces, but private subscribers at the rate of 10/- per year will be gladly accepted.

Will readers please notify change of address before the 20th of the months.

All correspondence to be sent to Rev. S.P. Toperoff, 5 Victoria Avenue, Sunderland.

"Be strong and of good
courage, be not afraid neither
be thou dismayed, for the Lord
thy God is with thee withersoever thou goest."

Joshua, 1:9.

*Edited and issued monthly by the Minister
and sent to you with the good wishes of
your friends at home.*

November 1944.   Vol. 3, No. 2.   Kislev 5705.

Chanukah.

Before the next issue of the Bulletin we shall have Chanukah with us, "The Festival of Light" has always inspired Jews with hope and courage which we need more than ever today.   The small band of Jewish warriors saved the situation in 168 B.C.E. when the conflict between Jews and Greeks began.   The Temple was then defiled, heathen sacrifices were offered up, scrolls of the Law were burned, Synagogues destroyed, and innocent people put to death.   But this did not break the spirit of the Jews.   On the contrary it encouraged them still more to defend and fight for their rights.

Judas Maccabeus and his followers fought for the four freedoms for which we are fighting today.   They cleansed the Temple of all its impurities and re-dedicated it with the pure light of the Torah.   This was the fight of Judaism against Hellenistic culture over 2,000 years ago.

Today, the same struggle manifests itself.   The Temple of Humanity has been defiled by the putrid race theory of the German herrenvolk.   The boosting of the Jewish bogy has been executed with exemplary thoroughness by the Nazis and it has seeped into the minds of millions who never gave a thought to Jews.   If ever it was time to say that Jews are news, it is today.   Of no people can it be said that the majority are held responsible for the sins of the few.   Yet the whole Jewish people are taken to task in Palestine because of the terrorist activities of an unknown gang of young hot-heads.

What does the future hold out for us?   If German militarism was overthrown tomorrow, anti-semitism would not be uprooted.   The evil has been done.   The Temple of humanity has been paganised by the poisonous propaganda of Nazism.   What is our duty as Jews?   Our enemies would like us to deflect from our course.   But no!   We must go on building the Jewish Homeland undeterred by the stumbling blocks that are put in our way. We are determined to overthrow the heathen altars of race prejudice and intolerance.   This will not be easy.   Super-human efforts on behalf of all Jews will be needed to re-educate the masses to an understanding of the Jew and his religion.

First and foremost we must be fired with resolve to be united and build the Temple of old.   As in 168 so today Scrolls of the Law have been burned, Synagogues have been destroyed and innocent people have been brutally murdered but the Chanukah lights still burn on, lasting witnesses to the immortality of the Jewish spirit.   We have already lived to see Synagogues re-opened in Italy, France, Belgium and Holland.   We can imagine the thrill that must have filled the hearts of the Worshippers who crowded the Synagogues to offer up prayers of Thanksgiving.   Like the Maccabeans of old they are cleansing the Temple and re-kindling the lights one by one.

All the synagogues had been defiled, some used as Gestapo quarters, barracks and stables, whilst others have been completely destroyed.   But the lights of Chanukah will be re-lit and they will all shine forth as beacons of light, hope and inspiration.   Where the synagogue is no longer it will in the meantime be superceded by the Mobile Synagogue one of which was recently consecrated by the Chief Rabbi in London.   These Mobile Menorahs will carry light into the blind desolate wilderness left by the

Nazis.

The spirit of Judas Maccabeus still lives. Chanukah comes as a timely reminder that the sadism and ruthless extermination of Fascism to enslave the world by brute force will not and must not prevail. "Not by might nor by strength but by my spirit, sayeth the Lord". If we are to enjoy a lasting peace the spirit of Chanukah with its eternal message of light and freedom must flood the earth as the waters covered the sea.

May you enjoy a peaceful Chanukah.

DO YOU KNOW?

1. Who was the first Jewish Barrister?
2. Who is the youngest Wing-Commander in the R.A.F.?
3. Who was the first American soldier to land in France?
4. What does the initial "G" stand for in the name of the famous actor, Edward G. Robinson?
5. Who invented the smoke screen?
6. When was the Jewish method of slaughtering animals, Shechitah, introduced in the German army?

Answers to the above on Page 5.

HERE AND THERE!

MAZELTOV.
Congratulations to:-
Weddings - Miss Freda Oler on her marriage to Pte. Weiner, U.S.A.
Dr. J. Stone on his marriage to Lucille Supper of London.
Engagements - Miss Hilda Yudolph to Pte. Joe Goodman R.A.S.C. (overseas) of Pinner, Middlesex.
Miss Shiela Brown to Theodore Jackson.
Birth - Mr. & Mrs. Julius Cohen on the birth of a son.
Dr. & Mrs. Goodman (Miriam Winberg) on the birth of a son.
The following is the syllabus of the Sunderland Young Zionist Association for the past few weeks.
"Jewish and other Justice", Aubrey A. Gordon.
"Jewish characters in Literature", Rosalie Gillow.
"The Woman's Place in Palestine", Sonia Sumner of Newcastle.
"Jewish Humorism", Fay Merskey.
"The Jews in England in the Middle Ages", Charles Cohen.
"Spinoza", Harold Merskey.
"A musical evening", Commentator, Charles Cohen.
"Why a Jewish State", Israel Wilonitz.

The congratulations of the Sunderland Jewish Community are due to Miss Phyllis Heilpern who has accepted an invitation to take up the post of Senior Mistress at the New Hasmonean Grammar School, London. Phyllis Heilpern will be missed as she was the inspiration of Habonim and Habonot. She sacrificed her leisure for the Zionist cause and as chairman of the S.Y.Z.A. for a number of years she helped to build a strong and informative Zionist Youth. Her departure will be felt but we are happy to know that she is taking up important work in the sphere of Jewish education.

3.

The other day a quiet and simple ceremony took place in Sunderland. It was attended by only six people and the occasion was the departure of Sol Novinski for the south. We naturally could not allow such an event to pass unnoticed and the Community was only too pleased to show its appreciation of the worth of one of its members for services that were given continuously over a long number of years for the Jewish youth of the town.

The presentation made by the Rev. S.P. Toperoff took the form of a wallet of Notes and a beautiful dressing case suitably inscribed. To many of you in the forces, the departure of Sol will mean a real wrench, for I know that you passed through his hands either as Scouts, Members of the Dramatic Society or of the Lit. However I am happy to add that the wrench will not be complete for we shall still hear from him through the medium of our Bulletin.

I remember well when I asked him to write of reminiscences for the Bulletin, how keen he was to make further contact with his young friends far from home and whom he could not see at the Lit because of circumstances that were beyond his control. His articles make most interesting reading and I venture to suggest will be the source of a future history of the Lit.

In his work for youth, Sol fortunately acquired that youthful interest in all matters which we hope will always remain with him. He was the soul and guiding spirit of Jewish Youth in all its manifold activities, and he was instrumental in uniting them to meet regularly for literary, cultural and dramatic work. There in the Jewish club-room, whether in the Synagogue Chambers at Moor Street or Unity Chambers or the Communal Hall, Ryhope Road, the Jewish Youth of the town was trained to foregather every Sunday evening under the leadership of Sol to discuss, debate or dramatise various aspects of the Jewish problem.

There Youth dilated, digressed and divined on every possible topic that the imagination conjured up. We often refer to the past as those good old days. They will return, Jewish youth must prepare now the way for a virile, healthy and Jewish Lit.

Whilst you are away from home the Lit is still functioning. This is as it should be. We must, however, remember the pioneering work of that small circle of stalwarts who over 30 years ago laid the foundations of Jewish Youth activity. Of that small circle of workers, pride of place must be given to Sol Novinski for his untiring efforts and selfless devotion to the cause of Jewish youth in Sunderland.

EN PASSANT   -   INQUISITOR

Imagine my chagrin, disappointment, despair, despondence (ad. nauseum) to discover that my journalistic effort is not so vital to Bulletin Production as I had hoped. The magazine goes to "press" and does not find it necessary to wait for my contribution........ I remember the time ..... alas! An involuntary sigh escapes me when I recollect how the Editor used to 'phone, write and way-lay me until my article appeared..... but now! The old order changeth indeed!! One can work one's fingers to the proverbial bone in public service, only to be discarded like an old glove after having served one's nefarious purpose - life is very hard. This month's Inquisition has been in readiness for three weeks so that our noble Editor could not make any more feeble pretexts. I've cudgelled my brain for libellous matter, but all in vain - ah! But who know what the next month portends?

Hi-de-hi to you all.

4.

FLASH

Is it true that a renowned crooning member of the B.L.A. misses his Tait-a-Tait in Newcastle?

On dit that a certain celebrity who dabbles in "chemical research" finds £5 an unlucky sum.

Who is desirous of paying a return visit to Croft? Vive les Americains!

Rumour hath it that the Chester Chapan has great reason to rejoice — roll on reunion!

Which juvenile member of the R.A.F. has many "fancies", but has to be content with a leek?

Where is D.A.?

Is the Beer King of France as convivial as ever?

On dit that the Bournemouth climate is extremely (em)bracing!!!

Can I ever thank C.M.M. for his more than acceptable gift, my "hints" seem to have fallen on fertile ground. How's Jane?

Rumour hath it that Sunderland's loss is going to be London's great gain? (If ever a town suffered).

Are the Pyramids and Mumps synonymous, Corporal?

How does Louis Bromfield II enjoy bridge-ing the gulf with the Brigadier?

Which road LEEDS to the BLOOMS?

IN RETROSPECT.

And so the "Lit" moved into Unity Chambers. Two rooms were placed at its disposal. The smaller, furnished as a private office was used as a Reception Room for Lecturers. After the meeting the male members davened "Maariv" here. A number of these members were thus able to attend the meetings and not miss their "Kaddish". I was one of these men and am very grateful to the Society.

The larger room had a small dais at one end, a Gas Fire with broken asbestos, and was dignified by the name of Hall. The winter of 1924/5 was rather severe and at times the attendances were small. Then the members would sit around the gas fire and in this intimate atmosphere would hold their discussions and debates. Sometimes I would encourage them to talk of their interests and ambitions for the Society. I discovered they were interested in Local Government, the League of Nations, and that there was a strong desire to meet their local M.P.'s.

Often during an interesting talk, the gas fire would go "Plop", back-fire and make a terrible smell. After turning off the gas and allowing the asbestos to cool it would be lighted again and the discussion was resumed. In this atmosphere was formed the friendly policy for which the "Lit" is justly famed.

It was during these talks that I became aware of a quiet but gently insistent voice. It was the voice of a new member, one Simon Light. He was giving the "Lit" many new ideas and more important still they were backed with experience gained in a Literary Society in Manchester. He was prepared to carry out his suggestions. He soon became a Committee Member.

The name of "Literary and Debating Society" was changed to Literary Circle and any sections formed, or to be formed were known as "Circles". This was Simon's idea. He was planning for the future.

The Dramatic Circle was formed and he was Chairman, a position he held for twelve years. Mrs. Robinson, a brilliant elocutionist and myself acted as coaches and work was commenced.

Next month I will write about lecturers who visited us at Unity Chambers. Cheerio,

SOL.

.5.

SEARCHLIGHT ON SPORT   - By Argus .

By the time this article is read by some of you overseas it may be
completely out of date and the League North championship may be decided.
At the moment Sunderland are slightly ahead of Huddersfield by virtue
of a superior goal ratio. Ratio and not average, I think, is the proper
word.   You don't divide the goals "against" into the goals "for to get"
an average.

We in Sunderland are just hoping the championship will land here, but
everything depends upon the players available for the last five games.
It is a worrying time for a Manager for sometimes he does not know until
an hour or so before the start what team he will have out.   Consequently
he has to keep back three or four reserve players and so weakens the
reserve side in their game.

Only once this season have Sunderland had the advantage of the
services of Horatio Carter.   That was at York and he was the means of
passes to his old colleague Eddie Burbanks which produced five goals -
four of them scored by Whitelum.   The centre forward with 18 goals to
his credit at the time of writing, is leading scorer in the northern
section.

At York we played a young back from the reserve side named Stelling.
This is a Washington boy who shows much promise because he is such a big
hearted youngster.   His one fault appears to be the length of his stride.
A player with a long stride when running is easily knocked over because of
the lack of body balance.

League clubs are now considering the changes which should take place
in post war football and they have until December 31st to submit their
suggestions to the League Management Committee.   The Players Union also
have ideas, especially about salaries.   They are meeting the Management
Committee in January.

One definite thing is that the Football League will have nothing to do
with Pools.   The other definite thing is that whether they like it or
not Pools will still be run because the public want them.

Answers to Questions on Page 2.

1. Sir Francis Goldsmith, advocate of the abolition of Jewish disabilities
and after 1860 spokesman of the Jewish Community in Parliament.
2. Hyman Baron, the 20 year old son of Mr. and Mrs. Max Baron of Bulawayo.
3. Lt. Abraham Cotiotti of Jewish-Spanish parentage commanded the first
wave of assault boats which landed allied troops between La Havre and
Cherbourg.   His boat touched the beach within sixty seconds of the
appointed hour.
4. "G" stands for Goldberg, the actor's original name.   When he went on
the stage he added Robinson but retained his proper name in the initial
"G".
5. The use of smoke in war is mentioned in Exodus 14, verses 19-20.   The
Israelites were protected by it during their march from Egypt to the
promised land.
6. After a series of scientific experiments Shechitah was introduced
generally in the German army in 1894.

6.

NEWS LETTER FROM THE HOME FRONT.

As the winter once again rolls on and the naked trees stand shivering in the howling wind we are reminded that this is the Season of the Lit. Indeed the Lit has just started its Winter Session with a healthy vigour that suggests a promising year. Several young folk, only just having reached the age limit, have become members and many of the older staunch supporters have also paid their subscriptions. Some had hoped to gain the benefits of the Lit without paying any subscription but they have been stung by strict action on the part of the treasurer.

The first literary meeting on Oct. 22nd was an inter-debate with the newly formed South Shields Society. The debate was on Co-education with Charles Cohen and Vera Segal (of Shields) proposing and Joyce Gattoff (of Shields) and Esther Cowan opposing. There was an audience of over forty and, after nearly a dozen speakers from the house a show of hands rendered "co-ed" victorious by a large majority.

There was a very well attended Social and Table Tennis Tournament the following week and the week after that (Nov. 5th) there was a talk by Mr. Leon Hirshberg of the County War Exective Agriculture Committee on "The Economic prospects of Palestine" --- a really interesting lecture which was an eye-opener on a great many aspects of the problem.

Sunday 12th November was a great day at the Lit. It started off at 3.30 with a concert organised by Mr. Arthur Smith, the band leader. This was attended mostly by children who no doubt thoroughly enjoyed every minute of it - and also of the tea afterwards which finished about 6.0. The smallness of the audience can be attributed only to the high price of the tickets. At 7.30 the dance started and soon a large gathering filled the floor, stepping to the strains of a seven piece band, which with the lady vocalist, made this dance really outstanding. Needless to say the days events were earmarked to help pay for the piano which the Lit has just bought and which was put into use for the first time at this dance. The required amount has not yet been raised but the Lit Committee is working hard and friends are donating so generously that I feel confident that the outlay will be soon refunded.

The Lit programme this Session is as good as ever. It is to include debates, lectures, socials, music recitals, dances and all the jolly affairs that have become synonymous with 'Lit'. I often think that Shakespeare must have had one eye on the Lit when he said "Age cannot wither her, nor custom stale her infinite variety".

Every member of the Lit, past present and those in the Forces will all wish to join me in sending very best wishes to Sol with sincere hopes that he soon settles down in his new surroundings making many new friends. But we look forward to reading his articles in future as we have done up to now.

I'll be with you again next month, Forces, so until then, good luck and cheerio.

Yours,
Also After Gen.

IN APPRECIATION

1. The Sunderland Jewish Bulletin.
Has gained world wide renown,
Bringing to each one of us
News from the dear home town.

2. To the Editor our gratitude is due
For his tireless toil and labour,
In order that we may all derive
Much pleasure and joy from his paper.

7.

3. To Sol our thanks ,we herewith tender
    For the reminiscences he recalls to mind
    His In Retrospect we all enjoy,
    Such talent as his is indeed hard to find.

4. To Inquisitor in humble praise
    We raise our hats and wonder when
    Her satire and wit will cross our path
    And we stand revealed by her fiery pen.

5. To all contributors old and new,
    To Argus and Also After Gen,
    Congratulations to you for making a success
    Of the Sunderland Jewish Bulletin.

                                L.A.C. H.M. Shochet, R.A.F.

EXCERPTS FROM LETTERS.

L/Cpl. Pearlman P., C.M.F. writes: I was very impressed with the people
I met at Florence and surprised at their knowledge of English. Florence
University is the foremost in Italy on literature and Florentines are
reputed to be the most intellectual in Italy. Everyone was tremendously
friendly and despite the lack of frenzied enthusiasm I got the impression
that they were even more pleased to see us than the Southerners.

Bedded in a vineyard near a hamlet about 12 miles outside the city
for a few days, I made the acquaintance of a family from whom I got
personal details about the Jewish community of Pisa, Leghorn and Florence.
Unlike the Roman and Neapolitan communities, they were thriving and proud
of their local history dating back to 1500 C.E., refugees from the
Spanish Inquisition and highly thought of.

I was asked for dinner and on declining I was surprised to
receive the assurance that there wouldn't be meat or bacon. Considering
the marked absence of knowledge of Hebrew customs and Kosher laws
hitherto noticed in a fairly extensive experience of Italian Jews, it was
amazing to be told this in such an out of the way spot.

Eventually in Florence, the Germans stayed on the other side of
the River Amo, running through the town and made their nearness felt
with machine gun, mortar and artillery fire. Republican Fascists and
German soldiers in civilian attire stayed on this side of the river and
unsportingly sniped at ourselves and partisans who had emerged from
heaven knows where, dressed in white blouses, the gayest coloured of neck-
erchiefs and armed to the teeth with rifles, machines guns, hand
grenades and even knives. If Italians could fight as well as they
dressed Mussolini might now be administering Palestine.

Once installed in the most comfortable house available, I
immediately pursued enquiries about the Jewish community and fortunately
was in a position to do so. It was not long before I met Jewish people
and heard of the most harassing and heartrending experiences and
ingenious attempts to avoid detection by the brutal S.S. and cruel
Fascists.

Florence unlike Rome, did not have a Pope with wide influence to

8.

protect its Jews nor was refuge in the city so easy to find. The courageous and persistent protests of the highest Catholic dignitary there, was of little avail, consequently their fight for very existence was a much harder and of course prolonged one. Generally it was not starvation, living in wretched cellars, changing residences week after week, living in the humblest of conditions in the country, the use of every device to avoid detection such as the pose of being a member of certain professions, false identity cards that was the worst feature of their lives, but the constant mental strain. One young man who being a Jew was brought to my notice went into hysterics recounting his experiences and grabbed me by the epaulettes and screamed "Help me, help me, you must help me."

After calming down I conducted him downstairs, a weak pathetic figure and was introduced to his pretty wife and child. A calmness which I did not feel while watching that child eating my sweet ration on my knee and the happy look on his wife's face brought a feeling of shame to that man at his behaviour, that he could not hide.

I think the most interesting case I encountered but not by any means the most touching, was that of Signore L. who lived in Trieste, where because of its proximity to the Austrian border, the Jews have fared even worse than Florence. An excellent linguist she broadcasted news over the Italian radio in Italian, French and German. With the introduction of racial laws in 1938, she arrived one morning to be told she was summarily dismissed. Her English was fairly fluent also.

Conditions generally for Jews in Italy were quite tolerable until the German occupation immediately after the Italian Armistice in 1943. At that time she left Trieste and lived in the country with her aged mother, being obliged to leave her husband and son. The Germans caught up with them and now she knows nothing of her mother. Being in a terribly nervous condition, she asked to go to hospital for treatment for internment and after several requests she accepted the magnanimous German offer of treatment in a lunatic asylum. After a week in this place she found she couldn't bear it any longer and asked to be returned. Eventually escaping she made her way to Florence, where an anti-fascist family whose address I was given when in Rome, befriended her and that was how I made her acquaintance. It was too risky for her to live with these non-Jewish people who were persona non grata with local fascists, so they booked a room in the best hotel in Florence and gave her the title of Countess di !!! of the province of Naples and invented a story of her being. One of the household acted as her personal maid and she managed to play her part through. I was able through her knowledge of history and art to appreciate better the priceless treasures and monuments of this city.

When I left Florence after four weeks, about seven hundred Jews had appeared in the town. The A.M.G. issued them immediately with ration cards and took steps to have their property restored. The larger of the two shools in this place is reputed to be the second most magnificent in the world and compared favourably with the renowned buildings of this city which were damaged beyond use by mining, the smaller one in which services were held twice daily was always well attended. Florentine Jews are Zephardic, their praying seemed to be sincere and of understanding of what they were saying, with a lack of frenzied fanaticism displayed in Zephardic shools of my experience.

Zionist societies functioned here, the most enthusiastic being the Mizrachi Group and very keen in their ideals they appeared to have been indeed. Back in my present unromantic station, there are few Jewish civilians but many Jewish service personnel including one Palestinian A.T.S. Sergeant and several W.A.C.S. Services are held regularly and a bible and discussion group functions actively where feelings on opinion run high.

V.A.D. Olga Grantham, S.E.A.C.: I am stationed in a most delightful spot about 5,000 ft. up, amongst the hills.   The climate is wonderful, cold mornings, bright sunny afternoons and cold evenings.   I am fortunate enought to be in a bungalow with three other girls, while the rest are all in tents.   We have our own servant to bring us early morning tea, clean our shoes, see to our bath water, in fact to generally minister to our welfare.   I think the most interesting and unusual procedure I came across was in Poona.   I took myself along with a Jewish officer I had met on the boat, to Shool on Yom Kippur, and as you can well imagine the moment we had entered we were the objects of vast interest.   It was all very strange to me to see Jewish women in saris, men in their long white shirts like coats and little fez hats, while the little boys and girls were dressed in European style.   When the women became at all weary, either of the service or of fasting, they just wrapped themselves in a blanket, lay on the floor and fell fast asleep.

Cpl. Cyril Behrman, M.E.F. writes: Last Shabbos was a great joy to me, as my first Bulletin arrived.   I can't really explain to you the great pleasure I found reading it through over and over again.   I have been to Shool a number of times in Cairo but regret to say it lacks the hamisher feeling I knew so well in the old home town.   I read in the Bulletin a letter from Sgt. Franks, but I had no idea who he was.   Last Sunday I visited the Jewish Club in Cairo, there I met him, he informed me he left Sunderland at the age of five.   I also meet Cyril Mincovitch each week, we find a lot to talk about, In Cairo there are two clubs, one is a Palestinian Club, I'm sorry to say I visited it once but find no time to visit it again.   My first and only brief stay was on a Friday night.   An American Chaplain was sitting at the top of a large table giving a very interesting talk.   Round the table sat a large crowd of Palestinian A.T.S. and men.   Most of them were paying no attention at all, just talking in their little groups.   I could have forgiven them for that, but 9% of them, both sexes were smoking.   Needless to say I left there disgusted but not before expressing my view to the Chaplain, who was in the same mind as myself.

Cpl. Norman Cohen, C.M.F. writes: I was "out of the war" for a few hours some weeks ago when I visited a neutral republic (someone composed a song about the place) and met there the only Jews living in the republic, husband and wife, both refugees from Vienna.   They were delighted to see me, the first British Jew they have set eyes on since the war and peppered me with questions about events in the world at large.   They gave me a message to deliver to some relatives in Vienna.   I'll deliver it, that is if the people are still alive.   Sorry Inquisitor if you think I'm neglecting you but I'm not a publicity agent.   However to oblige you, one of these days I'll write and let everyone know how good you are.   I'm a splendid liar.

The following letters were also received and gratefully acknowledged by the editor: A/c Landau, B.L.A.; Sgt. N.J. Franks, M.E.F.; Cpl. I.J. Charlton, INDIA; Horace Stone; Sgt. Alan Foreman; A.C.W.1 Sylvia Penn; Pte. Sol Cohen; Cpl. I.W. Brewer; L/Cpl. P. Pearlman, C.M.F.; A.C.1 Winburn C.; L/Cpl. L. Altman, INDIA; S/Sgt. J. Rosenthall, P.A.I. FORCE; Fus. B. Freeman MALTA FROCE; F/Lt. D. Cohen, INDIA; L.A.C. Harold Shochet, S. AFRICA.

LATE NEWS: Congratulations to Mr. & Mrs. Lionel Gillis of Rectory Terrace on the occasion of their silver wedding, and to Basil Taylor on his promotion to Warrant Office.

The Bulletin is issued free to members of the Forces, but private subscribers at the rate of 10/- per year will be gladly accepted.

All correspondence to be sent to Rev. S.P. Toperoff, 5 Victoria Avenue, Sunderland.

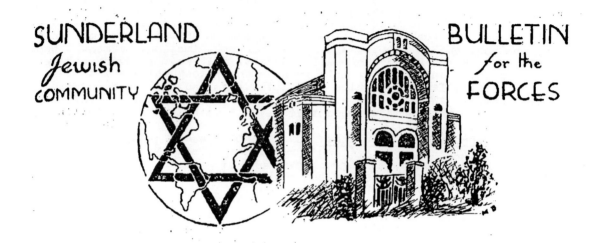

"Be strong and of good
courage, be not afraid neither
be thou dismayed, for the Lord
thy God is with thee withersoever thou goest."

Joshua, 1:9.

*Edited and issued monthly by the Minister
and sent to you with the good wishes of
your friends at home.*

December 1944   Vol. 3. No. 3.   Tebeth 5705.

I have much pleasure in publishing an article specially
written for the Bulletin by the Rev. Rothwell Richardson, Vicar of St.
Barnabas, Hendon and the Honorary Secretary of the Council of Christians
and Jews.

The Editor.

A Message of Appreciation and Hope

It was with genuine satisfaction that I received a kind invitation
from our mutual friend, the Rev. S.P. Toperoff, to write something for
the Bulletin circulated amongst members of the Jewish community serving
with the Forces at Home and abroad.   The reason for my satisfaction was
threefold.   To help, even in a small way, such a worthy endeavour to
maintain for those, who are perforce absent, some regular contact with
home is indeed gratifying to reader and writer alike.   Then, personally
there is a fellow-feeling which one has, having passed through some
experiences of active service oneself, for all those who are now engaged
in a struggle in many respects akin to that of 1914-18.   Another reason
yet remains, deeper perhaps than either already mentioned, the serious
concern which any considering Christian or Jew must have for the future
well-being of Jewry throughout the world.   This brings me to a common
cause of national importance.

There has come into existence, during war years, a National Council
of Christians and Jews and quite recently a Local Council in Sunderland.
Leaders of the religious and social life of the community have united for
"the promotion of mutual understanding and good-will between Christians
and Jews in all sections of the community, especially in connection with
problems arising from conditions created by the war".   In spite of all
that has happened in the past, one is happy to say that at present there
is a growing opinion and resolution that there shall be in the future a
closer co-operation of Christians and Jews in study and service directed
to post-war reconstruction.   Hyamson in his History of the Jews in
England at the conclusion of chapter XXXV, having referred to Jewish
emancipation, writes thus, "The next generation looked more to the wider
than to the narrower sphere of activity.   As a consequence England now
receives more from prominent English Jews than does Anglo-Jewry".   Those
of you who are now serving may not all be prominent Jews but you are,
undoubtedly, engaged in a 'wider activity' and the people of England,
together with the whole civilised world is receiving and will continue to
receive thereby, more than your own people.   There are many in England
who realise this, and are anxious that you should know that your service
and self-sacrifice is becoming more fully recognized and appreciated.

In conclusion may I quote some words of Lionel de Rothschild to be
found in A Book of Jewish Thoughts: - "To-day we are all privileged to
live in danger, to endure hardship, to make sacrifices, for the preserva·
tion of our country and civilization".   May it be granted to us, both
Christians and Jews, to co-operate more closely in the realization of
those ideals we may hold in common now and in the future for the well-
being not only of Jewry but of Humanity.

Rothwell Richardson.

2.

HERE AND THERE!

MAZELTOV!

Birth - Congratulations to L.A.C. and Mrs. Ernie Cohen on the birth of
a son.

Sunderland Senior Zionists - The Society has been reorganised and the
following are the officers : Chairman, Ald. J. Cohen; Vice-Chairman,
Julius Behrman; Joint Treasurers, H. Book and W. Morris; Hon.
Secretary, Ratcliffe Gillis.

Ladies Zionists - Mrs. A. Blakey is the new Chairman and Mrs. L. Davis
is Hon. Secretary.

Young Zionists - The new Chairman is Miss Pearl Berg.

Jewish Women's War Services Committee - The Society is now represented
on the Council of Social Service and the Standing Conference of Women's
Organisations. The new Hon. Secretary is Mrs. L. Davis.

Representative Council - The local T.A.C. (Trades Advisory Council)
recently took the initiative in convening a meeting of representatives
of every organisation in the town with a view to forming a Representative
Council that would unite the various bodies in the town and speak with
one voice on all matters affecting the welfare of the Community. There
was a good attendance and after some discussion it was resolved to call
a further meeting.

78 Wounded Soldiers from Sunderland Hospitals were entertained to
a Christmas Party on 13th December by 80 of the staff of Books Fashions
Ltd., in Ewesley Road Church Hall. Mrs. Book acted as Hostess and
Harry Wighar's Band and Concert Party provided the musical programme.
Tea and ice-cream were provided for the men and each soldier was given
a book of Savings Stamps.

SEARCHLIGHT ON SPORT - By "Argus".

As "Press day" is early this month owing to the pending holidays,
I am unable to relieve either your mind or my own on the League championship question. At the time of writing Sunderland's chances depended
entirely upon getting four points out of Gateshead and Newcastle United
defeating Huddersfield once or drawing twice. If both lost points then
Derby County might have stepped up to the top.

It is poetic justice that when we lost a point against York city at
home, Harry Thompson for whom we paid £7000 when we secured him from
Wolves should be the man who made York into a good team, and that "Raich"
Carter is getting goals to keep Derby County on our heels.

But in my judgment, Sunderland's main trouble has been missed
penalty kicks which have lost two points at least, and bad goalkeeping
which lost two goals in the home game against Huddersfield, all three
against York City, and at least two at Huddersfield.

Heywood is over six feet in height. He is good at anything coming
reasonably straight but a cross from the wing across the face of the goal-
and you begin to quake in your shoes. Anything crossed within six yards
of the goal line should be the goalkeepers but somehow Heywood is all at
sea with such a position and loses my confidence in him.

The absence of Jimmy Gorman owing to a nasal operation has given a
youngster named Stelling his opportunity. Stelling belongs to the
Herrington district and though slight in build has a big heart. His one

Dec   3.

fault is an inclination to make his tackle a fraction too soon and may
thus be easily side stepped, but experience will cure this weakness and
fancy he may make a good back in the process of time.

Freddie Laidman is back again to a holding battalion in the North
East.   Freddie is a P.T. Corporal and his move from Brancepeth to the
South was due to a "friendly" argument with a Sergeant - and he wasn't
singing "If the Sergeant drinks your rum, never mind".   Anyway he is
back again playing for Sunderland, and very welcome he is, because he is
a useful whole-hearted little player.

The Cup-ties begin at the Holiday period.   We open with two games
against Newcastle United.   As last season, the top 32 clubs go into th
the first round

IN RETROSPECT.

The list of Lecturers invited to address the "Lit" was the direct
result of the heart to heart confidences exchanged round the back-firing
gas fire.

Mr. F.E. Rowlands started the ball rolling.   A man of rare understanding, the other man's point of view always received, and I have no
doubt still receives his earnest of consideration.   He succeeded me as
Chairman of the Y.M.C.A. debating class.   Under his leadership Murray
Muscat spoke on Zionism.   Maurice Share spoke on some aspect of law,
and the Lit met the class in an inter-debate on Zionism.   This debate
was based on Murray Muscat's lecture and was very interesting and showed
a sympathetic understanding of this Jewish question.

The next lecturer was a Schoolmaster, whose name I regret I have
forgotten.   As Chairman I introduced him and his subject to the meeting.
I spoke for three or four minutes.   He commenced his lecture with the
complaint that I had stolen the beginning, middle and end of his lecture,
then he spoke for about an hour.   His subject was Disarmament.

Mr. Luke Thompson M.P. also paid us a visit.   He was accompanied
by his charming wife.   Mr. Thompson, then known in the town by the
affectionate nick-name of "Lucky Lukey", had a style all his own when
addressing the meeting, he would fling out his arms and say, "My friends".
Then with his sweeping gesture that seemed to gather his audience to his
bosom, he would in beautifully modulated speech and persuasive tones
deliver his lecture.   After moving a handsome vote of thanks to the
Chairman, Mr. Thompson and his wife stepped down from the dais and
mingled with his audience, many of whom were his personal friends.   So
genially and friendly was he that we all felt we had known him for many
years.   We were all captivated by Mrs. Thompson's charm.

I had the pleasure of chairing another meeting when he addressed
the Society as Sir Luke Thompson.   I will write of this meeting in good
time.

Next month - "More Lecturers".

Cheerio,

SOL.

4.

NEWS LETTER FROM THE HOME FRONT

It came as a relief to know that the Lit was carrying on its literary activities in the old style. The Live Newspaper Night on November 19th was quite up to the standard of the last few years and I thoroughly enjoyed it. The two most humorous articles were the first instalment of a love serial by Pearl Berg and small adverts by Reeva Cohen. Other articles were contributed by Leslie Epstein, Charles Topaz, Charles Cohen and Aubrey Gordon, who acted also as editor. It was soon over, however and I would have liked to have seen more people taking part as there is much good talent in the newer members of the Lit.

The following week was a very pleasant social. The radiogram provided the music for dancing and there was also table-tennis and darts. There was a good attendance and, like most socials, it gave people a chance to gossip and circulate any local "scandal" that might be in the air!

The Balloon Debate on December 3rd was also well attended, though this too finished very quickly. Considering all the speeches were ex tempore I think they were pretty good. The existence of the following people were put to trial:- Hitler, Aneuran Bevan, Tommy Atkins, Ann Shelton, Frank Sinatra, Winston Churchill, a High School Girl, Raymond Gram Swing and the Chancellor of the Exchequer. I was very surprised to see Raymond Gram Swing, the American Commentator, came out top by a long way! The number of those taking part was quite up to standard but the speeches were for the most part remarkably short. They also lacked a great deal of the bright wit that one expects at this sort of function. Nevertheless a jolly good effort - better luck next time!

There was nothing on at the Lit on Sunday 10th December because a cabaret and party had been arranged in aid of the Children's Forest Campaign. This was held by kind permission of Professor Ted Levey and Miss Belle Cowan at the Windsor Hall. It was raining heavily but the people poured in just the same until there were nearly 150 happy faces in the Hall. Some rather clever tap-dancing and singing was exhibited by youngsters and there was "I want to be an Actor" by Rosalie Gillow, and the other usual party events. I believe something like £25 was raised - a financial success!

Here are the main features of the Lit programme for the rest of the session:- December 19th Chanukah Dance; 31st, Party; January 7th, Debate; 14th, Dance; 21st, B.B.C. Night; 28th, Social; February 4th, Prize Paper Night; 11th, Social; 25th, Dance; March 4th, Debate; 11th Social; 18th Mock Parliament; 25th, General Meeting.

A conversation I overheard in a cafe ; - Two men who had met for the first time since boyhood days; the first - "Yes I'm very happy, my wife's an angel"; the other - "You're lucky! Mine's still alive".

Good luck Forces, everywhere.

Yours,

Also After Gen.

EXCERPTS FROM LETTERS.

W/O Basil Taylor, India, writes: It is really most refreshing to be kept well informed of what is going on back in Sunderland, and to hear how old friends are getting along in different parts of the world. For myself I have been kept rather busy of late, which I find is quite a change from the normal course of things. In out of the way places such as this the biggest worry is filling in ones spare time. By normal standards I suppose, living conditions in these parts would be considered very primitive but after a while none no longer attaches such importance to the absence of town life, and I personally must admit I find things very comfortable. During my leave in Bombay I came across a book called "The History of the Bene Israel in India". This I found gave a very interesting account of some of the earlier Jewish settlers in this country. It showed that Jews were in the habit of travelling far across the seas, even in Biblical times.

A/c Arnold Landau, B.L.A. writes: I have been stationed in Belgium for seven weeks now, and it has been my longest stay in any place, since I arrived on the continent. I am in quite a large town at the moment, and of course one of the first things I looked for was a Jewish congregation. Unfortunately as has been the case in many places, there are none to be found. There were quite a large number of Jews in this town pre 1940, some managed to get to England but the others were deported to Poland, and other places in Eastern Europe. Many of the Christians here asked the inhuman Germans what the Jews had done to deserve such a horrible fate. The answer more or less in every case was: "Hitler says the Jews must be destroyed, so we are doing it". Some of the finest citizens in the town were Jews but they all were the victims of Teutonic insanity. I shall never forget to my dying day neither shall I forgive the German nation for their inhuman treatment of my brethren.

L.A.C. C.M. Marks, C.M.F. writes: I had the honour of singing "Maftir" in the morning service on Yom Kippur, something of which I was very proud of and justly so considering the congregation of servicemen which must have been at least 800 strong. I wonder if any more of my colleagues overseas had the same enjoyable experience.

Cpl. I.J. Charlton, India, writes: I spent Rosh Hashannah and Yom Kippur in Calcutta and renewed acquaintances with the American Chaplain The great snag this time was the tremendous number of lads there and no matter where the Chaplain arranged his services for Rosh Hashannah there was a large number who were unable to get into the Shool.
A satisfactory solution was reached for Yom Kippur when two services were held, one being conducted by the Chaplain which was a shortened service and attended mainly by the American troops. An over-flow service was held which was conducted by a London officer a Lt. Lancer who was helped by Pte. Morris of Barrow (whose Brother incidentally, P. Morris, lives in Sunderland) and we had a full service 'davening' throughout the Yom Kippur day.
In the intervening days we had several morning services for

EXCERPTS Continued

'S'lichas' and my tefillin which accompanied me so far in my kit bag came out and did their duty - or should I say - I did my duty by them!!

Apart from Dave Morris (Mentioned above) there were also two other chaps in Calcutta with whom I had 'come out' and joined on a 'minyan' on the boat. I also had the good fortune to meet a boy from home again in the person of Mat Pearlman, who, since I last saw him last Yom Kippur eve had seen a lot of action in the seige of Imphal. Altogether I had a very enjoyable time in Calcutta and one morning I had the unique experience of learning 'blat gemorra' with Lt. Lanser. In a synagogue in a purely native quarter of Calcutta we found a most amazing library of Hebraic books, which though in poor condition and all haphazard must be one of the worlds unique Hebrew Library. The synagogue itself was unlike any other in India, more of a house and certainly very poor though meticulously clean. It was really hard indeed to refuse a pressing invitation from the 'shamos' to spend Yom Kippur with them in prayer.

Sgt. Norman J. Franks, M.E.F. writes: I spent four days in Palestine and should like to mention the very hardworking A.T.S. nursing orderlies whose industry and sympathy seemed to be doing much to further the understanding between Jew and Gentile whilst I was in hospital.

I visited Nahalal, the oldest Moshav in Palestine and situated in the Plains of Jezreel some sixteen miles from Haifa. The Moshav is the type of settlement wherein all the members hold a portion of land which is cultivated by them and their family without the aid of outside manual sources. A common pool of farm implements is held, the produce which varies from Horseradish to Honey, is disposed of through a central agency but otherwise the farmer is not tied by any regulations other than those becoming good citizenship and good neighbourliness.

Here the situation differs from the Kibutz, a representative sample of which I visited next. Ein Hashofet, in the Hills of Ephraim. The land here is held communally. Everything is done on a communal basis - eating, washing, working, playing. Perhaps in such places one may find the only working examples of Communism, though to mention the term in connection is certainly frowned upon by the members of the Kibutz.

It appeared to me that one of the two types of existence, the Kibutz appeared to be less exacting in the physical sense, in that the work is evenly apportioned, whereas in the Moshav one family of three worked an area equal to that owned by their neighbours who had a family of five. Perhaps the Moshav is an incentive to a higher birthrate.

One particularly noticeable fact occurred on my return to Haifa. Out in the country, the Arab and Jew are on really good terms, but in the city the sullen dislike of the Arab for Jew is too obvious. Returning to Cairo I was fortunate to meet two Sunderland boys. Leaving the town when but a child, they did not know me, but we were introduced through the Bulletin, being read by a LONDON boy! The boys Cyril Behrman and Cyril Mincovitch, looked well and gave me news of my relatives back home for which I was thankful and we parted with the promise of further meetings.

7.

EXCERPTS Continued

Pte. Claude Brewer, C.M.F. writes: In Tripoli I saw my first example of Nazi terrorism on the Jewish populations, and what I saw, although small and minute, compared with the atrocities in Europe, was enough to make me realize what we Jews are fighting for in this war.

From Tripoli to North Africa I met quite a number of French Jews, and spent Rosh Hashannah and Yom Kippur on the outskirts of Bizerte. During my short stay in Sicily I did not meet one Jew, as the Germans deported them to Northern Italy.

On my third day in Italy last November (1943) I had a pleasant experience which I must relate to you. It took place high up in the mountains of Southern Italy, a few minutes after we had stopped for the night in a little village. I had not gone two yards from the lorry when someone came up to me and asked in broken English, if there were any Jews in the unit, you can imagine his surprise and delight when he found out I was a Jew. He asked me to his house and to bring any other Jewish friends that I had with me. Three of us eventually arrived at his house and we partook of our first Yiddisher meal for quite a long while. All our conversations were in Yiddish, and it turned out that he was an interned Austrian refugee, who with other internees had been set free by the advancing Canadians. Here also we heard tales of atrocities which we thought could only be fiction, but were true. I have not done much more travelling since then, having been stationed in Naples for over a year now. I had the good fortune to meet Cpl. Philip Pearlman in Shool last Pesach, and although I go the the Jewish Club here quite often, I have not met any other Sunderland boys. There are quite a number of Jewish troops in this area and it might be of interest to sportsmen to know that the Table-tennis tournament which is run every week at the royal palace here has been won seven out of eight occasions by Jewish boys either Palestinian or British.

I am looking forward to the Chanukah Festival of which I shall forward a report to you (if possible) in due course.

The following letters were also received and are gratefully acknowledged by the Editor:- Fus. B. Freeman, MALTA FORCE; V.A.D. Olga Grantham, INDIA; Pte. Douglas Goldman, ENGLAND; S.B.A. Aaron Goldblatt, ENGLAND; L/Cpl. P. Pearlman, C.M.F.; Dvr. Lionel Gillis, B.L.A.; L/Cpl. Lionel P. Altman, INDIA; Capt. Ellis Dresner, B.L.A.; L.A.C. Maurice Dresner, ENGLAND and L.A.C. H. Davis, ENGLAND.

The Bulletin is issued free to members of the Forces, but private subscribers at the rate of 10/- per year will be gladly accepted.

Will readers please notify change of address before the 20th of the month.

All correspondence to be sent to Rev. S.P. Toperoff, 5 Victoria Avenue, Sunderland.

Sunderland Jewish Community
Bulletin for the Forces

1945

note: missing pages
March - Volume 3 No. 6 - pages 2 & 3

SUNDERLAND Jewish COMMUNITY

BULLETIN for the FORCES

"Be strong and of good
courage, be not afraid neither
be thou dismayed, for the Lord
thy God is with thee withersoever thou goest."

Joshua 1:9.

*Edited and issued monthly by the Minister
and sent to you with the good wishes of
your friends at home.*

January 1945   Vol. 3, No. 4.   Shevat 5705

"Quietness and Confidence"

It is true, I think, to say that with many at this time imagination is exceptionally active.   The products of the imagination may or may not resemble actualities and it is a consolation to remember that we can, happily, accept or reject the results of imagination.   Recent events especially on the Western Front have caused some to imagine that adversity continues to hinder the satisfactory progress of the cause of liberty and freedom for the peoples of Europe.   The actual position, however, is far from hopeless, if we are willing with quiet patience to review the course of naval and military operations during the last twelve months.   Take for example, the line of the German armies on all fronts a year ago and that line as it stands today.   Surely we have reasonable cause not for depression but for a high hope and a good courage.

There are also, unfortunately, those who are despondent about possible conditions on the Continent and in Great Britain after the war. Here again the imagination is, all too often, allowed to function almost uncontrolled with depressing effect.   Already there is to be heard that "It will be all the same as after the last war", implying the promises of politicians unfulfilled and the aspirations of the people thwarted by expediency or indifference.   But this must not of necessity be so;   much will depend on the mental and spiritual out-look of the people.   Legislation will no doubt play an important part in the future re-conditioning of the life of the community but legislation is not wholly independent of the people under a democratic constitution.   Hence it is the people, the kind and character of the people, including those returning from the Forces, who will be a potent factor in directing the course of future affairs.

But why do the people imagine a vain thing; because they lack a quiet patience and a sure confidence.   Even men and women in the Forces may be unduly influenced by an unhappy imagination at this time.   Permit me to remind you, one and all, wherever you may be, of words written and preserved, providentially as we may well believe, "For thus saith the Lord God, the Holy One of Israel; In quietness and confidence shall be your strength".

ROTHWELL RICHARDSON.

Once more I have pleasure in publishing an article by the Rev. Rothwell Richardson, Vicar of St. Barnabas, Hendon and the Honorary Secretary of the Council of Christians and Jews.

The Editor.

HERE AND THERE!

Mazeltov:
Congratulations to:-

Births   - Mr. & Mrs. Louis Refson on the birth of a son.
              Mr. & Mrs. George Wolfson (Rose Topaz) on the birth of a son
              Mr. & Mrs. Osher Joseph (Emma Joseph) on the birth of twins
              (boy and girl).

Engagement - Mona Levine to Charles Aronson of Largs, Ayrshire.

New Doctor - Congratulations to Ralph Blakey on having attained his
              medical degree.

2.

Representative Council - A meeting held recently and sponsored by the
T.A.C. was presided over by its Chairman Ralph Minchom. The special
speaker was Counc. A. Moss, J.P. of Manchester who gave an inspiring
address on the advisibility of forming a Representative Council in Sunderland.

The Surgeons' Hall Journal which is published each term by the
students of the School of Medicine of Edinburgh is edited by Henry
Goldman. Circulation of the magazine is over 1,000 copies in world
wide distribution.

EN PASSANT   -   INQUISITOR

I can visualise the welcoming smiles of relief, joy and exuberance
on the physiognomies of my readers when they are confronted with my
article once more! Grateful to discover that I am reinstated in editorial favour!! Their expectant optics peruse the "flashes" hurriedly, and
then they either grin embarrassedly (what a good sport am I) or relievedly
(thank heavens for one more month) hoping to gain pleasure from someone
else's discomfiture....... There is little need for worry these days, as
years of joyous journalism have removed the sting from my contributions.
I have learned compassion, and tolerance of human frailties. Relax, my
blood-hounds are on the prowl no longer..............
    Hi-de-hi to you all.

FLASH
Rumour has it that Chaplains and Nurses are being seen a lot together
this S.E.A.C. on!
We are gratified to learn that the Idol of India will be in England this
year. Our gain, yea, verily!
On dit that the Taxi Syndicate all go huntin', shootin' and fishin'
together in Scotland. No grouse?
They say that the "cook" of Leeds has a new "cookie". Anything
cooking?
If you want to know the time, don't ask a P.C. ask J.B. of course!
Who is known as "shepherd", sorry, "doctor of the hills"?
How long does it take for henna to arrive in England from the Middle
East? How is the "colour" problem?
Rumour hath it that Harrogate has once more become a famous spa since
the arrival of Sunderland's Royal Visitors!
We are sorry that the Cingalese Shiek is not able to be with us any
longer. Are we not "Intelligent" enough?
Who prefers an "eye for an eye" rather than a "tooth for a tooth"?
Rumour hath it that L.B. (M.E.F.) is just living for February, Any
more grateful patients recently?
A cognac for the crooner! Appreciation at home and abroad, some have
greatness thrust upon them.
Is an important person enjoying his LEV(ine)? Any complaints? Do
prenez garde when driving cars near the Gas Office.
Which pearl of a girl is shortly expecting a diamond?
Who said "engineering" works in London was a very good idea?

3.

SEARCHLIGHT ON SPORT   -   By "Argus"

It may be old news to you now that Sunderland failed in their bid for
the championship, but there can be no disputing the fact that the best
side we met in the first half of the season was the championship winners.
Huddersfield.

And yet Huddersfield went to their fifth game in the qualifying
competition for the League cup before they won a game on January 20th.
It is indeed surprising how badly good teams fare in Cup Games - and
Huddersfield are no exception.

Sunderland's trouble appears to be the back division and I am just
a little worried as to what is likely to happen when the war is over.
Gorman won't do for after the war - that's definite. Alex Hall though
he is still playing in Scotland, is not likely to come back to the game
after the war and Johnnie Feenan, who returned to his native Ireland to
become a driver, is not playing at all so he can be counted out.

I have hopes of Stelling, and Eves may improve when in full training,
but Eves and Gorman are not a "pair" and the adoption of offside tactics
by Gorman when he is not capable of playing it effectively has led to
goals. Candidly it is a good job we have a player of Lockie's ability
to cover this pair, but he cannot be expected to be pulling them out in
every game.

Cliff Whitelum has now scored over 30 goals this season, but take a
note for future guidance of a young centre forward whom Manager Murray
has signed - a boy named Harrison. He is still at a Secondary School
and has scored 24 goals for his school in the morning and over 60 for
Crookhall Juniors in the afternoon games. That is good going even for
a boy.

There are several good juniors on the Roker Park books and just the
day before I wrote this Billy Murray signed a Sunderland outside left
named Chilton who has been playing for the B.L.A. against Belgian
teams.

IN RETROSPECT

Mrs. Mundella (wife of the Principal of the Technical College)
spoke to us on the work of the Drug Traffic Committee of the League of
Nations. She was Secretary of the Sunderland League of Nations Union.
A live wire indeed was this little lady. Her information on the work
of the League was colossal and we spent a most interesting and instruct-
ive evening.

Mr. Charlton Deas, Head Librarian of the Sunderland Libraries also
spoke to us. His subject was "Work among the Blind". This was a
lantern lecture. We saw pictures of the blind feeling the specimens
of animals and birds in our Museum, learning to use their hands in place
of their lost sight. We also saw pictures of the models they had made
showing their impressions of the things they had "seen through their
fingers". This is an expression used by the Lecturer who declared that

4.

the blind see largely through the medium of their delicate sense of touch.
He also told us that we should speak to the blind as if they had their
sight.   Ending with an appeal for the better understanding of the
problems of the blind, he finished one of the most heart stirring lectures
ever delivered before the "Lit".
   We also had the pleasure of hearing our Honorary President, Dr.
Silverstone.   Essentially a young people's Minister, his talk was bright
cheerful and informative.   Dr. Silverstone had a fund of funny stories
to tell us.   One I particularly remember.   A Curate feeling embarrassed
by the attentions of the ladies in his Parish took a post in a neighbouring Parish.   After a couple of months he paid a visit to his old Parish.
Enquired of his successor how he got on with the ladies of the Parish.
"Oh!" said the young Curate.   "I take refuge in numbers".   "Ah!" sighed
the former Curate, "I tooke refuge in Exodus".
   Our membership was steadily growing and we decided to move to larger
premises.   Also the demands of the Dramatic Circle had to be met and a
suitable platform was needed.   We moved to the Railway Institute, Burdon
Road where we held a concert and some interesting meetings.
   I will write about our sojourn there next month.

                    Cheerio,
                         SOL.

                    ───────────

                    NEWS LETTER FROM THE HOME FRONT

   Hello again,   Forces everywhere!   Here I am sitting shivering
in the midst of a typical English winter recording for you all the red
hot news of Sunderland youth.

   On December 17th, the last night of Chanukah, I went down to the
good old Communal Hall wondering how this year's Chanukah Dance would
compare with previous ones .   Memories of past years fleeted through my
mind, for at Chanukah the Lit always holds one of its three big annual
dances.   And this year the same atmosphere was still there,   Quite a
large crowd danced merrily to the perfect rhythm of the band and many
munched sandwiches and swallowed lemonade at the Canteen on one corner
of the Hall.   Eight candles flickering at the front of the stage,
reminded me that this was a continuation of all past Chanukah dances
and the hope entered my mind that maybe by next year ..... you know!

   Many people also enjoyed the Social the following week, the most
noteworthy point of which was that several new records - the latest hits-
had made their appearance.   Not before time either for many of the
records previously played must, I feel sure, have been there for
years.   And were those darts new ones too?   But the ping-pong balls were
a little dinted - still like many other things, I suppose they too are
scarce.

   Then on the last night of 1944 I, and a host of others, flocked to
the Hall to what was described as an American Party.   It looked as if it
had been carefully planned but somehow I was disappointed.   The gay
jolliness that is necessary for any kind of party just was not there.   It
may have been of course, that the ages of those present varied from 16
to - well I'd better not say!   It follows then, that games that one lot

would enjoy would almost certainly bore another lot. Everyone did, however enter the right spirit for the "Grand Old Duke of York" and some of the other games but there was just that something lacking throughout the party and I am not prepared, or indeed able, to say what.

The more intellectual members of the Lit had their fling on Sunday January 7th when a debate was held on the subject that "Control is inconsistent with freedom". All the leading parts were taken by new-comers to the Lit - the Proposition by Charles Slater and Julian Isaacs and the Opposition by Harold Merskey and Charles Cohen. After a few speeches from others the house divided giving the propositon a small majority.

That's all for the present, Forces, so until next time - Cheerio and, as always, good luck.

Yours,

Also After Gen.

EXCERPTS FROM LETTERS

L.A.C. Charlie Marks C.M.F. writes: Your mention of mobile synagogues is the first I have heard of a very fine practical help needed by so many of our boys throughout the various theatres of war. I should like to enquire if a Chaplain is going to travel around with these mobile synagogues, because if not, although the spiritual background will be there, the absence of a minister will be very greatly felt.

Lieutenant Mordaunt Cohen S.E.A.C. writes: As for the Jewish soldier, not all are as fortunate as those from Sunderland. We are kept in touch with the hometown through the medium of the Bulletin and every Chanukah receive a gift from the Jewish Women's War Service Committee. I think I can safely say that practically nothing has been done by the Jewish Hospitality Committee for the troops in this command. The lads out here feel that they are forgotten by the community. Something must be done for them. Nice leave centres, an occasional parcel or a few books. This must be taken up now, before thousands of troops are sent here after the war in Europe is over. The organisation must be got under way. If the Troops in Italy, France, Belgium and M.E.F. can be catered for (and we don't begrudge them) then surely the chaps out here do deserve some small consideration.

Sgt. Sam Freedman B.L.A. writes: I took the opportunity yesterday of attending a Chanukah service held in a small town in Holland. I should point out of course we mostly turned up some twenty minutes late. Some short time after this late commencement, I was delighted to see Sollie Gillis (of crooning fame) enter. Of course we had a regular gossip of home, and very pleasant it was too.

S/Sgt. J. Rosenthal, Paiforce writes: Regarding some reference to the local "Boy Scouts". Perhaps you don't know that I was the first Sunder-land Jewish Scout and formed the first patrol in 1914. We were honoured by being presented to the late Col. Vaux at a gathering of all the Durham County Scouts and were the only Jewish Scouts between Leeds and Edinburgh.

6.

EXCERPTS Continued

A.C. Harold Shochet, S. Africa writes: Here, in this part of the Transvaal, Judaism as a religion barely exists, and I feel most positive that were it not for the social aspect of life, which, to most people is the main essential, it would fade away completely.   Religion and all it entails seems vastly remote from our co-religionists whatsoever be the cause.   Progressing on a fair scale, Zionism is certainly rearing its head high, and, in an endeavour to bring home the real thing a Kibbutz has been established on the outskirts of Johannesburg, on an estate aptly named Balfour Park.   Here can be seen S.African Chalutzim at work, especially at week-ends in the fields, girls and boys of rather tender age indulging in extremely hard work, contending with a climate similar in many respects to that of Eretz Yisroel.

Cpl. Cyril Behrman, M.E.F. writes: Have just returned from 14 days leave in Palestine, four days were spent in travelling and I had ten clear days to see Palestine.   I stayed most of the time in Tel Aviv with a family named Magid (Mrs. Magid's mother is a sister to Mrs. Tow of Sunderland) Tel-Aviv is the most wonderful town one could ever wish to see - everything is so modern and clean.   There are over 200,000 Jewish people living there.   It was so wonderful walking around the streets knowing everyone you pass were of the same faith, bus-drivers, window cleaners, even shoe-shine boys and the road cleaners were Jewish.   I was also in Jerusalem for two days and saw quite a lot of it, I visited the tomb of Rachel, went through the old city, the Wailing Wall and many other interesting places.   It was very sad just seeing how thousands of poor Jews live.

Pte. C. Brewer C.M.F. writes: The first night of Chanukah being Sunday a large service was held in one of the large theatres in this town.   A service was held and afterwards a concert was given by various members of H.M. and Allied Forces.   The place was crowded to capacity.   It was my good fortune to meet, before the service, another Sunderland boy - L/Cpl. P. Pearlman.

W.O.1 I. Levine of New Delhi writes: It is exactly three years to the day since I left Sunderland on this great adventure and I am therefore indulging in the luxury of becoming retrospective and getting really home-sick!!   How well I remember my last Sunday evening which incidentally was spent at the Lit.   There was a debate followed by the usual dancing to the gramophone (radio?!!) and of course "Ettie" Rosenthal's delightful meat sandwiches etc.   Then the usual whisperings - "Are you going to so and so's party?"   And I was!!   Ralph Freedman and I went along to a party at Muriel Sugden's place.   Since that day in December '41 I've seen so much - what a grand feeling it is to know that my "tour of duty" is coming to an end.   What will I find on my return?   Has Sunderland changed much? Has the air at Seaburn still got the same delightful "tang"?

V.A.D. O. Grantham S.E.A.C. writes: I am still kept hard at work and busy, but it really is terrific fun working with Indians.   When I first started I almost had to draw diagrams to make myself understood, but now, having acquired a smattering of the language I manage quite well.   I shall probably arrive home having forgotten how to speak English.

EXCERPTS Continued.

Arnold Bloomberg from S. Rhodesia writes: En route for my destination I arrived at Bulawayo, during my six days stay I got to know the place inside out. The town itself is built in the American style with streets running at right angles to the Avenues, and all the streets with numbers and not names. The majority of cars there were American also the hamburger stalls which line the streets add to its American appearance. During my travels which have been far and wide I have learnt that a Jew is always recognised by another Jew as a long lost brother. This I consider is one of the marvels of our religion and it certainly helps one a lot, to get so far from home among strangers, to realise what it means to be a Jew. Up to now I have just about seen all of Rhodesia from the Air, which is definitely the best way to get about here, the roads being so bad and the trains being so slow.

A.C. D. Rosenthal from Port Elizabeth S.A. writes: Since I last wrote I have been around in Port Elizabeth and I find its Jewry most hospitable. They go out of their way to contact any Jewish fellow from England and go even more out of their way to entertain them. I've not as yet met one anti-Zionist, indeed they are all extremely pro-Zionist. I contacted an old native of Sunderland, Edward Jacobs, whose kindness had made life away from home lots easier.

Cpl. I.W. Brewer, England writes: I thought the idea of an article by a non-Jew minister was an excellent idea. It helps greatly to create that spirit which is so essential in having an understanding with our neighbours. The Society of Christians and Jews meets quite regularly here and Rev. Josephs addressed the meeting a fortnight ago on Jewish Customs. The next speaker a regular member of the society is the Arch Deacon of Chester.

L/Bdr. S. Gillis B.L.A. writes: Last week I went to an E.N.S.A. show by Josephine Baker, the celebrated French comedienne and singer, and during the show she inaugurated a little competition on the stage for everyone who cared to make an appearance. There were only five of us, the prize was a bottle of cognac, which I won, Miss Baker persuaded me to give two encores, and I had great difficulty in getting off the stage.

A/C A. Landau, B.L.A. writes: I am now in a town a little larger than the previous one in which I was stationed, as usual I enquired about a Jewish congregation, but again I received the agonising reply - all have been deported. It seems that only in the few large cities in Belgium is there any sign of Jewish life whatsoever. Even though the Germans sowed Anti-Semitic hatred in Belgium, it did not bear much fruit among the people, as the majority were horrified at the bestial treatment meted out to our co-religionists.

The following letters were also received and are gratefully acknowledged: L/Cpl. L. Altman, INDIA; A.C.2 C.D. Cohen, ENGLAND; Fus. B. Freeman, MALTA FORCE; L.A.C. M. Dresner. ENGLAND; L.A.C. J. Gordon, B.N.A.F; L.A.C. I. Davis, B.L.A., L.A.C. B.A. Cohen, B.L.A., L.A.C.W. S. Leslie, ENGLAND; A/C J. Clarke, SCOTLAND and Cpl. J. Charlton, INDIA.

The Bulletin is issued free to members of the Forces but private subscribers at 10/- per year will be gladly accepted.

Will readers please notify change of address before the 20th of the month.

All correspondence to be sent to Rev. S.P. Toperoff, 5 Victoria Avenue, Sunderland.

SUNDERLAND
Jewish
COMMUNITY

BULLETIN
for the
FORCES

"Be strong and of good courage, be not afraid neither be thou dismayed, for the Lord thy God is with thee withersoever thou goest."

Joshua, I : 9.

Edited and issued monthly by the Minister and sent to you with the good wishes of your friends at home.

February 1945.   Vol. 3, No. 5.   Adar 5705

Purim

Purim which we now celebrate is the most popular season of the Jewish calendar, this popularity is due to the religious and national significance which the story of Esther teaches. It has been our unfortunate lot throughout our sojourn on earth to meet in every age with a Haman who has planned and schemed to destroy us. But rightly Jews have always out-lived their tyrants.

There is good reason therefore for the gaiety fun and hilarious enjoyment on Purim in which young and old take part. It is a people's Festival. It appeals to all. Even the unobservant and the unorthordox know that as long as the spirit of Purim is with us we shall live and rise above the dictators and Hamans of our age.

What are we fighting for today? Surely it is to uproot and annihilate the regime and system of the modern Haman whose evil designs and intentions would have exterminated the whole Jewish Race. And in this the sixth year of war we should be happy to celebrate Purim in the old style. For the great and mighty armies are rolling on to deal the final blow at the heart of the enemy. We should rejoice and thank God that the end is in sight.

There are however some misgivings in the hearts of Jews even at this hour when we stand at the threshold of victory. Will the over-throw of Hitlerism bring sure Peace and contentment of mind? The future is very uncertain. In liberated France though the Nazis have been hounded out the spirit of Amalek and Haman still flourishes. Where it is undiplomatic to spread its poisonous propaganda openly, it carries on its foul work furtively underground. Again in Belgium, thousands of Jewish refugees who escaped from Germany and Austria have been classified 'enemy nationals by the Belgium Government. Is this what we are fighting for? And even in the lands of the free the outlook is far from bright. It is estimated that in America there are more than 800 societies which are actively engaged in supporting a full programme of anti-semitism.

But in spite of these evil omens we mean to celebrate Purim. We must never despair. We must never become despondent. On the contrary we must strengthen our belief in our future and listen to the echo of Mordecai's voice who proudly proclaimed that he was a Jew. You who are fighting on different fronts, remember that you are descendants of Mordecai. Go back to your ancient heritage. Put your hope and trust in your religion your people and your land. Don't assimilate and forget your distinctive Jewish characteristics. We must follow Mordecai and Esther and never allow ourselves to be crushed by the forces of anti-semitism.

The story of Purim has an eternal message for us. Conscious of our Jewishness and proud of our mission on earth we shall go forward and rebuild our nation to the glory of God and man.

2.

A Personal Note.

I must sincerely thank all those who were good enough to send me letters of good cheer and also the many friends in Town who were so kind to me during my recent illness. I was deeply moved by this spontaneous outburst of concern.

We were all grateful to the Rev. Rothwell Richardson who stepped into the breach and wrote two articles for the Bulletin. Unfortunately he is now indisposed, and we all wish him a speedy recovery.

DO YOU KNOW?

1. Do women play an active part in the affairs of the Yishuv in Palestine and how do they compare with those of other countries.
2. Which English Essayist was prejudiced against Jews and Quakers.
3. Who invented the smoke-screen.
4. Who are the "Sobotnicki"?

Answers to above on Page 4.

HERE AND THERE

Mazeltov

Congratulations to:-
Birth   - Mr. & Mrs. G. Rabbinowitz on the birth of a son.
Engagements   - Miss Flora Blair to Richard Artman of Nottingham.
                   Miss Anita Freedman to Harry A. Slyper B.Sc., of London.
                   Miss G. Isaacs to David Tagger of Leeds.
New Recruits. - We are pleased to welcome the following three new recruits
                   E. (Archie) Gillis, Philip Linke and Miss Dinah Levinson.
Mentioned in Dispatches.
      Congratulations to Cpl. Harry Black who has been mentioned in Despatches for distinguished services in the Middle East.
Educational Success.
      Congratulations to Miss Edith Goldberg, who has received her B.A. Degree from Manchester University.
A Reminder.
      Subject to the exigencies of the service leave will be granted for Passover. You are therefore advised to make immediate application to your C.O.
Norwood Orphanage.
Arnold Wendorff who is a member of the Go-Ahead Concert Party that entertains War Workers, was responsible for a variety concert that was recently held in the Communal Hall. The proceeds of the concert, £30, was raised for the Norwood Orphanage.
Fancy Dress Ball.
      A children's fancy dress ball and cabaret took place at Windsor Hall by kind permission of Prof. & Mrs. Levey in aid of the Childrens Forest. The first prize was awarded to David Joseph as Carmen Miranda. The second prize was awarded to Lionel Burnley as Mrs. Mopp. The third prize to Carol Book as Eastern dancer. The fancy dress parade was followed by a cabaret performed by the pupils of Belle Cowan. £33 was raised for the Childrens Forest in Palestine.

3.

J.W.W.S.C.

The Sunderland Jewish Women's War Services Committee thank those overseas who wrote such appreciative letters in acknowledgment of the Chanukah parcels they received. The Committee takes this opportunity of wishing all forces a pleasant and happy Purim.

IN RETROSPECT

In the Railway Institute the Lit found everything necessary for meetings and the members looked forward to a long and comfortable stay, but this was not to be. We held a debate, a hat night and a dramatic reading. A musical recital given by a professional lecturer on Gilbert and Sullivan's operettes was a great success.

I ventured to lecture on the life of Sir Henry Irving and his art. The highlight of the half session spent there was the Concert. The Dramatic Circle took its first bow in the one act play "The Monkey's Paw" by W.W. Jacobs. The play was diligently rehearsed and I think gave the audience quite a thrill. Hyman Muscat as the lovable old father was outstanding. Dorrie Behrman played the mother and Leo Gillis the ex-sergeant major. Arnold Brewer acted the messenger. He was also responsible for the scenery. I prompted by candle light and felt very nervous. I also remember a delightful dancing turn by a grand-daughter of Mr. Israel Jacobs and a burlesque ballet dancing act by two young men from Newcastle. Each, clad only in singlet, two tin pan lids and a ballet skirt. Their show was a cross between an all-in wrestling match and gymnastic display. It was hilariously funny.

Some time later I was informed by the Secretary of the Institute that his fellow members objected to strangers using their premises and, would the Jewish Literary Circle agree to breaking their agreement with them. Feeling very unhappy and rather indignant, the Lit Committee had to look for other premises. The Y.M.C.A. stepped into the breach and lent the Lit their hall after their bible class had been held, enabling the Committee to keep faith with its members. Later the good old Unity Chambers welcomed the Circle with open arms.

The Dramatic Circle held its second show at the Co-Operative Hall Green Street. This meant extra expense and much work. The effort however paid and gave the Circle much satisfaction.

About this time Bessie Cohen our Honorary Secretary resigned, and Dorrie Behrman (who had acted as her assistant for some time) took full responsibility. I feel sure she did not know the amount of work that lay ahead of her, but knowing her and my Committee as I did I faced the future with confidence. It was I who did not realise what lay before us.

As a representative member of the New Synagogue Building Fund Social Committee, on the senior building Committee, I had seen the amended building plans and my hopes for the Lit ran high. When the building was nearly complete, Messrs. M. Jacoby, D. Berger and S. Goldberg were elected Hall Sub Committee. The Literary Circle applied for the use of the Hall and after explaining its aims permission to "Come Home" was granted.

Next month - "The Lit comes home"!

Cheerio,

SOL.

EN PASSANT - INQUISITOR

Before continuing my usual journalistic flow may I quote an extremely clever extract from my contribution September 1942 in which I very aptly wrote - "I beg to draw the attention of my ever decreasing followers to the fact that all characters mentioned below are purely fictitious and any similarity to any living person is purely coincidental. Anyone daring to identify themselves with my celebrities will be brought up for libel". Remember? Well, don't forget!! I'm s-s-s-supposed to have b-b-b-been intimidated - like the dolly in the popular hit, my knees should be a-knockin'. I ask you! Do you for one moment think I am going to dis-appoint thousand, nay dozens, of readers by curbing my poison pen at this stage of publication? (Eliza Doolittle could answer more appropriately than I) Perhaps I could emulate my superiors and take a vote of confid-ence - - - - When I am ultimately brow beaten (which will be at the cessation of hostilities) I'll throw in the sponge, but at the moment I'm thriving on, at long last, being in the news!!!
In conclusion Forces, I'll be sue-ing you!!! And remember the pen is mightier than the sword!!!

FLASH
Which member of the M.E.F. has been receiving CORPORAL punishment?
Has the Algerian Sheik from the White House been restored to humour yet?
Yes? No?
So Norman the Conqueror .... well..... nice work. It makes me think! (Try and figure this out)
Rumour hath it that a search party is on the look out for the Lass of RICHMOND Hill. Good hunting.
Who prefers two days in London rather than reporting for duty? I'm with you every time.
Who always says "I'll have to tell my Dad"?
We hear that the first Sunderland Jewish Boy Scout is often first in other things too - - - - -
Which medico has been seen walking furtively along the BURMA road? Or was he just tse-tseing me?
5279! 5279!! 5279!!!
Does a certain lieutenant drink whisky for medicinal purposes only?
Who are the "Big Three" who write this column for me? How are the mighty fallen?
PERMIT or not to permit?
Who aDAWS to be known as the Almond King?
Who's recently had his calling out pains? What's afoot?

Answers to Questions on Page 2.

1. In the British Parliament there are 14 women amongst a membership of 615. In the House of Representatives of the United States 6 of the 436 are women, and in the Elected Assembly in Palestine there are 7 women amongst 71 members.
2. Charles Lamb.
3. The use of smoke in war is mentioned in the book of Exodus 14 verse 19. The Israelites were protected by it during their march from Egypt to the promised land.
4. There is a sect of Jews in Palestine who are descendants of the Sobotnicki who were Russian Sabbatarians who left the Orthodox Church in the 15th Century and accepted Judaism.

5.

SEARCHLIGHT ON SPORT   -   By "Argus"

I had hoped to delay this article for a few days to give you a more definite idea of the possibilities of Sunderland surviving the qualifying rounds of the League Cup.

At the moment of writing it looked as though they required two of the four points at stake in order to go into the first round, so if they win at Hartlepool, it wont matter much what happens at Middlesbrough.

There has been a great deal of comment about Raich Carter being left out of the recent English team. Just to show that he is not a past number, Carter dashed down to Sunderland on a 48 hour pass to play against Gateshead and - well, he simply made Sunderland team into a working machine. Raich I anticipate, will be in the R.A.F. team to oppose the Army at St. James Park on March 10th. If he is not, the North East will indeed be disappointed for many have booked just to see the Carter-Matthews wing.

Sunderland will have the services of Arthur Housam for a while, The deaths of both his father-in-law and his mother-in-law in a very short period and the illness of his own wife has meant his release for a period on class W/T reserve to look after the "pub".

Arthur Wright, like Bradwell, has been in Cherry Knowle for an operation, but is back to home duty again and I see he has been selected to play for Western Command in March. Wright came home on leave from B.L.A. and went into Hospital for a knee injury.

In the case of Sid Bradwell, who was in para-troops, smashed up his leg very badly in Holland and the fracture is now out of plaster, but he still needs two sticks. Sid thinks, however, that they have made a good job of it and that he will be all right for football.

Nearly half of the Durham County Junior side which is representing Durham in the F.A. Counties Cup are on Sunderland's books as amateurs. When this war is over I fancy Billy Murray will be able to pull out for the reserve team some really promising youngsters, including a centre forward named Harrison who has scored over 80 goals this season.

NEWS LETTER FROM THE HOME FRONT

By no stretch of the imagination could I call the Lit dance on January 14th a success. It wasn't bad but that is about all I can say. The weather was drastic; consequently the gathering was small and the band was also lacking in numbers. The following week there was a B.B.C. Night which in its own small way was quite good. There was a General Knowledge Bee, a Tune Titles Quiz, a Film and a Radio Quiz. Those who were there enjoyed it.

The Social on January 28th was one of the best I have been to for a long time. There was Table Tennis, Darts and dancing to the radiogram. There were nearly forty people present, mostly gossiping at first but later nearly all were "paired off" and stepping out in time to the new dance records.

The biggest success of the year was the Cup Night on February 4th. Yes, it really was Cup Night for the cup was presented to the winner for the first time for several years. Perhaps this was the cause for the number of competitors but whatever it was there were more than there has been for quite a few years. The Adjudicator was Mr. R.I. Minchom B.A. (Oxon) A.M.I.E.E., A.M.I.P.E. and he did the job exceedingly well giving much sound general advice on reading papers. My memory was sent

8.

feeling back when the Chairman, Aubrey Gordon, introducing the Adjudicator said that Mr. Sol Novinski for many years had had that task and that the Lit's thoughts were still with him. The new Adjudicator, he went on, would ably step into the breach. I thought of all the previous competitions - of the wrangly and arguing by the competitors. But I can honestly say that this years winner deserved the cup as much as anyone I remember. He is Charles Slater who gave a clear and well delivered paper on "A New League of Nations"? Myer Robinson came second with a paper on "The Jewish Day School" and others taking part were Leslie Epstein, Julian Isaacs, Charles Cohen, Philip Winburn and Charles Topaz. In presenting the cup the Adjudicator said that the standard of the papers was high all round and congratulated the Society on its achievement.

There was a Social on February 11th, and this was also very pleasant. It was indeed enjoyable dancing to the latest records and the newest tunes, of which the Lit now possesses over twenty, and there was Table Tennis too. February 25th is a red letter day, for the Lit is holding a Bring and Buy Sale in the afternoon and a dance in the evening. The proceeds, I believe, are to wipe out the piano debt. I will give you the 'gen' about these events next time so, in the meanwhile, good luck and cheerio for now.

Yours,

_____Also After Gen._

EXCERPTS FROM LETTERS.

<u>Sgt. P. Pearlman, C.M.F. writes:</u> Again I've been fortunate enough to obtain an interesting job, as some of the most famous people of Italy as well as the most notorious are interned here, you can well imagine how enthralling it must be for me as interpreter.

<u>Pte. M. Pearlman, S.E.A.C. writes:</u> I find many things of interest in your ever popular growing paper, but above all, it keeps me spiritually in touch with my beloved town and many old friends, whose names appear periodically in the headlines of the different articles. At the moment I am in action somewhere in Burma, miles away from civilization and any Jewish Community of any description.

<u>A/C Arnold Landau, B.L.A. writes:</u> Unfortunately I wasn't able to attend a Chanukah service but that did not stop me from observing this, a great Jewish festival and I lit what candles I could scrounge, and sang Mo-oz Tsur, being Chazan and congregation all rolled into one. By the way some of the lads may be interested that I am attached to a unit, one of the personnel of which is Bobby Gurney, the Sunderland centre-forward. He was very pleased I came from Sunderland and we've had many a chat about football and the old home town in general.

<u>Sgm. I. Rosenthal, S.E.A.C. writes:</u> During the whole of the North Burma campaign I have been with the 36th Division and have travelled by land sea and air, on foot, in jeeps and jeep trains by day and by night. I have covered the whole of the Railway Corridor from Myitkyina to the Irrawaddy and now beyond, and it is perfectly obvious that I'm not finished, not by a very long way. This advance has not allowed me a lot of leisure in which to maintain my contact with the Western world. Your

Bulletin, however has been reaching me quite regularly and through it I have been able to follow events at home and keep track of many of my friends in their wanderings over the world's troubled surface. I thank you for it. Unlike the majority of my Jewish comrades-in-arms I have been unable I regret very much to say, to attend any kind of service whatsoever for more than fourteen months. Leave has not been granted to me since July 1943 except for two days in the latter part of that year when I spent Rosh Hashannah in Bombay. Since then I have been almost constantly in action, in Arakan, a short rest in Assam where I had two attacks of Malaria and now here. I had thought of following Buddha, but I can't stand the look on his face! Something must be done though, quite seriously, I'm not at all satisfied with the way things have gone and I feel I have a strong case to put forward when the time comes. Perhaps my pessimism regarding times to come will prove unfounded, it remains to be seen.

Cpl. I.J. Charlton, R.A.F., India writes: When reading the recent copies of the bulletin I really can't restrain a feeling of envy for those of my fellow members of the forces who are privileged to make frequent visits to European cities of world renown and there come into contact with members of the local Jewry, even though such meetings at times must be rather painful. My experience of the 'country-side' and local inhabit-ants in this area can be very simply and fully described by the words:- Jungle and lower class Indian native.

Cpl. A. Bergson in England writes:- The Forces certainly do 'Land' us in some queer places. Though T.G. I myself have had the good fortune to do most of my army service as a "Fire-side soldier" I am nevertheless fully conscious of the debt we all owe to the local boys' for the great job of work they are doing on almost every battle front. "The Sunderland Jewish Community may be well proud of her sons." was the remark passed by a non-Jewish Padre when I showed him a copy of the Bulletin. May I mention for the information of any of the Sunderland boys who may be on leave in Palestine that my father who resides at 2, Rabbi Akiba Street, Bnei-Brak, Palestine, would gladly entertain them at his home and would be especially pleased to have any of them for Pesach.

Surg.Lt. H.B. Minchom, Burma writes: This letter comes to you by the courtesy of two lamps in my tent which I share with a few others. The Bulletin has arrived and after the first page was read I was interrupted by two of the others, a doctor and a paymaster who wanted to know what propaganda it was. When I finished it I passed it on, much to their interest. There was one serious point of contention when Argus was quoted saying that Sunderland was at the top of the League it was dismissed as Jewish American Plutocratic Propaganda.

The following letters were also received and are gratefully acknow-ledged :- Fus. B. Freeman, MALTA FORCE; L.A.C. J. Gordon, B.N.A.F.; L.A.C.W. Slater L, ENGLAND, L.A.C. Davis I., B.L.A.; L.A.C. Davis H. ENGLAND; Cpl. A. Bergson, ENGLAND; Pte. D. Goldman and Pte. E. Gillis, ENGLAND.

The Bulletin is issued free to members of the Forces but private subscribers at the rate of 10/- per year will be gladly accepted.

Will readers please notify change of address before the 20th of the month.

All correspondence to be sent to Rev. S.P. Toperoff, 5 Victoria Avenue, Sunderland.

SUNDERLAND *Jewish* COMMUNITY

BULLETIN *for the* FORCES

" Be strong and of good courage, be not afraid neither be thou dismayed, for the Lord thy God is with thee withersoever thou goest."

Joshua, I : 9.

Edited and issued monthly by the Minister and sent to you with the good wishes of your friends at home.

March 1945   Vol. 3, No. 6.   Nisan 5705

Pesach

What is in a name?

The Festival which we celebrate in the months of Nisan is called as you know, Pesach or Passover. It is derived from the Bible although there the name given is "The Festival of Unleavened bread or Matzos". However, the name Passover is far more popular and universally used amongst our people.

The reason must obviously be that "Passover" applied to the Paschal offering which played such an important part in the exodus of Egypt. The name of the sacrifice has clung to us in preference to Matzos. The reason being that we are a people of sacrifice. Which race has made more sacrifices for its preservation and life than the Jewish race?

Sacrifice is interwoven with Jewish history. Indeed we should not forget that we observe Passover not in the eating of unleavened bread alone but in celebrating a festival which emphasises more than anything else the importance of Freedom for which Jews are continually fighting and striving.

Today too, we prefer to call this festival after the Paschal sacrifice because we are fighting now for the same freedom for which our ancestors fought in Egypt. We fight to worship the one true God and not a glorified idol of man's imagination. The full story of Jewish sacrifice and self devotion to duty in this war is not yet known for we belong to the "forgotten army". Our exploits and deeds are publicised only when they are bad. The feats of heroism and daring of self sacrifice and loyalty are hidden behind un-Jewish names. But the message of Passover is one of hope. With hope and confidence in a brighter and happier future we should unite and have faith in our cause.

What is in a name?

In ancient Egypt the Angel of Death passed over the houses of the Israelites, the doors of which were splashed with blood. It is true to say that hardly a Jewish house stands in the old time communities of Poland, Germany, Austria, Holland and Belgium. Now that these countries are being liberated it is our fervent prayer that the Angel of Death will pass over Israel and grant us a respite of torture, suffering and death.

In that one word "Passover" lie our hopes and aspirations. We pray that war with all its bloodshed, suffering and misery pass over from off the face of the earth, that the tyranny of the German war machine pass over out of existence for all times, and that the hatred of the Jew fostered by the Fascist Propaganda pass over into the limbo of oblivion, that pogroms, religious and racial persecution be no more and that in the words of the Hagaddah we may acknowledge God and "sing a new song".

May we usher in a new order, a new life that will enable us to re-build the shattered and scattered communities of Israel and may the Powers help us to strengthen Jewish life in Palestine so that the Jewish National Home become not a dream but a practical reality in our days.

4.

He described the historic House of Commons and the many ceremonials. He also described how a division was taken, and the members loyalty to the Speaker. Speaking from the floor of the hall he drew a plan of the floor of the House with his stick, and described how a member would cross the floor, how a new Member was introduced and many other ceremonials. Not only did he give the audience this picture, but he told them the historic meaning of these and many other manifestations of England's constitutional rights. This interesting lecture concluded with an invitation from the honourable gentleman to any member of the "Circle" to see the House under his guidance when in London.

After the lecture I invited Sir Walter to see the new Synagogue upstairs. Reaching for his hat, he expressed his delight at the opportunity. Standing before the "Bima" I explained to him the ceremony of taking the Torah from the Ark, placing it on the reading desk, reading the law, and putting it back again. After admiring the building he took leave of the members downstairs, and thus a memorable evening in the annals of the Literary Circle ended.

Next month, "Mr. Reah, R.A. speaks to us."

Cheerio,

SOL.
_____

NEWS LETTER FROM THE HOME FRONT

The Bring and Buy sale on February 26th came off as successfully as I had anticipated. There were three stalls and an ice-cream counter. The ice-cream was sold at 6d. and was really delicious. It was the first I had tasted since the ban was lifted and the creamy flavour reminded me of the old days. There was a food stall, a refreshments stall, selling lemonade and tempting sandwiches, and a book stall upon which there was a good display of books, magazines and odds and ends. Most things went very quickly as there was a fair crowd of mothers and fathers who had come along for the School Prize Distribution which was held in the Hall during an interval in the Sale. The fact that events clash like this shows lack of co-ordination amongst the various bodies who use the Hall.

All this was in the afternoon, at night there was the Lit's annual Purim dance which, this time I am glad to note was free to members. There was naturally a large gathering including a few "out-of-towners". The band was again good and everyone had a grand time.

The following Sunday, March 4th, the Lit turned from social enter- tainment to more serious consideration of world affairs. There was a debate on "That after the war women should return to the home". Theo Benjamin proposed with Charles Slater opposing. Upon such a controver- sial subject I had expected a "hot" debate but in fact only very few spoke for the opposition. This was most surprising especially in view of the fact that there was quite a large number of girls present. The vote gave the day to the proposition so it seems likely that the old, and so far satisfactory domestic arrangement will continue in future as in the past.

I was interested in the Mock By-Election the week after. There were four candidates, Julian Isaacs for Labour, Myer Robinson as independant agriculturist, Charles Slater, the man of the people and Philip Winburn

5.

for the Conservatives.   Each put up his respective case amid all the
thumping and heckling that is usual at political meetings and, incidentally, Labour won!

Any of you who will be home for Pesach should remember the joint
F.Z.Y. and Lit dance on Monday 2nd April.   It'll be worth going to.

That's all for now, keep smiling and best of luck.

Yours,

Also After Gen.

_____

Answers to Questions on Page 2.

1. Ramoth Hashavim in the plain of Sharon in Palestine is inhabited by
   400 Jews mainly German immigrants and they have 35,000 hens producing
   three million grade A eggs each year.
2. Jacques Offenbach, 1819 - 1880, the son of a Chazan.
3. The late Chief Rabbi of Turkey, Chaim Bejereno Effendi.
4. The Puritans in 17th century England.

_____

SEARCHLIGHT ON SPORT - By "Argus."

Well the die has been cast.   Sunderland are not in the first round
of the League Cup competition.   Against all opinions to the contrary,
Middlesbrough pulled some thing out of the bag - and put both points into
it.

I have never met anyone yet who can explain why a team which ran so
strongly for the first half of the season championship slumped badly in
the second half for the second successive year.   The only theory I can
advance is that they either played with a lot of luck which has now
deserted them or they cannot stand the pace.   There may be another
explanation but I leave you to guess at that - no pack drill.

You know luck does run in cycles.   When I say to people that Jimmy
Gorman was never a back in the £6000 class they point to the grand game he
played in the Cup Final.   I have always to admit that but my long
experience teaches me to watch for points and in the cup final he had one
of the luck cycles.   Every ball came to his right foot.

If the results have not been what we expected - or shall I say hoped
for?- it is at least pleasing to record the rapid advance of Stelling as
a back.   I know he is a little rash at times, but experience will cure
that.   Some of the "devil" can be taken out of a man's play, but if he
has not the "guts" when he starts it will never be put into him later.
"Guts" is a crude word but it is very expressive.

I think the policy to be adopted now should be the playing of some
of the more promising youngsters on the Club's books.   I know that
involves risk of defeat, but if you are going to satisfy yourself that you
have a potential first team player, that is a risk which must be taken.
/I fancy you will all agree that if he is not a potential first-teamer,
then its a waste of time keeping h

6.

The man who disappoints me most is Harry Bell, the Castletown and England ex-schoolboy. He has not made the frame and good ball playing is no use if he cannot stand up to it. And Bell definitely cannot. Besides he refuses to play for the reserve team. If that is an example of thinking he is a ready made player, its time he came back to mother earth. The worst thing a youngster can get is a hat larger than normal. Enough said.

A Story of Two Great Jewish Scholars.

Ibn Ezra (1092-1167) a great Jewish scholar and writer was once afflicted with an ulcer in the throat and decided to visit Moses Maimonides (1135-1204), whose fame as a healer of all kinds of diseases had spread throughout the entire world.

As was the usual habit of Ibn Ezra he did not disclose his identity upon coming to the home of this illustrious physician and most eminent savant. When Maimonides saw this patient who had come to him to be cured, he immediately knew that he was Ibn Ezra, for he had been informed that the latter was travelling in that vicinity, but he said nothing.

Then they began to discuss various Jewish matters as scholars are wont to do. When Ibn Ezra told Maimonides of his ailment, the latter replied:- " As the Shabbos begins this evening I have no time to examine you, but I shall prepare a certain medicine which will be ready after the Sabboth; meanwhile I shall be honoured to have you as my guest at the evening meal."

Maimonides was accustomed to invite the poor Jews of the city to his home so that they might partake of the Shabbos meal with him, and therefore when Ibn Ezra arrived that evening he found that many men were seated at the table. On the table there was placed in front of every guest a plate with a candle. Then the servants came and began to serve the soup, and after this had been done they placed some milk in every plate.

When Ibn Ezra saw what had been done he shrieked out very excitedly- "Oh that is terrible, how can you permit meat and milk to be mixed together with the candle?" No sooner had he utted these sharp cries than the ulcer within his throat burst.

Maimonides saw that his plan had worked out as he wanted it and proceeded to explain the whole matter to the surprised Ibn Ezra. "I knew who you were from the very first moment and therefore realised that there was only one thing that could cure you. I arranged the meal purposely in this fashion because I was sure that this would cause you to become very much alarmed, hence shriek out and the ulcer would be burst. But the food is not what you think it is. The candles are made of chicken fat and the milk is of coconut. Now you have been cured and I am satisfied."

7.

The Festival of Spring.

The people of Israel celebrates now its Spring Festival. The Festival of Redemption and of hope for the bright future. Spring brings courage to the oppressed and unfortunate; it promises them a change in their lives. Even if the days of winter drag on and the roaring storm winds bring on their wings the black clouds which darken the face of the sun; whilst every blossom fades and every nest is forsaken, whilst desolation, rain, storms and hoar frost rule with a firm hand and tens of thousands of creatures of the world perish and die off .... At long last Spring comes with all the splendour of its beauty and its passionate yearning for life, renewing the face of the World and Nature.

And you O Israelite, even if the days of sorrow are long and the dark years seem without end let there be no despair. The sword will not devour for ever, neither will the proud hand rule for all time. Though the beasts of prey howl and yelp and perform a dance of devils around the vineyard of Israel, storming it with violent anger, saying:- "Let us go and destroy them utterly".

You ..... neither be afraid nor despair. "For even if you pass through fire and water I shall be with you. I will guard you until the days of spring are here and then you will laugh at them for they will have perished for ever and thou shalt be firm and blossom once again, thou shalt increase and grow strong and become the glory of the Peoples."

(Culled from the Torah Va·avodah Library No. 4.)

The following letters were received and are gratefully acknowledged by the Editor: A.C.Landau, B.L.A.; L.A.C. Davis I., B.L.A.; Cpl. N. Cohen, C.M.F.; Cpl. Altman L., India; Pte. L. Marks, England; Fus. B. Freeman, Malta; Olga Grantham, V.A.D., India; Gunner Abrahams P.A.I.; Pte. Pearlman, S.E.A.C.; L.A.C. M. Dresner, England and Sgt. Sarabouski, South East Asia.

The Bulletin is issued free to members of the Forces but private subscribers at the rate of 10/- per year will be gladly accepted.

Will readers please notify change of address before the 20th of the month.

All correspondence to be sent to Rev. S.P. Toperoff, 5 Victoria Avenue, Sunderland.

SUNDERLAND Jewish COMMUNITY — BULLETIN for the FORCES

" Be strong and of good courage, be not afraid neither be thou dismayed, for the Lord thy God is with thee withersoever thou goest."

Joshua, I : 9.

Edited and issued monthly by the Minister and sent to you with the good wishes of your friends at home.

April 1945.   Vol. 3, No. 7.   Iyar 5705

The War is coming to a successful close.

Our men are on German soil liberating thousands of German prisoners of war and more civilians.   What is the reaction of our men to the non-fraternisation order issued by the Supreme Commander?

We as Jews have suffered more than any other people.   Close on five million Jewish Civilians have been starved to death, burnt, slaughtered and executed.   Our men will certainly not wish to fraternise with Germans who allowed this wholesale extermination policy of Jews to be executed with such sadism and thoroughness.

Yet the feelings expressed by Lionel Gillis in a letter in this issue should not altogether surprise our Christian friends.   Mercy, pity, love, are words which are written large in our Bible.   Jews have been called Sons of the Devil, Whited Sepulchres, hypocrites and heretics.   Jews have been burnt in the thousands throughout the Middle Ages in the name of Religion.

But what was our reaction to those who in the name of God have burnt us at the stake.

We knew they were inspired by a blind hatred of Jews which throughout the ages hardened into suspicion and mistrust.   But we persistently carried on with our way of life and customs and would not be intimidated by any false teachings though we suffered terrible humiliation, degradation torture and death.   This has been our unfortunate lot now for many centuries.

So today. Many of our Christian friends would not believe the atrocity stories in Germany, Poland, Rumania and other countries.   They preferred to pass them off as "mere propaganda".   The Germans they said are not as cruel as pictured by these so called Jewish propagandists.

Now for the first time non-Jewish War correspondents have given eye-witness accounts of the horrible scenes they saw at the Concentration Camps at Buchenwald, Belsen, Nordhausen etc.   Many correspondents have broken down in their description of these German torture-chambers and hell-dungeons in which thousands of human beings (civilians remember) have been bludgeoned, kicked and starved to death in the most abominable manner imaginable.

Is this what the German Herrnvolk "Supermen" have tried to foist on the world?   Is this the New World they have tried to introduce into every country they have occupied?   The blood of these innocent creatures cry out to the world and plead that their memory shall never be forgotten. Never again must the world allow itself to become so morally debased.

We as Jews have good reason to hate and detest for all times the German way of life.   We warned the world but the warning was unheeded. We were from the outset Enemy No. 1.   We were Hitler's first target in 1933.   We suffered the worst indignities of the Concentration Camp long before a shot was fired in this war.   Yet we do not ask for the annihilation of millions of Germans.

2.

All we ask and pray for after the removal of the arch criminals is that Jew-baiting which Hitler himself publicised and propagandised, be uprooted from the face of the earth. We plead that never again must it raise its monstrous and ugly head.

To achieve this we need the co-operation of all the peoples of the world. We need most urgently the active help of the Church and all organised Religion to instil into the hearts of its adherents, not a suspicion of the Jew but a respect and love for God's ancient people who have preserved the Law of Truth and loving kindness in the midst of persecution and held aloft the torch of Freedom and Justice.

DO YOU KNOW?

1. How many Jews lived in Palestine in Roman times?
2. Who is in command of the recently formed Jewish Brigade Group and how many countries are represented in it?
3. Who is "Rabbi Talmud"?
4. Which was the first Parliamentary Borough to be contested by a Jew?

Answers to the above on Page 5.

HERE AND THERE!

Mazeltov!
Congratulations to:-
Births   - Mr. & Mrs. G. Behrman on the birth of a daughter.
               Dr. & Mrs. L. Collins on the birth of a daughter.
               Mr. & Mrs. A. Refson on the birth of a son.
               Mr. & Mrs. M.B. Wolfe on the birth of a son.
Engagements - Miss Sheba Pearlman A.T.S., on her engagement to Cecil Cohn of Leeds.
               Miss Dorrie Behrman on her engagement to Harry Cohen of London.
Bar Mitzvah - Congratulations to Harold Benjamin son of Mr. & Mrs. Benjamin of Wroxham Court.

T.A.C. Annual Metting. The first Annual Meeting of the Trades Advisory Council took place in the Communal Hall with Mr. R. Minchom in the Chair. Reports of the year's work were given by both the Chairman and the Hon. Secretary, Mr. M. Burnley. Alderman Marcus Bloom of West Hartlepool, Representative on the National Council of T.A.C. addressed the meeting on the importance of the T.A.C. The executive and Committee were re-elected and the Hon. President, Rev. S.P. Toperoff in the course of his remarks thanked Ald. Bloom for his address. On the motion of Mr. R. Share a vote of thanks was accorded to the Chairman and Secretary for their work.
Council of Christians and Jews.
Under the auspices of the Council of Christians and Jews a Film Show and Social was held at the Communal Hall. The arrangements were in the hands of the Jewish Committee who acted as hosts. The Ministry of Information was good enough to include in their show two Zionist Films lent by the Zionist Organisation. They were "A Day in Dagania", and "The Land of Promise". Following the Film Show there was a Social, and tea and biscuits were provided by the Ladies of the War Services Committee. The Chairman of the Council, the Rev. A.G. Utton, briefly explained the function of the Council and a number of new members were enrolled.

3.

Youth Study Group
A Sunderland branch of the Jewish Youth Study Group was formed at the house of the Minister where regular Shiurim in Tenach (Prophets) will be held on alternate Sabbath, conducted by the Minister. Regular discussion on topical Jewish problems will also take place. The subject of the first discussion will be "Religion and our careers in life".

SEARCHLIGHT ON SPORT - By "Argus"

We are drawing near to the end of another season and wondering what is in store for the next. You may recall that before the turn of the year I told you of the decisions of the Football League - that if war in the west ended before the opening of the season 1945-46 League Football would be resumed on the basis of pre-war with the exception that there will be no promotion and relegation.

That may be all washed out at a meeting of the Clubs at Manchester in May for both Arsenal and Birmingham put forward grouping schemes combining the First and Second Division Clubs into areas with the idea of reducing travelling - a scheme which Sunderland will vigorously oppose on the grounds that they will have considerable cross-country travel with little financial return and it is easier to get to London and good gates.

Therefore until the May meeting we do not know what is to happen, but it is a certainty that Second League clubs will support the proposals as they are going to get better opposition.

Another thing which is troubling clubs is the fact that the Football League has ordered that every amateur placed on the retained list must be re-signed at the end of this season. Sunderland have many good amateurs who might now have been professionals but for the war. Many are in the Forces and cannot be contacted; others are being allowed to play elsewhere - and it is a thousand pounds to the proverbial hay seed that the clubs they are with will try to get them to sign for them and Sunderland will lose quite a few.

The first professional signing by Manager Murray was the securing of the transfer of Cyril Brown, Brentfords inside forward who is back to his old job as a clerk in Ashington Colliery Office. He is now 25 and a really good player. If you think of £500 you will be somewhere near the transfer fee - and at that he is a bargain price.

Brown ought to give to the attack that additional bit of craft so necessary when Raich Carter cannot play excepting on his leaves. Raich by the way, made a great hit on being recalled to England's team and he is regarded in Scotland as Enemy No. 1.

Many inquiries come to me from overseas to settle arguments about Carter's age. He is now 32, and though he is quickly turning grey, he is young enough and good enough, for a few seasons yet.

4.

IN RETROSPECT.

Once again the seating capacity provided by the Society was taxed to its utmost. The Lit was indeed fortunate in having the enthusiastic attendance of non-members. The Lecturer was Mr. Rea. R.A. (Headmaster of the Sunderland College of Arts and Crafts). He described his visit to the ancient and beautiful city of Prague. The lecture was illustrated by lantern slides. As it was impossible to fix a sheet on the beautifully polished partition at the top of the hall, it was hung on the wall where the mirror stands now. Incidentally this screen was a bed sheet belonging to our old friend and oft-times confederate Ette Rosenthal. The chairs had to be reversed and Mr. Rea and I sat at the side of the door.

In the course of his talk the lecturer told us that Prague possessed the oldest Synagogue in Europe. Describing the old building he told us there was to be seen a hole in one of the walls through which the Jewish women could peep and watch their men folk at prayer. I remember also many beautiful pictures of boulevards, gardens and ancient buildings. These slides were beautifully coloured. Mr. Rea told us he had taken the photographs himself, turned them into lantern slides and painted them. You, who know his work, can visualise the wealth of colour and artistic craftsmanship we enjoyed that evening. After the lecture he asked to see the Shool. I gladly, indeed proudly, escorted him upstairs. After admiring the design of the chandeliers and the curved blue ceiling spangled with stars, he remarked on the colour scheme, the pews, as he called the seating, and finally his eyes came to rest on the Ark. After a long and evidently careful scrutiny, he turned to me and said: "Byzantine architecture, correct in every detail".

Meanwhile the finances of the Society were worrying the Committee a great deal. The constant hire of chairs etc. had drained its resources. The Dramatic Circle however, came to the rescue. It would stage a three act play. But, it had no stage! "The Prudes Progress" a play by Jerome K. Jerome and Eden Philpotts was decided upon. This it was hoped would raise sufficient money to pay for a temporary stage. The seating accommodation would have to be bought later.

Next month I will tell you about this play and how Mr. Morris Davis. came to the rescue with regards to seating.

Cheerio,

SOL.

NEWS LETTER FROM THE HOME FRONT

As usual Pesach brought with it the end of another Lit year. The Annual General Meeting was held on March 25th and there was a good attendance. The general atmosphere was brighter than the last few years and the younger crowd especially showed a marked keenness to be elected to the Committee. In his report, Chairman Aubrey Gordon outlined the years events which, he pointed out, included several achievements such as holding a dance in aid of the U.P.A., entertaining non-Jewish wounded soldiers from Cherry Knowle and, though certainly not least, the purchase of a long needed piano. The membership, he added, was over 40 — an increase of ten over last year. Leslie Epstein presented the accounts which were passed without much questioning. These, he explained, showed that, despite a liberal expenditure on gramaphone records and other things, the

cash in hand was larger at the end of the Season than at the beginning.
Aubrey Gordon was re-elected Chairman for the coming year with Pearl Berg
and Philip Winburn as Vice-Chairmen, Theo Benjamin treasurer and Reeva
Cohen secretary.   A committee of six was also elected with a good
representation of the younger members who have shown themselves extremel
keen in all literary events.

I hope to review the whole Session in a later issue of the Bulletin
when there is space but there is no need to doubt that the Lit will soon
return to its former strength and the good old days will once again retu
Only one point worth mentioning is that the Lit does not seem to have an
preparations for a Welcome Home or Re-Union party.

The joint Lit and F.Z.Y. dance on Monday Chal Hamoed Pesach, which
I mentioned in the last issue, was very successful.   There was a large
crowd many of whom were from Newcastle and Shields.   Max Davidson, a
member of both the Lit and F.Z.Y., led his newly formed band which, thou
not yet perfect, played quite well especially in the second half after
the Cabaret.   It was announced that over £12 had been raised in aid of
the Red Cross Palestinian Prisoners of War fund.

The Lit Committee I hear, has been in session to draw up the Summer
Programme which is to include several rambles.   Of course until about
October there is no regular Lit meeting on a Sunday evening but if the
weather bears up to expectation that will not be missed.

I hope to be with you again next month so cheerio for the present.

Yours,
_____ Also After Gen.

Answers to questions on Page 2.

1. According to Roman Records Jewish Palestine maintained 3½ millions;
   that is more than four times as many as any other subsequent rule
   succeeded in maintaining in that country.
2. The Commander of the Jewish Brigade is Brigadier E.F. Benjamin.   53
   countries are represented in the Jewish Brigade.
3. No such person ever existed except in the ignorant mind of Capuchin a
   great mediaeval scholar.   This proves how little of the Talmud was
   known by the so called scholars of the Middle Ages.
4. Shoreham was contested by David Salomons in 1837 but he took his seat
   with the passing of the Emancipation Act in 1858 as Member for
   Greenwich.

_____

EXCERPTS FROM LETTERS

Warrant Officer Isadore Levine, Indian Command writes: Last night I
attended the first Communal Seder, which was held at the Imperial Hotel,
New Delhi.   There were over 350 Service personnel present and the fact
that we Jews are spread to the four corners of the earth was very much in
evidence and amply illustrated by the varied nationalities present.
Glancing around whilst the Service was in progress, I observed an Austral
ian Sergeant engrossed in conversation with a W.A.A.F. from London.- a
Dutch Naval Officer sharing a Prayer Book with an American nurse - a very
tough looking Corporal in the "Chindits" (Wingate's original Expedition)
several Indian girls wearing exquisite "Saris" and representatives too

numerous to mention from all the Arms of the American, British and Colonial Forces. The Management of the Imperial Hotel were unable to provide wine glasses for so large a gathering and so tumblers were issued in lieu. It was rather difficult to drink the four traditional glasses of wine from a "pint glass" and so we comprised at the ratio of one tumbler equals two Wine glasses.

Last week I was 'on tour" with my Colonel and as we visited Agra I managed to take some photographs of the famous "TAJ MAHAL". It is undoubtedly the most magnificent work of its kind in the world. The entire "TAJ" is constructed of marble and the gardens and tiny lake that surround it make a delightful setting. The "TAJ" by moonlight is reputed to be the most beautiful sight in the world, but I think the lights of Bombay will look even better - when I am on that ship!

Sergeant Philip Pearlman of C.M.F. writes: The Seder Services at Rome were well catered for and all meals were obtainable at the Jewish Club. Kneidlach were also included in the menu at every lunch - excellent Palestinian Matzo was available in unrationed quantities. The second Seder (under the influence of four large "Coisos" of delicious Palestinian Wine), we continued the celebration after the Hagadah in the open square in front of the building where the Sedarim took place and danced a frenzied Hora.

Considerable jubilation and pride was voiced about the exploits of the Jewish Brigade now in action. Its activities have received prominence not only in all Forces' Newspapers but also in the Italian Press, which published a message from General Mark Clark to its Commander.

Jews of Rome as do all Jews in Italy who have been in contact with Palestinian Units are more conscious of their Jewishness. Frequently seen in the streets of Rome are people wearing a badge in the shape of a Magen David on the blue background. These are on sale at the Jewish Club in Rome. The Shools are better attended. Their economic condition has generally improved, with prices of every commodity continually rising, a decent living is made by buying and selling.

Corporal Joe Charlton of S.E.A. Air Force writes: The first Seder was held in the largest hall in Calcutta at an American Camp with a capacity of over 950 but even this was totally inadequate. During the Seder we were honoured by the presence of General Stuart accompanied by Sir Reg. Storrs (a former Governor of Palestine) first of whom addressed us, the latter showing a terrific knowledge of Hebrew, Yiddish and also of Jewish life and Customs.

Quite a full programme of entertainment was arranged for us and we were fed at the Judean Club by the generosity of the firm of B.N. Elias & Co., who stood the full cost and also entertained us to a swimming party and tea at one of their recreation Clubs adjoining one of their Jute Mills. We all had terrific afternoon and what a tea! We had to stagger back on to the Lorries.

Driver Lionel Gillis, B.L.A. writes: Your Editorial on the Sacrifice of the Jews, which is denoted by Pesach and the fact that the Angel of Death passed by the Jewish Homes, because their lintels were marked with blood, has certainly been brought home to me over here. It has become apparent to me that the Jewish pre-war population has not only been rased as a Religion - but also individually. So far in Germany I have not been able to find any.

My feelings on Germany are very mixed. There is certainly no fraternisation, but often there appears the spark of pity for these wretched old people and young children. The ordinary soldier has a certain degree of mercy in his make up and it is operating overtime now. This policy of non-fraternisation is alright for the moment – but, sooner or later it will have to be modified or it will break down completely. It is just as unnatural for the Allied Soldier not to speak to old people or children as it is for Soldiers to stop smoking or drinking beer. Even with the impulse of hatred for the Germans, which every Jew possesses, I still could not find it in me to kill these defenceless civilians, as some of our unpractical Newspaper-letter writers have advocated. We have a Prisoners Camp near here and passing it with a comrade, we watched how these Germans stood meekly in line awaiting transportation to the rear. What a wealth of scorn a Welsh boy put into one descriptive word which suited these Prisoners – "Supermen".

Lieut. Mordaunt Cohen of S.E.A.C. writes: Its a long slice of one's time to be overseas for nearly four years. Still I have seen some of the world and other people and it has helped me to appreciate the eternal problem of our people in true perspective. I am sure that most of the lads who have seen other countries will come back home with ideas quite different from those of the older members of the Community

Corporal Cyril Behrman of M.E.F. writes: I have just returned from my second visit to Palestine after spending a wonderful holiday. We visited a Settlement in which we saw real life. It's just like one happy family. Each member has a job to do and they go about it in a very wonderful fashion. It is unfortunate however that Jewish Traditional Practice is very lax in the Settlement.

Fus. Freeman of Malta writes: On my leave for Pesach I visited some Catacombs where the Phoenicians lived over two hundred years ago; they were still in very good condition. We all carried a candle and followed a guide who explained everything of interest to us. Every family had its house cut out in the rocks. For beds they had pits cut out in the shape of a bath. They were quite small and we were told that the people too were very small but quite strong. During the air raids a few thousand people lived in them. I also visited the Cathedral and was surprised to see a very fine painting on the wall done by an Italian artist. To my amazement I found that on the painting there were a number of Hebrew words I was proud to be the only one of the Company who could take down a copy of these words.

Cfn. Louis Olsberg, B.L.A. writes: The Shool I went to on Pesach was like a huge Cathedral inside. The Service was Turkish, an Organ and mixed Choir. We made the acquaintance of a gentleman who suggested a Beth Hamidrash and there I found the real old type of froom people. After the service my hostess gave me a yellow Mogan David with J in the centre that the Boch made all the Jews wear. I was given it as a souvenir. I also was given a small enamel flag with the Mogan David on. I was told that everyone will now recognise me as a Yiddisher Soldat. Many Jews told me how happy they all were when the R.A.F. passed over, they realised then that they were not forgotten.

Letters also received and acknowledged:– Sgt. Ralph Freedman, ENGLAND; W/O Basil Taylor, INDIA; Cpl. Lionel Altman INDIA; L.A.C. Cohen B.A., of B.L.A.; Pte. Claude Brewer C.M.F.; A.C.1 Davis, ENGLAND; A/C Landau, B.L.A.; S/Lt. Barry Gould, NIGERIA; Cpl. Rupert Levy, C.M.F.; V.A.D. Olga Grantham S.E.A.C.; Cpl. Gerald Shochet, B.L.A. and S/Sgt. Jacques Rosenthal, M.E.F.

The Bulletin is issued free to members of the Forces but private subscribers at the rate of 10/- per year will be gladly accepted.

Will readers please notify change of address before the 20th of the month.

All correspondence to be sent to Rev. S.P. Toperoff, 5 Victoria Avenue, Sunderland.

SUNDERLAND
Jewish
COMMUNITY

BULLETIN
for the
FORCES

" Be strong and of good courage, be
not afraid neither be thou dismayed, for
the Lord thy God is with thee withersoever
thou goest."

Joshua, I : 9.

*Edited and issued monthly by the Minister
and sent to you with the good wishes of
your friends at home.*

May, 1945   Vol. 3, No. 8   Sivan 5705

Victory is here at last.   Services of Thanksgiving have been held in every place of Worship.   We are all elated and grateful to God for having delivered us from the iron grip of a most terrible tyrant.

Once again the words of a Christian Cleric have been realised.   "The Jews have always stood at the graves of their persecutors".   But this time unfortunately more than a quarter of world Jewry, over four million Jews have been brutally murdered and done to death.

Hitler more than once expressed the wish that no matter what the issue of the struggle, as long as Jewry is totally annihilated his purpose will have been realised.

Has he realised his purpose?

He has certainly broken up and shattered many Jewish Communities, he has reared a generation of Jew-haters and spread the poisonous propaganda of Anti-Semitism throughout the world.   But Jewry is still alive and we mean to live.

We know however that we have a terrific job to do.   We must take up the threads of Jewish life and strengthen and revitalise the Jewish consciousness whereever it still lives or languishes.   We have to rebuild the broken Communities.

We have to infuse new life in the dry bones of the valley of the shadow of death left by the trail of the Concentration Camps.   We have to rehabilitate those who were fortunate enough to be rescued alive.

But the same old question presents itself, Wohin?   Where are they to go.   Is not this the opportune moment for the opening wide of the gates of Palestine and giving the worst sufferers of War a haven of refuge.

Victory in Europe is here but it is so far a victory of a feat of arms, of daring exploits on land on the sea and in the air.   We all pray for a moral Victory, a victory of the spirit, a victory of right over might.

We have with the help of God overthrown the might of the greatest enemy of mankind but we have not yet enthroned the power of RIGHT.   We owe it to the four million Jewish dead.   We owe it to the millions who have made the supreme sacrifice.   We owe it to the martyred souls of all races and creeds who died so that we may live.

The future is in the balance.   We pray and trust that Humanity will not be wanting.

DO YOU KNOW?

1. Which Jewish Lord Mayor showed an amazing feat of Horsemanship in a Royal Procession?
2. Why were Jews believed to be possessed of witchcraft in the early ages?
3. Who was the discoverer of colour photography and invented the capillary electrometer.

2.

4. Of whom was the following recorded in the Customs Records on his entry
   into Germany – "Today 70 Oxen 20 pigs and one Jew passed the Customs!
   barriers" ?

Answers to the above on Page 5.

HERE AND THERE!

Mazeltov!
Congratulations to:-

Births	– Dr. and Mrs. Geewater (nee Sonia Rawlinson) on the birth of a son.
	Cpl. and Mrs. N. Berg of Glasgow on the birth of a son.
	Sgt. and Mrs. Ralph Freedman on the birth of a daughter.
	Mrs. and Mrs. Jack Bergson on the birth of a son.
Engagements.	– Miss Lorna Maccoby on her engagement to Cpl. Bernard Mayer of the Australian Army.
Wedding	– Miss Dorrie Behrman on her marriage to Mr. Harry Cohen of London.
Promotion	– Congratulations to Captain Mordaunt Cohen who has been appointed Staff Captain at Brigade Headquarters.

Sgt. S. Freedman. – We are happy to state that Sgt. Freedman who sustained
injuries when he ran over a German mine whilst travelling in a truck is
now progressing favourably. We are pleased to include a letter from him
from a Convalescent home in England.

Bede Debate – At the Bi-Annual Cup Debate of the Bede Boys' Debating
Society John Jacobs was awarded the Cup by the Headmaster, Mr. G.A.
Bradshaw.

Mr. R.I. Minchom. – Mr. Minchom has been elected a member of the
Committee of the North East Section of the Institute of Production Engineers.

Council of Christians and Jews. –
    Under the auspices of the Council of Christians and Jews a very
successful meeting was arranged at the Town Hall when Rabbi Dr. Altman,
Communal Rabbi of Manchester delivered a most inspiring address on the
occasion of the first Annual Lecture of the Society. Dr. Altman spoke
on "The Image of the Jew" and gave a brilliant exposition on the causes
and the cure of Anti-Semitism.
    Councillor John Young J.P., the Mayor, presided in the presence of
over two hundred and fifty people.
    Votes of thanks were accorded to the speaker and the Mayor by the
Rev. A.G. Utton and the Rev. S.P. Toperoff.

Ladies Zionists.
    A Public Meeting arranged by the Women's Zionist Society was held at
the Communal Hall. Dr. Anni Samuelsdorff of Palestine was the special
speaker and Mrs. A. Blakey presided. Mrs. Kissman and Mrs. Mendelson
also addressed the Meeting.
    Dr. Samuelsdorff visited the North East to be present at the Women's
Regional Zionist Conference held at Newcastle. Twenty delegates from
Sunderland were present at the Conference.
    A comprehensive vote of thanks to the speakers was given by Mrs. M.
Joseph.
    The young Zionists were entertained by Mrs. L. Davis who gave a talk
on "The Jew in literature". Miss Pearl Berg was in the Chair.

3.

Sunderland & South Shields Jewish Refugee Hostel.
The General Meeting of the Hostel took place recently and the following were elected:- Mr. J. Behrman, Chairman; Rev. S.P. Toperoff Vice-Chairman and Treasurer; and Mr. M.B. Wolfe, Hon. Secretary.

WELCOME HOME!

We are happy to have once again with us Leonard Lerman who has been away for five years, three years of which he was a Prisoner of War.

He was captured at Benghazi in Libya and after two months was transferred to an Italian Prisoner of War camp. He spent some time at the following camps:- Naples, Lucca, Macerta, Verona.

With the Unconditional Surrender of Italy Leonard was transferred to Germany staying for different periods at the following Camps:- Innsbruck Moosberg, Lamsdorf and Brucx, in Sudetenland.

On the whole the treatment was pretty rough and there was plenty of beatings. On the forced marches which he endured many times Leonard saw many Polish Jews and others beaten up and shot. The whole German people were responsible for the crimes and bestialities of the Nazi Regime.

A Welcome of cheer and comfort will go out to Leonard from all at home and overseas and on behalf of the Sunderland Jewish Community we are delighted to have him with us.

We trust that he will now enjoy a well-earned rest.

IN RETROSPECT

Owing to the lack of accommodation in the Communal Hall, the Dramatic Circle, since leaving Unity Chambers, were holding class in the Talmud Torah Meaburn Street. But, these rooms were unsuitable for rehearsing a three act play. Permission was granted, and the school room at the old Shool, Moore Street, was once again put into use. Owing to lack of floor space, the tables were put together and on these, (the platform of the Lit's very first concert in 1912) the Dramatic Circle rehearsed its first three act play. Rehearsals were held every Sunday afternoon during the Summer. The Circle opened its second season in the Communal Hall with this play. The Hall was quite literally crowded, many people standing the whole evening. At the final fall of the curtain Mr. Sol Gillis the Congregations President came on the stage and expressed his and the audiences thanks. The audience called for the producer. I shall never forget the thrill I had when I faced that vast sea of faces. Thanking the great assembly, I explained the Circle's ambition to furnish the Hall and called for continued support. Another play "Fanny and the Servant Problem", by Jerome K. Jerome was put into production and performed at the end of the session.

Meanwhile a one act play by P.G. Wodehouse entitled "A Little Fowl Play" was given by the Circle in the Edward Hall (Victoria Hall) during the great bazaar held by the New Synagogue Building Fund. Good going was it not!!

4.

Then came the Lit's first piece of real good luck.   An offer by
Mr. Morris Davis to put into the Communal Hall as many chairs as the
Circle required, to be paid for at its own convenience.   A fine gesture
I assure you, and one that was much appreciated by the Committee and
Isaac Brewer, its much worried Treasurer.   Now that we had a platform
our ambition was to open a third session with a variety concert.   A
concert party accepted our invitation and gave us a very splendid show.
It may be of interest to you to know that this party was the cradle of
those well known music hall artists, Bob and Alf Pearson.

Next month I will tell you of the One Double O Club and how we
bought a piano.

Cheerio,
SOL.

NEWS LETTER FROM THE HOME FRONT.

I never thought when I accepted the honour of writing a monthly
letter in May 1943, that exactly two years later, I should have the
pleasure of penning a Victory Letter.   Nor, indeed, did I think, four
weeks ago, that before I had the chance to write to you again we should see
total victory in Europe.   What, you must be asking, was Sunderland like
and how was the grand news greeted at home.

The news of the absolute surrender of the German forces seemed imminent for so many days before it actually came that it was received with
comparative calm.   The news came in a Forces Programme announcement that
the German Command had ordered unconditional surrender.   This was at 3.0
p.m. on the Monday (May 7th) and where I was, some 100 people stood alongside me around a loud speaker - they were full of excitement.   Immediatel
ly wild cheering went up and within a very short time townsfolk were
hustling about; people dashing home, where possibly, hoping to be in time
to hear the P.M.'s official declaration - which did not come until 24
hours later.   Flags quickly appeared as if from nowhere and streamers and
bunting found their way to the most inaccessible places.   Loud speakers
were to be seen around the Town Hall ready for the Mayor to speak one hour
after the official declaration.   Everywhere seemed to hum with busyness;
young folk sang (and yelled) and faces wore a constant smile.   Yet there
was an air of calmness despite all - an air which seemed to say "That's
one job well done; now for the next."

Both VE Day and the next were spent rather as well earned holidays
than as an opportunity for excessive rejoicing.   The cinemas were full but
no more than any other holiday, the streets were busier than they have
been for a long time and Seaburn had a good complement of visitors -
especially on the second day which was one of the hottest so far in the
year.

The Lit, too, did its share in an unselfish way by organising a
"Surprise Party-Cum Dance" and inviting all the Jewish youth organisations
in the town, irrespective of age.   This was on VE day plus one and the
Communal Hall was decorated with flags and bunting as well as could be in
the present shortage.   I entered the Hall to find everyone in a large
circle enjoying the game of musical Parcel which gave rise to much fun.
There was not much in the line of games, for dancing to Max Davidson's band
occupied most of the time.   Most people and especially the members of the

5.

younger organisations, had a jolly time though I look forward with eagerness to a grand re-union party when you will all be back home again in the
not very distant future.

Hoping to see at least a few of you very soon and wishing you all
the best of luck.

Yours,

Also After Gen.

Answers to Questions on Pages 1 and 2.

1.Sir George Faudel Philips, Lord Mayor in 1897 instead of driving before
the Queen in his State Coach, followed the ancient practice of riding on
horseback preceding Her Majesty. On the occasion of the Diamond Jubilee
of H.M. he rode from the Temple Bar to St. Paul's attired in full regalia
and holding aloft the great sword of State - a feat which evoked a storm
of wild enthusiasm from the crowds all along the route of the procession.
2. The masses of the people were unlettered and did not understand the
civilizing influences of Jewish teaching which stressed justice, brotherhood, love and peace. The prejudice against Jews was so strong that
instead of respecting them for their teachings which were obviously ahead
of the times, non-Jews were taught to suspect the Jews for possessing
mysterious teachings which were beyond the spheres of human reasoning and
therefore akin to witchcraft.
3. Gabriel Lippman (1845-1921), was Professor of Physical and experimental
mathematics at the Sorbonne. In 1908 he was awarded the Nobel Prize for
Physics.
4. When Moses Mendelsohn (1729-1786) Philosopher and pioneer of German
enlightenment entered Berlin the above record was made by the customs
official. His Phaedon (1767) which established the belief in the
immortality of the soul, one of the most widely read and translated works
of German Literature, put him in the forefront of European Philosophers.
The Berlin of the 18th Century was no different from the Berlin of the
20th century in treating the Jew as merely another animal.

SPORTING REFLECTIONS - By "Argus"

I am writing this on the eve of the final day of the season 1944-45
the day before Sunderland played Gateshead in the final of the competition
now known as the Tyne, Wear, Tees Cup, the results in which also count
in the League table.

I cannot, therefore, give you the result, But I can give you some
indication as to how the season's play of the Red and White's has struck
me. The first half of the season was much better than the second
half, but one has noted a definite improvement since Brown was signed
from Brentford and Laidman returned to the Half Back line. Brown can
hold the ball and take it forward; Laidman can hold it too, but he is
inclined to play across the field instead of advancing towards Goal. In
addition, Brown can shoot accurately, while Laidman, without his body
over the ball, invariably lifts the ball high. Brown is going to be
useful in the post-war transitional period.

6.

In the last month of the season, we signed a 16½ year old inside forward named Hetherington who lives at Shiney Row. Make a note of this for future guidance. Hetherington is the best young forward Sunderland have signed since Raich Carter. He is a natural Footballer with a body swerve either way. He is well built too and can do the 100 in 10 and 2/5 seconds, which is a proof of speed.

Manager Murray is cutting down his list of amateurs. He has been holding private trial games and sorting the wheat from the chaff - in other words, retaining the best of them.

Next month I may be able to give you a better idea of prospective candidates for places in the senior team when I have the full list of signings.

You will know by now that in the coming season First and Second Divisions are lumped together and divided into South and North Leagues. I imagine it will work out all right. but Sunderland were dead against the proposal because it may mean financial loss in meeting Second Division clubs and cross country travel.

EXCERPTS FROM LETTERS

<u>Sgt. S. Freedman from England writes:</u> I was never a believer in the philosophy that one gained comfort from the fact others were "worse off" than oneself, but have found it to be true whilst in hospital.   Strange indeed! I have improved tremendously during the past two months and get around quite well.
     I was particularly interested in Lionel Gillis' letter on fratern- isation. I spent several weeks as an interpreter in P.O.W. Camps in Holland and Belgium and I can endorse his remarks that the non-fratern- isation policy is doomed from the moment of its conception. As he so rightly points out, even we Jews who have more reason than the rest of the world to hate Nazism and the Nazis are moved to some degree of pity. Whether this is a virtue or a vice only the future history of Anti-Semitism (and I'm afraid there will be such a history) will reveal.

<u>Cpl. Lionel Altman India, writes:</u> Life goes on pretty well the same except its got considerably rather uncomfortable. Still, if its anything we do know we are on the road to victory at last, and that the biggest struggle is over, surely there will never be any battles as we knew them in Europe, before the Germans were utterly defeated, by the three great powers, and the varied races and creeds under their joint command, to which the world, and civilisation owes so much.
     You must have been shocked as we all were by the terrible and almost unbelievable pictures etc. that have come from the Hell of Europe, the German Concentration Camps. There is no doubt now, these were no atrocity stories, it is fact that millions of innocent people, including a large majority of women and children were killed, murdered, tortured and experimented upon in cold blood, never has the world since the beginning of time experienced such sadistical madmen. How they can all be punished for these crimes, for wiping out millions of people, of all races and creeds, it is hard to know. We know of no laws to cover these exigen- cies, certainly death is practically impossible. Re-education is vital. It has certainly affected the whole of the world of human beings, and it

is hoped that our memories will not be so short this time, and that we will fight and work harder than ever to maintain the peace that will soon be ours P.G.

<u>Cpl. Joe Charlton, S.E.A. Air Forse writes:</u> I have very recently received from the chaplains office a copy of the Monthly news sheet 'Shalom' - which is the new organ of the Jewish troops in S.E.A.C. I can however say with pride, that the Sunderland bulletin has yet to be surpassed either by this paper, or its American equivalent, the Judean, which is a rather spasmodic publication.

<u>Pte. E. Gillis, writes:</u> In my short period of service I have had some amazing experiences, such as meeting a Frenchman serving in The Army Catering Corps, and approaching me he asked me to direct him to the N.A.A.F.I. as he had just arrived, but I had just arrived myself. Anyway we walked along, and he told me he was a Jew, and had managed to get to this country. I also met a Welshman who had been to Palestine, and who could speak Hebrew fluently.

<u>S/Sgt. J. Rosenthal, M.E.F., writes:</u> Here I have met Nat Goodman's brother-in-law and now have the pleasure in passing on to him my copies of the Bulletin. He enjoys them and it is nice to listen to our little community being praised for their attention to the troops while other towns seem to have forgotten their boys completely.

This place is rich in memories for our people. I've seen the Pyramids that we sweated to build and an old synagogue where Moses is reputed to have been before he left the land of Goshen, There is a portion of the Torah written by Ezra the Scribe.

<u>Capt. Ellis Dresner, West Africa Force writes:</u> I've been here 3 weeks now, and I must say I like it. There are much worse places than this. Its a great contrast to France and Holland and one finds much of great interest here, both as regards the country, the natives and the work. As you can see I'm now in a hospital, officially, although all my work is done outside; along the coast and up in the Bush with the Native Regiments. Its all most exciting - for the first six months anyway!

I've made one or two enquiries of C.E. and R.C. Padres, but cannot ascertain whether or not there is a Jewish Padre in West Africa. Certainly there's none in Gambia - as far as I know I'm the only Jew in this colony - I've met no others. Consequently, I attended no Service at Passover, for the first time in my life.

The following letters are also received and are gratefully acknowledged:- Cpl. Norman Cohen, C.M.F.; L.A.C. Julius Gordon, C.M.F.; Sgt. P. Pearlman C.M.F.; Fus. Freedman, MALTA FORCE; Pte. M. Doberman, ENGLAND; O.Q.M.S. J. Goodman, England; A/C Landau A., B.L.A.; Pte. D. Goldman, ENGLAND; Captain E. Dresner, WEST AFRICA FORCES; Captain M. Cohen, S.E.A.C.; L.A.C. Marks, C.M.F.; and Cpl. Charles Gillis, C.M.F.; Pte. S. Mincovitch, ENGLAND

The Bulletin is issued free to members of the Forces but private subscribers at the rate of 10/- per year are gladly accepted.

Will readers please notify change of address before the 20th of the month.

All correspondence to be sent to Rev. S.P. Toperoff, 5, Victoria Avenue, Sunderland.

SUNDERLAND
Jewish
COMMUNITY

BULLETIN
for the
FORCES

" Be strong and of good courage, be not afraid neither be thou dismayed, for the Lord thy God is with thee withersoever thou goest."

Joshua, I : 9.

Edited and issued monthly by the Minister and sent to you with the good wishes of your friends at home.

June 1945   Vol.3, No. 9.   Tamuz 5705

We are in the throes of a General Election, the first one for a number of years. During the war we were all united to overthrow the enemy. We sunk all differences and unitedly we strove to achieve the aim we set in front of us. In Europe at least we achieved that aim. We have destroyed the enemy. What is the task ahead of us?

Enough of destruction, now for measures of construction and work. We must build and recreate the shattered and broken Communities on the Continent.

It is natural for us as Jews to expect big things for have we not suffered grim and terrible disasters out of all proportion to our numbers. Yet so far there has been no talk of any large scale immigration into Palestine, the doors of which are still closed to the suffering martyrs of German Concentration Camps. But surely the salvaging of thousands of human beings who have endured indescribable torture and indignities should have first claim!

Why can we not be united in Peace as in War? War is synonymous with death, destruction and misery. Peace should bring new life, construction and happiness.

It is interesting to note that all the political parties in the coming election have stressed the importance of housing. We need new homes to house those that have been bombed out. How true is this of the Jewish home. Jews have been bombed out of Palestine for nearly 2,000 years. Within recent years facilities were granted to Jews to build a National Home. This then is our demand as it is the main plank of the programme of all parties.

Millions of Jewish homes have been destroyed on the Continent. Jewish life has been disintegrated and totally destroyed in many parts of the world. The once flourishing Communities in Poland, Russia and Germany will be no more. We therefore demand more homes in our own HOME.

Open the doors of Palestine to 100,000 refugees immediately and create a new haven of rest for the homeless and helpless Jews on the Continent!

There is no Jewish vote. We have sympathisers and friends in all parties. But we are entitled to ask for what we have fought and are still fighting - Justice!

DO YOU KNOW?

1. Which Jewish Chief Constable was murdered during the discharge of his duties?
2. Who was the first Jew to be knighted?
3. What is the "Flying Camel"?
4. What is the origin of the hymn "Leoni" commencing with the words - "The God of Abraham praise", as found in Church Hymn books.

Answers to the above questions on Page 3.

2.

HERE AND THERE!

Mazeltov!
Congratulations to:-

Engagements   - Pte. Leopold Levin R.A.P.C., to Miss Alma Connie, A.T.S.
                Manchester.

Weddings   - Miss Mona Levine to Charles Aronson, Glasgow.
                Miss Diane Levin to Wilfred A. Merkil, London.
                Miss Sheila Brown to Theodore Jackson.

Silver Weddings -
                Mr. and Mrs. M. Charlton on the celebration of their
                Silver Wedding.
                Mr. and Mrs. H. Stone on the celebration of their
                Silver Wedding.

Bede School Examination
        The following pupils have been successful in the recent Bede
School Entrance Examination:- Charles Brewer, Vivian Kelly, Henry
Olswang, Brian Posner, Ivor Sarabouski, Gloria Cohen and Thelma
Doberman.

Welcome Home Presentation
        At a reception in the Board Room of the Ryhope Road Synagogue
to Leonard Lerman, a silver cigarette case suitably inscribed was
presented by Mr. A. Merskey on behalf of the Congregation.   The Rev.
S.P. Toperoff and Mr. Jacob Clarke welcomed the first Jewish Prisoner
of War home and Leonard responded.

T.A.C.
        Under the auspices of the Trades Advisory Council a lecture was
given by the Rev. A.G. Utton (Chairman of the local Council of
Christians and Jews), on "the work of the Council of Christians and
Jews".   Mr. I. Minchom presided.   After a lengthy and fruitful
discussion in which many present took part, the Rev. S.P. Toperoff
proposed a vote of thanks to the Lecturer and Councillor Jackson
(Newcastle) accorded a vote of thanks to the Chairman.

        Members of the Area Council of the T.A.C. representing Newcastle,
Middlesbrough, South Shields and Hartlepool were present at the
Lecture.

Jewish Aged Home.
        A Conference of delegates representing Communities in the North
East took place at the Ryhope Road Synagogue Board Room to discuss
plans for the proposed Jewish Aged Home to be set up in Sunderland
to serve the Jewish Community in the North East.

———————————

3.

IN RETROSPECT.

A Concert Party means rehearsals! Rehearsals need a piano! So the Lit decided to buy one. A small sub-committee was formed and its members decided to run a series of small socials or dances with a novel appeal. A competition was to be held each evening and the word or figure 100 was the clue. Admission was 1/- and it cost 2d extra to enter the competition. The refreshments which included ices were to be a source of profit and placed in the capable hands of Rhoda Davis (now Mrs. Harold Olswang) and Dorrie Behrman (now Mrs. Harry Cohen). Enough money was raised to enable the Society to buy a second hand piano and the "Happy go Lit Concert Party" went into rehearsal. I have written about this party in my second letter to you in this Bulletin ("Peeps into the Past" series).

Meanwhile debates, discussion and lectures were taking place. During the summer, rambles were held and as One Double O socials had been so successful the Lit held a number of flannel dances.

The tennis club moved to new courts in Alexandra Road and a new ambition was born in the Society; to possess a sports ground of its own. The members worked hard and the Treasurer saved hard, but as you know, your motto will have to be "Some Day". But, do not lose heart. For my part, though perforce I must live many miles away, I will be a happy man when I hear of the accomplishment of this long cherished dream.

Expenses were rapidly mounting and Isaac Brewer requested a drive for new members. In my inaugural address at the beginning of each season I pointed out the benefits of the Society. Then the Committee members canvassed each person present. This was very successful and the practice was continued until 1934.

Next month I will write you about lecturers who spoke to us during this period. I think you will find them an array of brilliant men and women.

Cheerio,

SOL.

Answers to Questions on Page 1.

1. Henry Solomon for 13 years Chief Constable of Brighton and brutally murdered on 14th March 1944 at the age of 50.
2. The first Jew to be knighted was Sir Moses Montefiore.
3. The name was first given to the Palestine Flying Club founded in Tel-Aviv in 1933. One of the main activities of the Club was gliding and one of its aims is to turn its members into instructors.
4. A Methodist Minister the Rev. Thomas Oliver wrote the hymn to the tune of "Yigdal" which he heard at the Great Synagogue, London, where it was rendered by Meyer Leon the Choirmaster of the Synagogue.

4.

SEARCHLIGHT ON SPORT   -   By "Argus".

There are many doubts as to what is to happen in the coming Football season.   One after another of the clubs are beginning to think they may be involved in travel difficulties and are wondering whether they will be able to go through the programme they agreed to last month.   The two third division sections have already decided to ask the League to arrange fixtures on a regional basis, which destroys the decision already arrived at.

The trouble is that the Government have given no indication that there will be additonal travel facilities and there is also the question of getting service men to travel.   It has been relatively easy to get them on a day pass, but if overnight travel has to be undertaken, it won't be so easy.

The longest journey Sunderland will have to undertake will be to Chesterfield but that means leaving Friday afternoon.   The same applies to Lancashire games.

Manager Murray is not worrying however.   "All I can do is to put out the best available team", he says, "and trust to luck.   I guess I shall have some worrying days, but that's what a Manager is for – to do the worrying."

Billy has signed quite a number of his best amateurs, but he is still very much in the dark as to how many of his professionals will become available next season.

Tom Smith is to box at Roker Park ground on August Bank Holiday Saturday.   His opponent will be Kid Tanner and the promotion is to be for the benefit of Monkwearmouth and Southwick Hospital.   Tom will have to do some very serious training between now and August for as you know all his army fights in the past two years have been over three rounds. He has to go ten threes with Tanner - a big difference.   I have always contended Army bouts have not shown Smith to advantage for he needs four or five rounds to get thoroughly going.

NEWS LETTER FROM THE HOME FRONT.

I was not thrilled at the Social Evening at the Lit on Sunday June 3rd, but it was a good way to fill in an evening.   A few service personnel, stationed in the district, numbered amongst the gathering of between thirty and forty.   The radiogram was as usual, the piece de resistance for there is now quite a selection of recent dance records. Table tennis is always an attraction and it is necessary to book up your game at least half an hour beforehand.   I was glad to see a new set of darts though the dart-board could do with an overhaul - or at least a new set of wires.   No doubt this will be attended to in due course but the Lit must always be up to scratch.   One innovation which has every-one's whole hearted support is the sale of refreshments.   This has been done at such affairs as dances but I do not remember ever having a glass of lemonade or cider at a Lit Social and it certainly does prove welcome after a few quicksteps to American dance bands!   The circulars had also indicated that ice-cream would be served but apparently this was unobtainable

5,

rather a disappointment when you are expecting it. If the Lit circulars are going to warrant one's attention they must not raise false hopes or expectations.

There have not been any other Lit events since I last wrote so I have space now to give you the review of last Session which I promised. As a whole the last few sessions have been a struggle against ever increasing difficulties. But grim determination on the part of the few remaining members has brought the Lit through six war-time seasons - through bombing and fierce set-backs to witness the first steps in the direction of peace. In view of all the difficulties a membership of over 40 for last Season was an achievement of which the Lit may well be proud. The events had not the variety of pre-war days - but we cannot expect that. Only one outside lecturer, for example, could be brought because of the inability to furnish a sufficiently large audience. This may be possible for the coming Session and I hope the Committee will consider it. The Prize Paper Night, or Cup Night as it may again be called, was the most successful one during the war with a turnout of seven contestants. In the summer the Lit entertained some thirty non-Jewish wounded soldiers from Cherry Knowle to a tea-party and the expressions of thanks by the men themselves indicated the success of the effort. Five dances were held to keep the finances stable which cannot be an easy task when so many former members are away from home. Yet I was glad to see that the amount spent on records was double that of the previous year and only the very latest were obtained - a sound investment!

A few events, at various times during the Session were, despite every endeavour and much hard work, simply a 'flop'. But this must not discourage for under such circumstances the fact that the Lit functions as well as it does is in itself a credit to Sunderland's young folk - past as well as present, for without the reputation I doubt whether the same tenacity to keep going could have existed. Let's all hope that the coming session will prove to be a great stride on the road to normal times and success of pre-war magnitude.

Cheerio for now and all the very best,

Yours,
Also After Gen.

EXCERPTS FROM LETTERS.

L.A.C.W. Leonie Slater writes: Victory in Europe was well celebrated on the South Coast, as in every other community, and you will no doubt have heard on the radio that Portland was honoured (should we say that) by three German U-boats, one of which (U.776) is now on display at Westminster Bridge. I went to see these U-boats while they were docked at Portland. As I stood on the Pier and looked down on this weapon of war, which had it not been for the foresight of the British Navy and Royal Air Force, might have won the war for Germany. I thanked God that He had delivered us from the hands of that inhuman race, and that our people were now free after so many years of indescribable suffering. The Prisoners from the U-boats were taken to an enclosure very near to my billet. They were very young and in spite of their surrender, as arrogant as ever.

Sgt. P. Pearlman, C.M.F. writes: I had the experience of seeing films of German concentration camps in the company of Germans, their reactions were varied, some appeared even to smile. I had occasion to speak to

6.

several German women recently who were the equivalent of A.T.S., they stiffened up when I told them I was a Jew, but on the whole they are broken. One of them under a very summary interrogation, wept. I had the feeling it was more of shame at having to be interrogated by a Jew rather than having to relate about the disastrous condition of her family in Germany.

Cpl. I.J. Charlton, R.A.F., S.E. Asia Air Force, writes: You may deem it queer but where I am in the very midst of another war, fought no less fiercely but in far worse climate and geographical conditions, the occasion of V.E. Day was of no great personal significance to us. True we were delighted to hear that the years of oppression for the many millions in Europe were ended. Also we were happy in the knowledge that no more of the blood of our fellow combatants would be shed. We were relieved to hear that this meant the end of the fear of aerial bombardment to which our near and dear ones were subjected. However apart from the older men in the lower release groups we will all have to finish our tour out here, and probably our hardships will not be alleviated - so why rejoice! We were all disgusted when listening to the wireless after Mr. Churchill's speach, when people throughout the U.K. were giving impressions of their feelings, on V.E. Day the general train was - "I am happy, the war is over" - no thought for the millions fighting the Jap for whom the war is far from over - ask a man in Burma or Borneo if the war is over! I have summed up my feelings of this V-day and if they are bitter they are true and highly representative.

Pte. M. Pearlman, S.E.A.C. writes: When I entered Rangoon, this once beautiful city of Burma nearly 14 days ago, my first thoughts were are there any Jews left who have survived the Japanese tyranny, and if so, is there any Shool still standing undamaged, that they may go to, to pray, without being prevented and annoyed. I found the synagogue untouched and still standing in all its glory, but I am sorry to say, no community. There are only a handful of Burmese Jews who had remained to guard this holy house of worship. For $3\frac{1}{2}$ years they had gone through torture and misery with only one thought, that one day, the enemy would be driven out of the country and they would be spared to re-open their synagogue.

Capt. Mordaunt Cohen, S.E.A.C. writes: Reference to the remark in "News Letter from the Home Front" that the Lit does not seem to have any preparations for a Welcome Home or Reunion Party. In arranging any such function it should be borne in mind that the war is not over merely with the defeat of Germany. Perhaps I may suggest two or three functions to welcome home members of the forces who've served overseas. If these were arranged to coincide with certain Yomin Tovim at various intervals one could ensure that nobody was left out of the celebrations. The struggle against the Hun has been a long one, especially for us Jews. Only now does the world realise how our brothers on the continent of Europe have suffered during the past 12 years. We have known of the horrors of the concentration camps but the complacent nations have turned deaf ears to the voices crying out from the wilderness of Europe. Let us hope that the German nation reaps its true desserts. While I quite agree with the sentiments expressed by Lionel Gillis, let us not fall into the trap which has been so often set and say "only the Nazis are bad, the majority of Germans are alright." When one recalls the S.S. women torturers of the Belsen concentration camp and the truculent arrogant German youths who revelled in taking up arms against the allies how can we say that we should exude brotherly love towards this nation of sadists. We must not make the same mistake about the Germans as our ancestors did nearly 3,500 years ago, over "Amalek". You might think that I sound bitter but when you consider that certain people have spent ten years of their lives fighting Germany in two wars, it is time that the Huns were taught a lesson once and for all. You should hear what my Brigadier has to say about them. He'd solve the German menace in one generation.

L.A.C. Charles Marks, C.M.F. writes: Pesach today must have a more than usual significance to the Jewish serving men and women for after all, at the actual time for which we celebrate, was there not a great march taking place. A march of a captive people to liberation; and today is not the same thing happening? People who have and still are suffering are at last seeing an end to their trials and hard fought battles. More so the Jew than anyone else is seeing the end in sight. But what of the new beginning? Surely we wont have to start another battle - a fight for freedom of religion. Are the free peoples of the world going to let themselves be educated by what has happened or are they going to carry on in the same stubborn way as before, looking down on the Jew, calling him names and making a mockery of his religion. Basically all worship one God, therefore there can be no possible difference between the Jew and his neighbours as regards religion. Previously I made the remark "looking down on the Jew", by which I didn't mean that we expected to be looked up to, as a master race, a people who can do no wrong. I merely meant that we should be placed on a level - on the same religious plane as the other civilised peoples of the world - after all what is religion but guiding principles of a persons life.

L/Cpl. C. Brewer, C.M.F. writes: Reading this months bulletin I am very glad to know that L. Lerman is back once again in Sunderland after spending many years as a prisoner of war. My only hope is that when the war is over in the Far East we may find alive some of the boys who have not been heard of since Singapore fell. Now that the war is over in Italy we in the Ordnance Corps have quite a lot to do, but we are also finding time to get our sporting activities going. I manage to get in a game of cricket nearly every week, and am also getting myself fit for basketball and swimming. At times I have come across many chaps from Sunderland who have recognised me from the time that I was a member of the Judeans, and used to play table tennis and football for them.

Letters were also received and gratefully acknowledge from the following:- Fus. B. Freeman, MALTA FORCE, Pte. D. Goldman, ENGLAND; L/Cpl A. Davis, ENGLAND; Gds. Philip Linke, ENGLAND; Capt. Ellis Dresner, W.A. FORCE; Dvr. Lionel Gillis, B.L.A.; A/C Arnold Landau, B.L.A. and W.O.1 Isadore Levine, INDIA.

The Bulletin is issued free to members of the Forces but private subscribers at the rate of 10/- per year are gladly accepted.

Will readers please notify change of address before the 20th of the month.

All correspondence to be sent to Rev. S.P. Toperoff, 5 Victoria Avenue, Sunderland.

———————————

SUNDERLAND
Jewish
COMMUNITY

BULLETIN
for the
FORCES

" Be strong and of good courage, be not afraid neither be thou dismayed, for the Lord thy God is with thee withersoever thou goest."

Joshua, I : 9.

Edited and issued monthly by the Minister and sent to you with the good wishes of your friends at home.

July 1945.   Vol. 3. No. 10   Ab 5705

Jews and the Crucifixion

A Brains Trust arranged by the local Council of Christians and Jews recently took place when a number of questions were discussed.   One question which called for some frank comments was "Does Christian teaching blame the Jew for crucifying Christ?"

Now you might think that this question is purely-academic and in any case does not affect the broad masses many of whom are at any rate irreligious.   This is however far from the actual fact.   This vital question does affect you and all of us as the death of Christ is the foundation and basis of Christianity.

All children are taught the gospel story in School and we as Jews shudder to think what impression is left on the plastic mind of the child who connects the Jew with Christ-murderers.   It matters little whether the child later on in life is indifferent to religion.   This story elaborated by all the gospel writers will have left an indelible impression on the mind of the child and nothing later on in life will explain it away.

Especially tragic is it for us when well-meaning Christians assert that if Jews accepted the blame for the crucifixion they would have saved themselves a great deal of suffering.   Throughout the Middle Ages the Church persistently taught its followers to look upon the small Jewish race as Christ-killers and in consequence as a people rejected by God.

This is one of the greatest misconceptions foisted upon the human race.   Clemenceau bitingly said: "It wasn't the Jews who crucified Christ, that was left for the Christian to do".

Why should such un-Christian dogmas be held by Christian people for it is on this basis that anti-semites have raised the superstructure of racial and religious propaganda.   It is hard to understand why we are still saddled with the blame for the crucifixion.

In the first place why should Jews today be called upon to admit their share in an act which took place nineteen hundred years ago.   You might as well condemn the whole of France today for the martyrdom of Joan of Arc in the fifteenth century.

Nor is the crucifixion by Jews an historical fact as some of our Christian friends imagine.   Modern Christian scholarship does not accept the crucifixion by Jews as an historical fact.   It is well known that the crucifixion never was a Jewish but a Roman form of punishment.   The death sentence too never took place on a Friday.   Further the offence with which Jesus was charged namely the claim of being the Messiah was not a criminal action in the eyes of Jewish law, the guilt for which was punishable by death.   A former Christian cleric wrote: "Fascism and all it stands for is the greatest curse in the world today.   Christianity was responsible for a great deal of Jewish persecution in particular the crucifixion story.   I have forbidden my teachers to preach or teach that Jesus was killed by the Jews".

2.

In some quarters it has been suggested that the denial by Jews of responsibility for the crucifixion was the cause of Jewish persecution. Did Hitler annihilate five million Jews because they did not accept blame for the crucifixion?   Is not this tantamount to admitting that persecution of Jews is justifiable in the eyes of the Church and that it will continue with the connivance of the Church as long as Jews do not publicly recant from a crime they are alleged to have committed nearly two thousand years ago?   It is a sad and tragic omen of the future and must dash to the ground all hopes for the realisation and implementation of the Atlantic Charter which definitely and unequivocally demands freedom of worship for all minorities.

I do not know of any condition laid down in the Atlantic Charter for the public disavowal of past errors or mistakes.   Such views will certainly not make for better relations and friendship between the two communities; it can only widen the gulf which already exists.   It is to be hoped that Christians will approach the subject in the spirit of Christian love and forgiveness.   Let them read the sombre and grim details of Jewish History.

Think of the Inquisition, auto-da-fe, Crusades and pogroms when Jews were massacred in their hundreds of thousands in the name of Christ. Think of the concocted stories of the blood libel, poisoning of the wells and the desecration of the sacred wafer - all supposed to be traced to the devilry of Jews.   Have we not suffered enough as the eternal scapegoat of history!   Surely the time has arrived to bury the hatchet.

Before we can begin to build the new post war world we shall have to rid ourselves of these tragic misconceptions about the Jew.   The Jew is no more responsible for the crucifixion than present-day Christians for the holy Inquisition or the Crusades.

Our Christian friends must re-educate themselves and learn more about Judaism and the origins of Christianity of which there is a lamentable ignorance.   Christians must regard Judaism not as a mere tribal religion that was superseded by Christianity but as a major religion a civilisation and way of life that is responsible for the ideals cherished by millions of peoples throughout the world for Justice, Righteousness and Peace.

DO YOU KNOW?

1.   Who is Modelliani?
2.   Who was: (1) The founder and first Mayor of Tel Aviv?
              (2) The first Poet Laureate of Palestine?
3.   When did Jews first come to England?
4.   Who wrote; "The Jewish Problem would be solved on the day when the last Christian was converted to Christianity"?

Answers to the above on Page 4.

3.

HERE AND THERE!

Mazeltov!
Congratulations to:-
Births   - Mr. & Mrs. Max Gillis on the birth of a son.
               Mr. & Mrs. Klein on the birth of a son.
               Mr. & Mrs. M. Pearlman on the birth of a son.
Engagement- Miss Eta Cohen of Cheltenham formerly of Sunderland to
               Ephraim Smith of Leeds.
Weddings   - Miss Anita Freedman to Harry Slyper of London.
               L.A.C. Harold Isaacs to Sheila Bloom of Leeds.
               Miss Ena Stone to Morris Rabin of London.
               Pte. Leopold Charles Levine to Alma Connie of Manchester.
Silver Wedding - Mr. & Mrs. A Benjamin.

Education Successes - Congratulations to Aubrey Gordon who has received
the LL. B. at Durham University.
In the list of successes of the Bede School Entrance Examinations the
following were inadvertently omitted:-
               David Joseph and Harold Linskill.

Squadron Leader Sydney J. Pollock
      Congratulations to Squadron Leader Pollock of Air Sea Rescue work,
who has been awarded the D.F.C.   The citation runs as follows:- "He
displayed great courage in effecting the speedy rescue of a crew shot
down in Nundarbans, also for outstanding gallantry in flying operations
against the enemy."

Miss Gertrude Magrill
      Congratulations to Miss Magrill who has left Bristol to take up a
Senior post with the Ministry of Health in the Midlands.   Miss Magrill
thus enjoys the unique position of being the first Jewess to hold the
important job of Regional Nursing Officer.

Jewish Women's War Services Committee.   Under the auspices of the
J.W.W.S.C. a most successful bazaar in aid of funds was held at the
Communal Hall recently.   There were several stalls, the following being
in charge:- Mesdames R. Share, C. Hall and Miss P. Wolfe in charge of
home-made cakes; Mesdames H. Stone, R. Collins, G. Lewis in charge of
grocery;. Mesdames L. Davis, L. Share, W. Morris in charge of fancy
goods; Mesdames A. Blakey, D. Cohen, M. Davis, M. Joseph, C. Rawlinson
in charge of Cafe, and Mrs. L. Mincovitch in charge of the Ice Cream.
Mrs. R. Share formerly opened the Bazaar and more than £80 was realised.

Council of Christians and Jews.   The Council held a Brains Trust at the
Y.W.C.A. the Rev. A.G. Utton was the Question Master and the following
were the members of the "Trust"; the Rev. H. Ross, the Rev. S.P. Toperoff,
Miss Moul and Mr. R. Minchom.

United Palestine Appeal.   Following a reception at the residence of Dr.
and Mrs. A. Blakey, Rabbi M. Shenck of Australia was the special speaker
at a public meeting in the Communal Hall when he spoke on the position of
Jewry in the world today.   Mr. A. Merskey Chairman of the Appeal
Committee presided.

4.

ROLL OF HONOUR

Died on Active Service - We are sorry to have to record that Gunner David Davis, only son of Mr. & Mrs. A. Davis of Belle Vue Park has died from Cholera whilst a prisoner of war in Japanese hands.
    The whole community share the grief of the family.
    May his dear soul rest in peace.

SUNDERLAND YOUNG ZIONIST ASSOCIATION

On July 1st we held a Conference with representatives of Newcastle F.Z.Y. We were fortunate in having with us Hannah Stein, President of F.Z.Y. and Bettina Frankenstein, Organizer of F.Z.Y.

Hannah Stein urged our Society to organize a book drive for the book starved Jews of Europe who are still in what were once concentration camps. We wish to ask the whole community to co-operate with us in this campaign. With the help of Hannah a programme was arranged for the next four months. It includes talks on such subjects as "Structure of the Histadrut", "Taxation in Palestine", "United Synagogue versus Beth Din", "Meaning of Assimilation". It also includes debates, discussions, a Hat Night, an Oneg Shabbat, a live Newspaper, a musical evening, a Brains Trust and a Quiz Night.

It has also been decided that there is a possibility of a summer camp being held in the Northern Area. Arrangements for this are going well ahead. Any inquiries about this camp should be made to Miss Pearl Berg who was elected Joint North Regional Officer with Miss Rita Birk of Newcastle.

Answers to Questions on Page 2.

1. When the Italians joined the war at the side of the Nazis the Germans searched for a typical painting of outstanding merit for exhibition in Germany. They chose a masterpiece by Modelliani as they were ignorant that he was a Jew.
2. (1) The founder and first Mayor of Tel Aviv was Meir Dizengoff 1861-1936.
    (2) The first Poet Laureate of Palestine was Chaim Nachman Bialik, 1874-1934
3. Jews first came to England in the days of William the Conqueror. They were exiled in 1290 and returned under Cromwell.
4. Heinrich Heine 1797 - 1856. Heine was one of the greatest poets on modern Germany, essayist and satirist,

---

IN RETROSPECT.

Hitherto I have written this history entirely from memory, but I have come to the time when membership expansion, new activities and events have followed each other so rapidly that I find it necessary to "Pin Point" my narrative as it were, and give you dates occasionally. These will all be verified and I wish to thank my many friends who have and will, help me in this respect.

B.

The "Lit" moved into its proper Home (the Communal Hall) in 1928 and within one year there were so many young peoples activities that the hall was occupied five nights a week.

During November 1929 these young people suffered a grievous loss. The Rev. Muscat (Hon. President of the Lit, Chaplain to the Scouts and generally the young people's friend) died. All activities closed down immediately for a full week as an outward sign of mourning. In 1930 the Society opened a Memorial Fund. The subscribers were to be only members of young peoples societies with which the reverend gentleman had worked. The list was closed in a fortnight and a memorial window was placed in the Shool.

The silver cup was presented for the first time to the winner of Prize Paper Night. The honour went to Daniel Mincovitch.

Rabbi Cohen of Sheffield spoke to the Society. His subject was "Superstitions, their derivation and meaning". On the whole the lecture was humorous. I particularly remember his story of the Rabbi who visited a theatre. The cast comprised a large chorus of beautiful girls. Before leaving the theatre he cut his finger nails, allowing the ends to fall to the floor. When the manager asked him the reason -- well - you know the superstition and the answer!

Mr. A. Armstrong, a friend of our Vice-chairman Joe Topaz, spoke to the Circle on "English Folk Music". Possessor of a fine baritone voice, he gave those present illustrations. His singing was delightful and much appreciated. Finally he got his audience to sing with him. He was so delighted with this display of enthusiasm that he promised a return visit. In all, he spoke and sang to the Society three times. One of his recitals was entitled "Folk Songs of Many Lands". I was particularly impressed by the sadness of the Russian songs. Clearly expressive of the life of the Russian peasant in days gone by. Mr. Armstrong always ended his recitals with the audience singing lustily with him "Blaydon races" and "Dashing away with a smoothing iron" - his signature tunes as it were.

Next month, Dr. Marion Phillips, M.P., visits the Lit.

Cheerio,

SOL.

NEWS LETTER FROM THE HOME FRONT

Hello, again, Forces everywhere. Here we are well on into the summer again though the weather so far has been very changeable, with some sunny and warm periods. The home town is gradually but surely regaining some of its peacetime character. The other Sunday, Seaburn saw a stream of cars lined up along the 'front', the like of which I have not seen for quite a few years. The sun shone down on the familiar promenade now free from threatening barbed wire and Warning Notices. Kiddies paddled on the edge of the water, swallowing as much ice cream has had not already trickled down their clothes. In fact Seaburn was looking up - even the tents and deck chairs had re-appeared and clothed the beach like a patch-work quilt. The tramcars now also run to Seaburn via Roker, a route which until recently had been closed for security reasons since the commencement of the war. Barricades, blockhouses and blast-walls have almost entirely vanished from Sunderland's landscape never, we hope, to

6.

return.

Yet despite this surrounding atmosphere of a world attempting to return to normal life, of people trying to forget the misery that has blackened the last few years in Sunderland, the Communal Hall is as drab as ever.   The paint-work is in a state of depression and the general appearance gives one a feeling of gloom.   If this hall is to be inviting to the folk who return home from the Forces it must be changed entirely - it must be bright and breezy.   The walls must be pleasantly decorated and not, as now, painted in scullerylike fashion.   The Communal Hall can be and must be, made into a first class hall - a pleasure for our young folk and older ones too, to frequent.

There was a Lit Social on Sunday 24th June but there was only a smallish gathering.   There was dancing, table tennis and, of course much chatting.   As usual the buffet proved popular and on the whole the evening was very pleasant though many people had apparently decided to make the most of the fine weather while it lasted.

Arrangements are in full swing for the summer dance on July 29th for which already a great number of tickets has been sold.   This looks as though it might prove to be an outstanding event and I'll give you all the gen about it next time.   Until then, Forces, good luck and keep smiling.

Yours,
Also After Gen.

SEARCHLIGHT ON SPORT - By "Argus".

In another month from the penning of these lines Football, such as it is, will be in full swing again.   Some of the Football League Clubs are already getting "windy" about the prospects of having to renew £8 per week contracts with players who, after a lapse of six years may have reached the age when Footballers like flies, (in some parts) disappear in the winter time.   The Service players will get £4 per match and some of the "big bugs" are already grousing that they will get only half of what the "demob" man will get.   But the "demobbed" man has to keep himself and his family out of his £8.

Manager Billy Murray is just hoping for the best.   He has got Tommy Urwin in part-time charge of the coaching of the juniors and there may be some news shortly of Alex Hastings.   He is on the short list for the Managership at Chesterfield, but he may stay at Roker if he is offered a Scouts job.

Tom Smith is boxing Kid Tanner at Roker Park ground at August Bank Holiday week end.   I saw him box at Tottenham the night Jack London lost his heavy-weight "crown" to Woodcock.   Don't believe the stories of London's apologists that he lost the title because he did not hear the count owing to the noise.   I have no doubt he could not hear it, but it was not because of the noise.   It was because Woodcock's punch had robbed him of his senses.

Jack London never was championship class - Woodcock is.   The fact that he was an Amateur champion enabled him to become a boxer as well as a fighter, and if he can put another stone on he will be much better.   I think Woodcock will go far in the game.

One of the Glasgow newspapers recently had a cartoon of an officer complete with Sergt. interviewing a Tommy.   Said the Officer: "I see you

were a Carter in civil life - are you going back to your old job?"
Tommy; "No sir, I'm gonna make a change.   The word Carter has too many
painful associations for me."
     See the point?   The "Tommy" was Bobby Brown, the Scottish Goal-
keeper.

EXCERPTS FROM LETTERS.

<u>Capt. Ellis Dresner, West Africa Force</u> writes:- There's quite a large
though floating Jewish population here, and I was fortunate enough to be
able to attend a Thanks Giving Service in Freetown on V.E. Day plus one.
There were about 20 service men - officers and other ranks of all 3 services
at this service which was held in the Toc H.   It gave me an opportunity to
meet the other Jewish personnel in the Colony - one of whom turned out to
be Sub.Lieut. John Samuels, formerly of Sunderland.   The Service was conducted by a civilian in the Colonial Administration - a London man, and was
a very commendable effort for the 'back of beyond'.
<u>W.O.1 I. Levine, India Command</u> writes:- V.E. Day was celebrated in "The
Imperial City" with great pomp and splendour but beneath the surface one
could sense a feeling of 'reserve' and 'restraint'.   After all, OUR main
enemy in THIS theatre of operations has still to be eliminated as he doubt-
less will be, and in record time, we hope but it's difficult to feel really
"free" and imagine final Victory has been achieved when you're liable to
don a suit of "jungle green" and be sent "up the line" the next day.   Naturally we know that our dear ones can once again "light up" wihtout fear of
the "flying bomb" and a million and one other war time dangers, fills us
with a sense of great joy and thankfulness, but WE HAVE NOT WON YET nor
have we yet WON THE PEACE IN EUROPE.   Let us by all means celebrate but
with the sober knowledge of what still has to be achieved.
<u>Dvr. L. Gillis, B.L.A.</u> writes:- Last Friday night, a man, a German Wehr-
macht soldier came along and asked for 'Gillis'.   I went out and he said
'Shalom Aleichem', to which I gave the traditional reply, but I was not
convinced.   He told me that, one night he had asked one of our men if we
had a Jew among this unit and he had been told my name and where I lived.
As I have said I was not convinced as I realised the 99% possibility about
it. We spoke, he in German at first, and I in my Yiddish-German, then later
on we finished in Hebrew, and I was convinced.   His story I may add is a
perfectly natural one, and I quite believe him.   During the last few years
he has simply not told anybody he was a Jew, and being a man with no family
he has never been suspected.   He has purposely kept out of any medical
examinations in the army, and I know that this is quite easy, so that his
Jewish Origin should not be discovered.   Now he is really worried, as if
he goes to the Military Government and tells them he is a Jew, he will
undoubtedly be killed by his German 'comrades'.   What a position for a man
to be in.   Can we judge him and can we blame him?
     Letters also received and gratefully acknowledged by the Editor from:-
L.A.C. Maurice Dresner ENGLAND; A/C Arnold Landau, B.L.A.; Fus. B. Freeman
MALTA FORCE; Pte. M. Pearlman, S.E.A.C.; Cpl. Joe Charlton, S.E.A. AIR
FORCE; Capt. Mordaunt Cohen, INDIA COMMAND; V.A.D. Olga Grantham, S.E.A.C.;
Cpl. L.P. Altman, INDIA COMMAND and L/Cpl. C. Brewer, C.M.F.

     The Bulletin is issued free to members of the Forces but private
subscribers at the rate on 10/- per year will be gladly accepted.
     Will readers please notify change of address before the 20th of the
month.
     All correspondence to be send to Rev. S.P. Toperoff, 5 Victoria
Avenue, Sunderland.

SUNDERLAND
Jewish
COMMUNITY

BULLETIN
for the
FORCES

" Be strong and of good courage, be
not afraid neither be thou dismayed, for
the Lord thy God is with thee withersoever
thou goest."

Joshua, 1 : 9.

*Edited and issued monthly by the Minister
and sent to you with the good wishes of
your friends at home.*

ust 1945   Vol. 3, No. 11   Ellul 5705

By the time this issue reaches you it will be very near to the New
ear.   Since the publication of this Bulletin this is the first time that
he ancient Jewish greeting "A Happy New Year" will really mean something
o many of us.   War with all its deadly and pernicious results has at
ast come to an end.   Who has not suffered from this ghastly Holocaust?

For the first time war has been brought to the hearths and homes of
he people and many will remember for a long time the shocks, fears and
nxieties that their prolonged strength has brought.

Nationally we Jews have suffered more than any other people on
arth.   Our losses are more than five million souls and important centres
f Jewish life have been wiped out.   But we are the "People of Hope",
e are looking forward to a really happy New Year.   Many of you will be
oming home in the course of the next few months and we all look forward
o your active interest in the general welfare of the community.

Nationally too, we look forward to a happy New Year.   We are not
nmindful of the difficulties that lie ahead, we know the road will not
e strewn with flowers.   We have hope however in the justice of our
ause.   We know | that Anti-Semitism
ill not dis- | appear, it may even
ecome aggrav- | ated, but we are
anguine enough | to believe that
alestine will | eventually become a
ewish state and | that facilities will
e granted us to | offer a new lease of
ife to the | remnant of Jews that
ave miraculously | escaped death at the
nds of the | Nazis.

> The Editor and Staff
> send New Year Greetings to
> all serving in the Forces.
> It is our Prayer that the
> coming year herald a new
> era of lasting Peace.   May
> you be inscribed in the
> Book of Life.

It is a pious wish and a
umble prayer but we mean to make the coming year a happy and fruitful
ar for all Israel.

May our prayer be heeded and our wishes be granted by the Almighty.

A happy New Year to you all.

DO YOU KNOW?

Who wrote - "The Jews are a frightened people.   Nineteen centuries
of Christian love have broken down their nerves"?
Who was first to conceive the idea of the motor car?
When and by whom was the Palestine Orchestra founded?
Which Christian author calls one of the characters of her book
"Klesmer", the Yiddish for "musician"?

Answers to the above on Page 3.

2.
HERE AND THERE

MAZELTOV!
Congratulations to the following:-

Births   - Mr. & Mrs. Grunblatt (nee Celia Leslie), on the birth of
a son.
Mr. & Mrs. Charles Goldman, on the birth of a daughter.
Mr. & Mrs. Teacher on the birth of a daughter.

Engagements   - Miss Hazel Merskey to F/Sgt. Walter Gallick of London.
Miss Devora Pearlman, L.L.B, to Joseph Wineman of Bucks.

Educational Successes - Congratulations to:-
Derek Abrahams, who has been awarded a State Scholarship
to Cambridge.
Theodore Benjamin, who has passed the Preliminary Exam.
of Chartered Accountants.
The following who have passed the School Certificate:-
Leonora Jacobs, Rose Schlasinger, Sonia Clark, June Davis, Phyllis Hurst.
The following who took part of the examination and passed:-
Blossom Greenwald, Beryl Schwam and Beryl Wilder.

Promotions   - Congratulations to Major George Magrill of Edinburgh,
formerly of Sunderland.

Departure of the Rev. A.I. Burland.

After 15 years loyal service to the Sunderland Hebrew Congregation,
Mr. Burland is relinquishing his post and is shortly leaving for
Manchester.   Throughout his stay with us, he has endeared himself to
all and proved to be a popular figure in the life of the Jewish
Community.

We wish him God - Speed to his new post and trust that he will
enjoy happiness and success in his future work.

IN RETROSPECT.

Another musical Lecture that stands out in my memory was given
by the Rev. Oler L.R.A.M. His subject was the life and works of
Mendelsohn.

Mendelsohn's works were amply illustrated by members of the Society
including the Lecturer himself.   There were present many well known
musicians and at the conclusion of the Recital some of these gentlemen
paid a handsome tribute to the artists and congratulated them on the
high standard of their performance.   The Lecture was an outstanding
success.

I delivered a Lantern Lecture on Belgium and gave a number of my
adventures and impressions.   (This by the way is a hint to some of you
much travelled men and women of the Services.)

Dr. Marion Phillips M.P. visited the Society.   She was accompanied
by a number of her supporters, many of whom I remembered from my Y.M.C.A.
Debating Class days.   These lectures, however were not political but

3.

arose out of a purely friendly desire of the members to meet and get to know their political representatives as ordinary men and women; and to know their interests and ideals. Dr. Marion had not been speaking long before it became evident that her life was devoted to the brightening of the domestic lives of the ordinary working men and women living in dull and drab surroundings. At the conclusion of the Lecture she expressed the desire to see the Shool. I was very happy to escort her and we went upstairs. After inspecting the ground floor we went up to the gallery.

She was much impressed by the symmetry of the building and view from the first two rows of seats. "But I like the more subdued cathedral atmosphere in a place of worship" she said. We were about to leave by the south door when she turned, and looking round the building said "If at any time I should like to come here and sit quietly and rest and think, may I do so?" As I answered "Yes certainly, doctor" I thought she looked very tired and oh, so sad. She gathered her cloak about her, and wearily left the Shool.

Next week I shall write you about Joe Topaz's regime and "Peter Button speaks".

Cheerio,
SOL.

Answers to questions on page 1.

1. Israel Zangwill.
2. Siegfried Marcus.
3. In 1935 by the violinist Bronislaw Huberman who chose the 75 players from numerous refugee Continental musicians. The orchestra recently celebrated its one thousandth public concert performance.
4. George Eliot in "Daniel Deronda" refers to the hero of musical art as Mr. Klesmer.

NEWS LETTER FROM THE HOME FRONT

Only three months have passed since I put pen to paper to write of our V.E. celebrations and now, much sooner than I had dared to hope, I can tell you how Sunderland greeted this grand news of Jap defeat. Like last time we were kept in suspense for about a week expecting at any moment that hostilities would be ended. Although in other towns rejoicing was in full fling a few days before V.J. Day, Sunderland showed no sign of over - excitement. On Tuesday evening August 14th the radio told us to stand by for an "important announcement" sometime during the evening, and at mid-night the Prime minister transformed a hope into a reality. Then good old Sunderland lit up! Crowds in Fawcett Street forced the Mayor to keep his rash promise that he would speak from the Town Hall one hour after the official declaration and sure enough at 1 o'clock in the morning he spoke impromptu to the cheering crowd. But his official speech was made at 11 o'clock the next morning when Fawcett Street was, literally, thronged.

4.

Wednesday and Thursday were public holidays and, as might be expected in Sunderland, it rained both days!   Decorations again found their way to the dizzy heights all over the town though I don't think there were as many flags as appeared on V.E. Day.   On Wednesday there were long queues for all picture-houses the whole day, and dances were packed at night.   I "scouted" the town for you around midnight and it was busier than it often is during the daytime.   Young folk (and not-so-young) danced and sang gaily and people rang A.R.P. bells and swung gas-rattles without regard to noise.   The terrace of Mowbray Park resounded with notes of accordians and singing, and occasional fireworks exploded giving those near a sudden start.   In the small hours of the morning weary but contented folk wended their way through the lighted streets homeward.   Thursday saw more persistent rain which must have dampened the emotions of many, but the fun was on the same lines as the previous day.

And so the sun has broken through the black clouds of war.   Nice work lads (and lasses too!)- you have done a great job and we're waiting to greet you home.

The Lit had a dance on July 29th and, though not too well attended by the younger crowd this time, was very jolly.   The seven piece band excelled and the buffet was again more than popular.   The Lit should soon be preparing its winter syllabus about which I will give you the 'gen' as soon as it comes to hand.

An officer friend reports over-hearing the following in the Mess. "What on earth is this stuff?".   "It's been soup, Sir".   "I want to know what it is, not what it's been"!

Keep smiling forces and best of luck.
Yours,

Also After Gen.

SEARCHLIGHT ON SPORT   -   By "Argus".

I am penning these notes on the eve of the opening of another season and only a few days after we have celebrated V.J. Day.   It is appropriate therefore that I should congratulate you all upon the success of the campaigns you have taken part in, and though your worries are not over, they soon should be.   I hope when you all meet in Sunderland in a welcome from your Community I shall have the pleasure of joining you to celebrate the occasion.

Season 1945-46 reminds me I am growing older, though I don't need the date to impress that upon my mind.   I first commenced travelling with Sunderland in 1909, and since 1919 have travelled continuously.   One of these days, perhaps, I shall get to know something about this ball-game which so many thousands go mad about.   Perhaps that little comment fits

5.

in with your idea of your humble servant.   Anyway it does in quite a number of places where in the past I have created rows on a Saturday evening.   The bigger the row, the more readers the next week.

But what are the prospects.   Well to be quite frank I cannot tell you.   Everything depends upon how the players become available from week to week, and how they become available under the much discussed "A" Scheme.

What I can tell you is that in the practice games, public and private, I have seen more young players of promise than in the past twenty years.   Billy Murray with three teams running has to find at least 36 players each week, but as he has over a hundred to select from, that should not be difficult.

The latest acquisition on professional forms is a boy from the Normanton district of Yorkshire named Dunn.   I should not think he is more than 5'6" but he is stocky, and he was so good in the final practice game that Manager Murray did not let him out of his sight before he had signed professional forms.

For some weeks at least we shall have the help of Major Laurie, who is stationed on an Ack-Ack site in the area,   He is a Dundee right half and a top notcher.

Bert Johnson expects to be demobbed in October and Burbanks in that month too, but Carter is in Group 32.

Cheerio for the time being.   You'll be hearing from me next month.

EXCERPTS FROM LETTERS.

L/Sgt. Altman, L.P. India Command, writes: The newsreels arriving out here lately have been of the various concentration camps the Allied Armi have found in Germany and some of the occupied countries.   Horrific sti are the pictures of Belsen and Buchenwald, atrocities for which the pape had in some measure prepared us.   In some measure only, for its somethi else to actually see Death ovens, piles of bodies, etc.   It is a good thing, perhaps at this moment that the easy-going run of adults should see with their own eyes the starvation and torture they had only read about before.   But they should have been reminded that they DID read about it not this year or last, but SEVEN and EIGHT years ago, when they paid little attention.   The usual comment of "atrocity story", or "the Jews made it up" etc... The Manchester Guardian, The News Chronicle, The News Statesman, the Jewish Press, and other journals gave us the facts while our politicians flirted with that madman Hitler, and the "man-in-street" preferred the "dogs".   It wouldn't do any harm to remind people that if they felt more strongly, or felt at all then, events might not have proved so encouraging to the Nazis.   But, to do that needed a

6.

responsible and intelligent film journalism, which we did and still do not
seem to have. The newsreels of Belsen and Buchenwald terribly
informative as they are, neglect even to remind us (since people need
reminding) that many of the sufferers in concentration camps were and
still are Germans and Jews. I imagine we shall go back after the war
to the newsreel of "society snippets", and the picture page?? There
is every sign we shall, although some of the latest films by the M.O.I.
have been good. But we seem to have left it to the Americans to
produce the film "What we are fighting for"... Time marches on... but
not evidently round our way at home! The need is crying for education,
NOT armaments, they will never stop wars, - they might start them. There
is the biggest education job in the worlds history ahead of us in Europe, -
without all the country's like India etc. where the people generally are
still illiterate. I think all the worlds fundamental problems are
attributable to lack of education - just pure ignorance if this can be
rectified, civilization must progress - and rapidly; otherwise if we
continue as we have done for the last 40 years, we shall finish ourselves
off completely.

V.A.D. Olga Grantham India writes: Calcutta which I visited is a very
dirty, overcrowded, and badly laid out city, and so after poking around
the native quarters, and the bazaars, I decided to move on. In one of
the bazaars I stopped to buy a charm bracelet, and got quite a surprise
to discover that the charms were very tiny shields of David in gold and
blue. After a chat with the native woman who was selling it, I
discovered that she originated from Persia, but she had became completely
Indianised, was wrinkled and very dark and wore a sari notwithstanding
all this she had not forgotten her Yiddish, which issued forth fluently
when I tried to beat down her price! Needless to say, she won.

After leaving Caloutta I spent two more days in the train, and
arrived at Lucknow, a much cleaner and pleasanter city than Calcutta
but overpoweringly hot, with a damp humidity which hung in the air like
a blanket. The heat was so intense, that all I could go and see was
the Residency, famous for the fact that it held out during the Indian
Mutiny, and also because it never dips its Union Jack. After leaving
Lucknow, I travelled farther north two more days, and arrived in Naini-Tal
a peace-time hill station, situated 7,000 feet up in the hills, foothills
of the Himalayas.

This is a beautiful place, in the centre of the town is a huge lake,
with shops, cinemas, cafes, and one or two houses set round it whilst
surrounding the entire compound are these ranges of beautiful mountains.
I yachted and boated on the lake, played lots of tennis, and got up very
early one morning to climb Chuna Peak, the highest of all the peaks. It
took $2\frac{1}{2}$ hours of solid climbing to reach the top, but the view was so
magnificent it was worth all my pains. As it was a very clear morning,
the snow capped tops of the Himalayas were clearly visible, and they
just look grand and proud, standing out very clearly and sharply against
the sky. I passed an extremely pleasant 18 days here, but soon found
myself back on to a train where I remained for 5 days, until finally
returning once more to the fold.

7.

Pte. M. Pearlman S.E.A.C., writes: The news of Japan accepting Unconditional Surrender has just reached us, we have God to thank for this miracle, it means thousands of lives being saved and Peace for the world at last. It is also a fitting time, Rosh Hashana and Yom Kippur in three weeks, surely the world, not only Jews will turn more to religion, and realise that we must have peace and goodwill amongst each other.

Driver Pollock, B.L.A. writes: I am stationed in a small town called Bad Segeburg near Lubeck, and I have met the only Jewish man that survived from the 30 families that once lived there. Strange as it be, he is now the assistant Burgomaster of the district.

I took him some of your cigarettes of which he was very grateful - so I think it is only fair that I should also express his thanks to you all.

Letters also received and gratefully acknowledged by the Editor:- A/C Landau, B.L.A.; L.A.C.W. Zelda Gillis, ENGLAND; Fus. B. Freeman, MALTA FORCE; Pte. Alan Pearlman, S.E.A.C.; Cpl. Phyllis Mincovitch, ENGLAND; Pte. D. Goldman, ENGLAND; Cpl. J. Charlton, S.E.A.A.F.; and L.A.C. I Davis, B.L.A.

NEW YEAR.

New Year dawns - what will it bring?
Breezes that will blow away
Darkling clouds that hide the day
Sunshine brightly glistening?

Will it banish sorrows, tears,
Hearts that heavy burdons bear
Misery and dull despair
Heritage of former years?

Will its message joyous be?
Will the tyrants iron hands
Fall from off all captive bands?
Will the chosen be set free?

New Year dawns - God grant it bring
Solace to each downcast soul
And as clouds of darkness roll
Sun with healing on its wing.

The Bulletin is issued free to members of the Forces but private subscribers at the rate of 10/- per year will be gladly accepted.

Will readers please notify change of address before the 20th of the month.

All correspondence to be sent to Rev. S.P. Toperoff, 5, Victoria Avenue, Sunderland.

SUNDERLAND
Jewish
COMMUNITY

BULLETIN
for the
FORCES

"Be strong and of good courage, be
not afraid neither be thou dismayed, for
the Lord thy God is with thee withersoever
thou goest."

Joshua, 1:9.

*Edited and issued monthly by the Minister
and sent to you with the good wishes of
your friends at home.*

September 1945   Vol.3   No. 12.   Tishri 5706.

It was with a great sense of relief and gratitude shared by the whole community that we heard the wonderful news that the following prisoners of war in Japanese hands are safe and sound.

We congratulate the families and relations of:-

Morris Mincovitch, Yankel Pearlman and
Nathan Ernstone.

"This is from the Lord, it is marvellous in our eyes.   This is the day which the Lord hath appointed, we will rejoice and be glad thereon."

The most heartfelt joy and happiness will naturally be felt by the immediate relations, but it is no exaggeration to add that we all feel this personal joy.   It is our ardent wish and hope that our "heroes" will return home very soon with the fervent will to forget as quickly as is humanly possible the nightmare of their experiences during the past three years.

The news has fittingly come through during the great season of prayer in the month of Tishri, which is replete with Jewish Festivals and Jewish ceremonialism.   It is our common Prayer that others too, from whom no message has been received will miraculously return.

During Rosh Hashannah and Yom Kippur we renewed acquaintance with several of our local men who had been away for a number of years.   May the prayers, hopes and aspirations of all be quickly realised so that their near and dear ones be reunited with them and very soon that the Sunderland Jewish Community may once again play its rightful part in Anglo-Jewry.

DO YOU KNOW?

1. What is Badchan?
2. Who was the first English Ecclesiastic who used Hebrew in his books?
3. Where is the Biblical allusion to the oriental habit of a servant responding to the hand clapping of his master?
4. What was directly responsible for the settlement of Jews in England?

Answers to above on Page 3.

HERE AND THERE!

Mazeltov!
Congratulations to the following:-
Births: Mr. and Mrs. Gordon (nee Anette Penn) on the birth of a son.
             Mr. and Mrs. S. Bergson on the birth of a daughter.
Engagements: Miss Blanche Book to Elia Perlman, L.D.S., A.I.L. of Newcastle.
Wedding: L.A.C. Israel Davis to Joan Rosenston of Harrogate.

2.

Congratulations to Mr. Ian Ross who has been elected Chairman of the Sunderland Gramophone Music Society.

Educational Successes.

The following have been successful in the School Certificate:- Moses Feld, Julian Isaacs, Harold Merskey, Norman Oler, Charles Slater.

Conference of Christians and Jews.

A Conference of Christians and Jews was held recently in Sunderland at the Jewish Refugee Hostel in Kensington Esplanade.   The principal Speaker was the Rev. W.W. Simpson of London, the Organising Secretary of the National Council.   He spoke at the afternoon session on "The need of our work - a survey of the present situation in the field of Jewish-Christian relations."   The Rev. Hector Ross, Chairman of the local Council, presided.

After tea the evening session was opened with a short address on "The future activities of local Councils" by the Rev. S.P. Toperoff and the Rev. Dr. Allen of Newcastle.   At both sessions there were good and fruitful discussions in which many present took part.

Delegates at the Conference came from Newcastle, South Shields and West Hartlepool.

IN RETROSPECT.

This brings us to 1931.   The "Lit" had now been in continuous operation for twenty years.

Joe Topaz (then Vice-chairman) consented to take office from me for one year in order to give me a much desired rest.   During this session I was presented with a handsome illuminated address signed by the heads of the Congregation and the "Lit" circle.

The Nussenbaum brothers (Friends of the new Chairman) gave the Society a cinema show, suitable music being supplied by Joe Topaz's radio-gram.   This event proved so successful and popular that it became an annual fixture.

Peter Batten, the editor of the Sunderland Echo spoke to the Society during this session.   He was entertained to tea before his lecture at the home of the chairman.   I remember Simon Light asking him why Zionism got such scant publicity in the Press.   Mr. Batten's reply was - "The Jew has no news value."   Quickly came the question,- "Then why, if a Jew breaks the law, do the papers make so much of it?" The answer was characteristic of the man.   "The Jew is a law abiding citizen, if he does good, it is not unusual, but should he break the law, it is unusual and that is news."   On the way to the Hall he asked how the Dramatic Society was progressing and informed me he would sooner be an actor than a producer.   Then looking at me very

3.

earnestly he said - "Suppressed personality", but then, he was a
publicist. Knowing him to be a very busy man I asked him what he
did in his spare time. He answered - "When the weather is wet, I
write articles for a rainy day." It can truly be said of him - "On
parade, work and wit. Off parade, journalism and joviality."

This session was notable for many fine inter-debates and I
remember one heart searching discussion on some characteristics that
made the Jew so noticeable in public. Did the members of the "Lit"
see into the immediate future? I wonder - for soon the Jew was, alas,
unfortunately to become news. Aye, even headline news. The Society
held two very fine concerts, a Locum Tenems Night and Prize Night.
Joe Topaz had a very busy session and acquitted himself with
distinction.

Next month - "The "Lit" goes on a Mediterranean cruise."

Cherrio,

SOL.

Answers to Questions on Page 1.

1. A professional jester in Russia and Poland who entertained guests
   whilst dancing, by jokes, comic and earnest songs, and mock
   argumentations on ridiculous and imaginary problems. He was
   also called "Marshallik".

2. The Venerable Bede in the 8th century alluded to Hebrew on
   several occasions in his books.

3. Psalm 123 verse 2 "Behold as the eyes of servants look unto the
   hand of their masters."

4. Not only Jews but Christians believed intensely in the coming of
   the Messiah and as a prelude the English invited Jews to settle
   in their country.

NEWS LETTER FROM THE HOME FRONT.

Once again the year speeds by before we have time to realise it
and suddenly we find ourselves at the threshold of a new Lit season.
For the first time for almost every present member of the Lit the
Session starts without fear of interruption from Alerts though the
other difficulties of war-time organisation have not yet disappeared.
The return to pre-war activities must of necessity be gradual but I
know that the Lit will seize every opportunity to take a step in that
direction. Just how long it will take for the Lit to flourish in
old style cannot yet be foreseen but already one can sense a difference

4.

between the programme that has just been drawn up and the programmes of the war years.

One great step, in my opinion, is the decision to invite two local men of note to address the Society.   That this is a bold and risky step in view of the possibility of a small audience I do not deny but without taking risks one rarely succeeds.   I sincerely hope that the older and past members will interest themselves in lectures arranged by the Lit and thus encourage, at a critical period, an organisation which has provided intellect for over thirty years. If this Season is a success, as I am confident it will be, the door will be open to those jolly days which seem to be in the dim past but which hold such happy memories for so many of us.

Other events, which I am informed, are on the draft syllabus are debates, dances, social evenings, a Live Newspaper Night and a B.B.C Night.   I will let you have the dates of these and of the two lectures as soon as they are made known.

The Season is due to commence on Sunday 7th October which is the first Sunday after the Yomim Tovim and I will have more "gen" for you about the opening events next time.

Until then, Cheerio and lots of luck.

Yours,

Also After Gen.

Letters have been received from the following and are gratefully acknowledged by the Editor:-

Cpl.Charlton,S.E.A.A.F.;   Sgt. Pearlman P, C.M.F.;   Cpl. Isaac Brewer, ENGLAND;   V.A.D. Olga Grantham, INDIA COMMAND;   Sgt. Ralph Freedman, ENGLAND;   L.A.C. Julius Gordon, C.M.F.;   Pte. Gwen Magrill, ENGLAND; A.C. Landau, B.A.O.R.;   Fus. Freeman B., MALTA FORCE;   Cpl. Cyril Pearlman, M.E.F.;   L.A.C. I. Davis, B.A.O.R.;   Cpl. Norman Cohen, C.M.F.;   Sgt. Altman, INDIA COMMAND;   Sgt. E. Kolson, S.E.A.C.;   Lt. J. Stone, INDIA COMMAND;   Sgt. Sarabouski, INDIA COMMAND; Capt. Mordaunt Cohen, INDIA COMMAND; and Pte. Max Pearlman, S.E.A.C.

5.

SEARCHLIGHT ON SPORT - By "Argus"

The first month of the Football season gone and where are we!
Evidently we are the strongest team in the Northern section for we
are holding the remaining twenty one clubs up.

It would take more research work than I am prepared to undertake
to discover whether Sunderland had ever been at the bottom of the
League before today, but I certainly cannot recall their being in that
position - not even in that fateful 1927 - 28 season when by defeating
Middlesbrough in the last game of the season the Tees-side club went
into the Second Division, whereas if the result had been reversed
Sunderland would have done so. Actually we never held bottom place.

It is quite easy to say what is wrong. The forwards are neither
hitting the goal or shaping like getting goals from attacks developed
in mid-field. There are too many players without the spirit and the
heart to fight for the ball.

It is not so easy to find the remedy. With only one man so far
released from the Forces - Bert Johnson - there is no choice of
players excepting young and inexperienced players, and it is my firm
impression that some of the players now in the senior eleven know it
and trade upon the fact. One might as well be frank about it.

Manager Billy Murray is the most worried man at Roker Park today.
He does not like it, but as I say, how is he going to remedy it!
Only by buying and though I know he has three players in his mind,
money is required. I have no doubt that will be forthcoming if the
position becomes serious, but quite frankly there is so much to do in
the near future that the Sunderland directors cannot afford to spend
money unless it is absolutely necessary.

Don't be surprised therefore if Sunderland just wait a while to
see which way "the cat jumps". There is nothing at stake this season
beyond building a team to face the future - a very important problem
and one which will not be easy to accomplish. You no sooner get a
promising player than the services claim him.

The Bulletin is issued free to members of the Forces but private
subscribers at the rate of 10/- per year will be gladly accepted.

Will readers please notify change of address before the 20th of
the month.

All correspondence to be sent to Rev. S.P. Toperoff, 5 Victoria
Avenue, Sunderland.

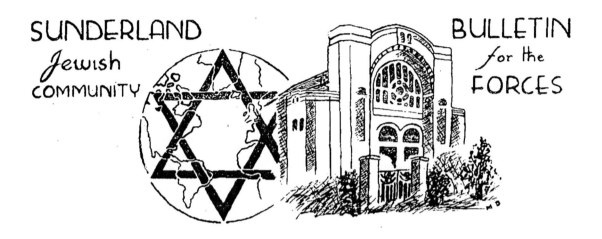

SUNDERLAND
Jewish
COMMUNITY

BULLETIN
for the
FORCES

" Be strong and of good courage, be
not afraid neither be thou dismayed, for
the Lord thy God is with thee withersoever
thou goest."

Joshua, I : 9.

*Edited and issued monthly by the Minister
and sent to you with the good wishes of
your friends at home.*

October, 1945.   Vol.3   No. 13.   Cheshvan 570

THE FUTURE OF THE BULLETIN.

Now that hostilities have ceased and demobilisation is releasing some of our men and women in the Forces, the future of the Bulletin must be discussed.

Several correspondents have already written asking that the Bulletin should continue to appear even after the last man has returned. Though the Bulletin is primarily for the Forces it has made a number of "friends" outside the Forces.

Through our contributor Sol Novinski we have enjoyed a regular glimpse into the past thus renewing our acquaintance with the early pioneers and champions of the Literary Circle. The story is not exhausted and once our appetites have been whetted we should like to read more of the pen-pictures of those early days.

Concurrent with the story of the past "Also After Gen" is giving us the story of the present. But outside the realms of the activities of the "Lit" past and present a local Bulletin can do much towards unifying and strengthening the manifold and varied activities of our Community.

I therefore invite the opinions of readers on the advisability or otherwise of retaining the Bulletin in our midst.

Concrete suggestions and proposals will be welcomed, for it must be borne in mind that whereas the expenses incurred in producing the Forces Bulletin have been defrayed by three local Gentlemen, the future Communal Bulletin will have to be self-supporting.

DO YOU KNOW?

1. Who began the Youth Aliyah?
2. Who founded the Habimah?
3. Who said "Jews are members of the Human Race, worse than that I cannot of them"?
4. Of which Christian Ecclesiastic is it recorded that he prohibited the foundation of a Society for the Prevention of Cruelty to Animals on the ground that it is a theological error to imagine that man has any duty towards the dumb creature?

Answers to the above on Page 3

HERE AND THERE

MAZELTOV!
Congratulations to the following:-
Births   - Mr. & Mrs. H. Brechner on the birth of a daughter.
          Mr. & Mrs. A. Davis on the birth of a son.
          Mr. & Mrs. S. Dent on the birth of a daughter.
          Dr. & Mrs. Jack Stone on the birth of a son.
Wedding - Miss Sylvia Penn on her marriage to Mr Arnold Sheckman of North Shields.

2.

IN RETROSPECT.

I forgot to mention that Mr. Stanley Ritson spoke to the Society during Joe Topaz's regime.   This eminent surgeon met many old friends after the meeting and spent quite a long time chatting with them.

The "Lits" latest venture to date was the promotion of regular socials, and it was felt that the summer dances needed just that extra push to make for success.   It was decided to hold a novelty dance.   Simon Light had a brain wave.   The function would take the form of a cruise dance. In other words, the Hall would be decorated to suggest the atmosphere of a luxury liner.   The Committee were enthusiastic and soon showed its genius for imagination and detail.   Shipping tickets were printed inviting members and friends to come on a Mediterranean cruise on the S.S. Yaki. Hiki. Haki Doola.   When the "passengers" arrived they had to enter the Hall by an improvised gangway and were met by the Purser (a Committee lady) dressed in white tennis frock and white doughboy hat.   The admittance ticket was checked and the "passenger" stepped on to the deck (the floor of the Hall).   The walls had been lined with posters showing beautiful sea and landscapes.

Harold Olswang provided a number of white washed old motor tyres. These were hung round the walls with the appropriate lashings of rope and represented life belts.   The North side of the Hall was roped off and furnished as a deck cafe.   I, as captain wore a blue jacket and white flannels, the jacket bore the appropriate gold lace and brass buttons, and complete with cap to match, I acted as M.C.

All the members of the Committee acted as stewards and were dressed in white and wearing white dough boy hats.   When they spoke to me they would come to attention and salute smartly.

Our old friends the Elite Orchestra obligingly "hotted up" some nautical airs during the evening.   The dance floor was crowded and being a hot evening, the cafe did a roaring business in ices and soft drinks, which were consumed through straws.   Deck games were also much enjoyed and I remember a horn pipe danced by some ladies of the "Lit Concert Party".   This dance caused quite a sensation and I do believe was one of the most successful functions ever held in the Communal Hall.   It was followed some time later by another novelty dance entitled "A Gretna Green Dance".   Unfortunately, I was unable to be present and cannot give you first hand details.   I was told however, that an anvil wedding was staged by our old friend Bobby Isaacs.

Between 1933 and 1936 the "Lit" had its busiest and most successful time.

Next month I will start to write about the Jewish Arts League, The North East Union and The Northern Federation of Jewish Societies.

Cheerio,
SOL.

3.

Answers to questions on page 1.

The credit belongs to two great women, a German Jewess, Frau Freier
who first worked out practical plans to enable children to attain a
life of security and freedom in the Jewish National Home.   In
Palestine Miss Henrietta Szold, at the age of 73 when looking forward
to retirement assumed the role of Mother to the Youth Aliyah.   More
than ten thousand children have been rescued from the Nazi terror
and brought into Palestine.

The Habimah Players were founded in Russia in 1917 by Stanislavski
who delegated one of the most talented of his staff the Armenian Poet
Vanchtangoff to the training of his group.   They perform in Hebrew
but do not restrict their repertoire to native playwrights and include
the translations of the best of established writers especially of
Shakespeare.

Mark Twain was the author of the statement.

Pope Pius IX 1846-1878 prohibited in Rome the Society for the
Prevention of Cruelty of Animals.   On the otherhand it is laid down
in the Talmud by the Rabbis that the Jew is forbidden to taste food
before he has fed the animal.

NEWS LETTER FROM THE HOME FRONT

The Lit Session for 1945/6 has commenced.   After a rather weak
~~or~~t of Social on Sunday 7th October there was a Presidential Address
~~th~~e following week by Vice-President Simon Light who spoke on "Reflection
~~to~~ a smallish though extremely interested audience.   From the Chair,
~~Au~~brey Gordon first read a message of good wishes from the President
~~So~~l Novinski.   Describing the Lit from its early days to the beginning
~~of~~ the war, Simon Light reminded present members that those "good old
~~da~~ys" could and would return.   He mentioned that our Lit was the first
~~Je~~wish Literary Society in the country and emphasised the part it had
~~p~~layed in the North East Union which so many of you will well remember
~~an~~d which the Chairman pointed out was that very afternoon in the course
~~o~~f reconstruction.

The Speaker reminisced about the Jubilee Year and also about various
~~d~~ramatic Festivals and illustrated his talk all the way through with
~~w~~itty and humorous episodes which made an hour and a half pass in no
~~t~~ime!   Old circulars, syllabuses, photographs and press cuttings helped
~~t~~he audience to realise the magnitude of many of the past events.   After
~~t~~he Speaker had worked up a spirit of keenness amongst members they were
~~a~~sked for suggestions; a number of those forthcoming were very
~~c~~onstructive and I feel that if the same enthusiasm prevails throughout
~~t~~he Season the Lit will be well on the way to its magnificent former self

From now onwards until Pesach there will be, to use the old tag,
something on at the Lit" every Sunday evening at 7-0.   I do hope to
~~s~~ee many more of you Forces at the Hall in the near future.   Already
~~t~~he boys are beginning to trickle home - some already released others
~~o~~nly on leave but it's a good sign.   As it will be of interest to many
~~o~~f you I shall make a special point of attempting to remember who puts
~~i~~n an appearance at the Hall and to give you the 'gen' each month.   Sol
~~W~~illis popped his head in the door at the Social but had to rush away

4.

as he was leaving the same evening.

That's all for now. Remember the dance at the Hall on Sunday the 28th October if you happen to be home. Best of luck to you all.

Yours,

Also After Gen.

EXCERPTS FROM LETTERS.

<u>F/Lt. Cohen, S.E.A.A.F. writes</u>: At the moment I am just over two hundred miles north of Singapore. I have been to Kuala Lumpur which is the capital of the Federated Malay States. It is quite a large town with white buildings populated mainly by Chinese. The word Kuala means Mouth of the River and Lumpur in English is Mud.

It is interesting to note that the Chinese are the business people of Malaya. There are quite a number of Indians too mainly from Madras and Southern India.

The rubber plantations in this district have not been cultivated since the Jap occupation. Quite near to my Headquarters is a shipyard where under enemy supervision the Chinese built boats which had a displacement of 150 tons and were about 170 feet long. They were quite well made and took approximately three months to complete. Everything was done by hand; even the stocks though a little primitive consisted of blocks of wood as supports. Many boats were unfinished when we arrived and one had even been given its first coat of paint.

<u>Surg. Minchom, Colombo, writes</u>: I have met many of the ex-prisoners here and heard the tales of their captivity. They do not bear repetition and not far from me now is a camp of Javanese who can only compare with the inhabitants of the Belsen camp. Yet all the prisoners say that Thailand was the worst place. Can you wonder at my feelings waiting for news. Well it is over now, time will allay the hurts of 3½ years, and the ex-P.O.W's here are putting on weight at an extraordinary rate and look cheerful and happy in the extreme. Strangely enough they are not vindictive save against a few of the worst jailors and their only desire is not to see another Jap.

The Chinese have, if anything suffered even more than the British. Death or a terrible beating was the punishment for the least crime, yet they made every effort to help the P.O.W's. No one could speak too highly of them out here.

<u>Cpl. Charlton, S.E.A.A.F. writes</u>: On V.E. day we were left fairly cold, especially as we felt we were being forgotton more than ever, but on V.J. it was out turn to celebrate, now we could surpass London and verily indeed most of the world by our celebrations for we had something to celebrate. The victory service for the Jewish troops in Madras was held at the house of a private family (of whom more later) and was attended by about seventy of us. After the service we were indeed

5.

fortunate to hear a lecture by the Jewish Representative to the Cochin State Council on the history of that outpost of orthodox Jewry in Cochin.

A few days before Rosh-hashama we moved into a transit camp to await embarkation and were hourly expected to move, but I was fortunate enough to be able to spend at least the first two evenings of the festival Madras at the same people's house who had the J.J. service, and we were entertained to dinner by them each night.

A day later we embarked and found ourselves in comparative luxury on a trooper which is indeed rare. Tom Kippur found me still aboard the trooper preparing to make a beach landing on Malaya which is not the ideal place at that time. Anyway the next morning we were taken off on gun boats and then transferred to landing craft from which we eventually waded about 250 yards ashore, no joy ride with full pack bedding and arms and ammunition. The first night we spent in a rubber plantation at the side of the road where we built ourselves huts of rushes, banana leaves and anything else we could find. On the following morning we set out in trucks and eventually arrived at Kuala Lampur. The city is really amazing, finer than any city in India. The shops are full of pre-war goods which had been hidden during the occupation, and are now coming out at ever rising prices. Cigarettes are of more value than gold, and those with a surplus can get as much as $5 (11/-) for a tin of fifty.

This letter would not be complete without an appreciation of Mr. and Mrs. Wolff of Madras, who act as hosts each Sunday to the boys and at whose house the festival service has been held for years. I have seen more of India than most people, but believe me their's was the first real hospitality, and their's was the first house at which one felt really at home in a traditional atmosphere, it is rather strange that I was only acquainted with such hospitality in my last hours in India for I never found it before.

Letters also received and acknowledged: V.A.D. Olga Grantham, S.E.A.C.; Sgt. Lonnie Slater, DORSET; Fus. Freeman, MALTA FORCE; Pte. Douglas Goldman, SOMERSET; L.A.C. M. Dresner, ICELAND; L.A.C. I. Davis, B.A.O.R.; Pte. Leonard Lerman, SURREY; Cpl. C. Behrman, M.E.F.; L.A.C.W. Leslie S. YORKS.

We are pleased to publish short messages from Sgt. Maurice Mincovitch and Bombardier E.J. Pearlman just released from Japanese hands.

Bombardier E.J. Pearlman:-

After nearly four years of captivity in Japaneze hands, my relief and joy at being back with my family, relatives and friends in Sunderland is beyond expression.

The City of Rangoon was memorable for the meeting between my brother Mottle and myself. It was fitting that we should meet on the first night of Rosh Hafhana when everybody's thoughts are with ones family.

6.

As P.O.W. we always managed a Service on Shabbos morning under the Auspices of Arkus (No.2 Camp Dentist) who is a member of the Blackpool Community.

We must thank God for the peace which has brought to an end all our miseries, and that this peace will be very lasting.

Signed,

E.J. PEARLMAN.

Maurice H. Mincovitch:-

Home! a rather fond hope for the past four years, has at least become a reality!

When I think of myself as I was just over two months ago, and then think of myself as I am now, I have to keep pinching myself to be reassured that it is not just a wonderful dream.

I had not been aware of the existence of the Bulletin until I met Mottie Pearlman in Rangoon. He lent me his copy, and the glimpse it gave me of home provided a great fillip to my already rising spirits, I must admit though, that the news of the various simchas made me a little uncertain as to my age. You see it's rather difficult to realise that boys and girls are apt to become men and women.

I should like to thank Reverend Toperoff for providing me with the opportunity of writing this message. I know you will all agree with me that he is doing a fine job of work.

Naturally I shall not say anything about my years in captivity, so I will conclude wishing you all a very speedy and safe return to the old home town.

Shalom,

MAURICE H. MINCOVITCH

The Bulletin is issued free to members of the Forces but private subscribers at the rate of 10/- per year will be gladly accepted.

Will readers please notify change of address before the 20th of the month.

All correspondence to be sent to Rev. S. P. Toperoff, 5 Victoria Avenue, Sunderland.

SUNDERLAND *Jewish* COMMUNITY

BULLETIN *for the* FORCES

" Be strong and of good courage, be not afraid neither be thou dismayed, for the Lord thy God is with thee withersoever thou goest."

Joshua, I : 9.

Edited and issued monthly by the Minister and sent to you with the good wishes of your friends at home.

November 1945   Vol.3   No.14.   Kislev 5706

"The lights of Europe have gone out".   This was the description
of the world at the outbreak of the 1914-1918 War.   Since then the
lights have reappeared, and become extinguished through the dark
forces of Hitlerism and now once again reappeared in all their pristine
glory.

Chanukah which we shall soon celebrate is the Jewish Festival
of Light, and for the first time in 6 years we shall celebrate
Chanukah this year with the lights full on.

Judaism always stresses the importance of light.   The Sabbath
and Festivals are introduced by the kindling of candles, the shedding
of more light on the Friday evening table, bringing brightness and
colour and cheer into the Jewish home.   So important was "light"
considered by the Rabbis that they make it synonymous with the "Torah".
In other words they meant to imply that Jewish teaching brings light
and enlightenment and not ignorance and darkness into the world.

Of the numerous testimonies to the light of Israel in the world
let us choose one by the Christian philosopher, Lecky.   "Whilst those
around the Jews were grovelling in the darkness of besotted ignorance,
whilst the intellect of Christendom enthralled by countless
superstitions, had sank into a deadly torpor in which all love of
inquiry and all search for truth were abandoned, the Jews were still
pursuing the path of knowledge, amassing learning and stimulating
progress with the same unblinding constancy that they manifested in
their faith".

The Jew has suffered much throughout his bloodstained and
martyred history because of the blind forces of ignorance, prejudice
and an unreasonable hatred from his enemies.

But with hope springing eternal in his breast he has always
kindled the Menorah of Light which throughout the ages has emblazoned
his trail and lit up an otherwise sinister and gloomy horizon.

Czecho-Slovakia, Hungary, Rumania, Holland, France-- these
countries come to mind.   Though torn by internal strife the aftermath
of total war-- they are gradually finding their feet, the torch of
Freedom burns dimly in these countries but slowly and surely the light
of Justice will help them to reassert their national independence.
One people alone- the Jewish people --that has suffered more than any
other on earth are enshrouded by darkness--- why?   Because they are
not allowed to return to their ancestral home.   Though Palestine, was
promised by 52 Nations and a guarantee given in 1917 that facilities
would be granted for Jews to build a National Home, nothing has as
yet materialised.   For Jews indeed the pronouncement by the Labour
Government to restrict immigration has been more than a disappointment
It has blackened the Jewish horizon, and Mr. Bevin's speech has come
as an anti-climax as we had laid so much store on the declared policy

2.

of the Labour Government before the General Election.

We must however not lose heart. "Put not thy trust in princes or in the son of man in whom there is no salvation" said the Psalmist.

Chanukah comes at an appropriate time as do all Jewish Festivals. Chanukah reminds us that the light of Israel still burns, the spirit of Israel is unquenchable, immortal and indestructible. The Menorah will be lit in the Homes and the Synagogues as a faithful testimony to the dogged obstinacy of Israel that it means to live and flourish in it's own land--- Palestine- promised to us by G-d.

Neither politics nor force will bring us back to the Holy Land which gave us and the world the eternal teaching of the Bible. In the classic words of Zachariah read on Chanukah "Not by might nor by power but by my spirit saith the Lord".

DO YOU KNOW?

1. Which Jewish character has become a Saint in the calendar of the Christian Church?
2. Why did Mahomet compose a special prayer to G-d to help him combat the Jews?
3. What percentage of Jews in Canada fought in the war?
4. What is known in Jewish History as the Mortara Case?

Answers to the above on Page 4

HERE AND THERE

MAZELTOV!
Congratulations to the following:-

Births   - Dr. & Mrs. J. Priceman on the birth of a daughter.
Engagement - Norman Cohen on his engagement to Miss Zelda Levin.
Marriages - Celia Davis on her marriage to Sam Lampert of London.
             Devora Pearlman on her marriage to Joseph Wineman of London.
Promotion - Dr. V.E. Gillis who has been made a Squadron Leader in the R.A.F.

SUNDERLAND YOUNG ZIONIST ASSOCIATION.

During the last few weeks Sunderland Young Zionist Society has been addressed by several of its own members including Mr. H. Merskey, Mr. Ch. Slater and Mr. L. Epstein. The society has also held a Hat Night and a very successful Live Newspaper Night which opened with an editorial given by Miss E.E. Heilpern and an article submitted by the papers' Parliamentary Correspondent. The paper then continued with the Scandal Column, 'Varsity News, Adverts., Sports News and Letters to the Editor.

On Wednesday, 14th November, the society sponsored A Variety

3.

Concert which was held in the Communal Hall in aid of the United Palestine Appeal.

The Sunderland Federation of Zionist Youth would like to thank Habonim for the good work they did in their campaign to pursuade members of our community to write to our local M.P's appealing for their support in the Jewish claim for 100,000 immigration certificates to Palestine.

[In a communication from the Senior M.P. Willey I was informed that over 100 letters were received from members of the Community and that each letter was acknowledged - Editor.]

The thirteenth annual meeting of the Women's Zionist Society was held recently at the home of Mrs. M. Joseph. Many new members were enrolled. The following were elected: Mesdames A. Rawlinson, President; A. Blakey, Chairman; L. Davis, Treasurer; H. Cohen, Assistant Treasurer; A. Merskey and Miss P. Wolfe, Vice-Chairmen; and Mrs. M. Joseph (31, Humbledon Park) Secretary.

DUTCH CHILDREN ENTERTAINED.

The Jewish Women's War Service Committee entertained a group of Dutch children (non-Jewish) at The Carlton Rooms, where a sumptuous tea was provided. The Dutch children were the victims of Nazi persecution and were spending a short period in Sunderland prior to their return to Holland.

JOEL INTRACT MEMORIAL HOME OF REST FOR AGED JEWS.

A meeting of the North East Home for aged Jews was held recently at the Communal Hall with Mr. M. Jacoby in the Chair.

The project was fully explained by the Chairman and many question were asked regarding the constitution of the new Home which should be open for Passover.

Mr. A. Merskey and J. Behrman are the local representatives.

The following were elected on this local Committee:-
Miss P. Wolfe, Mesdames R. Share, I. Isaacs, M. Pearlman, A. Merskey and H. Stone.

Messrs. H. Stone, M.A. Cohen, I. Gorden, R. Share, D. Pearlman, M. Greenwald and Miss Jean Merskey Hon. Secretary.

PRESENTATION TO PRISONER OF WAR.

In the presence of the Council of the Ryhope Road Synagogue and the families and relations of Mr. and Mrs. Maurice Mincovitch, a silver dish, suitably inscribed was presented by the Sunderland Hebrew Congregation to Sgt. Maurice Mincovitch to mark the occasion of his release from a prison camp in Japan.

Mr. A. Merskey presided, The Rev. S.P. Toperoff proposed the health and future happiness of the couple and Sgt. Mincovitch responded.   The toast of both parents was proposed by Mr. J. Clark to which Mr. R. Minchom responded.   Mr. I. Gordon proposed a vote of thanks to the Chairman, also thanked Mrs. Olsberg for providing light refreshments.

We have received a request from Cpl. Claud Brewer to publish his address.   Any local men visiting Naples will be welcomed by Cpl. Brewer whose address is:- 1054730 R.S.D.
557 B.O.D.   C.M.F.

Answers to questions on page 2.

1. Judas Maccabeus.
2. He was afraid of the active opposition and heroic fighting qualities of the Jews whom he tried to overcome.
3. The voluntary enlistments of Jews in Canada represent 8.82 per cent of the Jewish Population (168,367) whereas the total enlistments in Canada represent 6.91 per cent.
4. In 1854 a Jewish child of the Mortara family became ill and the Christian maid thinking that it would die, baptised it secretly. Following "confession" Papal soldiers forcibly removed the child (now 6 years old) to Rome where he was trained to become a priest. The "case" aroused world wide indignation and even Napoleon III protested to the Pope but to no avail.   Sir Moses Montifiore made the journey to seek an interview with the Pope but even this was refused.

IN RETROSPECT.

The "Lit" had joined the Northern Federation of Literary Societies and soon inter-functions with constituent Societies were being held.   The first of these was an inter debate with the Sheffield Jewish Students Society and was held at Sheffield.   A return visit took place the same season.

Then followed a regional conference of the Federation.   The delegates arrived on the Friday and attended Shool on Shabbos morning.   They were officially welcomed by the Circle at a full dress Ball in the evening.   The conference was held Sunday morning in the Communal Hall and was addressed by its Honorary President Mr. Neville Laski.   He stressed the importance of making and keeping contact with each other.   Mr. Abbs Moss, when expressing thanks mentioned the work of the Manchester Union of Literary Societies. I spoke in support of the resolution and said I thought the idea of a regional Union was very good.   Mr. Moss thereupon proposed "That a North East Union of Jewish Young People's Societies be formed", and so a new offspring of the "Lit" was born.

After the conference an excellent lunch was served while an orchestra played sweet music.

As Honorary President of the "Lit" I occupied the chair at a
mass meeting in the evening. Mr. Laski delivered his Presidential
address. The Communal Hall was crowded, about three hundred people
being present. As I faced that vast sea of faces I was thrilled.
When I rose to reply to the "Thanks to the Chair" Mr. Laski whispered
to me "Thank the Secretary for her splendid work". I assured him
I had not forgotten.

It is strange how these little memories remain with one,
indicating, as it were a person's character.

The Circle owes a deep debt of gratitude to Dorrie Behrman for
a magnificent piece of organisation. Not one little item was
forgotten and it is the little things that count.

The affiliation to the Federation opened out a wide field of
possibilities which the "Lit" was not slow to use. There followed
inter debates, two picnics, Summer schools and Drama Festivals.
Many firm friendships were made. The Summer schools were responsible
for at least one marriage, the Drama Festival another, and the North
East Union also had its share of romance. I suspect many other
happy events, but as I have only observation to go by, I will say
no more about this subject.

Later functions and return fixtures were held with the Manchester
Union, Sheffield, Birmingham, Liverpool and the Hull Judeans while
Leeds gave the "Lit" an excellent drama night. The lecturers who
spoke to the "Lit" numbered, among others, Miss C. Laitner of Sheffield,
Rabbi S. Fish also of Sheffield, Sidney Needoff of Manchester, Theo
Birks A.R.I.B.A. of Manchester and Rabbi Israel Abrahams also of
Manchester.

Next month I will give you a further list of some of the brilliant
lecturers who spoke to us, also "The Rev. S.P. Toperoff joins the "Lit".'

> Cheerio,
>> SOL.

NEWS LETTER FROM THE HOME FRONT.

Since last month the Lit has scored two grand successes, one
in the social line and the other on the literary side. The dance on
Sunday 28th October was indeed one of the best the Hall has seen for
at least a couple of years. There was a larger crowd than there has
been of late to dances, there were more of the older generation and
the jollity was at a very high level. Jack Usher and his band (who
play regularly at several dance halls in town) provided music of a
standard which merited the applause whilst the novelty dances proved
such a hit that almost everyone in the Hall joined in. The Communal
Hall took on a little of its old atmosphere no doubt greatly helped
by the fact that quite a few lads, who have been away from home so

6.

long, came down to re-visit the Lit. They included Yankel Pearlman
(home from Japanese hands), Sammy and Harry Isaacs, Julius Gordon
and Lionel Gillis -- and they all looked extremely well.   There was,
naturally, the running buffet but all the tasties were sold out
long before I got a look in.

The other interesting event was held the following week when
there was a talk by Mr. Jackson of the Blind Institute who addressed
the Lit several times before the war. He returned to speak on
"More Cockney Humour" and he held the audience (nearly forty strong)
in fits of laughter.   Mr. Jackson is a fluent speaker with a
natural sense of humour which made his jokes, all carefully chosen
from every aspect of Cockney life, come pouring forth in a smooth
endless stream.   I hope the Lit will provide us with more speakers
of Mr. Jackson's calibre and I also hope to see more of the older
members of the community taking an interest in this type of thing.

The Lit in these events has provided two forms of entertainment
of contrasting nature but each of the highest standard in it's own
sphere.

When the radiogramme went "on strike" during the Social on
11th November it looked as though the evening was going to be a flop
but Pearl Levey kindly stepped into the breach and tapped out dance
tunes on the piano for the rest of the evening.   In fact the Social
turned out more lively than it might have done otherwise!

I hear, by the way, that Jack Usher is again booked to play
at the Lit dance on 2nd December so I hope to see another crowd
on leave then.

Cheerio for now,

Yours,

Also After Gen.

SEARCHLIGHT ON SPORT - By "Argus".

For the past three weeks - that is to say the first three in
November - we were kidding ourselves that at last Sunderland had
begun to find their feet. We got five points out of six.

Then we were brought up with a jerk to the fact that everything
in the garden was not so lovely as some people imagined.   Preston
came and beat us 1 - 0, and the Sunderland side played just as
badly as they had been playing earlier in the season.   Fact is
they would be reliable or good enough until side is strengthened.

But while I am talking about strengthening the team Sunderland
directors are talking about transferring Carter.   They don't want
to part with him, but Carter has put forward the plea that his wife
is suffering from heart trouble and he desires her to be as near to

7. (

her parents as possible.   They are now living in Derby.

I have my own idea of all there transfers of stars.   They would never have arisen in most cases had there not been a war, or war service had counted towards benefit.   If you think that out, you will know the meaning without me saying so.

However, Carter has not gone yet, and while I write the only offe is from Middlesbrough - and Carter won't go there, for that is very little nearer to Derby than Sunderland is.

We have not got that back yet, and there is no sign of one.   It is not much good sighning a service-man who cannot get to Sunderland, nor a player in civilian employment who is under the Essential Works Order elsewhere.

Letters received and gratefully acknowledged by the Editor:-
Pte. M. Doberman, WESTGATE-ON-SEA; Pte. D. Goldman, GLAMORGAN; Cpl.
C. Brewer, C.M.F. Pte. E. Gillis, INDIA; Pte. L. Lerman, SURREY;
Pte. Mincovitch, NOTTS; Lieut. J. Stone, INDIA COMMAND; Cpl.
Charlton, S.E.A.A.F.

The Bulletin is issued free to members of the Forces but private subscribers at the rate of 10/- per year will be gladly accepted.

.Will readers please notify change of address before the 20th of the month.

All correspondence to be sent to Rev. S. P. Toperoff, 5 Victoria Avenue, Sunderland.

Sunderland Jewish Community
Bulletin for the Forces

1946

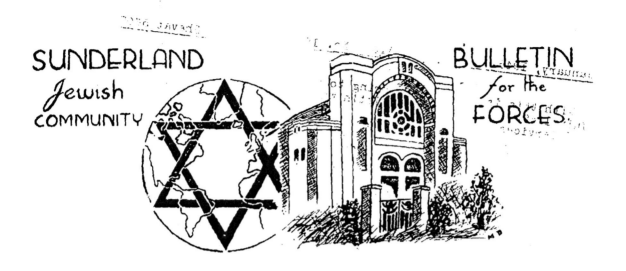

SUNDERLAND *Jewish* COMMUNITY

BULLETIN *for the* FORCES

" Be strong and of good courage, be
not afraid neither be thou dismayed, for
the Lord thy God is with thee withersoever
thou goest."

Joshua, I : 9.

*Edited and issued monthly by the Minister
and sent to you with the good wishes of
your friends at home.*

313

January, 1946.   Vol.3   No. 15.   Shevat 5607

With this issue we shall bring to a close a venture which was begun in July 1942.   This Forces Bulletin was originally intended for members of the Services.

Let us at this stage, then, recapitulate the events that led to the appearance of the Bulletin.   From the outset of the war when a number of our lads joined up as Territorials, the idea of a Bulletin was conceived and we felt that it would be the means of uniting the serving members of our Community whilst away from home.   As soon as the numbers warranted it, we mooted the idea, though we realised that there would be the difficulty of finance.   Other difficulties, too, appeared; should the Bulletin be restricted to members of the Ryhope Road Synagogue only, or to all members of the Sunderland Jewish Community who found themselves in the Services?

Both these problems were soon solved by the initiative and generosity of Mr. I. E. Cohen, who originally undertook to defray the expenses incurred in the production of the Bulletin which was to be sent to all Jewish serving personel of the Town.   With characteristic sportsmanship and a sense of duty, Mr. Cohen was joined by Mr. H. Brechner and Mr. I. Share who insisted on sharing the financial responsibility.   To this trio who made the production of the Bulletin possible, our sincere and grateful thanks are due in the first place.

The Editor must also acknowledge here the co-operation and valuable help given by the various Contributors.

The readiness with which "Argus" of the Sunderland Echo agreed to contribute a monthly article, will always be appreciated by members of our Community.   This is one of those silent expressions of understanding and goodwill which exist between Jews and Christians.   If such expressions were multiplied in more facets of the maelstrom of life, they would break down the artificial barriers that tend to cause division and strife.

We are particularly grateful to Sol Novinski for his pen pictures of early "Lit" life, for he has rescued from oblivion some of the most interesting episodes in the history of the Literary Circle.   We all look forward to the time when these articles will form the nucleus of a reliable history of the "Lit" which should prove to be most illuminating

We are also thankful to "Also After Gen" who gave us a monthly review of all that happened at the Communal Hall on Sunday evenings. I am happy to know that an appreciable part of the Bulletin was devoted to the past, present and future activities of the "Lit", thus constantly keeping alive the importance of the "Lit which, I hope, will now receive a fillip and healthy stimulus from those coming home.

No Bulletin, however, would be well balanced without a column in light vein.   No one - not even the Editor - understood ALL the baffling, intriguing and ingenious innuendoes which flashed through "Inquisitor's contribution, sparkling with wit, humour and satire.

2.

Could a Sunderland lad wish for a more puzzling and fascinating adventure in the arid wastes of the desert or in some lonely outpost, than trying to solve these hidden mysteries!

So much for the contents of the Bulletin.   We must not forget that we owe a word of praise and thanks to Maurice Dresner who designed the cover of the Bulletin, which has been much admired.   It truly pictured the movements of our men and women, who travelled to nearly every corner of the globe with the Magen David, always mindful of their Jewish heritage.

The Jewish Forces Bulletin will be no more.   We humbly suggest that it served a most useful purpose.   It provided a platform for the views and opinions of readers, many of whom soon took advantage of this feature.   They often thrilled the Editor and, I am sure, many readers with their descriptive and sometimes provocative outbursts of really good journalism.

The Bulletin will live as a monument to the war effort of Sunderland Jewry that sent nearly 150 men and women out of a total Jewish population of 900 souls to the fighting fronts of the world.   We are proud of Sunderland Jewry's war effort, both at home and abroad.   The full history has yet to be written.   Though the Bulletin will cease to function, its contents and its message of hope, fortitude, courage and faith in God will live on.   Our Rabbis remark that when one parts from the dead we use the expression "Go in Peace" but when we part from the living we say "Go unto peace".   We cannot conclude without saluting the memory of those serving men who have passed on to the Beyond.   To them the journey of life is over; to them we say "Go in Peace".   May their Souls be bound up with the bond of eternal life, and rest in everlasting Peace.

To the living we say "Go unto Peace".   Go forward towards an era of lasting and continuous peace.   May wars with their indescribable torture and misery be a thing of the past.   The mission of the living is to keep on striving and walking towards Peace, the goal of mankind. We must rid ourselves of the warmongers, haters and despisers of man. Never again must the seeds of discord be sown to allow racial and religious discrimination to stalk the earth.   We, as Jews, are proud of our war effort whether in England, America or Palestine.   None have been more loyal or patriotic.   Have we not a right then to demand to "Go unto Peace" for which we pray every day!

In conclusion, I would remind those of you still in the Forces that I shall be pleased to hear from you and hope to maintain contact. To the demobilized my earnest wish is that your peace-time labours be crowned with success.   We are all looking forward to the "Victory Reunion".   Good luck to you all!

Your Friend,

S. P. TOPEROFF.

3.

DO YOU KNOW?

1. On which problem did the White House in U.S.A. receive the largest monthly total of letters.
2. "Don't eat in the open streets 'don't eat with your fingers; don't eat standing; don't bolt your food". In which book of dietetics do we find the above quotation.
3. Who said the following:- "The Jewish Religion is a mother whom her two daughters have wounded a thousand times."
4. Till what age did the Jewish child attend School in the Middle Ages and how did he compare with the non-Jewish child?
5. What is the meaning of "Shoklen" and why do Jewish practise it?

Answers to the above on Page 5

We are pleased to publish the following message from

RABBI I. BRODIE.

SENIOR JEWISH CHAPLAIN TO H.M. FORCES.

I am very glad to have the opportunity of contributing a few words to the final issue of the Bulletin.

During the course of my visits to the different theatres of war, I often used to hear men 'grousing' about the apparent indifference to their welfare of the people at home. There were, however, Communities against whom such a reproach could not be made. These Communities, through their welfare organisations, kept in touch with those of their members who were serving in H.M. Forces, both at home and overseas.

I am glad to know, nor am I surprised to find, that the Sunderland Jewish Community has, particularly by means of the Bulletin edited by the Rev. S. P. Toperoff, endeavoured to keep in contact with Sunderland boys and girls. I have seen copies of the Bulletin and found them interesting. I am sure that the Bulletin has been a source of encouragement and inspiration, particularly to those of the Community who have served in distant lands.

Might I add that the Bulletin is another expression of the fine intimate Jewish spirit for which the Sunderland Community has been well-known. My congratulations to all concerned for services rendered and a job well done.

HOME THOUGHTS ON RETURN FROM ABROAD

AVE ATQUE VALE

BY

CAPTAIN MORDAUNT COHEN R. A.

It is strange being home after six years of war. The first couple

4.

of days, I seemed to be walking around in a trance, but gradually things are becoming normal. The town is still the same. Of course it has not escaped it's share of the air blitz, but all in all, very little noticeable damage - apart from John Street and Salem Avenue - has occured since I left for overseas. The weather of course is still the same and anyone coming home from the Far East will feel the change in climate.

I found the greatest change in the young generation. Boys and Girls of 10 - 12 when the war started are now grown out of all recognition in the majority of cases. Many contemporaries have not changed much, although most of them seem to have got married. The older generation are very much the same - a little older, a few extra grey hairs but still full of life. The past six years have indeed been a great strain for them.

Most noticeable is the fact that the womenfolk are still dressed smartly despite rationing and utility clothing. Rations are not comparable with what we receive in the Forces, but there is no real shortage, and what there is, is good.

The boys are slowly coming back from overseas either on repat or release, and by the middle of next year the vast majority should be in civy street. With this in mind, and now that the war is over, it has been decided, with much regret, to make this the final issue of the Bulletin. It was felt that, rather than let it peter out, to finish while it was still in it's prime.

On behalf of all the Sunderland Jewish members of H.M. Forces, I would like to thank the editor Rev. S. P. Toperoff for the sterling work he has put in for the past four years in bringing us all, through the medium of the Bulletin, a little nearer to the old home town. No effort has been too great for him, even in the face of difficulties and opposition. To "Argus" (Captain Jack Anderson) too, we owe our profound thanks for his sports columns. I found them more intimate than those in the Echo as I felt it was something special for our serving men and women. If life was played like English Sport there'd be no wars. Long may your pen flourish Argus!

To "Inquisitor" too, and our old friend Sol Novinski we owe our gratitude. They never failed to produce the laughs and the memories of old.

Last but not least we must thank those few members of the community who supported and financed the production of the Bulletin. Without their generosity the venture could never have been started.

I hope that we shall all be home soon and meet at a grand reunion party. It has been suggested that the entire Bulletin be reprinted together with a suitable forward to commemorate Sunderland Jewish Community's War Effort. Personally I think it an admirable idea and trust that if the matter is raised in the near future it will receive the whole hearted support of ex-service men and women.

·5.

In conclusion, let us put to good use our experiences of the past · six years to improve the community at large and see that war, envy jealousy and malice is banished for ever more from the face of the earth.

Shalom Lehitraoth Bekarov!

_____

Answers to questions on page 3.

1. During the thirtyone days of October 1945 President Truman and Secretary of State Byrnes received between them 61,665 letters and telegrams from American citizens in Palestine, urging them to open its doors wide to Jews. In comparison it is worth noting that · during the 86 days of August/October only 600 letters were received on the Atom Bomb.
2. This quotation is culled not from a modern medical book but from the Talmud (200 - 500 C.E.).
3. Montesquieu 1689 - 1755, the philosophical Historian.
4. The Jewish child left school at the age of 13 or 14 whilst the average non-Jewish child finished his education at 10 or 11 in the 16th century.
5. "Shoklen" refers to the swaying of the body to and fro by orthodox Jews, when praying or studying in olden times when books were rare several people read at the same time from one book which was usually large. As every reader was obliged to bend down in order to read a passage, this resulted in a continual bending forward. By imitation this habit gradually grew upon the pious and studious who always accompanied their prayers and reading by "Shoklen".

Another explanation given is that "shoklen" encourages religious ecstasy and arouses a natural enthusiasm.

My Dear Rev. Toperoff,

Now that I have once again returned to civilian life and have received a copy of your monthly Bulletin addressed to my home, I cannot help but think of the wonderful comfort the receipt of your Bulletin brought me when I was so many thousands of miles away only a few months ago.

Only a Serviceman stationed overseas can really appreciate what it means and feel like to receive news of your home town. It was to me, and I know to all my other Sunderland colleagues in His Majesty's Forces like a spiritual oasis in the desert of loneliness in which we · so often found ourselves.

So you can guess with what regret I learned that your Bulletin is now to cease publication. The reason, no doubt for this, is due to the number of Sunderland men in the Forces who have now, or will soon be returning to civilian life.

b.

When we will look back on our past in the forces, we will always think of the happy hours reading and rereading your Bulletin brought to us. Perhaps more than anything else it did make us feel proud to be members of the Jewish race and help us to carry on in the true Jewish tradition that would make us be worthy sons of our noble heritage.

I look forward to the spirit of Jewishness that your Bulletin fostered in wartime, to be carried on in times of Peace by the continuance of the monthly Bulletin to Sunderland Jewry. I feel sure that this can be made possible, and that you will not lack support in making the Bulletin a regular feature amongst the Jewish Community of Sunderland.

Pleace accept my warmest thanks to yourself and staff for all your untiring labours in making the Bulletin mean so much to all those Sunderland men in the forces who were privileged in receiving so much hope and comfort from your efforts.

Yours Very sincerely,

NAT GOODMAN.

Ex Warrant Officer.

NEWS LETTER FROM THE HOME FRONT

And so I put pen to paper to write my last News Letter for the Bulletin. I hope that during the last couple of years I have given you a little idea of what is going on here at home at the Lit. I have endeavoured to the best of my ability to give you a true and unbiased picture of the various events that have taken place in the Communal Hall. If you have enjoyed my short articles half as much as I have enjoyed writing to you I shall be more than happy.

I feel I could make no greater use of this last issue of the Bulletin than to grasp the opportunity to bring to your notice the grave situation in which the Lit now finds itself. For thirty four years the Lit has played a most important role in the life of the younger generations of the town. It has provided more than a mere meeting place for those with nothing to do -- it has actively knitted together Jewish young folk with a solid bond of Jewish friendship. Through its medium many have met Jewish friends and have taken an interest in affairs Jewish who, otherwise, would have been lost to the Community.

The Lit has had its ups and its downs but none will deny that these last few years have come as a terrific blow to such a flourishing Circle. Hard work and unbelievable keeness of those who remained have up to now pulled the Lit through six desperate years of war. Not once during that time was any event cancelled in advance through war reasons and more than once I have watched members' dancing round the hall to the radiogramme whilst outside bombs were falling less than half a mile away. We held on because we hoped that some day the Lit would regain its former prestige.

If the Lit is to see this Session through, there must be an awakening not only amongst the young folk but amongst their parents too. Two appeals I must make now. Firstly those of you still in the services -- why not send your 5/- membership subscription now? the Lit badly needs it. And to the members of our community at home please give the Lit your support. Attend lectures, talks and debates and may I even suggest you pop your head in at the door at Socials and dances to see how things are going?

Well, Forces and all my readers everywhere, I send my very best wishes for a speedy re-union with your dear ones. I hope, Members of the Forces, that you all soon return safely home.

Yours sincerely,

Also After Gen.

_____

STOP PRESS!

A COLLOSAL SOCIAL SUCCESS.

BY L.A.C. JULIUS GORDON.

30th December, 1945 will long be remembered for a singular function sponsored by the Lit. The occasion was the result of a special effort necessitated by an alarming situation in which the Lit, after six years of war-time struggle found itself. Something extraordinary just had to be done and the members of the executive and committee really got down to it in no uncertain manner. The effort proper was initiated by a house to house membership campaign which was affected with meticulouse thoroughness. So well had the circulars previously posted throughout the town their effect and so enthusiastic were the callers that the response was almost magical and a grand stimulous for the extraordinary effort which took place on the following Sunday. This too the form of a re-union Supper and Dance in the Communal Hall and all the hard work and untiring efforts of the splendid band of workers were surely rewarded beyond all expectations. One might say "The whole town was there".

As one who has recently returned from overseas I can hardly describe just what it did for those of us present who were pre-war Lit enthusiasts. Arriving shortly after 7 o'clock I found already some 60 or 70 guests seated at tables around the Hall tables arranged with a host of good things. The hall was resplendent with its mass of paper decorations as did also the stage which had been suitably embelished and adorned with flowers. A steward in evening dress greeted the guests as they arrived and directed them to their respective cloak rooms. Within a very short time one found oneself partaking of supper with no lack of neat little "Nippies" to attend to ones needs.

All ages seemed to be represented. Lit celebrities - many of them had not been seen for many a year - exchanged delighted greetings

•8.

and for an hour or so the supper continued in a convivial atmosphere - the radiogramme playing all the while - a steady flow of guests arriving. At 8 o'clock the tables were cleared and quickly removed, Jack Usher's band having meantime arrived and taken up its stand on the stage. Without any apparent interruption it was "on with the dance". By this time there must have been not less than 200 in the Hall, the music was good and the dance went with a swing. During a break in the dancing Mrs. Toperoff, deputising for Rev. Toperoff who was indisposed, urged all, in a delightful little speech, to continue to give support to the Society's activities, pointing out that it ought to be regarded by the congregants as a duty. The chairman of the Society, Mr. A. Gordon, in a clarion-call for support exhorted all pre-war members in particular, to rally around once more and for a whole hearted effort to restore the Lit "to its former grandeur". The success attending this effort was proof that the Community was fully behind the Lit, and with continued interest, some attractive functions, both literary and social, could be arranged. The membership as a result of the drive had passed all previous records and then stood at over 150. It was hoped, the Chairman continued, that the Dramatic and Arts Sections would be re-formed and that all interested would volunteer their services.

Mr. Isaac Brewer and Mrs. Leena Goldblatt expressed gratitude to the younger element who had so nobly carried on during the difficult war-years and Mrs. Goldblatt spoke feelingly of how much our old friend and President, Mr. Sol Novinski, would have enjoyed being present at such a unique and outstanding Literary Society function. This was heartily applauded.

The dance was one of the jolliest ever and if the dancing space was cramped - well who cared? Ice-cream was sold, there was a running buffet a raffle and two dutch auctions - all very successful and 11 o'clock saw us at the end of what surely must have been one of the greatest social events ever seen in the Communal Hall. I am sure that we all departed glad that we had not missed it and wishing the Lit every future success.

IN RETROSPECT.

From 1931 onwards much of my time was spent visiting Middlesbrough, Newcastle, Shields and West Hartlepool, for, as Chairman of the North East Union of Jewish Young People's Societies, I had much organising work to do. Simon Light became Chairman of the "Lit" and I am indebted to him for the following list of speakers.

Sam Phillips of Newcastle spoke to us on Disraeli. Mr. Israel Jacobs gave his Presidential address entitled "Communal Reminisences". In the course of his remarks he produced a paper of the notes of the opening speech given at the consecration of the Old Synagogue in Moor Street. It is interesting to note that this paper was discovered in Australia and sent to him by Abe Rothfield, who was one of the three original founders of the Society. Other lecturers were Rabbi Miller of Middlesbrough, Joe Gillis of Sunderland, who gave a film lecture describing his visit to Palestine, Rev. Drukker of Newcastle, Rabbi Shachter of Belfast, Barnet Janner, M.P., and Isaac Swift. These were just a few of the lecturers who spoke to us.

Much new blood was coming to the "Lit" about this time. First and foremost I must mention the advent of the Rev. S. P. Toperoff, he came in October 1934. I remember an invitation to his home and in the course of conversation I was impressed by his sincerity. A forthright man of decided opinions and yet able to see and understand anothers point of view. I came away with the impression that the young people of our Community had gained a valuable ally and friend. As I know him to be a very modest man and Editor of the Bulletin, I think I had better say no more about him.

Rita Olswang who was Secretary between the years 1934 and 39 and Isaac Brewer who was an honorary Vice-Chairman were also outstanding figures of the "Lit", while no history of the Society will be complete without mentioning Sol Cohen, who as Treasurer was responsible for the finances of the Society during this critical, but highly successful period.

Early in 1935 the Committee began to think about the preparations for the celebrations of the Silver Jubilee of the Society.

Through the good offices of Mr. Israel Jacobs, our Honorary President, the Jubilee Dinner and Ball were held in the Masonic Hall in Burdon Road. Professor Selig Brodetsky, of whom I have written in a previous contribution was our honoured guest. The Mayor and Mayoress, Alderman and Miss Summerbell were also present. Some 230 guests sat down to dinner. The old members of the "Lit" were there in full force and the dance programme contained old waltzes, two steps and veleetas. The good old lancers were not forgotten and were danced with more vigour than accuracy. For the younger members there were one steps, fox trots and tangos in plenty. And so 1911 and 1936 were joined on this great occasion.

And now dear friends, I must say "Farewell" for the Bulletin in its present form is concluding with this issue. If my writing has given you the smallest amount of pleasure, I am very glad. I know from experience in World War No. 1 how the receipt of a letter from my home town was eagerly looked forward to, and I am delighted if I have brought to you one tiny ray of pleasure.

If I have given your mind a little touch that has stirred within you memories of happy evenings at the "Lit" I am well content. I know that "Memories live longer than dreams" and there is no finer company to anyone who is far away from home. To you boys and girls in the Forces who are not yet demobolised, I wish you a speedy and happy homecoming.

And so, once again "Farewell",

Cheerio,

SOL.

10.

<u>SEARCHLIGHT ON "SPORT"- By "Argus".</u>

This is my Swan Song so far as the Bulletin is concerned. Usually one writes a Swan Song with more than a tinge of regret. In this case it is a pleasure, because it is a sure enough indication that, the war over, you are gradually but surely returning to your homes and your loved ones, and the necessity for this production is a diminishing quantity.

It has been a greater pleasure to write a few monthly notes for you than it has been to watch some of the football we have seen during the war period, and if my notes have enabled you to keep touch with sport at home then that is sufficient thanks so far as I am concerned.

It has not always been easy to find the time. Some of you may know I have carried out the duties of Military Welfare Officer in Durham County in "my spare time" during the whole of the war, and when you realise that I have averaged nearly 2,500 cases a year, you may guess that frequently it has been a case of putting in full time for welfare and spare time on my job as the Sports Editor of a newspaper. Combined with that I have acted as Chief Reporter until we get some of our staff back.

In this closing article I want to express my thanks to all of you who have written me appreciative words for my articles. I hope to meet you all at a re-union later in the year.

We are still in the English Cup as I write this. For how long is in the lap of the gods, and as you know the gods are not always kind. However, I can see improvement, and that is something to be thankful for.

I will let you into a secret as I close. Carter was transfer or £6,000; Willingham bought for £3,500; and Jack Jones cost £50

Cheerio for now, and those of you who remain in the Forces, may he group number advance quickly.

———————

<u>SUNDERLAND   JEWISH   WOMEN'S   WAR   SERVICES   COMMITTEE.</u>

The Sunderland Jewish Women's War Services Committee was formed January 1941 and has done excellent work throughout the war. It fitting that we record here, in the last issue of the Bulletin, manifold and varied activities in which the S.J.W.W.S.C. interested self.

The Society, a voluntary organisation, was divided into the llowing Groups:-

Secretarial workers to the Guild of Help.

Il.

Rota of workers for the Information Centre.
Sewing and mending for evacuees, under the auspices of the Guild
of Help.
Collection of cast off clothing for Blitz emergency.
More than 40 Blood Donors.
Knitting for W.V.S. to which we were affiliated.
War Savings Group, which was awarded Certificate of Merit.

In addition to the above Groups who worked conscientiously throughou
the War the Society also adopted a Minesweeper, the Canadian Corvette
"H.M.S. EYEBRIGHT" to which a crew of 58 Canadians were attached and
they were supplied with cigarettes, tobacco, sweets, magazines, knitted
comforts, portable gramaphone and records. We also collected books
for the Royal Naval War Libraries, sent consignments consisting of
250 sheets and 250 pillow cases to the Russian Relief Fund, about a
thousand garments for relief of Concentration Camp victims, and hundreds
of packets of food for Post-war Relief and Reconstruction abroad.

We were also asked by the ..A.C. to take charge of a Rest Centre
for homeless people, at the Communal Hall. At the suggestion of
Captain Anderson, the local Welfare Officer, we adopted the Camp
Reptian Station in Grey Road, to which monthly parcels of books,
stationery, cigarettes, cakes and biscuits were sent.

In 1944 we adopted ward 15 of the Cherry Knowle Emergency Hospital,
which monthly parcels are still being sent, and a group of volunteers
received permission to visit Jewish wounded in nearby military hospitals

The S.J.W.W.S.C. have representatives on the Council of Social
Service and the Standing Conference of Women's Organisations, recently
formed to unify and further the work of women in this country.

The following Organisations benefitted financially from our Society
A.F. Benevolent Fund, St. Bernados Home, Guild of Help, Seamen's
Mission, Mayor's Comforts Fund, St. Dunstans, Soldiers, Sailors and
Airmen's Families Association, Mrs. Churchill's Aid to Russia Fund,
Red Cross, W.V.S., and the Mobile Synagogue.

To the Executive, Group Leaders, and the many workers who
consistently carried on a grand job, the sincere and grateful thanks
of the Community are due. Our service men and women are particularly
grateful to the Sunderland Jewish Women's War Services Committee for
concern and interest in their welfare. I know how they appreciated
those welcome Chanukah parcels and gifts of cigarettes.

To all who have been associated with the Sunderland Jewish
Women's War Services Committee we say
THANK YOU!

All correspondence to be sent to Rev. S. P. Toperoff, 5, Victoria
Avenue, Sunderland.

There is no complete record of the Jewish men and women from Sunderland who served in the Armed Forces during the Second World War. However a list has been gleaned from the names mentioned in these Bulletins to which has been added some extras from personal knowledge. We apologise for any omissions.

Abrahams, A

Abrahams, David

Altman, L

Behrman, Cyril

Behrman, Gerald

Berg, Issy

Berg, Nat,

Bergson, Abe

Black, Harry

Bloomberg, Arnold

Book, Toby

Book, Wilf

Brewer, Claude

Brewer, Charles

Brewer, Harold

Brewer, Isaac

Brewer, Sylvia

Burnley, Eric

Caplin, Pearl

Caplin, Selwyn

Charlton, Joey

Clarke, J

Clarke, Joe

Cohen, BA

Cohen, Dereck

Cohen, Solly

Cohen, Dick

Cohen, Louis

Cohen, Mordant

Cohen, Norman

Davis, Abe

Davis, Austin

Davis, David

Davis, Hymie

Davis, Issy

Davis, Myer

Doberman, M

Dresner, Ellis

Dresner, Morris

Ernstone, Nathan

Forman, Alan

Franks, N J

Freedman, B

Freedman, Ralph

Freedman, S

Gillis, Archie

Gillis, Charles

Gillis, Ernie

Gillis, Lionel

Gillis, Max

Gillis, Miriam

Gillis, Solly

Gillis, Vicki

Gillis, Zelda

Goldberg, Victor

Goldblatt, Aron

Goldman, Douglas

Goodman, Nat

Gordon, Julius

Gould, B

Grantham, Gwen

Grantham, Olga

Isaacs, S

Issacs, Harry

Issacs, Sam

Jackson, Bernard

Joseph, Harry

Kersh, Charles

Kolson, Charles

Kolson, E

Landau, Arnold

Landau, Joey

Lerman, Len

Lerman, Sammy

Leslie, Syd

Leslie, Sonia

Levin, Leo

Levine, D

Levine, Issy

Levinson, Dinah

Levy, Rupert

Linke, Philip

Linskill, Jack

Maccoby, Chaim

Maccoby, Lorna

Maccoby, David

Magrill, Gwen

Magrill, Harold

Marks, Charles

Marks, Louis

Marks, Lionel

Minchom, Hymie

Mincovitch, Cyril

Mincovitch, Maurice

Mincovitch, Phyllis

Mincovitch, Sylvia

Oler, Freda

Olsberg, Luis

Olswang, Rita

Pearlman, Alan

Pearlman, Beril

Pearlman, Mottie

Pearlman, Miriam

Pearlman, Phivie

Pearlman, R D

Pearlman, Reva

Pearlman, Sheba

Pearlman, Yankel

Penn, Annette

Penn, Sylvia

Pollock, Sydney

Raymond, Morrie

Rosenthal, David

Rosenthal, J

Rosenthal, R

Schochet, Harold

Silverston, Harry

Slater, Lonnie

Soldinger, Phil

Stewart, Raphy

Stone, Horace

Stone, Jackie

Taylor, Basil

Van Der Velde, Addy

Weinthrop, H

Winburn, Charles

Winburn, Israel

It is sad to recall the five young Jewish men from Sunderland who made the ultimate sacrifice in this world conflict.

We remember them with pride.

David Davis

Bernard Jackson

Harold Magrill

Lionel Marks

Israel Winburn

If people were asked what was the most important operation which contributed to the success of the Allies in the Second World War (1939-1945) it would have to be the code breakers of Bletchley Park. Without their knowledge and information on the decoded enemy messages no planned operation could have been as successful as it was. Although members of this exclusive club talked very little about their involvement even after the war the Sunderland Jewish community are proud of the two members of the Beth Hamedrash who contributed to this vital work.

Hayim Maccoby

Joe Gillis

Lightning Source UK Ltd.
Milton Keynes UK
24 October 2009

145288UK00001B/50/P